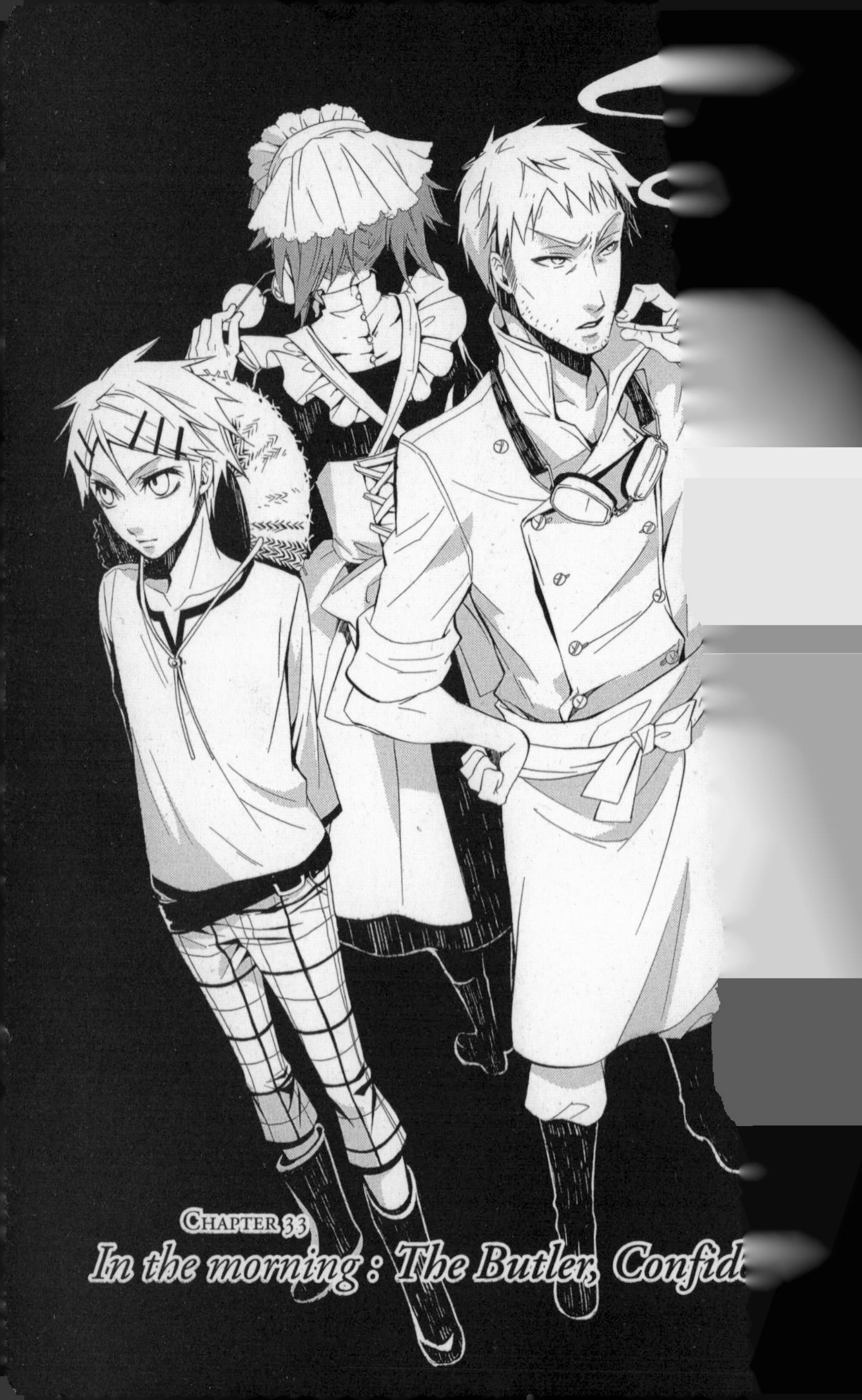
Chapter 33
In the morning : The Butler, Confid

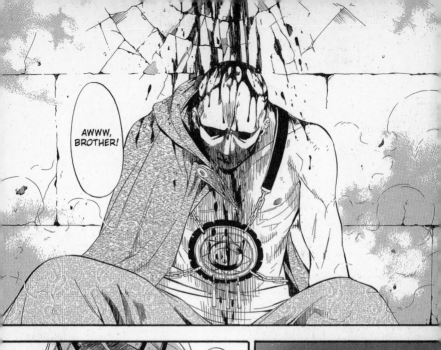

AWWW, BROTHER!

H"
ZA
(CRUNCH)

HOOOW AWFUL.

JUST LOOK AT ALL THE BLOOD THAT'S BEEN SPILLED!

H"
ZA

I HATE PAIN, YOU KNOW.

PIKU
(TWITCH)

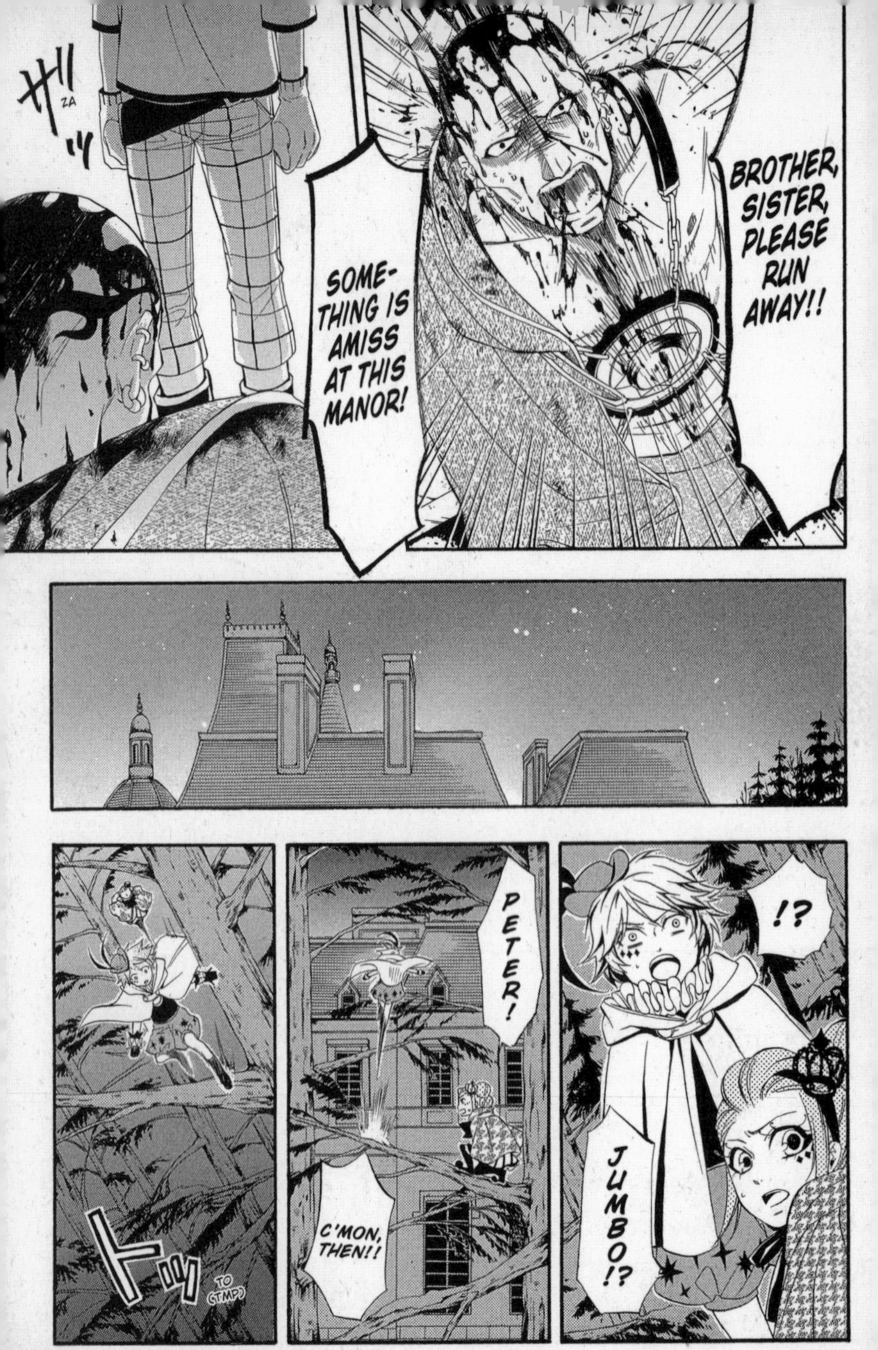
BROTHER, SISTER, PLEASE RUN AWAY!!
SOME-THING IS AMISS AT THIS MANOR!
ZA
!?
JUMBO!?
PETER!
C'MON, THEN!!
TO (STMP)

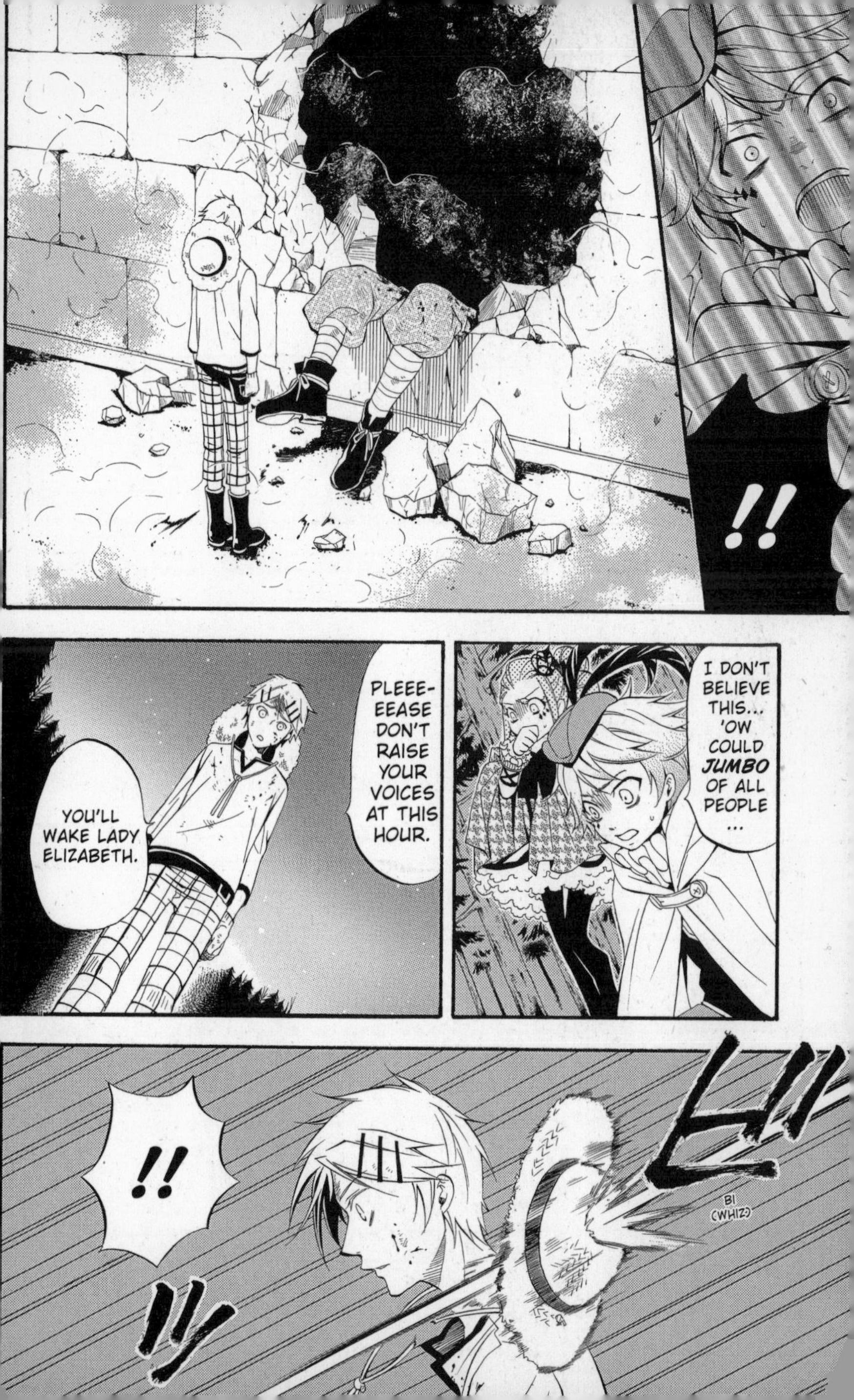
!!
I DON'T BELIEVE THIS... 'OW COULD *JUMBO* OF ALL PEOPLE ...
PLEEE-EEASE DON'T RAISE YOUR VOICES AT THIS HOUR.
YOU'LL WAKE LADY ELIZABETH.
BI (WHIZ)
!!

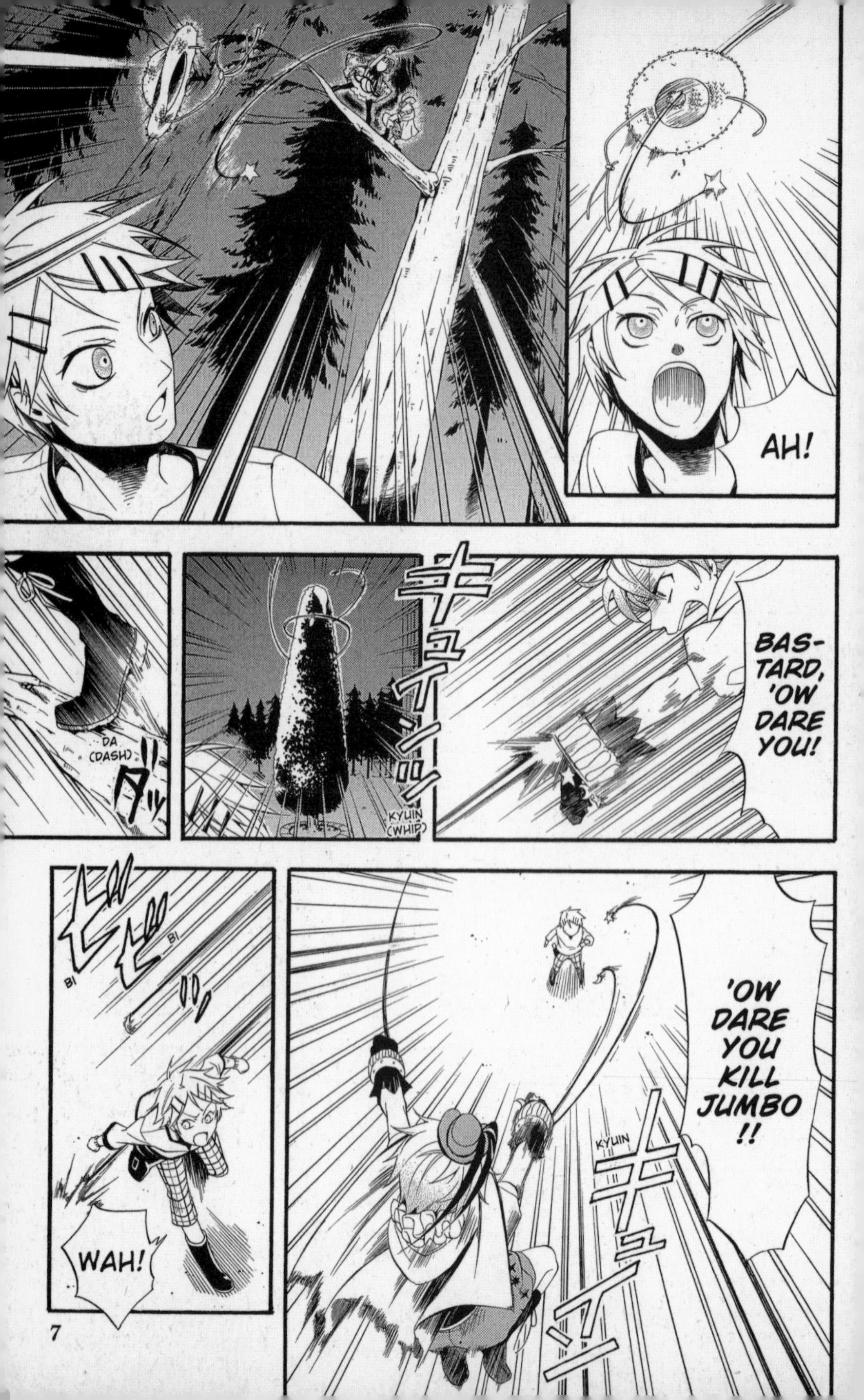
AH!
BAS-TARD, 'OW DARE YOU!
KYUIN (WHIP)
DA (DASH)
'OW DARE YOU KILL JUMBO !!
KYUIN
BI
BI
WAH!

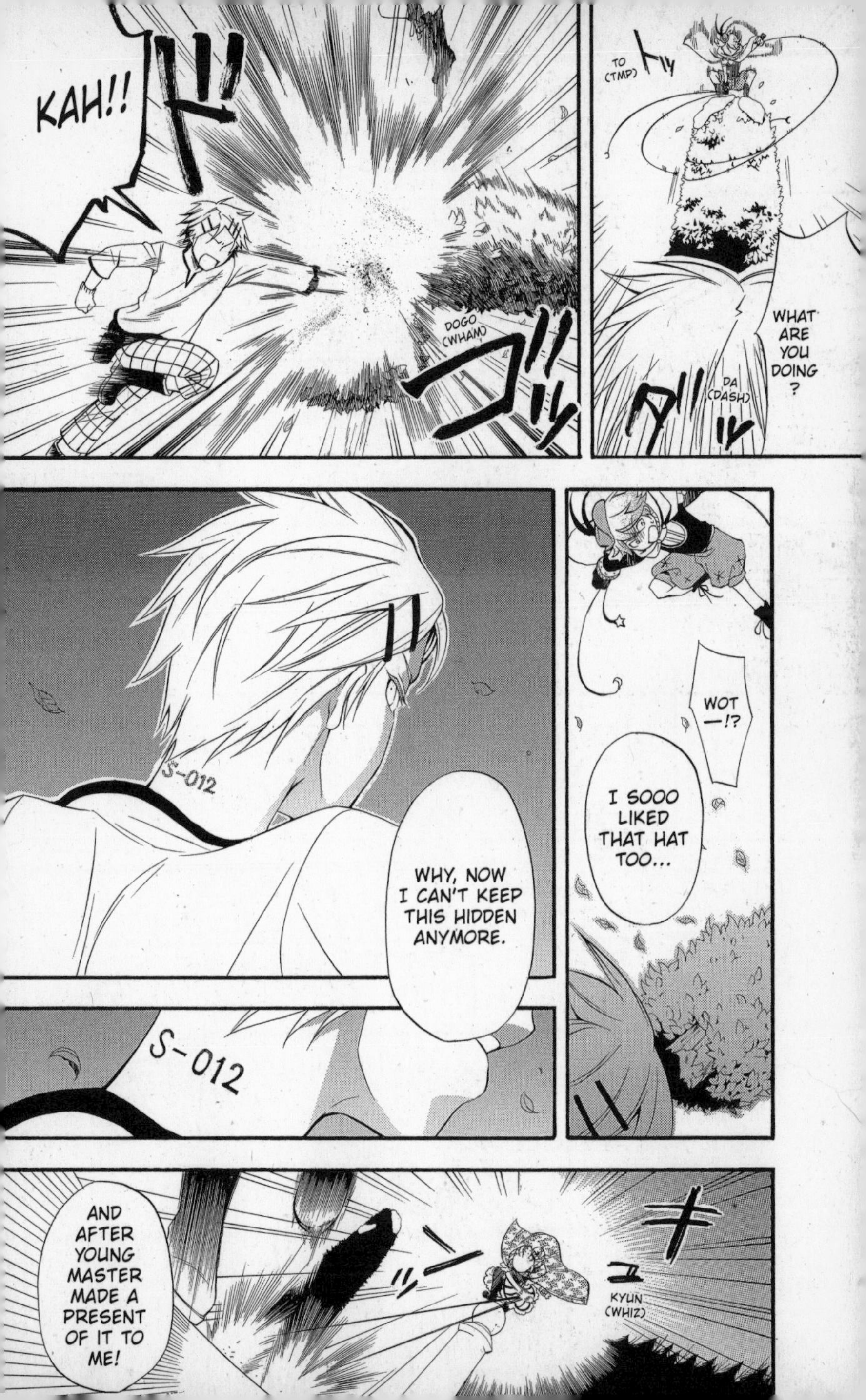
TO (TMP)
WHAT ARE YOU DOING?
DA (DASH)
KAH!!
DOGO (WHAM)
WOT—!?
I SOOO LIKED THAT HAT TOO...
S-012
WHY, NOW I CAN'T KEEP THIS HIDDEN ANYMORE.
S-012
KYUN (WHIZ)
AND AFTER YOUNG MASTER MADE A PRESENT OF IT TO ME!

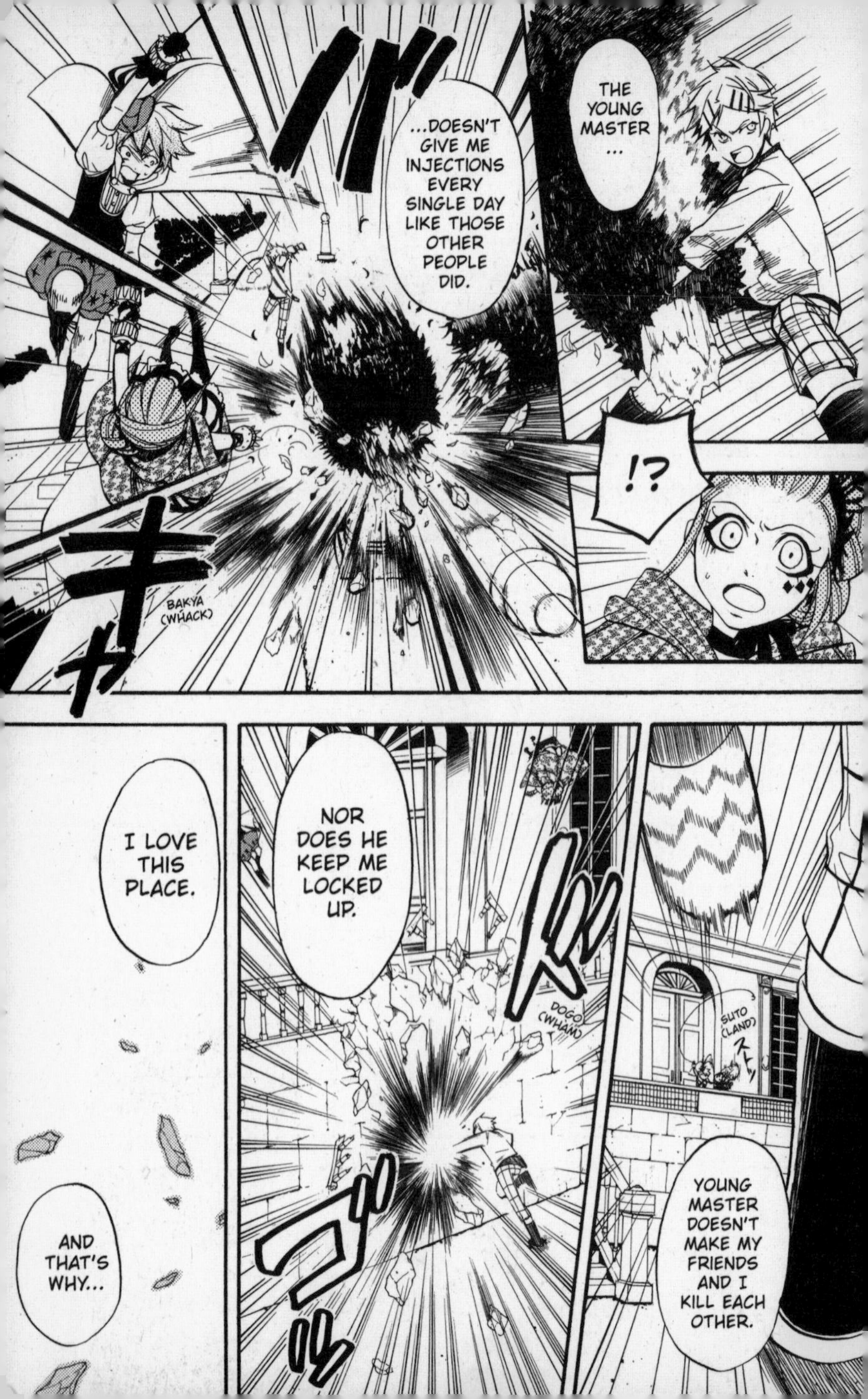
THE YOUNG MASTER...
!?
...DOESN'T GIVE ME INJECTIONS EVERY SINGLE DAY LIKE THOSE OTHER PEOPLE DID.
BAKYA (WHACK)
YOUNG MASTER DOESN'T MAKE MY FRIENDS AND I KILL EACH OTHER.
SUTO (LAND)
NOR DOES HE KEEP ME LOCKED UP.
DOGO (WHAM)
I LOVE THIS PLACE.
AND THAT'S WHY...

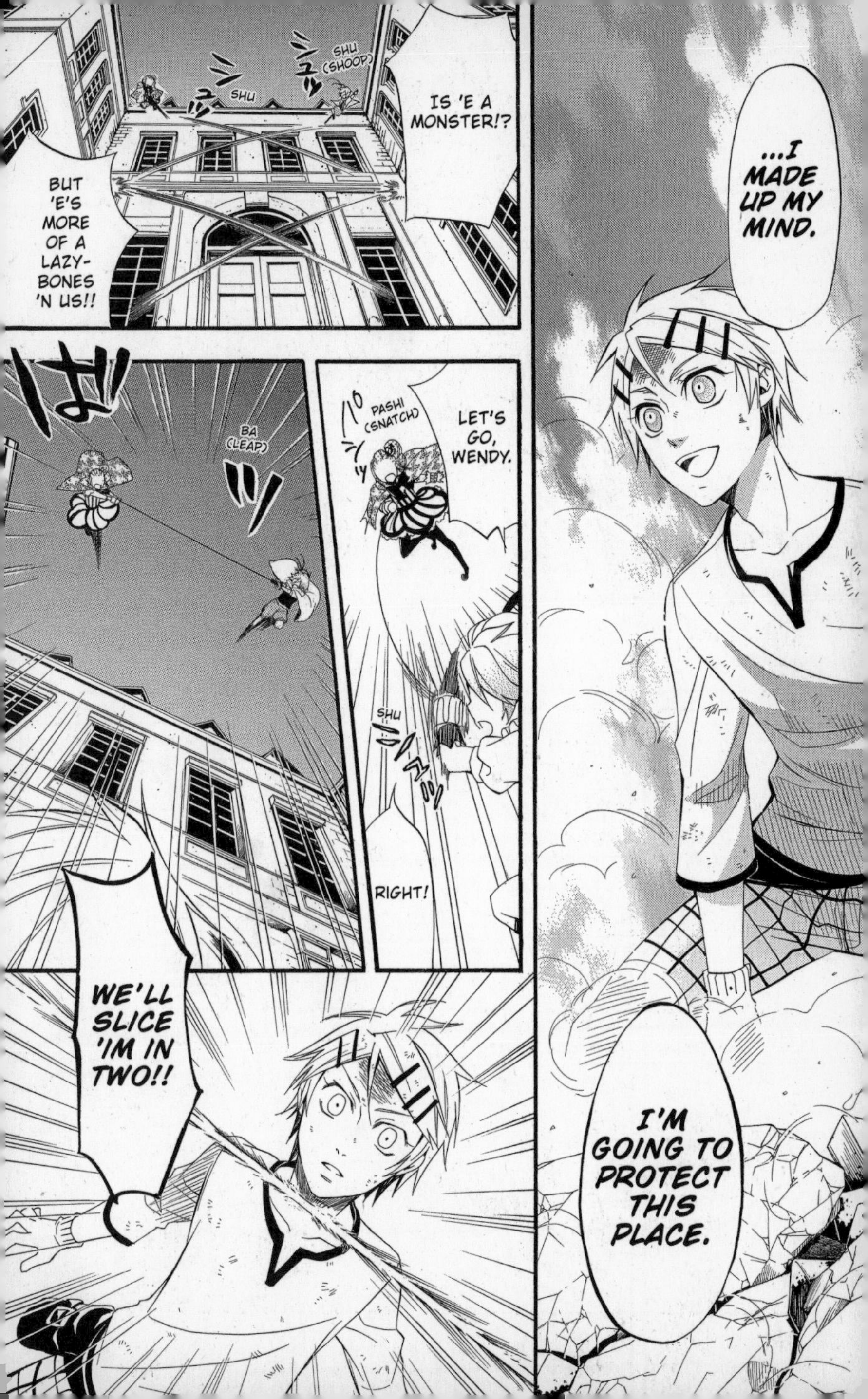

...I MADE UP MY MIND.
I'M GOING TO PROTECT THIS PLACE.
SHU (SHOOP)
SHU
IS 'E A MONSTER!?
BUT 'E'S MORE OF A LAZY-BONES 'N US!!
PASHI (SNATCH)
LET'S GO, WENDY.
SHU
RIGHT!
BA (LEAP)
WE'LL SLICE 'IM IN TWO!!

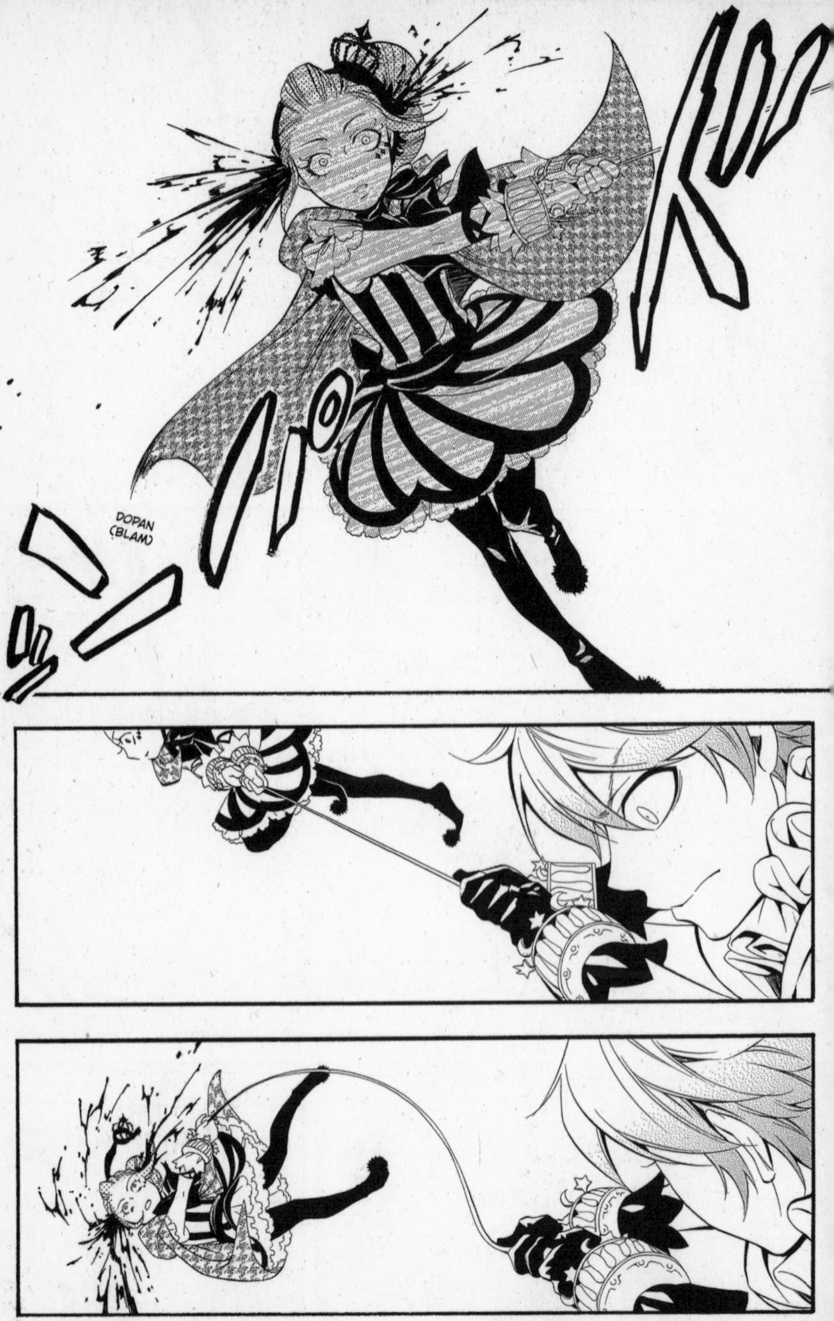
DOPAN
(BLAM)

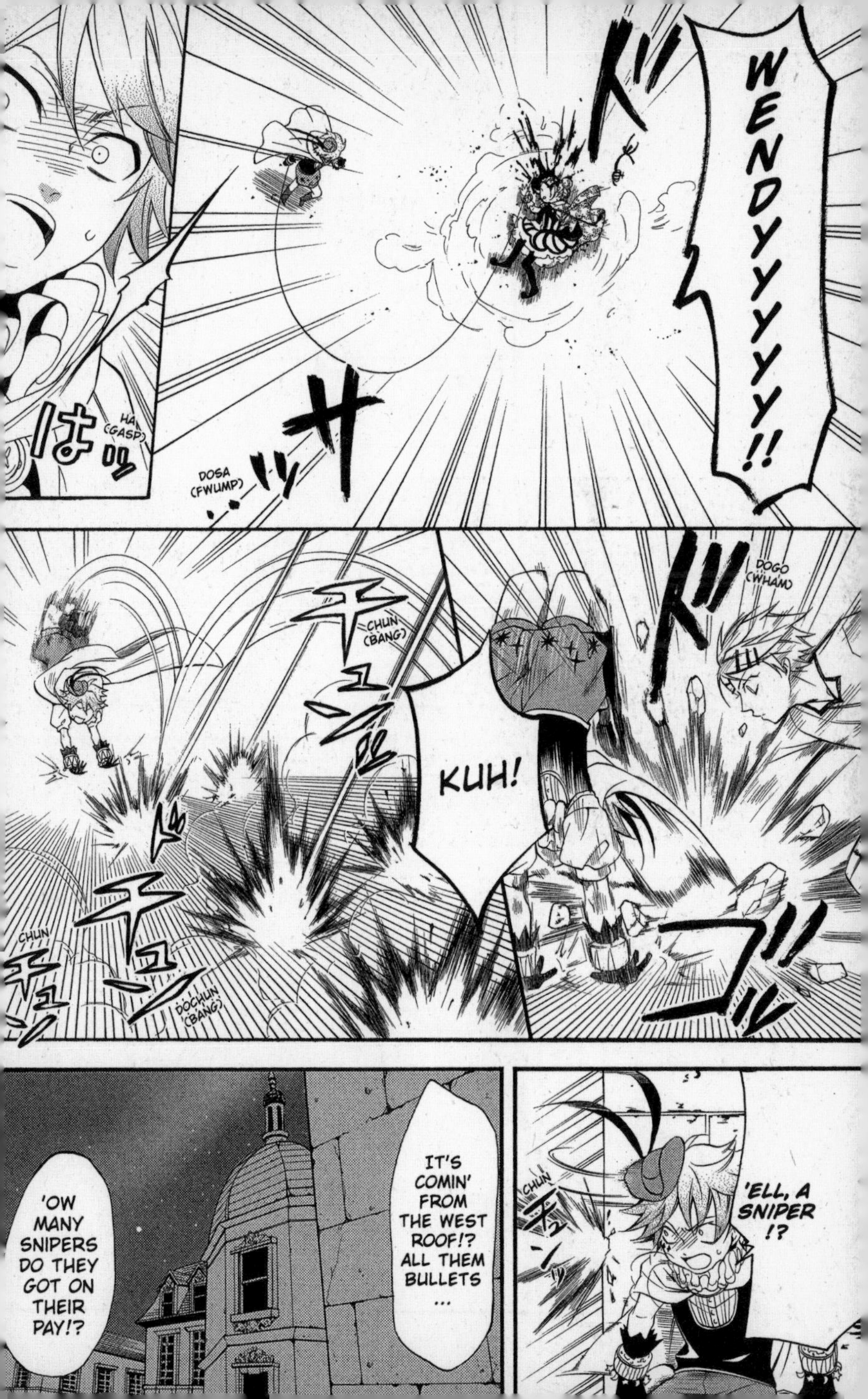

WENDYYYYYYY!!
HA (GASP)
DOSA (FWUMP)
DOGO (WHAM)
CHUN (BANG)
KUH!
CHUN
DOCHUN (BANG)
'ELL, A SNIPER !?
CHUN
IT'S COMIN' FROM THE WEST ROOF!? ALL THEM BULLETS ...
'OW MANY SNIPERS DO THEY GOT ON THEIR PAY!?

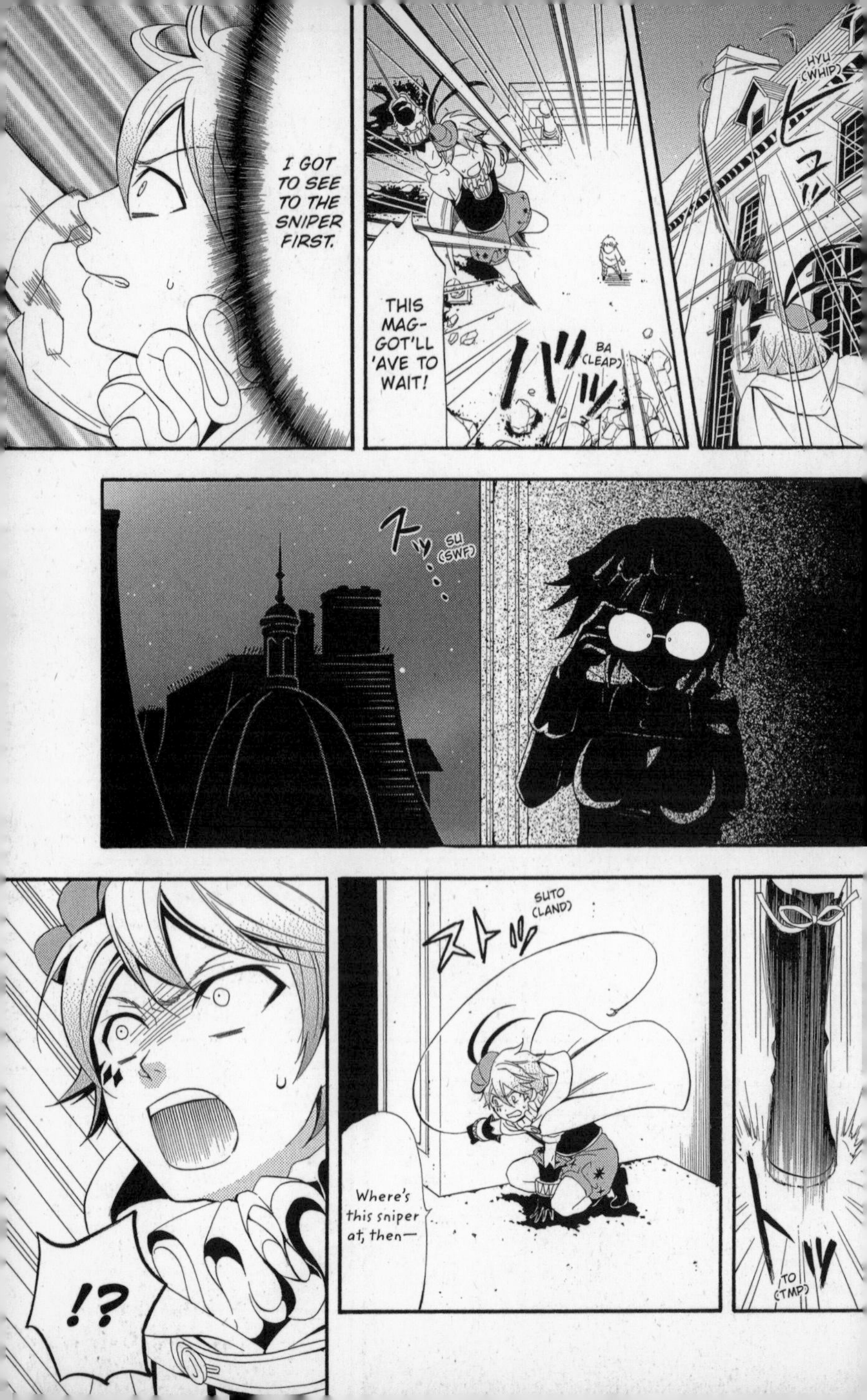
HYU (WHIP)
THIS MAG-GOT'LL 'AVE TO WAIT!
BA (LEAP)
I GOT TO SEE TO THE SNIPER FIRST.
SU (SWF)
TO (TMP)
SUTO (LAND)
Where's this sniper at, then—
!?

ズラッ
ZURA
(ENDLESS)

?

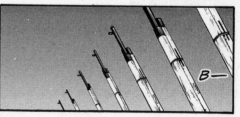

B—

BLIMEY!!

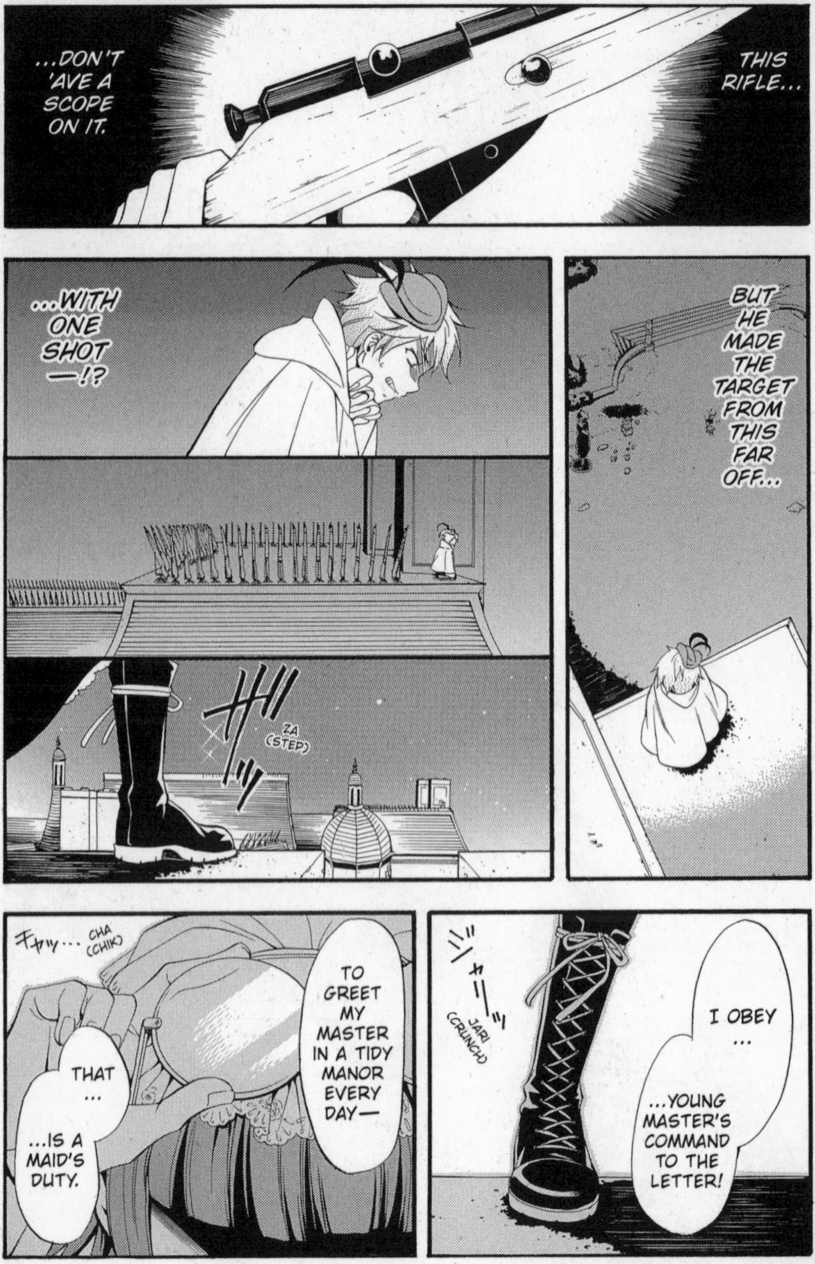
THIS RIFLE...
...DON'T 'AVE A SCOPE ON IT.
BUT HE MADE THE TARGET FROM THIS FAR OFF...
...WITH ONE SHOT—!?
ZA (STEP)
JARI (CRUNCH)
I OBEY ...
...YOUNG MASTER'S COMMAND TO THE LETTER!
CHA (CHIK)
TO GREET MY MASTER IN A TIDY MANOR EVERY DAY—
THAT ...
...IS A MAID'S DUTY.

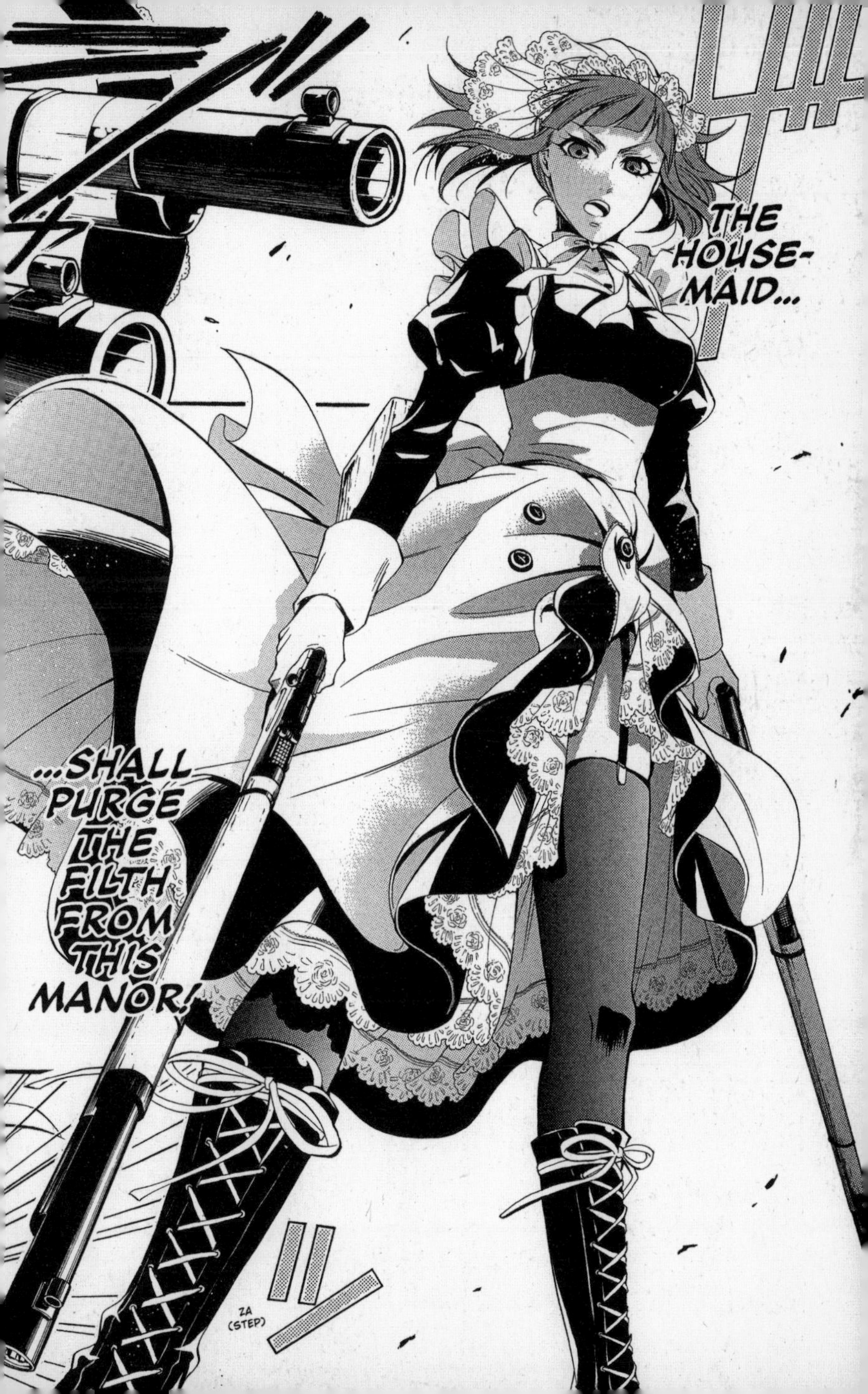
THE HOUSE-MAID...
...SHALL PURGE THE FILTH FROM THIS MANOR!
ZA (STEP)

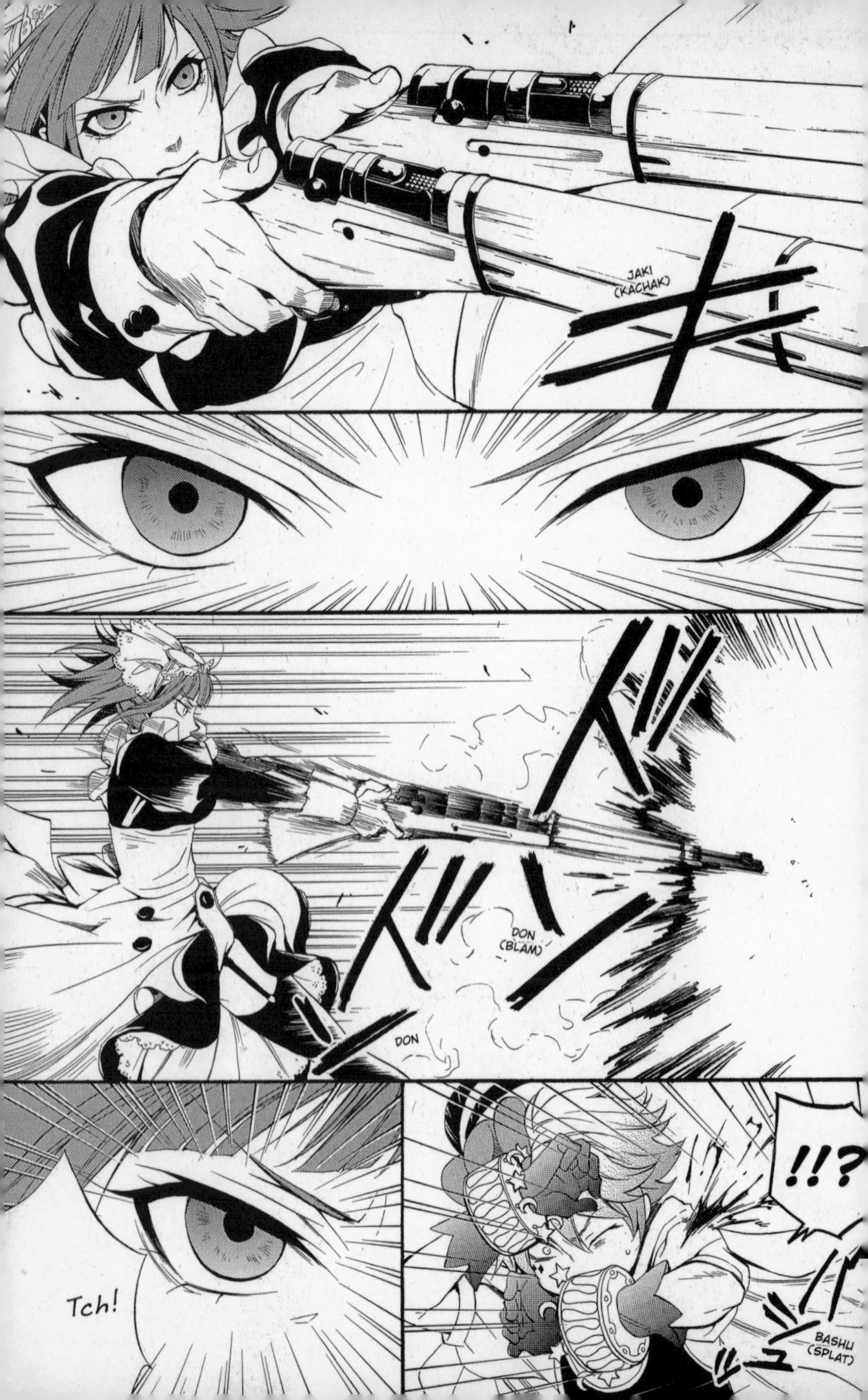
JAKI (KACHAK)
DON (BLAM)
DON
!!?
BASHU (SPLAT)
Tch!

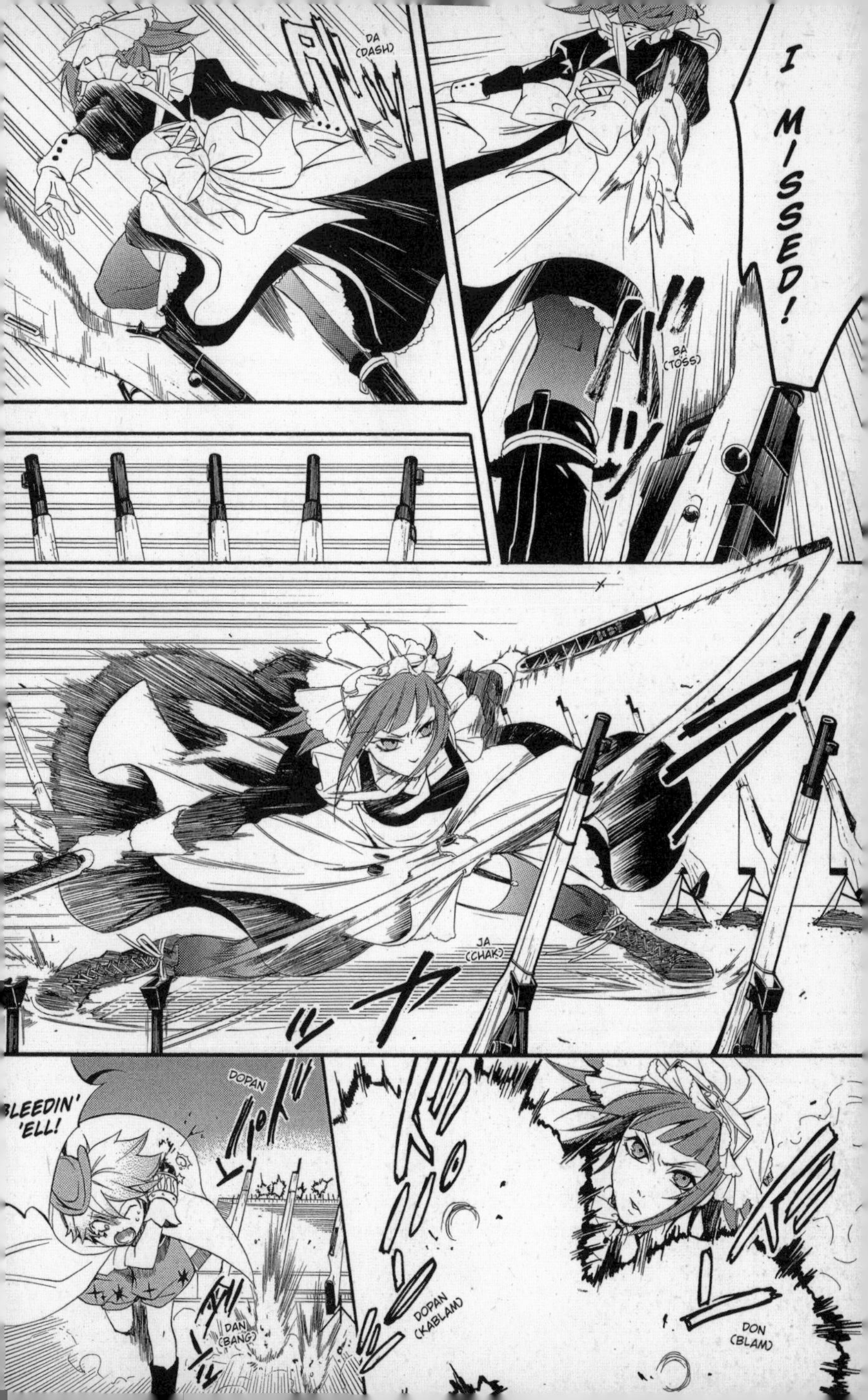
I MISSED!
BA (TOSS)
DA (DASH)
JA (CHAK)
DON (BLAM)
DOPAN (KABLAM)
DOPAN
BLEEDIN' 'ELL!
DAN (BANG)

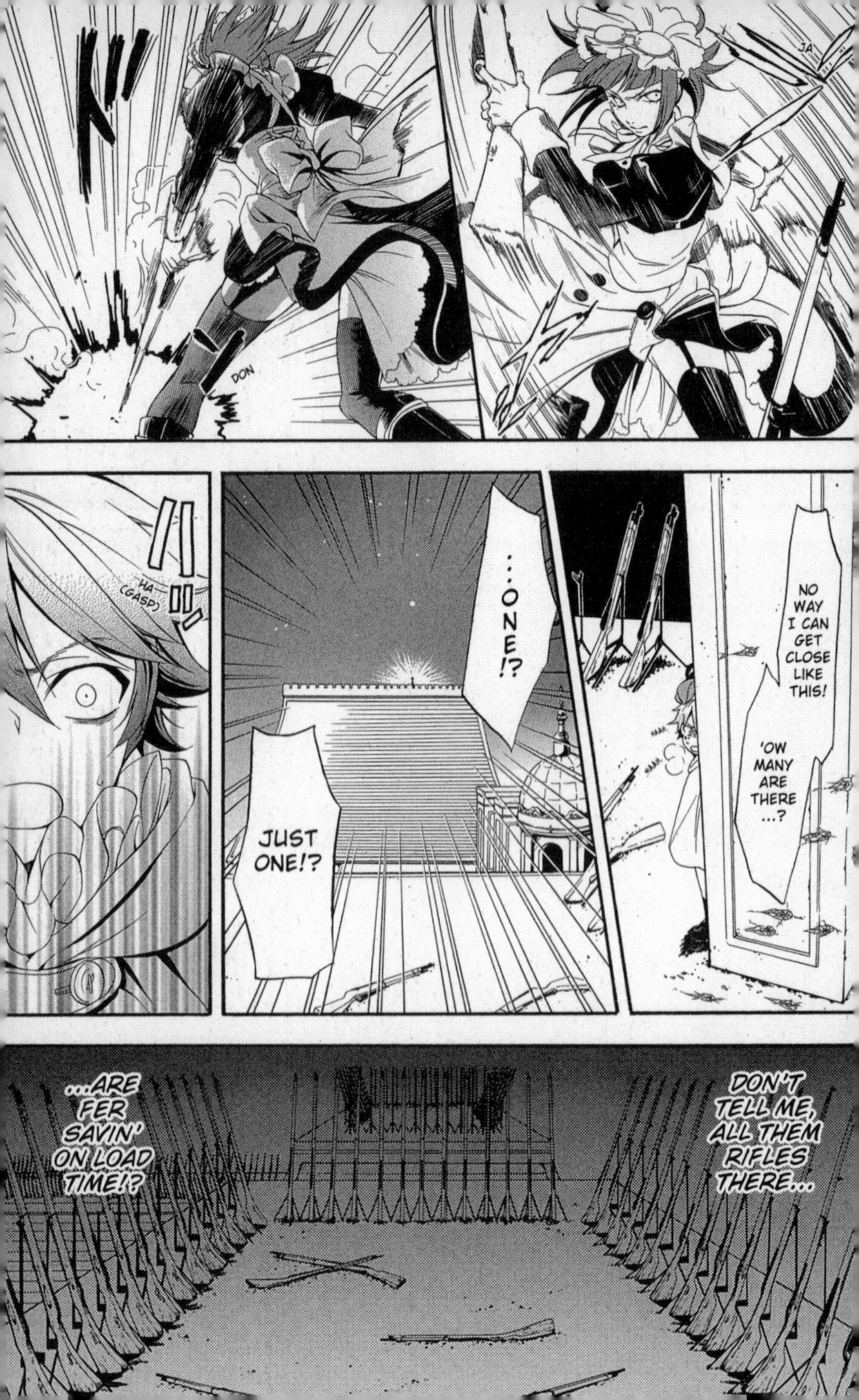
JA
ド
DON
NO WAY I CAN GET CLOSE LIKE THIS!
'OW MANY ARE THERE ...?
...ONE!?
JUST ONE!?
HA (GASP)
DON'T TELL ME, ALL THEM RIFLES THERE...
...ARE FER SAVIN' ON LOAD TIME!?

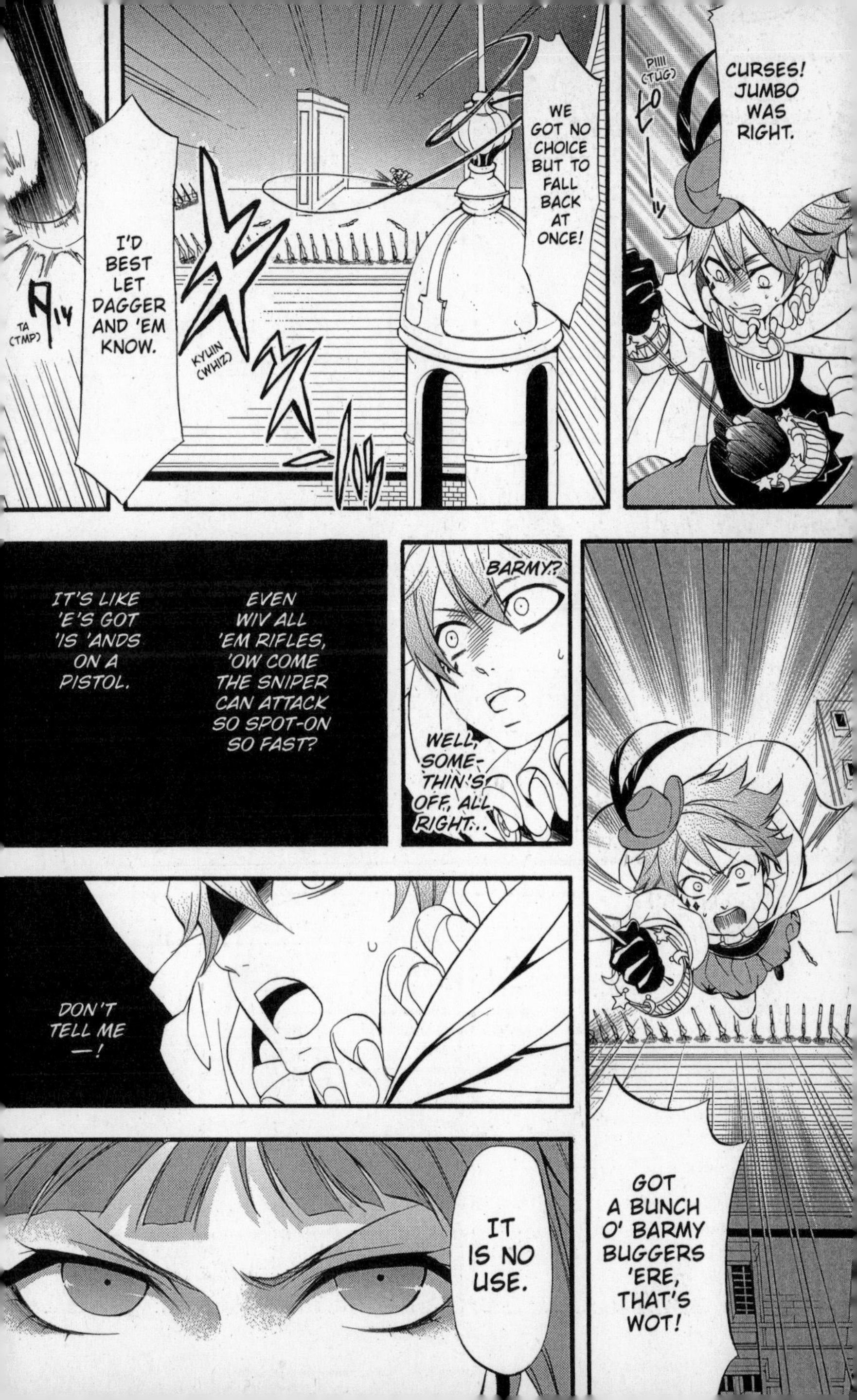
PIIII (TUG)
CURSES! JUMBO WAS RIGHT.
WE GOT NO CHOICE BUT TO FALL BACK AT ONCE!
KYUIN (WHIZ)
I'D BEST LET DAGGER AND 'EM KNOW.
TA (TMP)
GOT A BUNCH O' BARMY BUGGERS 'ERE, THAT'S WOT!
BARMY?
WELL, SOME-THIN'S OFF, ALL RIGHT...
EVEN WIV ALL 'EM RIFLES, 'OW COME THE SNIPER CAN ATTACK SO SPOT-ON SO FAST?
IT'S LIKE 'E'S GOT 'IS 'ANDS ON A PISTOL.
DON'T TELL ME —!
IT IS NO USE.

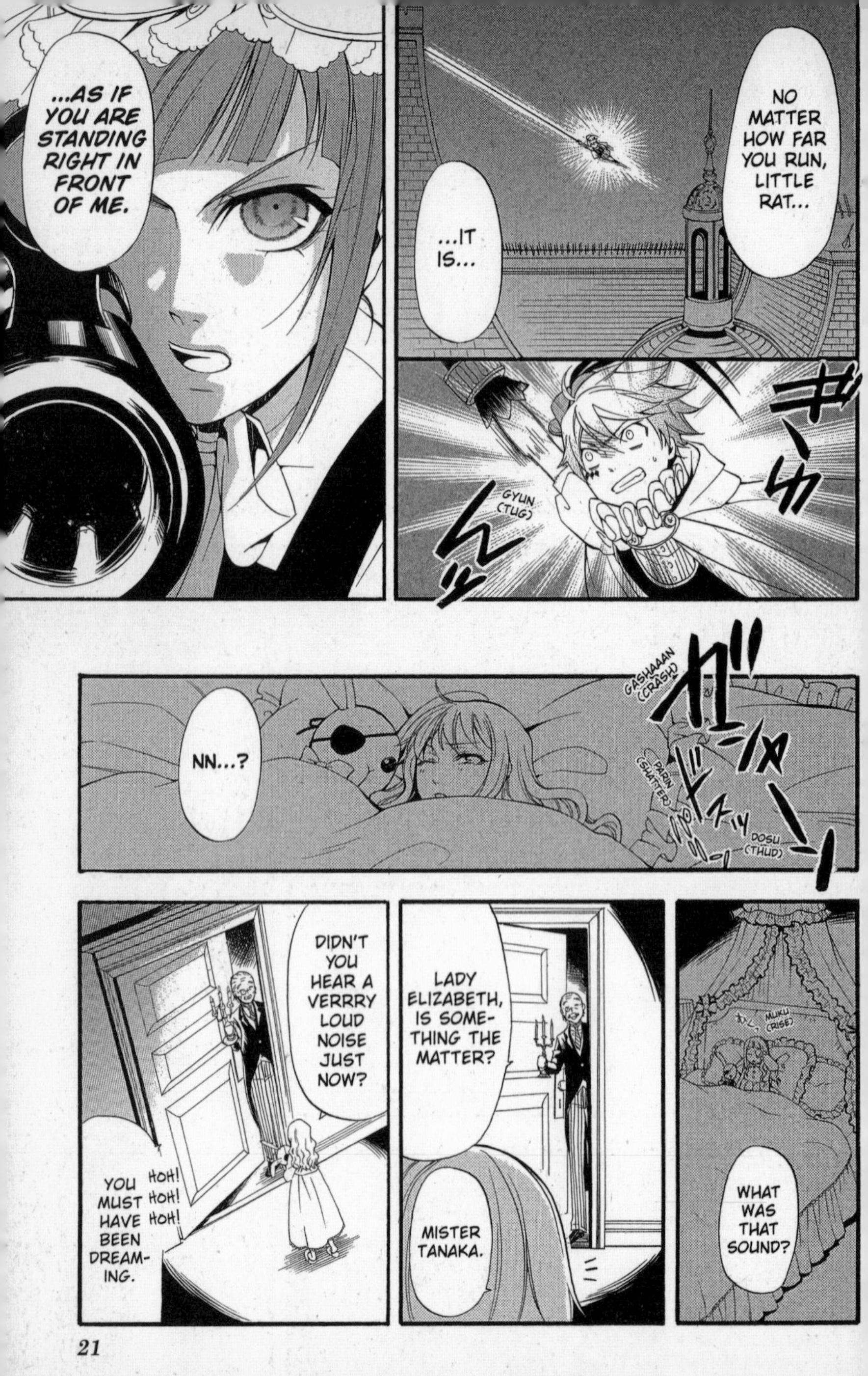
NO MATTER HOW FAR YOU RUN, LITTLE RAT...
...IT IS...
GYUN (TUG)
...AS IF YOU ARE STANDING RIGHT IN FRONT OF ME.
GASHAAAN (CRASH)
PARIN (SHATTER)
DOSU (THUD)
NN...?
MUKU (RISE)
WHAT WAS THAT SOUND?
LADY ELIZABETH, IS SOME-THING THE MATTER?
MISTER TANAKA.
DIDN'T YOU HEAR A VERRRY LOUD NOISE JUST NOW?
HOH! HOH! HOH!
YOU MUST HAVE BEEN DREAM-ING.

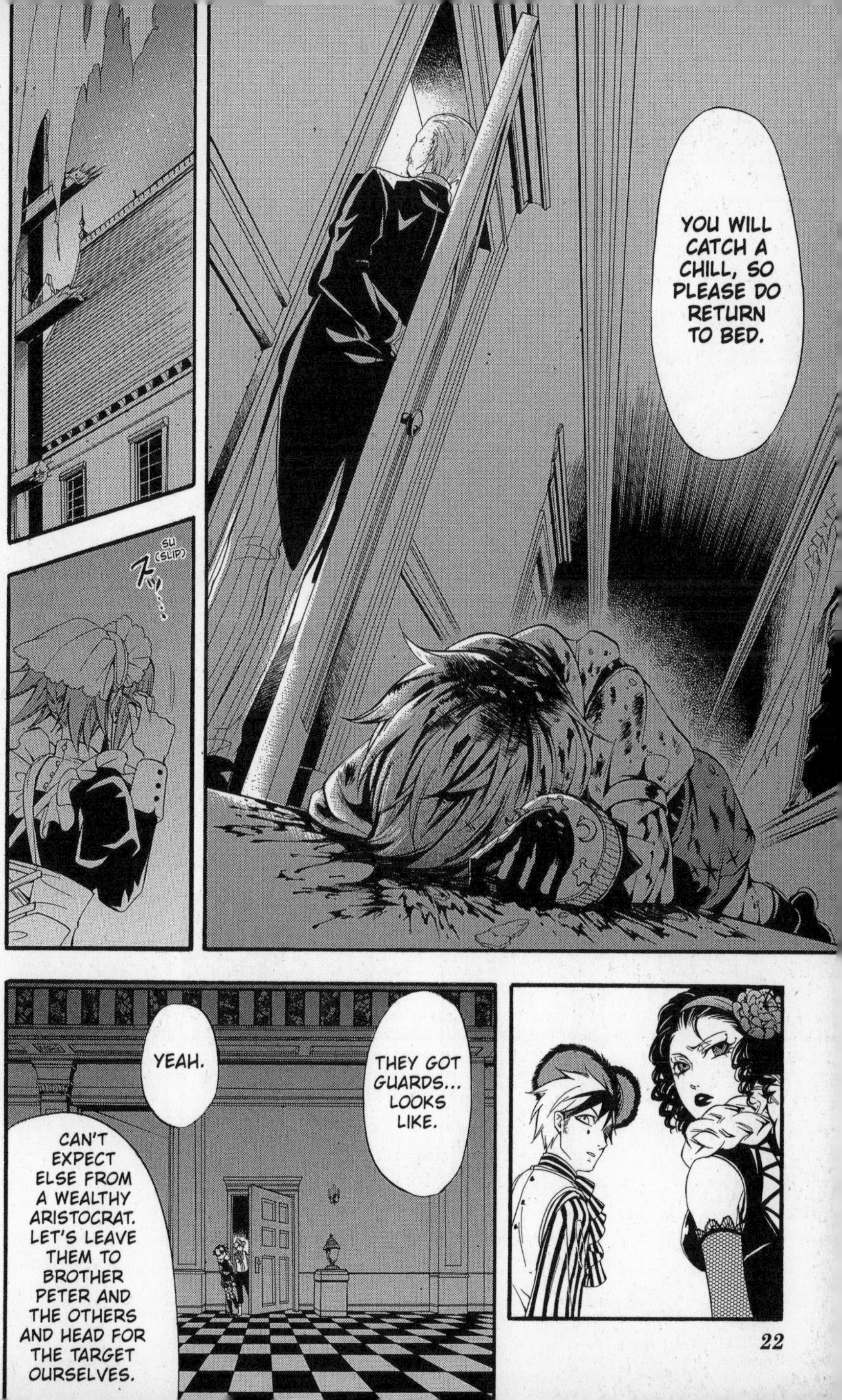
YOU WILL CATCH A CHILL, SO PLEASE DO RETURN TO BED.
SU (SLIP)
THEY GOT GUARDS... LOOKS LIKE.
YEAH.
CAN'T EXPECT ELSE FROM A WEALTHY ARISTOCRAT. LET'S LEAVE THEM TO BROTHER PETER AND THE OTHERS AND HEAD FOR THE TARGET OURSELVES.

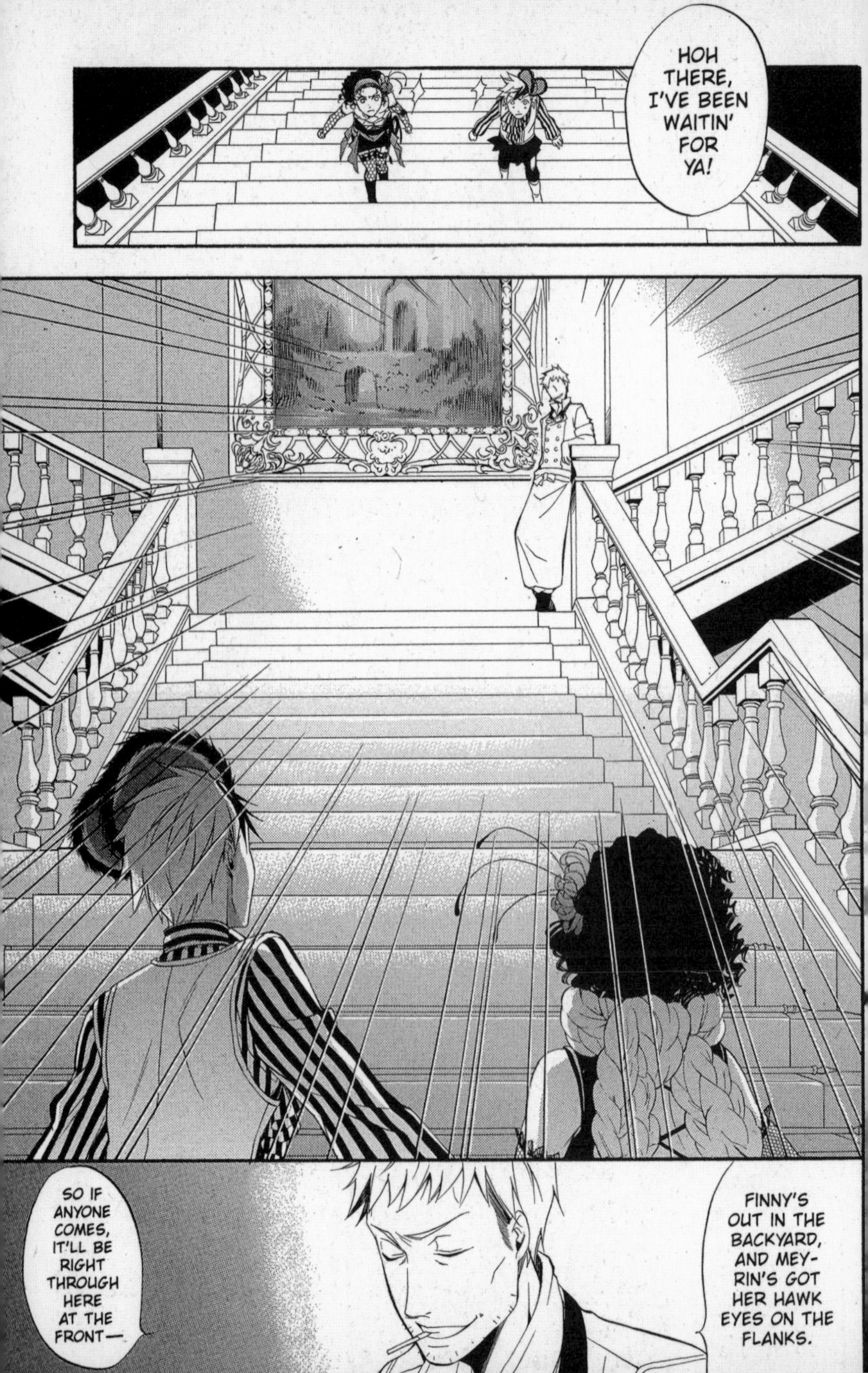
HOH THERE, I'VE BEEN WAITIN' FOR YA!
FINNY'S OUT IN THE BACKYARD, AND MEY-RIN'S GOT HER HAWK EYES ON THE FLANKS.
SO IF ANYONE COMES, IT'LL BE RIGHT THROUGH HERE AT THE FRONT—

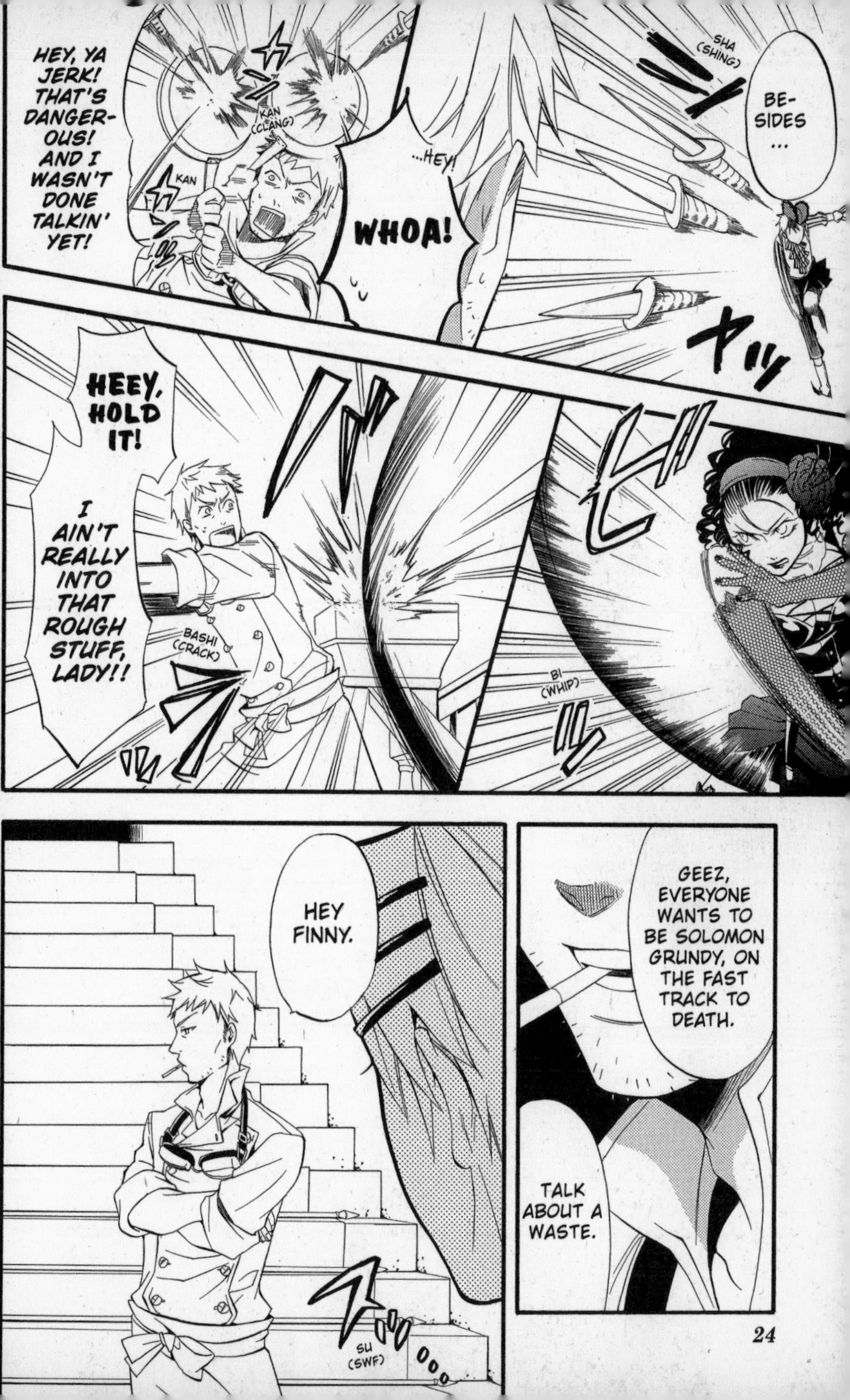
SHA (SHING)
BE-SIDES ...
...HEY!
WHOA!
KAN (CLANG)
KAN
HEY, YA JERK! THAT'S DANGER-OUS! AND I WASN'T DONE TALKIN' YET!
BI (WHIP)
HEEY, HOLD IT!
I AIN'T REALLY INTO THAT ROUGH STUFF, LADY!!
BASHI (CRACK)
GEEZ, EVERYONE WANTS TO BE SOLOMON GRUNDY, ON THE FAST TRACK TO DEATH.
TALK ABOUT A WASTE.
HEY FINNY.
SU (SWF)

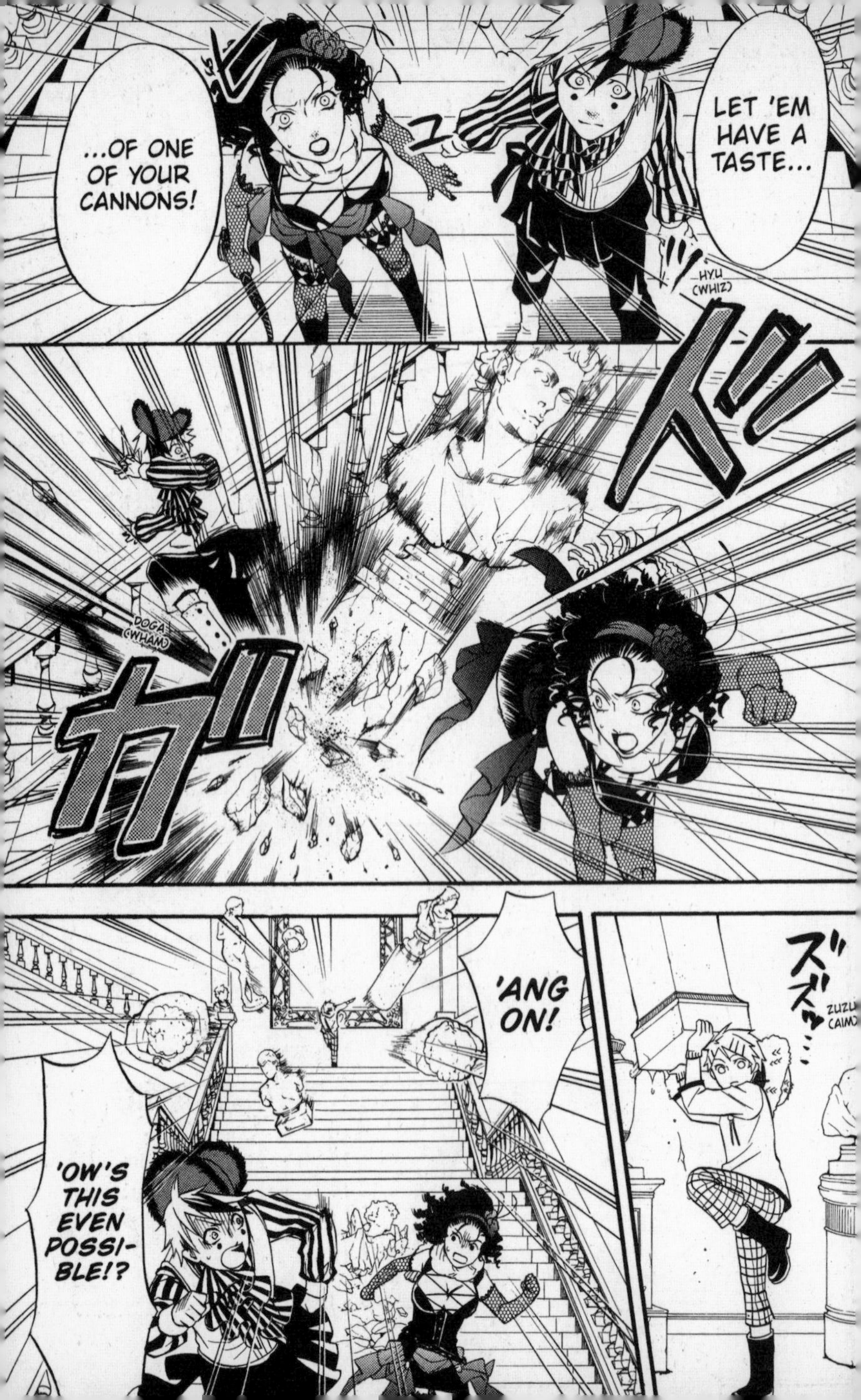
LET 'EM HAVE A TASTE...
...OF ONE OF YOUR CANNONS!
HYU (WHIZ)
DOGA (WHAM)
ZUZU (AIM)
'ANG ON!
'OW'S THIS EVEN POSSI-BLE!?

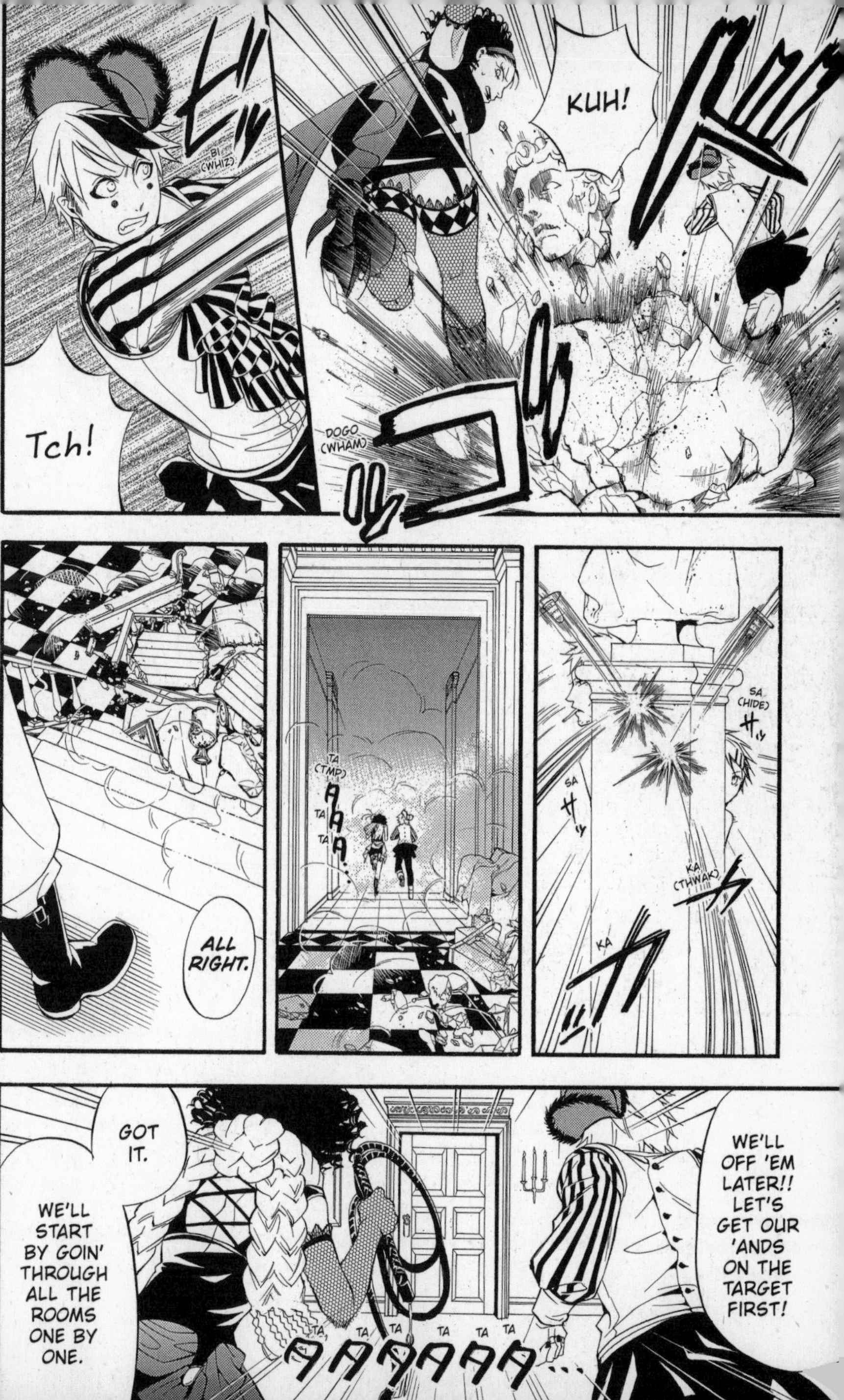
KUH!
DOGO (WHAM)
BI (WHIZ)
Tch!
SA (HIDE)
SA
KA (THWAK)
KA
TA (TMP)
TA
TA
ALL RIGHT.
WE'LL OFF 'EM LATER!! LET'S GET OUR 'ANDS ON THE TARGET FIRST!
GOT IT.
WE'LL START BY GOIN' THROUGH ALL THE ROOMS ONE BY ONE.
TA TA TA TA TA TA

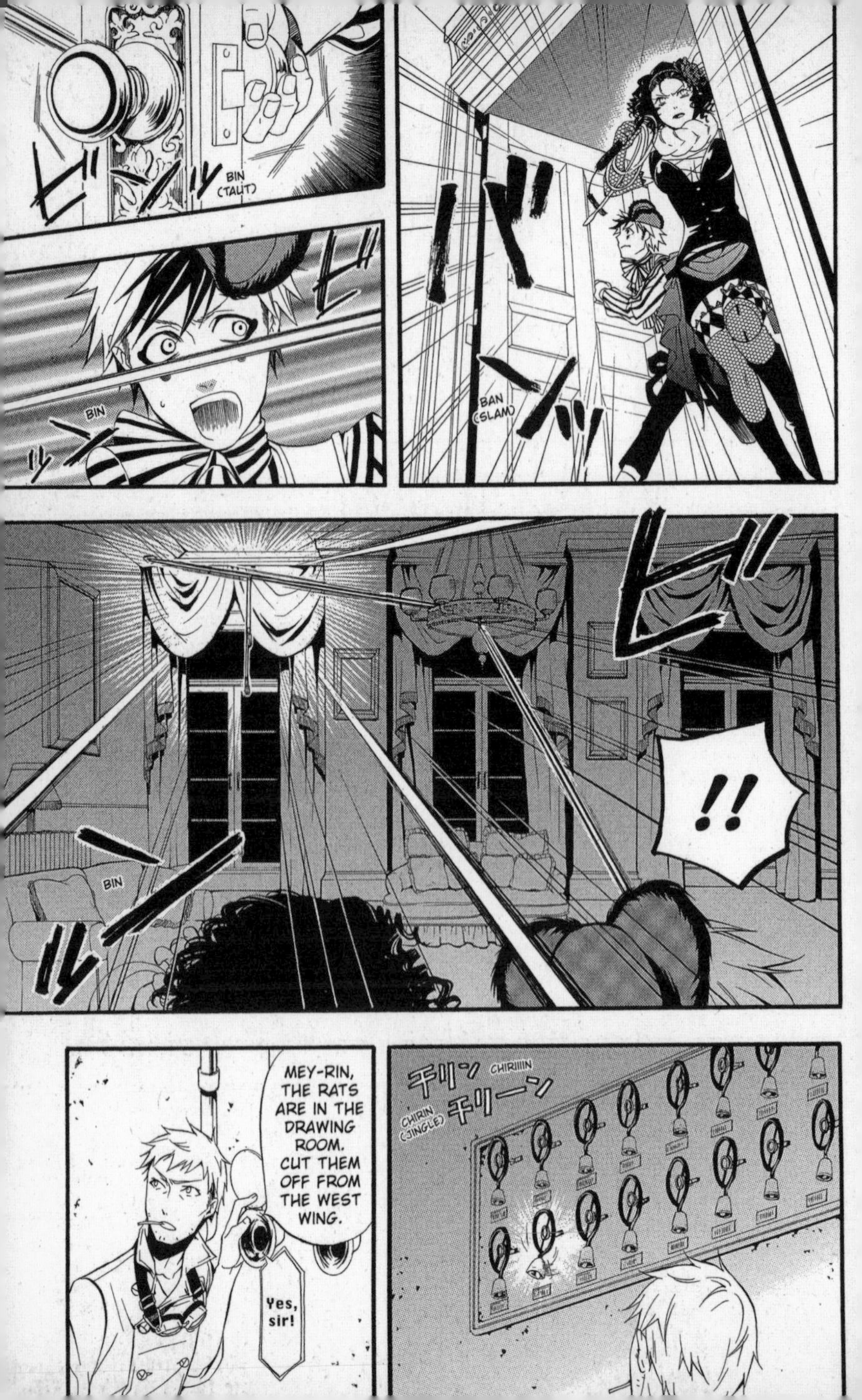
BAN
(SLAM)
BIN
(TAUT)
BIN
BIN
!!
チリーン CHIRIIIN
CHIRIN
(JINGLE) チリーン
MEY-RIN, THE RATS ARE IN THE DRAWING ROOM. CUT THEM OFF FROM THE WEST WING.
Yes, sir!

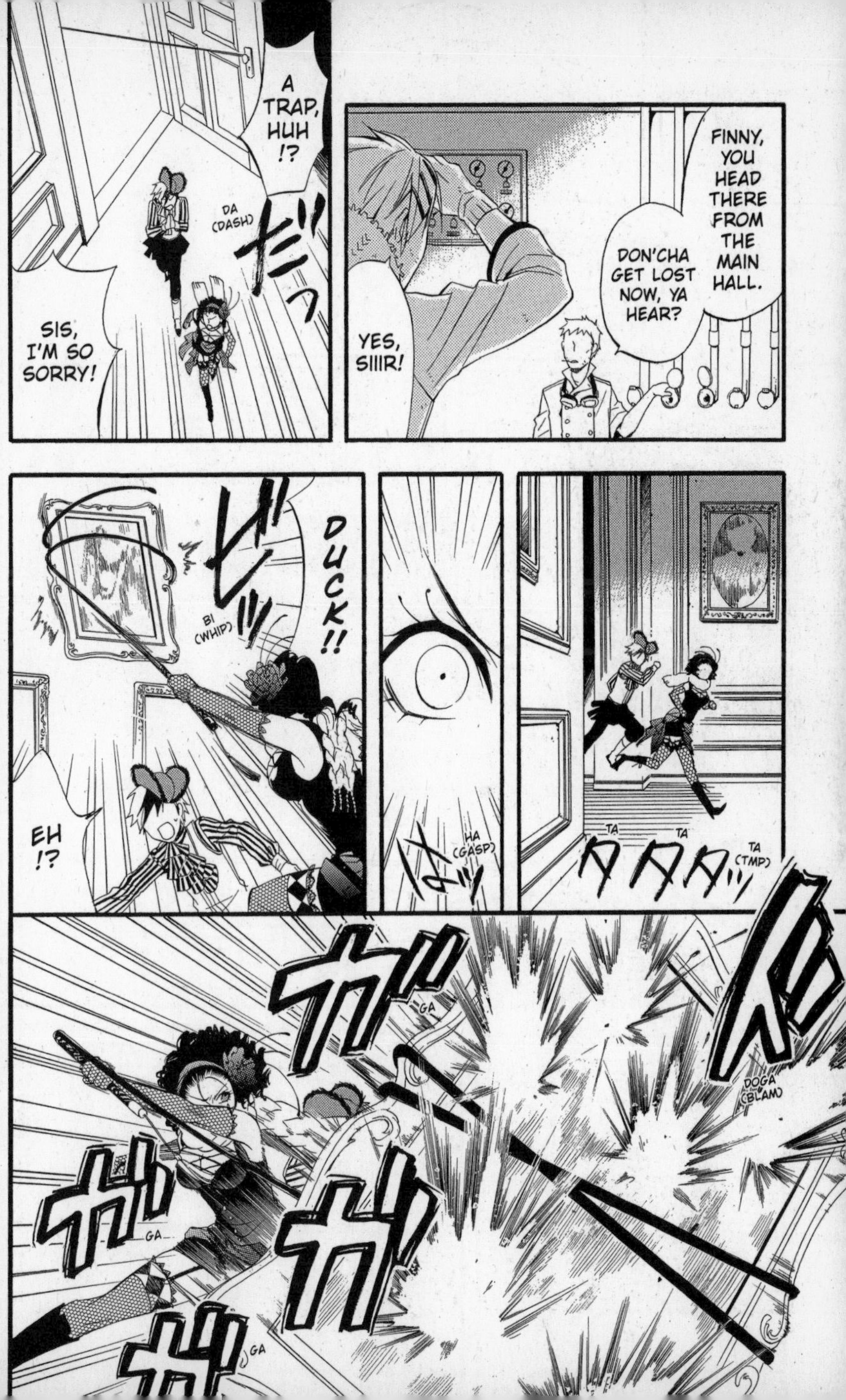
FINNY, YOU HEAD THERE FROM THE MAIN HALL.
DON'CHA GET LOST NOW, YA HEAR?
YES, SIIIR!
A TRAP, HUH!?
DA (DASH)
SIS, I'M SO SORRY!
TA TA TA (TMP)
HA (GASP)
DUCK!!
BI (WHIP)
EH!?
DOGA (BLAM)
GA
GA
GA

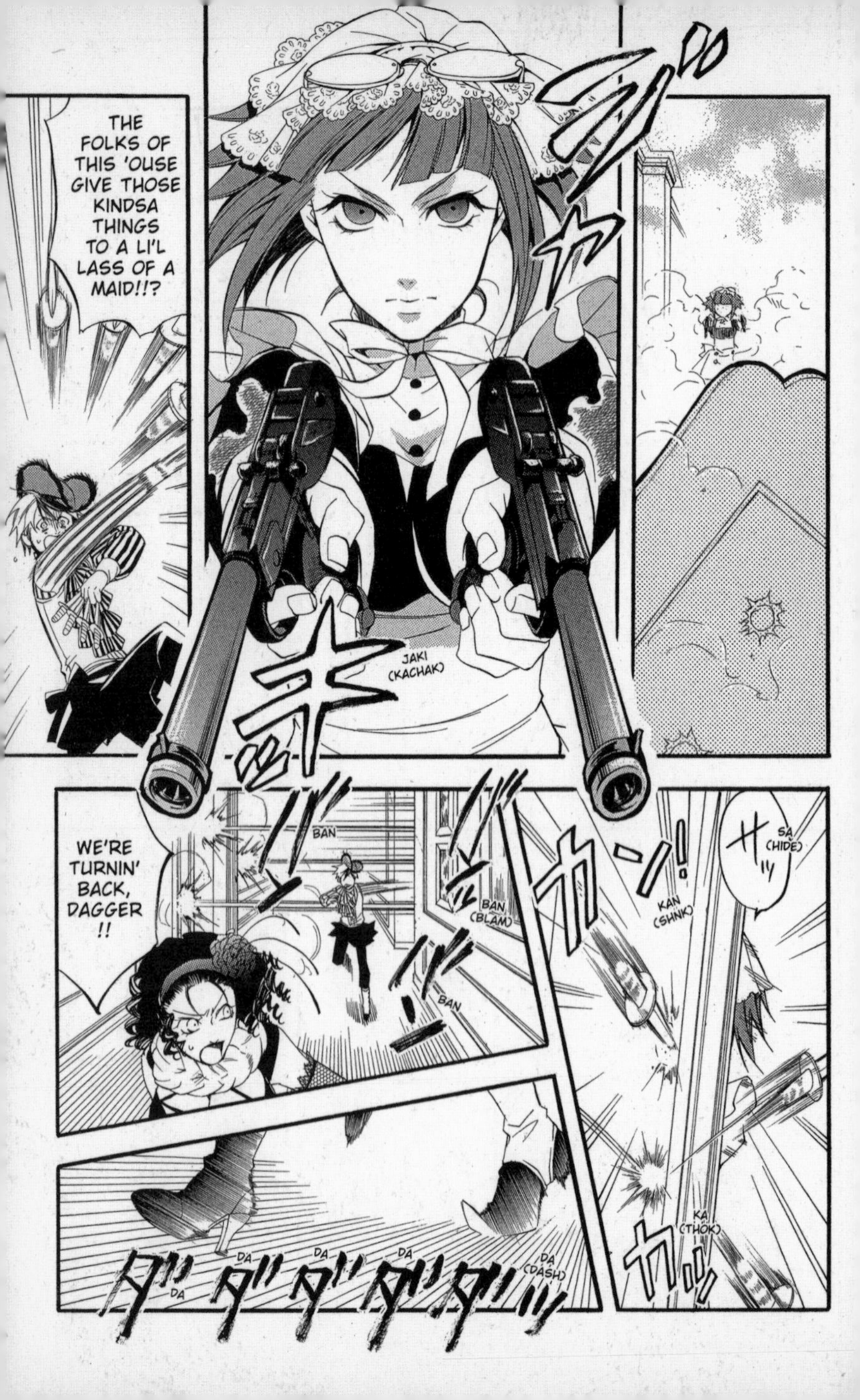

JAKI (KACHAK)
THE FOLKS OF THIS 'OUSE GIVE THOSE KINDSA THINGS TO A LI'L LASS OF A MAID!!?
SA (HIDE)
KAN (SHNK)
BAN
BAN (BLAM)
BAN
WE'RE TURNIN' BACK, DAGGER!!
KA (THOK)
DA DA DA DA DA (DASH)

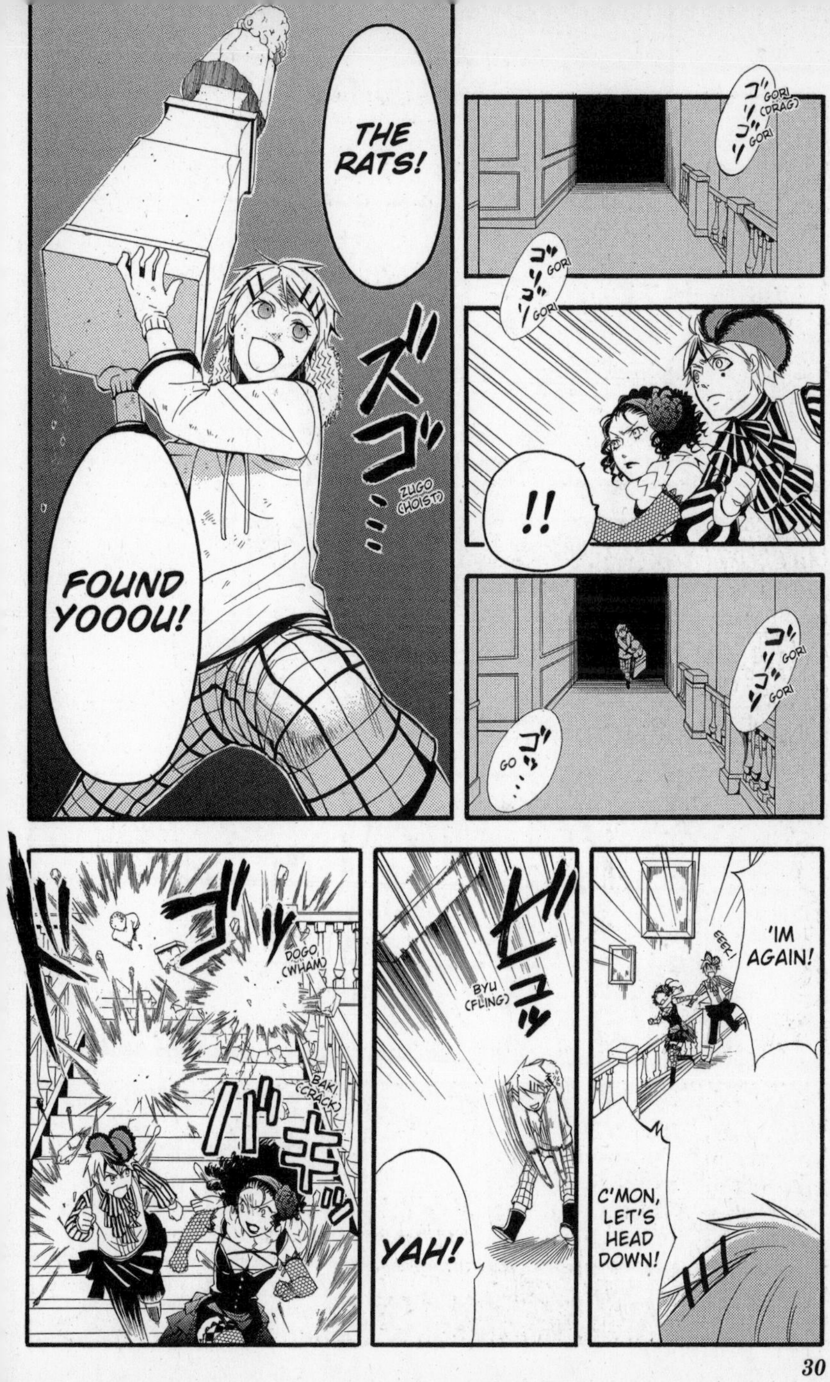

GORI (DRAG) GORI
GORI GORI
!!
GORI GORI
GO
THE RATS!
ZUGO (HOIST)
FOUND YOOOU!
'IM AGAIN!
EEEK!
C'MON, LET'S HEAD DOWN!
BYU (FLING)
YAH!
DOGO (WHAM)
BAKI (CRACK)

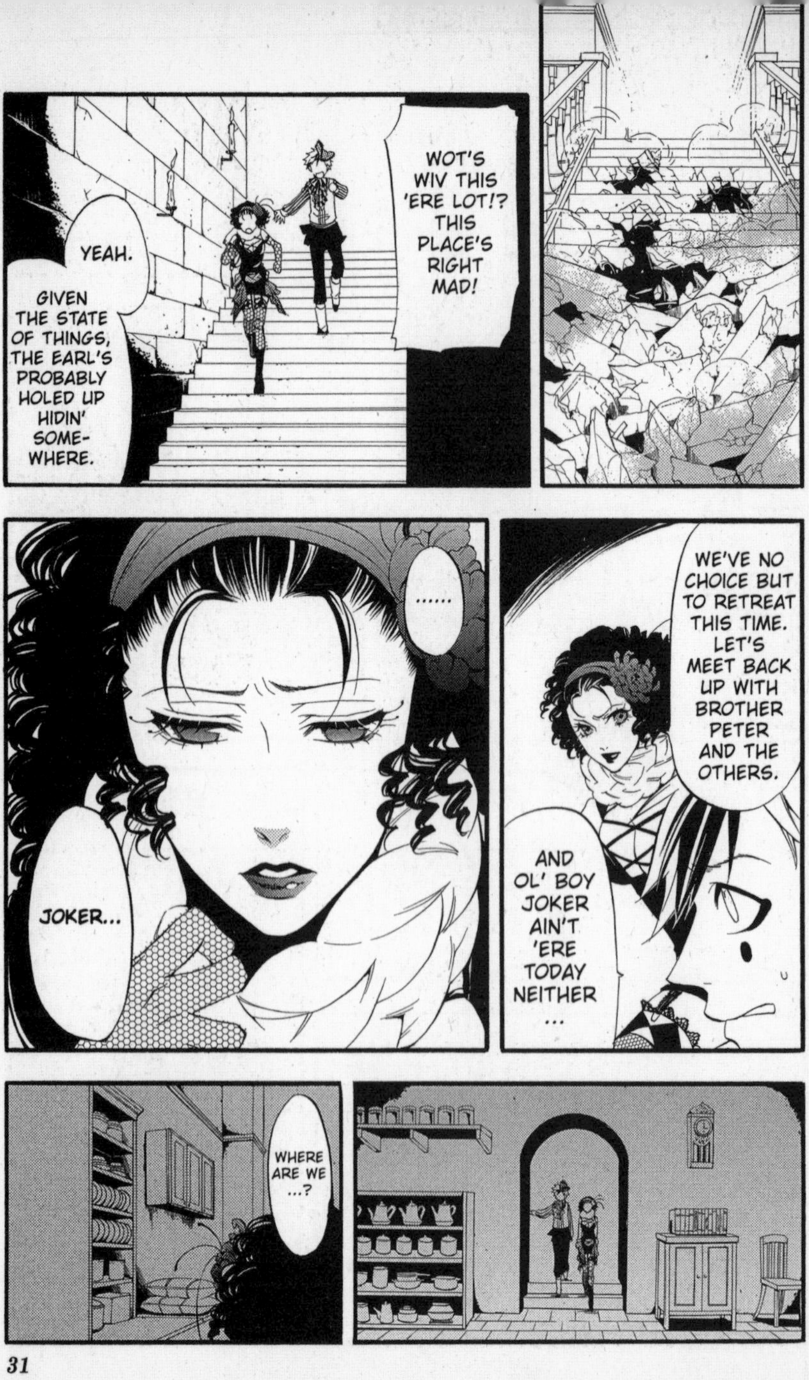
WOT'S WIV THIS 'ERE LOT!? THIS PLACE'S RIGHT MAD!
YEAH.
GIVEN THE STATE OF THINGS, THE EARL'S PROBABLY HOLED UP HIDIN' SOME-WHERE.
WE'VE NO CHOICE BUT TO RETREAT THIS TIME. LET'S MEET BACK UP WITH BROTHER PETER AND THE OTHERS.
AND OL' BOY JOKER AIN'T 'ERE TODAY NEITHER ...
......
JOKER...
WHERE ARE WE ...?

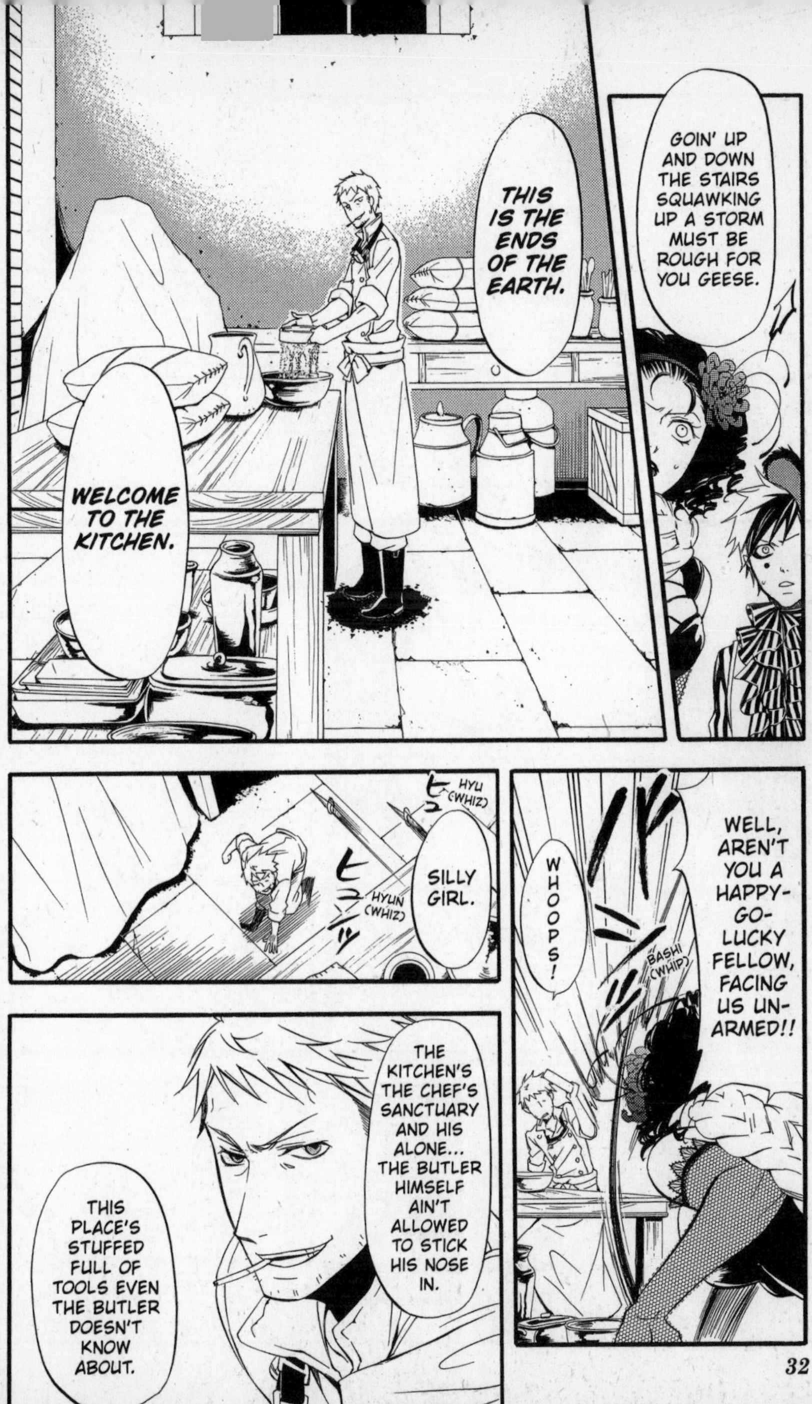
GOIN' UP AND DOWN THE STAIRS SQUAWKING UP A STORM MUST BE ROUGH FOR YOU GEESE.
THIS IS THE ENDS OF THE EARTH.
WELCOME TO THE KITCHEN.
WELL, AREN'T YOU A HAPPY-GO-LUCKY FELLOW, FACING US UN-ARMED!!
BASHI (WHIP)
WHOOPS!
HYU (WHIZ)
SILLY GIRL.
HYUN (WHIZ)
THE KITCHEN'S THE CHEF'S SANCTUARY AND HIS ALONE... THE BUTLER HIMSELF AIN'T ALLOWED TO STICK HIS NOSE IN.
THIS PLACE'S STUFFED FULL OF TOOLS EVEN THE BUTLER DOESN'T KNOW ABOUT.

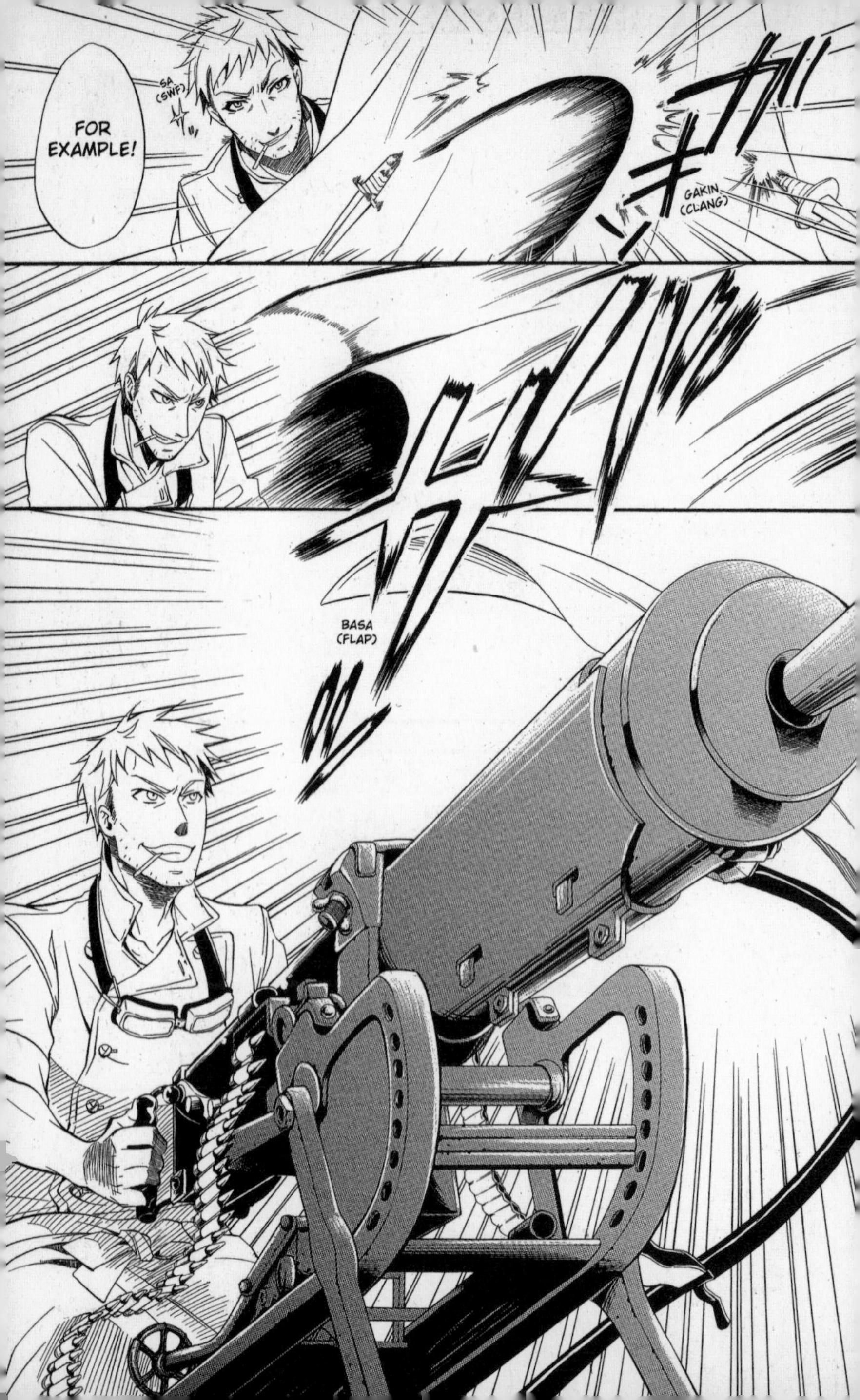
GAKIN (CLANG)
SA (SWF)
FOR EXAMPLE!
BASA (FLAP)

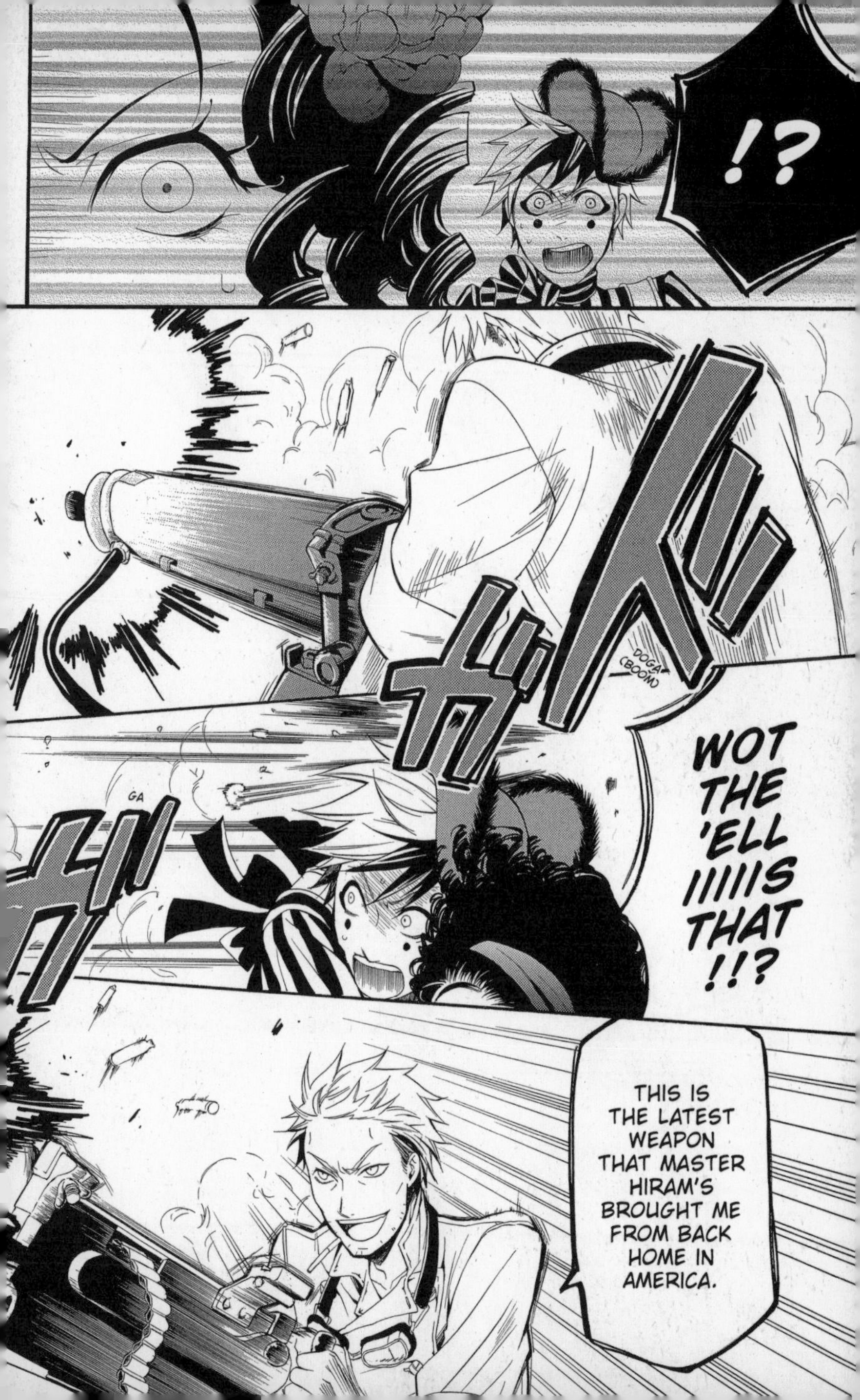
!?
DOGA (BOOM)
GA
WOT THE 'ELL IIIIIS THAT!!?
THIS IS THE LATEST WEAPON THAT MASTER HIRAM'S BROUGHT ME FROM BACK HOME IN AMERICA.

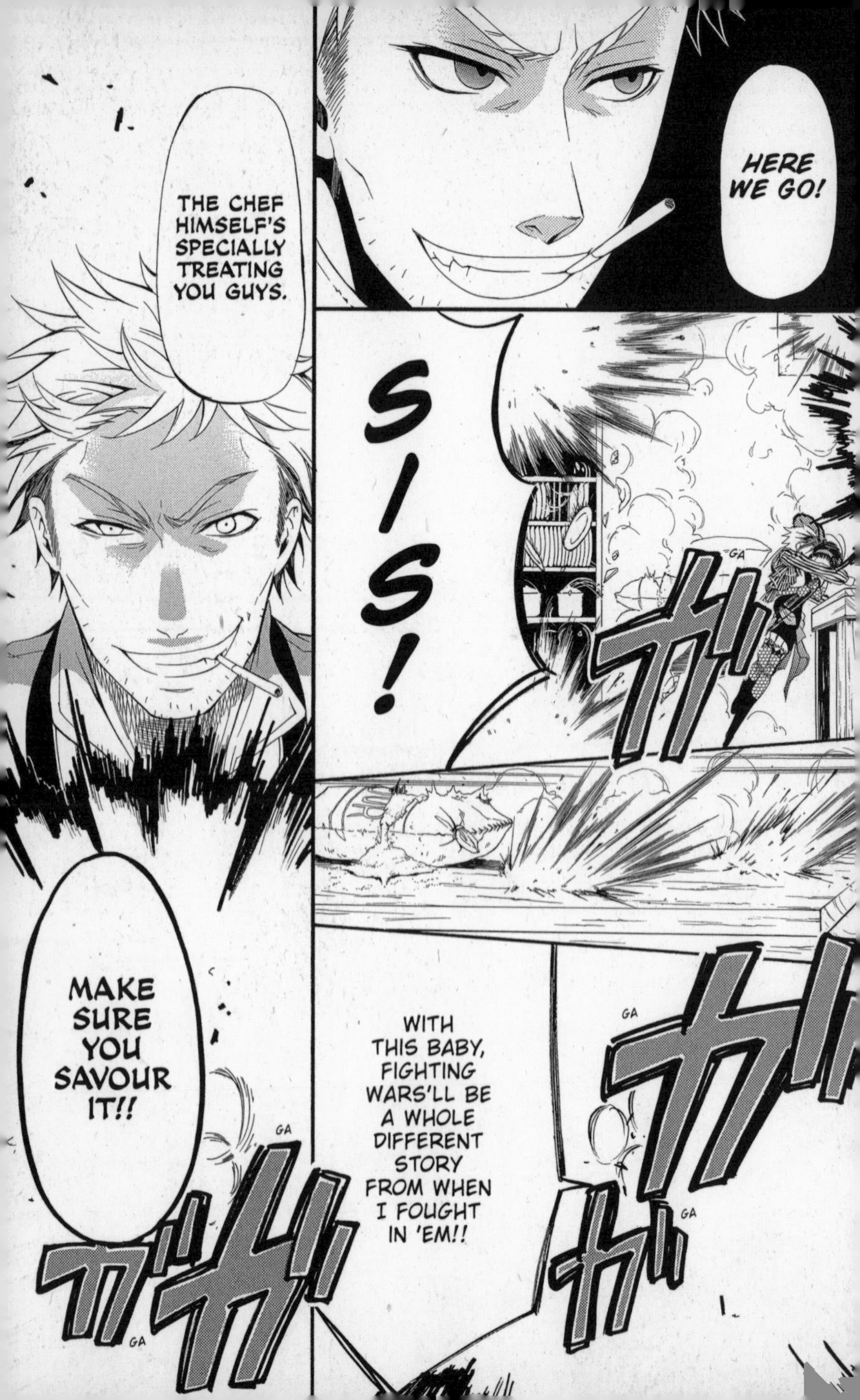
HERE WE GO!
SIS!
GA
WITH THIS BABY, FIGHTING WARS'LL BE A WHOLE DIFFERENT STORY FROM WHEN I FOUGHT IN 'EM!!
GA
GA
THE CHEF HIMSELF'S SPECIALLY TREATING YOU GUYS.
MAKE SURE YOU SAVOUR IT!!
GA
GA

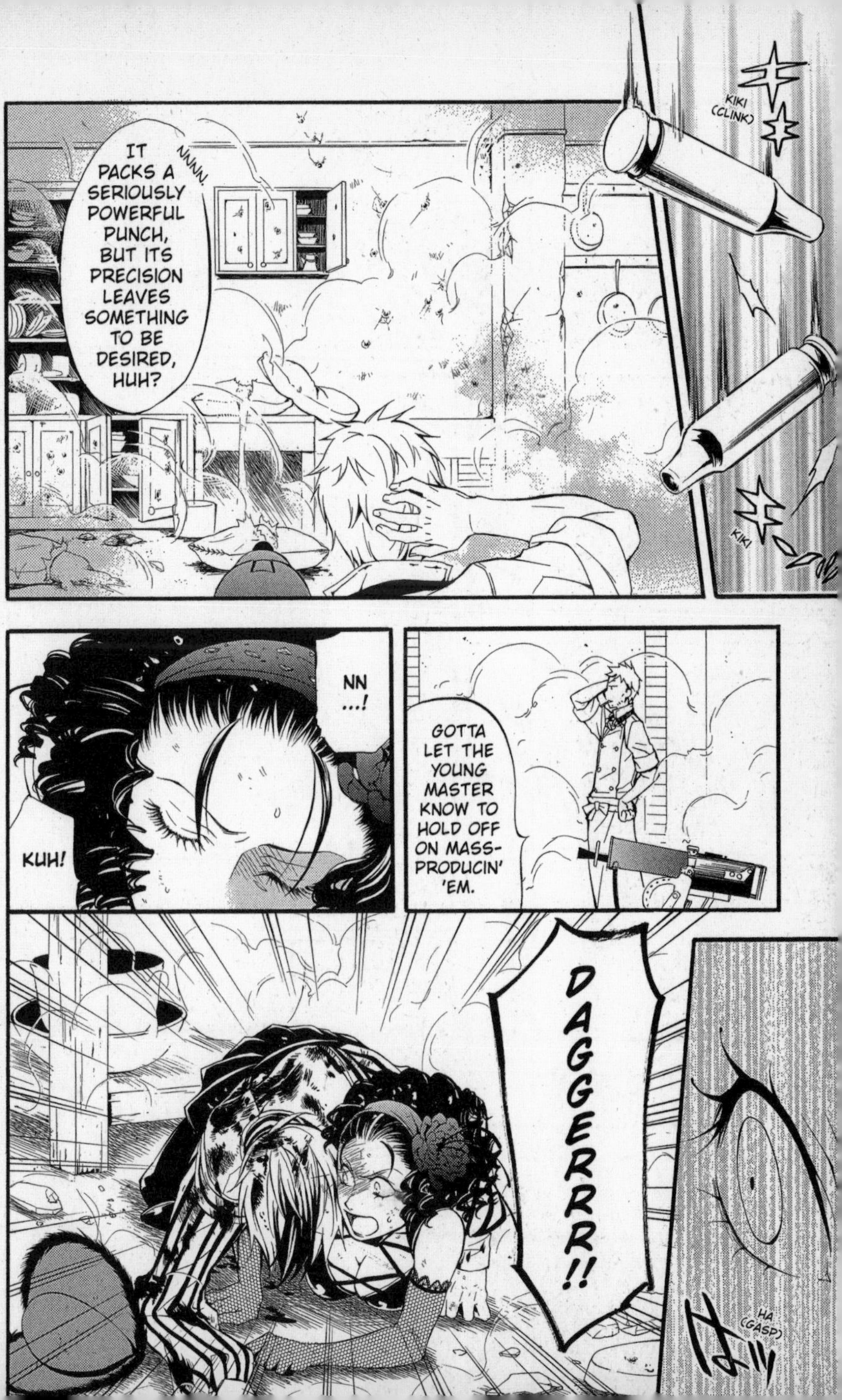
KIKI (CLINK)
KIKI
NNNN.
IT PACKS A SERIOUSLY POWERFUL PUNCH, BUT ITS PRECISION LEAVES SOMETHING TO BE DESIRED, HUH?
GOTTA LET THE YOUNG MASTER KNOW TO HOLD OFF ON MASS-PRODUCIN' 'EM.
NN ...!
KUH!
HA (GASP)
DAGGERRR!!

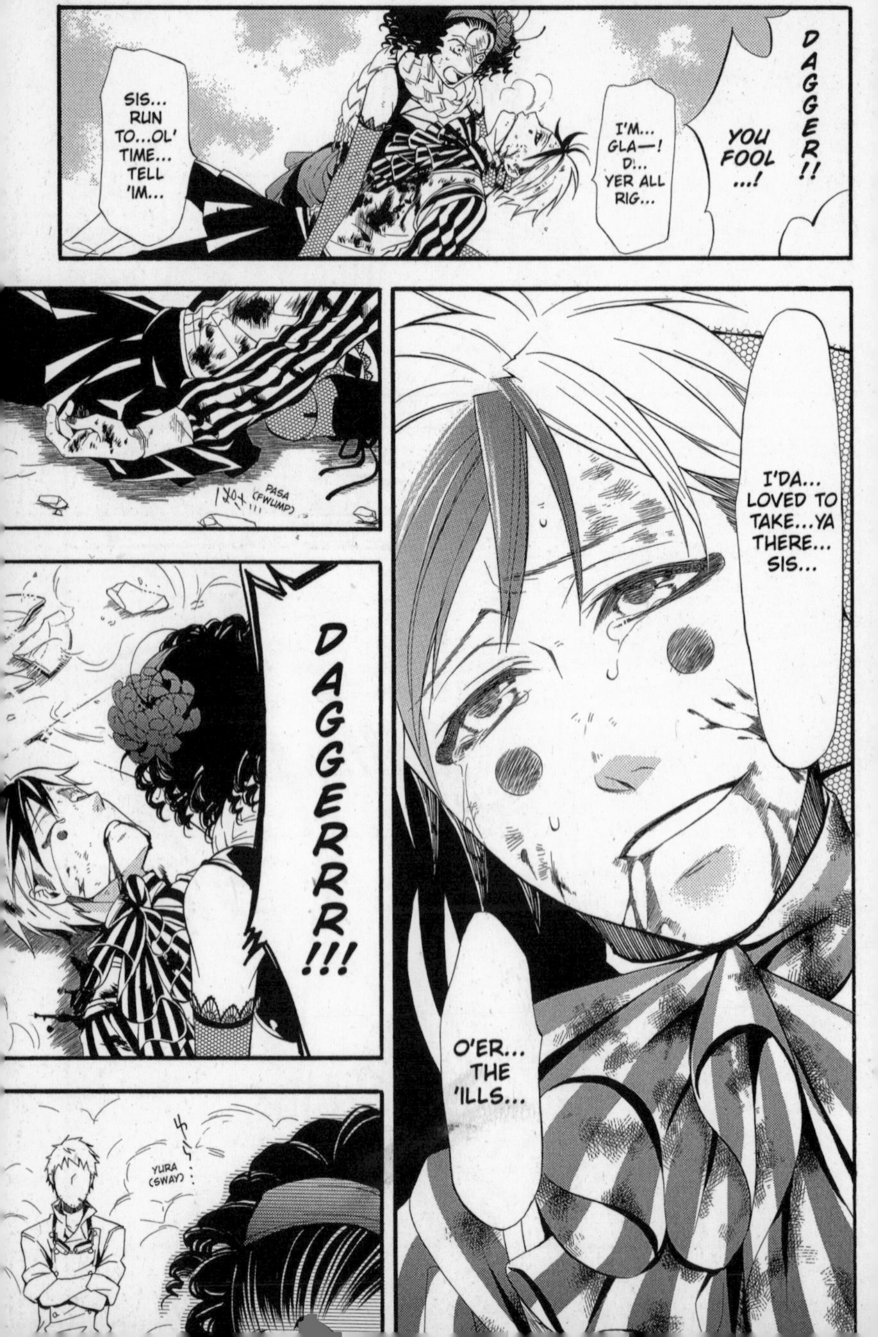
DAGGER!!
YOU FOOL ...!
I'M... GLA—! D... YER ALL RIG...
SIS... RUN TO...OL' TIME... TELL 'IM...
I'DA... LOVED TO TAKE...YA THERE... SIS...
O'ER... THE 'ILLS...
PASA (FWUMP)
DAGGERRRR!!!
YURA (SWAY)

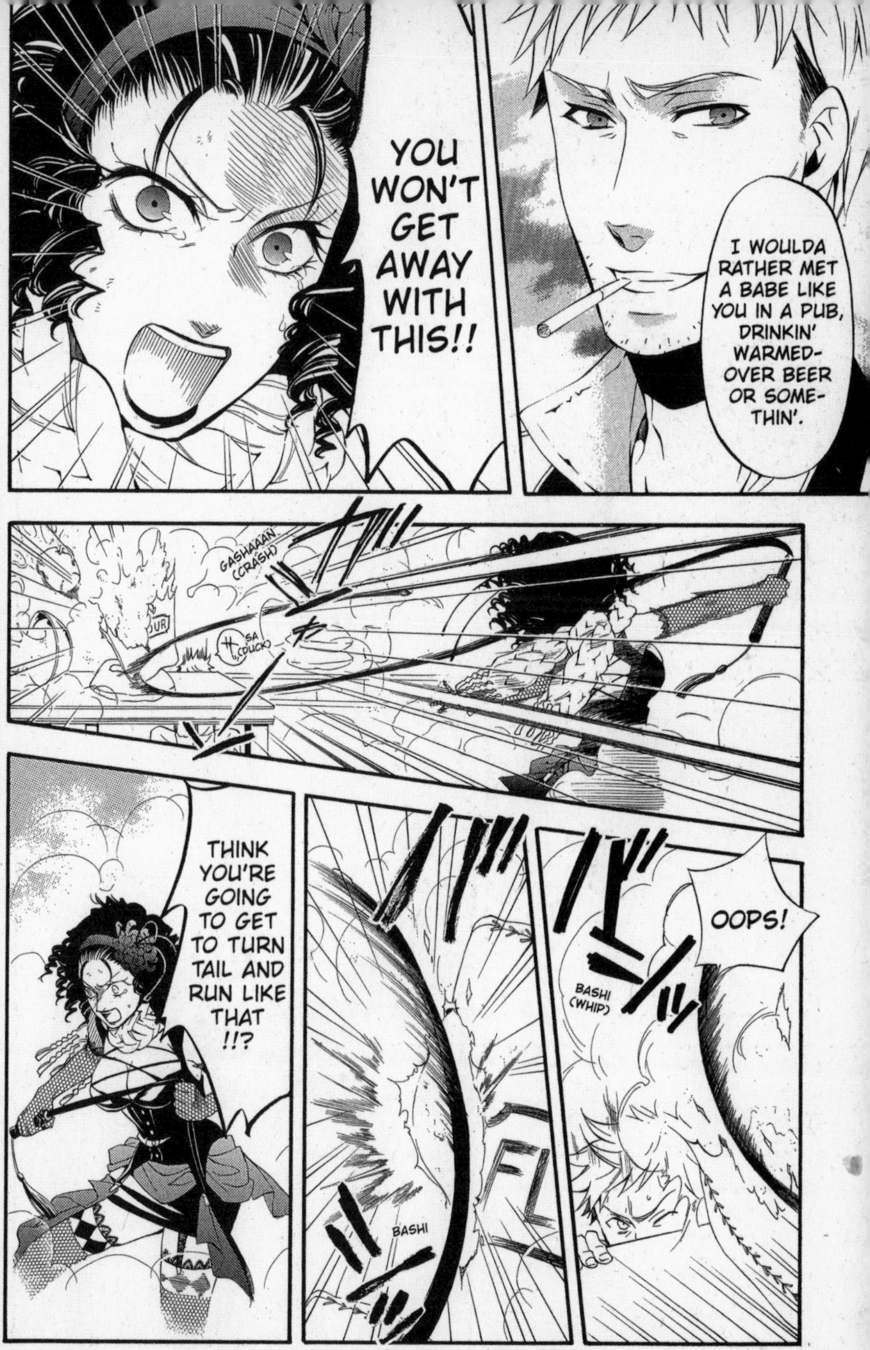
I WOULDA RATHER MET A BABE LIKE YOU IN A PUB, DRINKIN' WARMED-OVER BEER OR SOME-THIN'.
YOU WON'T GET AWAY WITH THIS!!
GASHAAAN (CRASH)
SA (DUCK)
OOPS!
BASHI (WHIP)
BASHI
THINK YOU'RE GOING TO GET TO TURN TAIL AND RUN LIKE THAT!!?

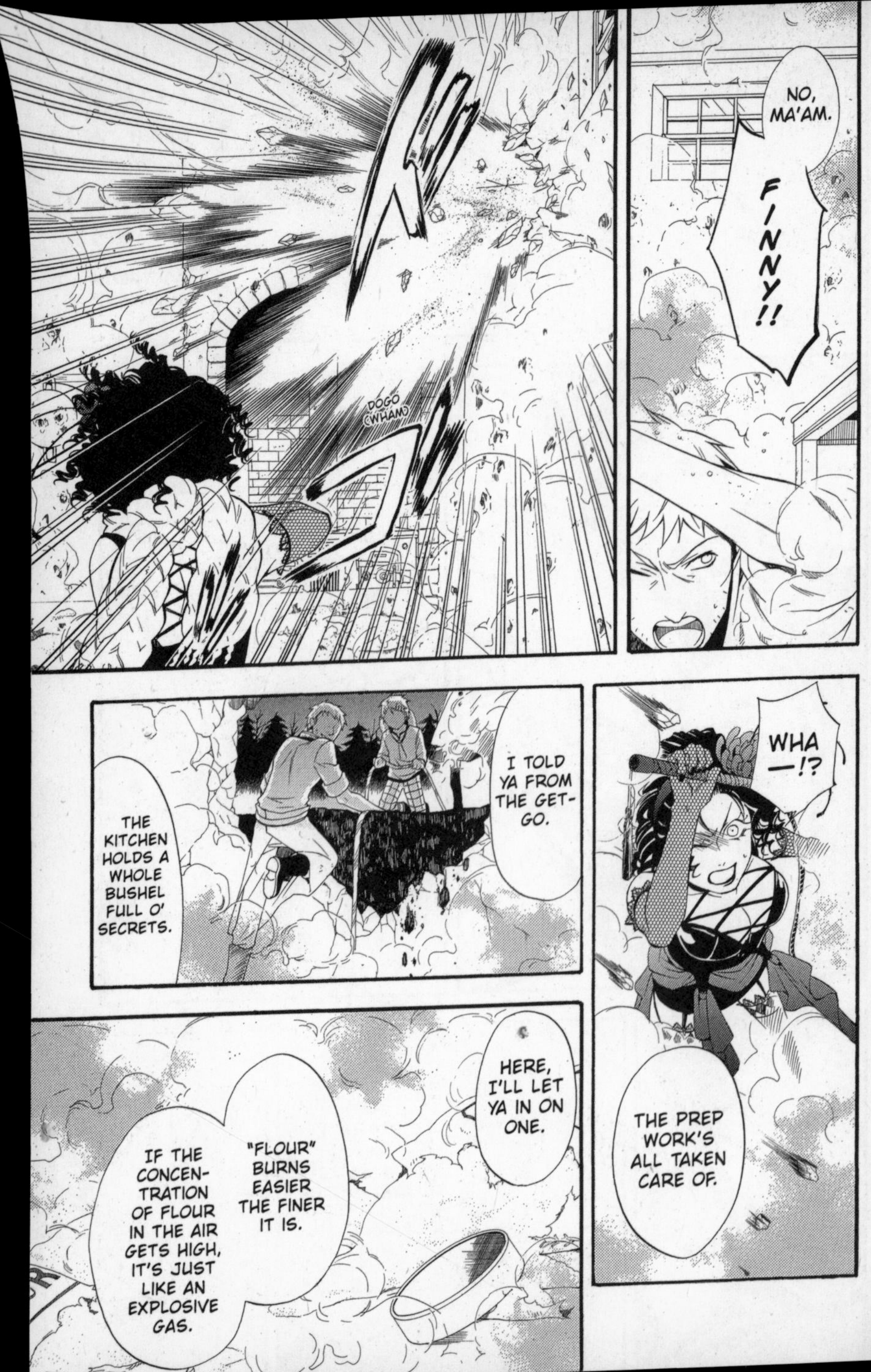
NO, MA'AM.
FINNY!!
DOGO (WHAM)
WHA—!?
THE PREP WORK'S ALL TAKEN CARE OF.
I TOLD YA FROM THE GET-GO.
THE KITCHEN HOLDS A WHOLE BUSHEL FULL O' SECRETS.
HERE, I'LL LET YA IN ON ONE.
"FLOUR" BURNS EASIER THE FINER IT IS.
IF THE CONCEN-TRATION OF FLOUR IN THE AIR GETS HIGH, IT'S JUST LIKE AN EXPLOSIVE GAS.

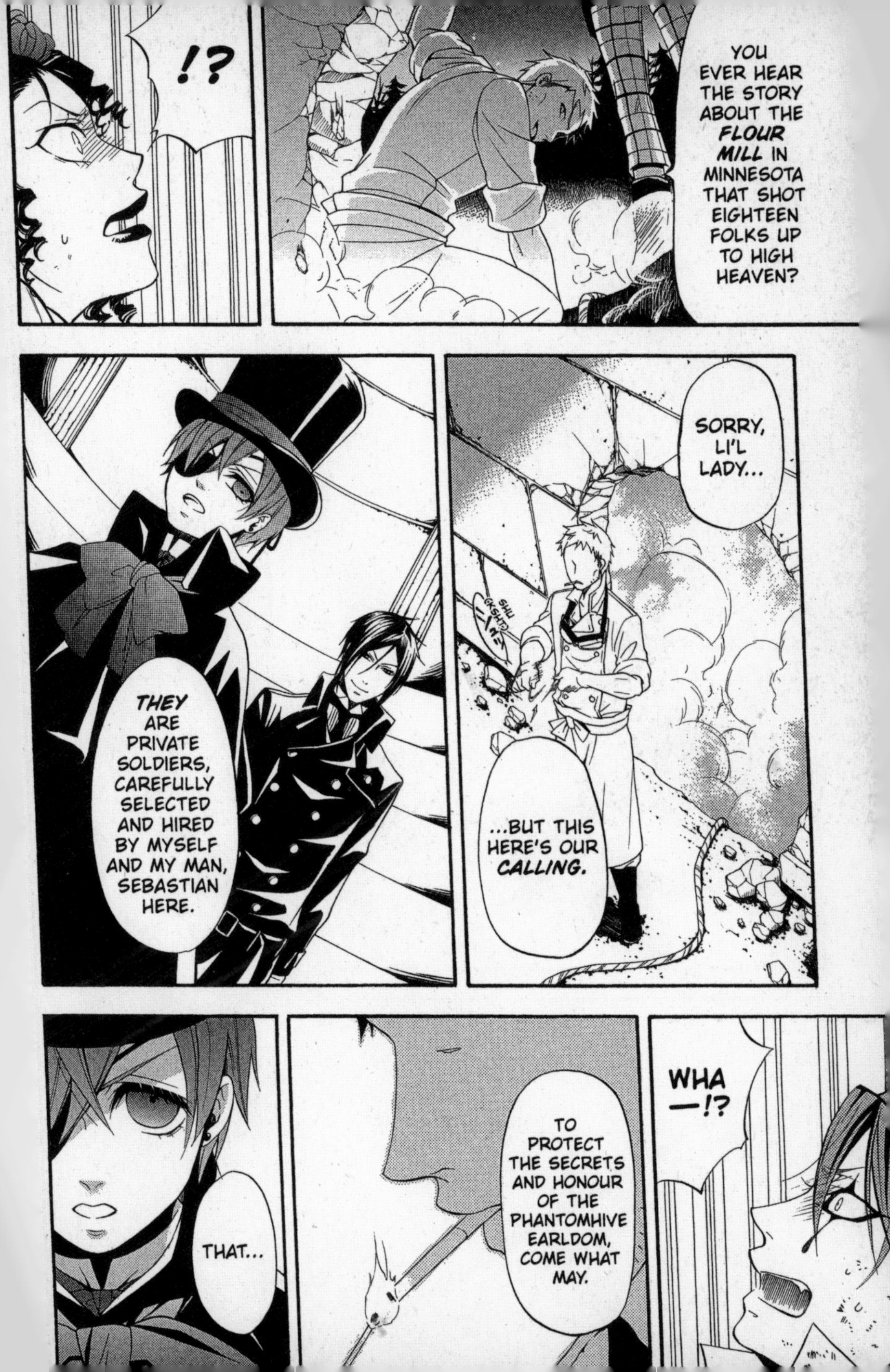
YOU EVER HEAR THE STORY ABOUT THE FLOUR MILL IN MINNESOTA THAT SHOT EIGHTEEN FOLKS UP TO HIGH HEAVEN?
!?
SORRY, LI'L LADY...
SHU GKSHT
...BUT THIS HERE'S OUR CALLING.
THEY ARE PRIVATE SOLDIERS, CAREFULLY SELECTED AND HIRED BY MYSELF AND MY MAN, SEBASTIAN HERE.
WHA—!?
TO PROTECT THE SECRETS AND HONOUR OF THE PHANTOMHIVE EARLDOM, COME WHAT MAY.
THAT...

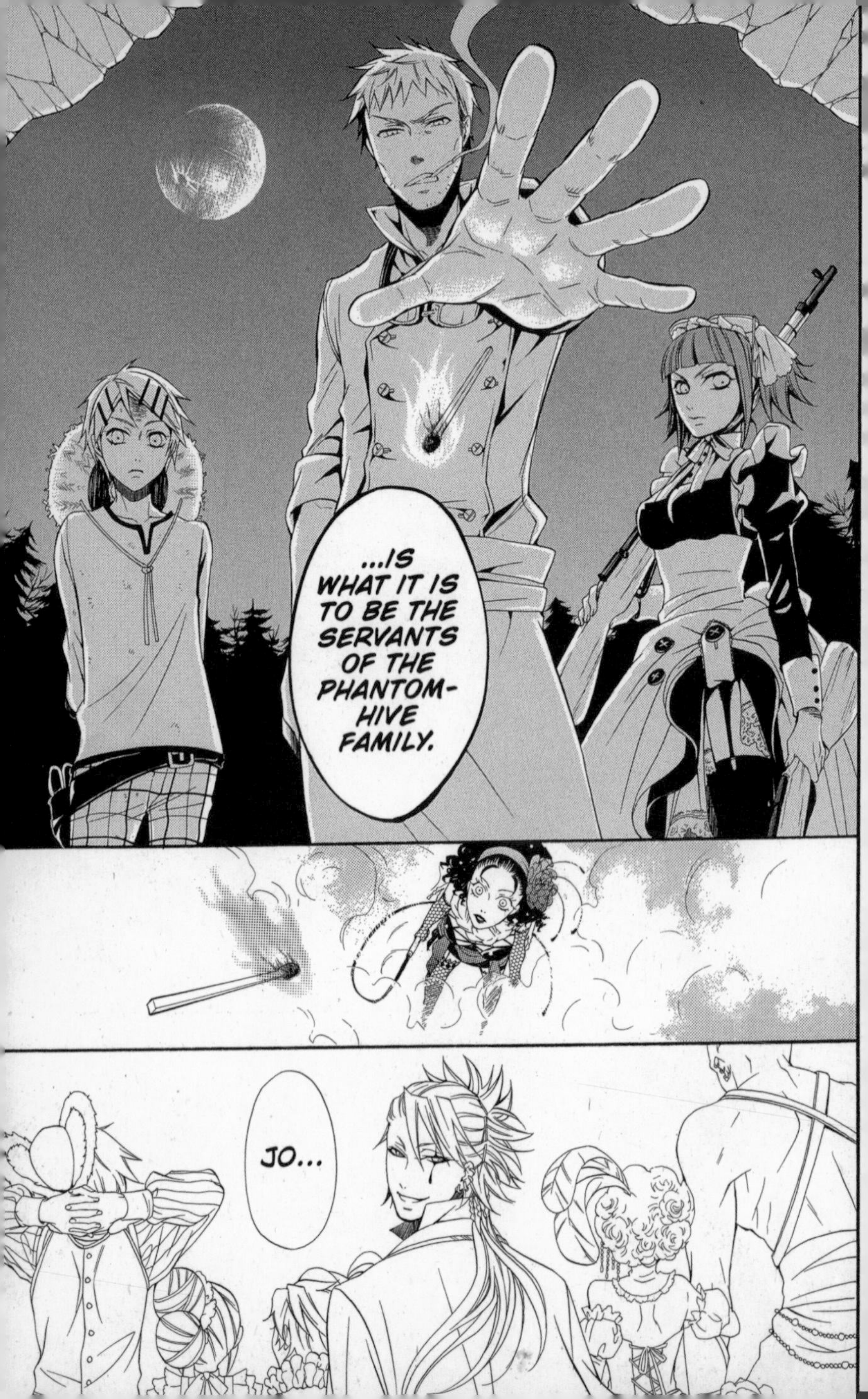
...IS WHAT IT IS TO BE THE SERVANTS OF THE PHANTOM-HIVE FAMILY.
JO...

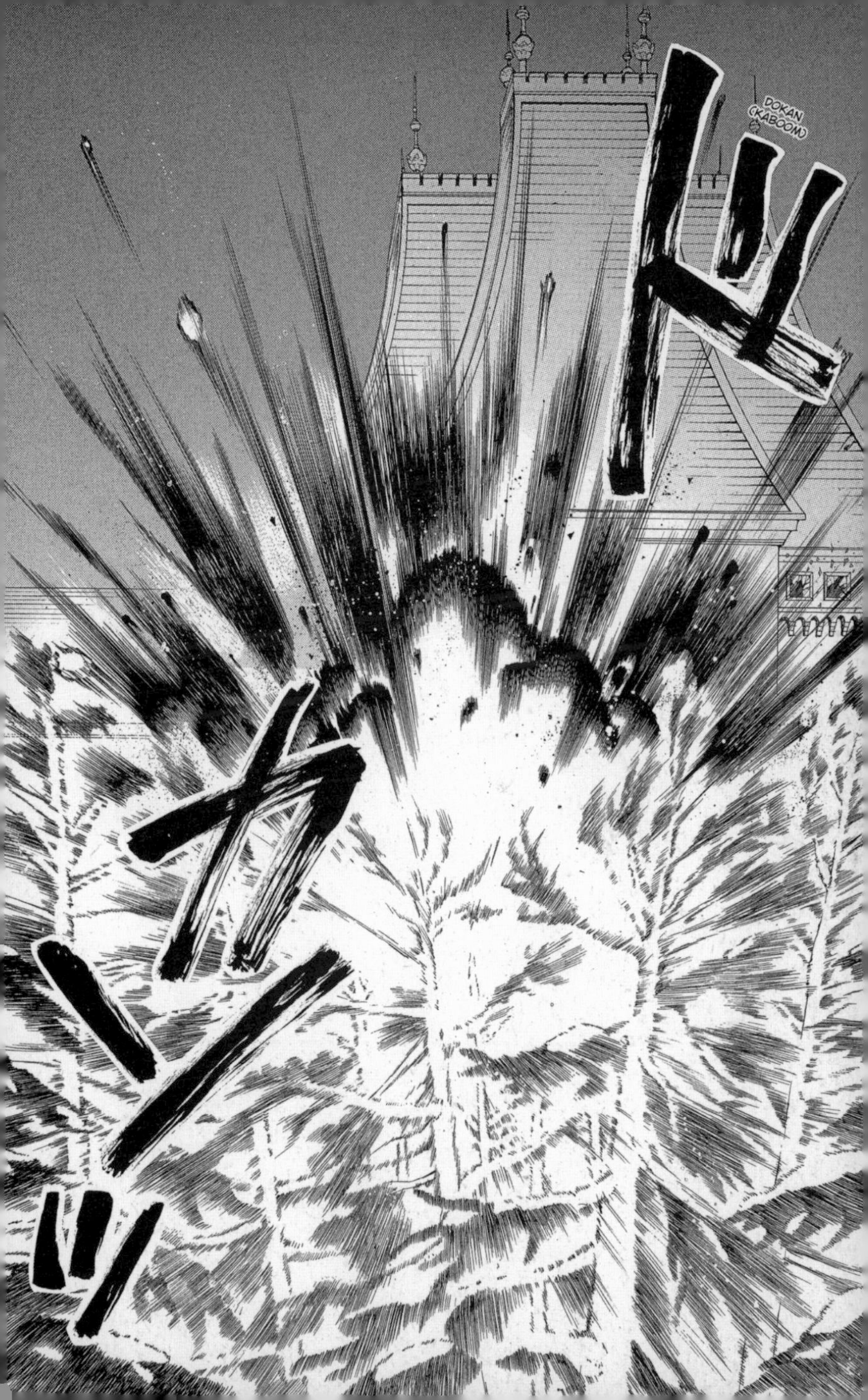
DOKAN
(KABOOM)

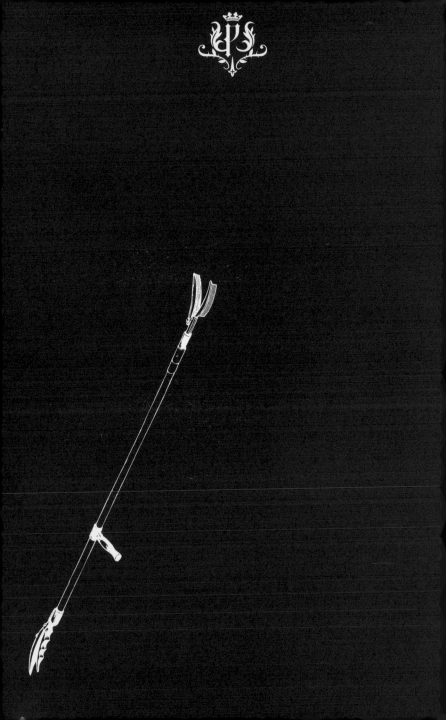

Black Butler

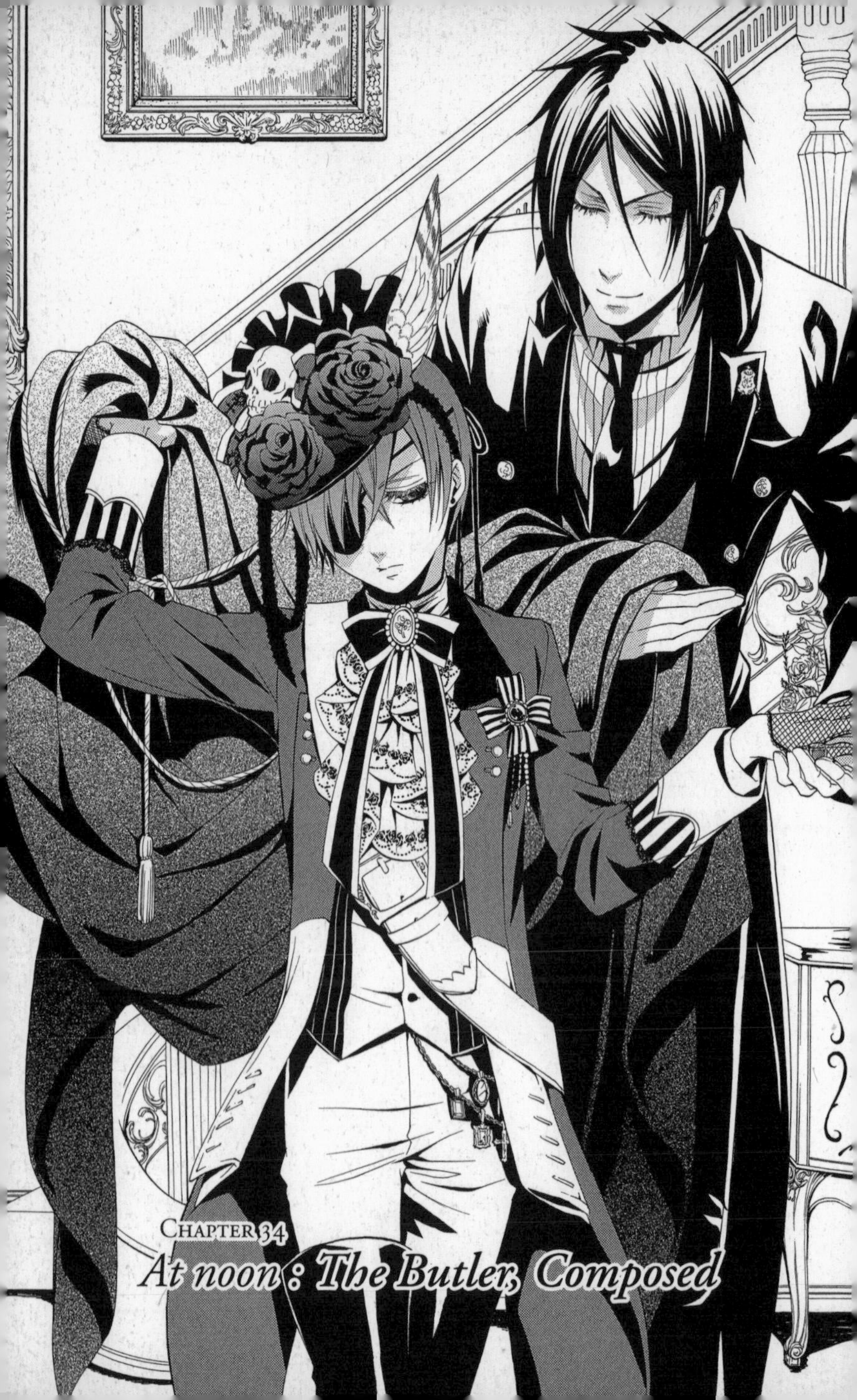
Chapter 34
At noon : The Butler, Composed

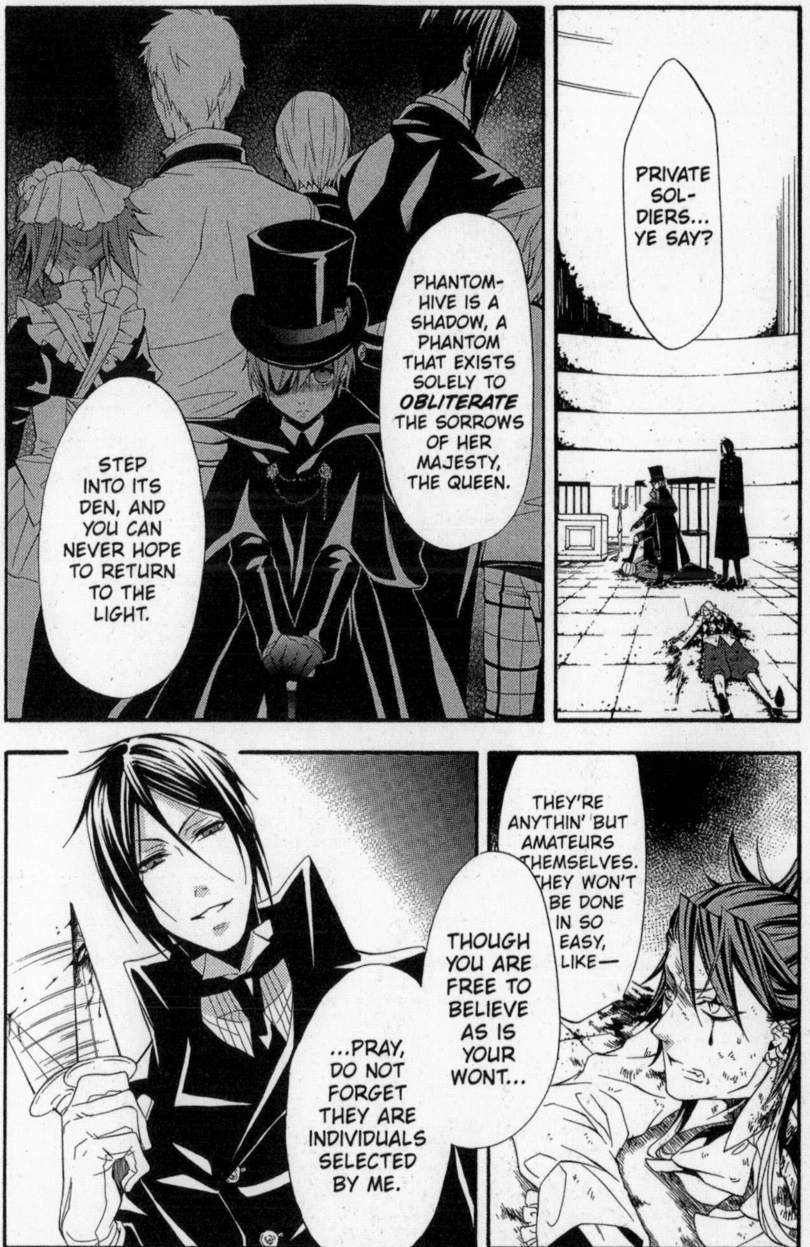
PRIVATE SOLDIERS... YE SAY?
PHANTOMHIVE IS A SHADOW, A PHANTOM THAT EXISTS SOLELY TO ***OBLITERATE*** THE SORROWS OF HER MAJESTY, THE QUEEN.
STEP INTO ITS DEN, AND YOU CAN NEVER HOPE TO RETURN TO THE LIGHT.
THEY'RE ANYTHIN' BUT AMATEURS THEMSELVES. THEY WON'T BE DONE IN SO EASY, LIKE—
THOUGH YOU ARE FREE TO BELIEVE AS IS YOUR WONT...
...PRAY, DO NOT FORGET THEY ARE INDIVIDUALS SELECTED BY ME.

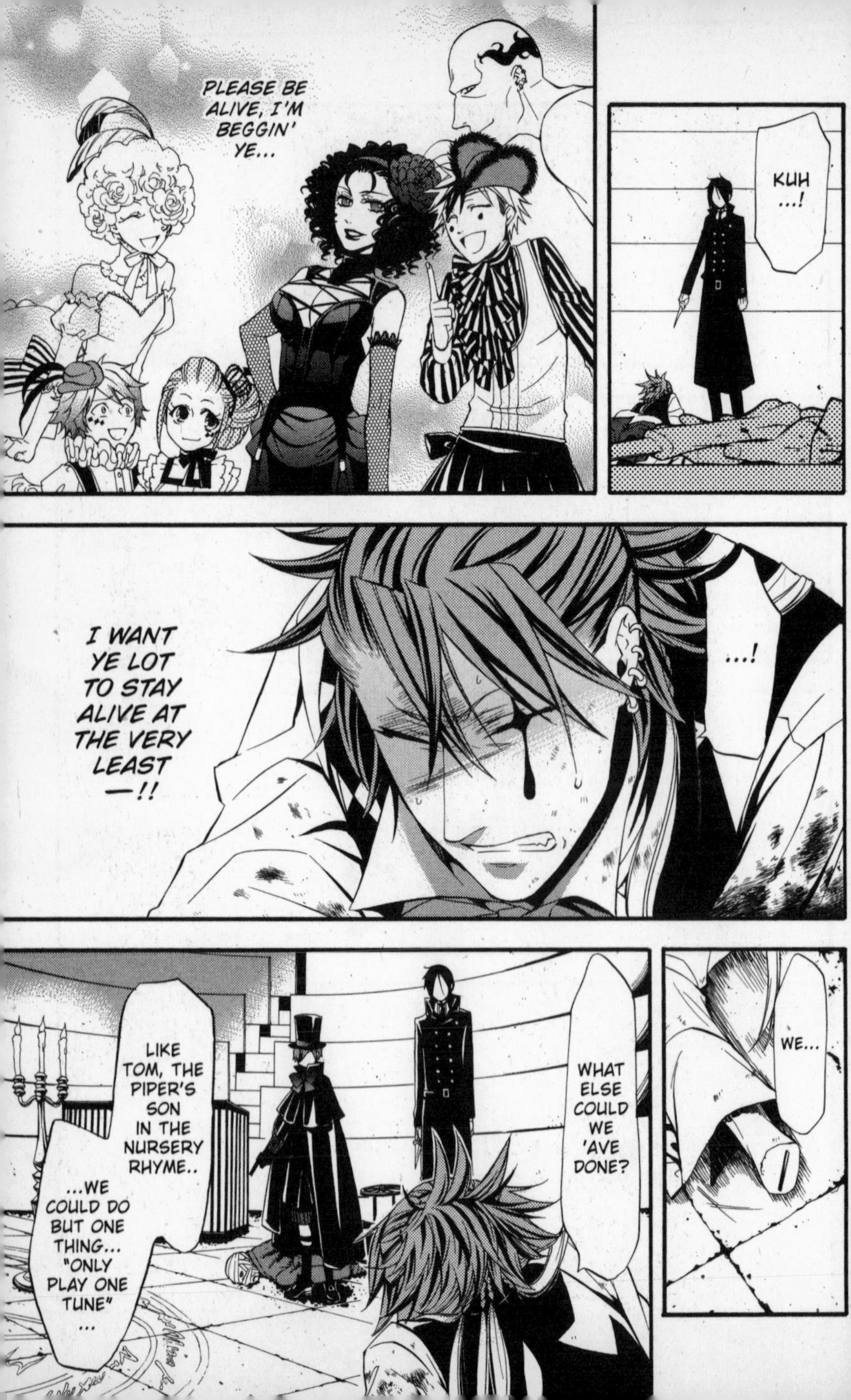
KUH ...!
PLEASE BE ALIVE, I'M BEGGIN' YE...
...!
I WANT YE LOT TO STAY ALIVE AT THE VERY LEAST—!!
WE...
WHAT ELSE COULD WE 'AVE DONE?
LIKE TOM, THE PIPER'S SON IN THE NURSERY RHYME..
...WE COULD DO BUT ONE THING... "ONLY PLAY ONE TUNE" ...

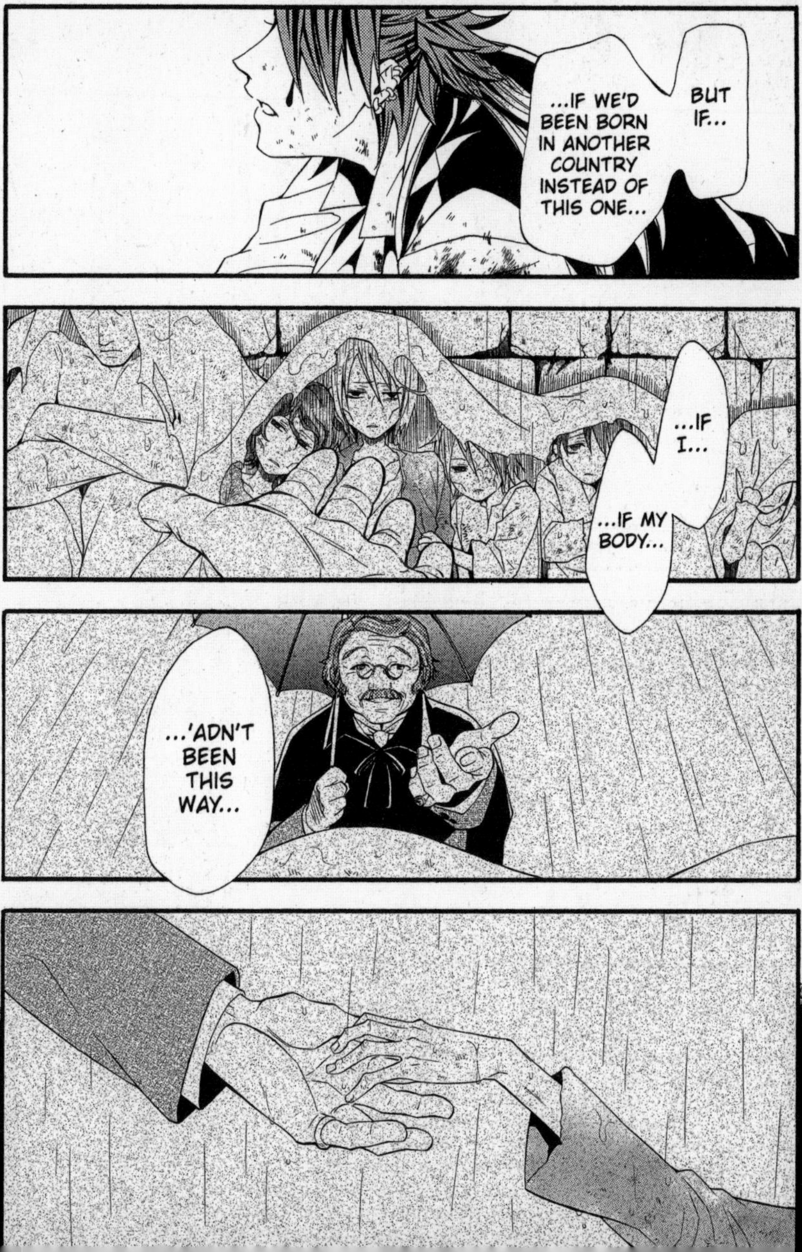
BUT IF...
...IF WE'D BEEN BORN IN ANOTHER COUNTRY INSTEAD OF THIS ONE...
...IF I...
...IF MY BODY...
...'ADN'T BEEN THIS WAY...

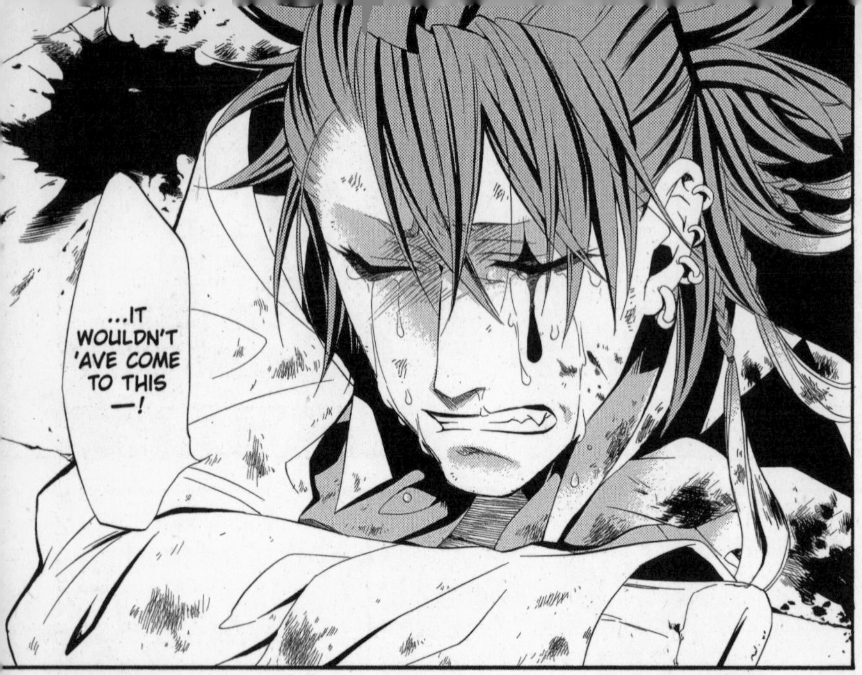
...IT WOULDN'T 'AVE COME TO THIS —!

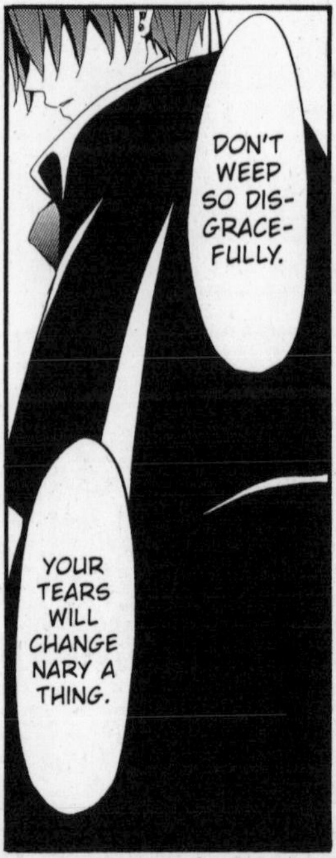
DON'T WEEP SO DIS-GRACE-FULLY.
YOUR TEARS WILL CHANGE NARY A THING.

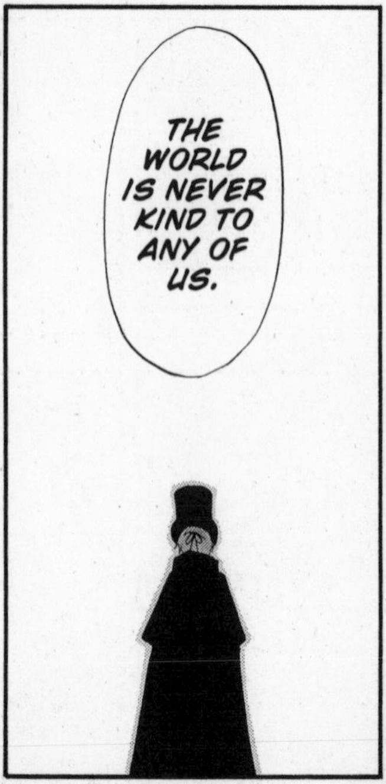
THE WORLD IS NEVER KIND TO ANY OF US.

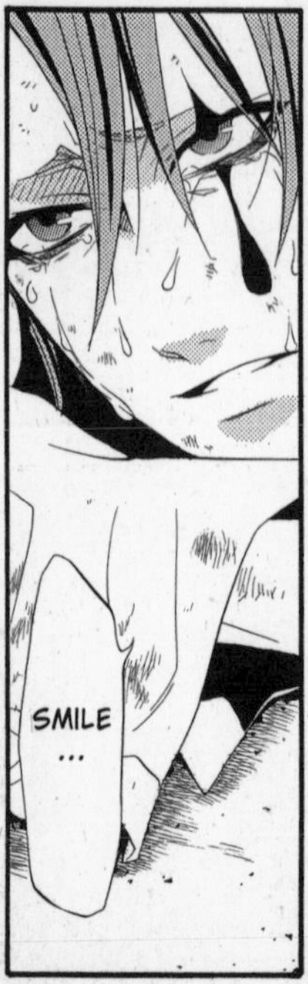
SMILE ...

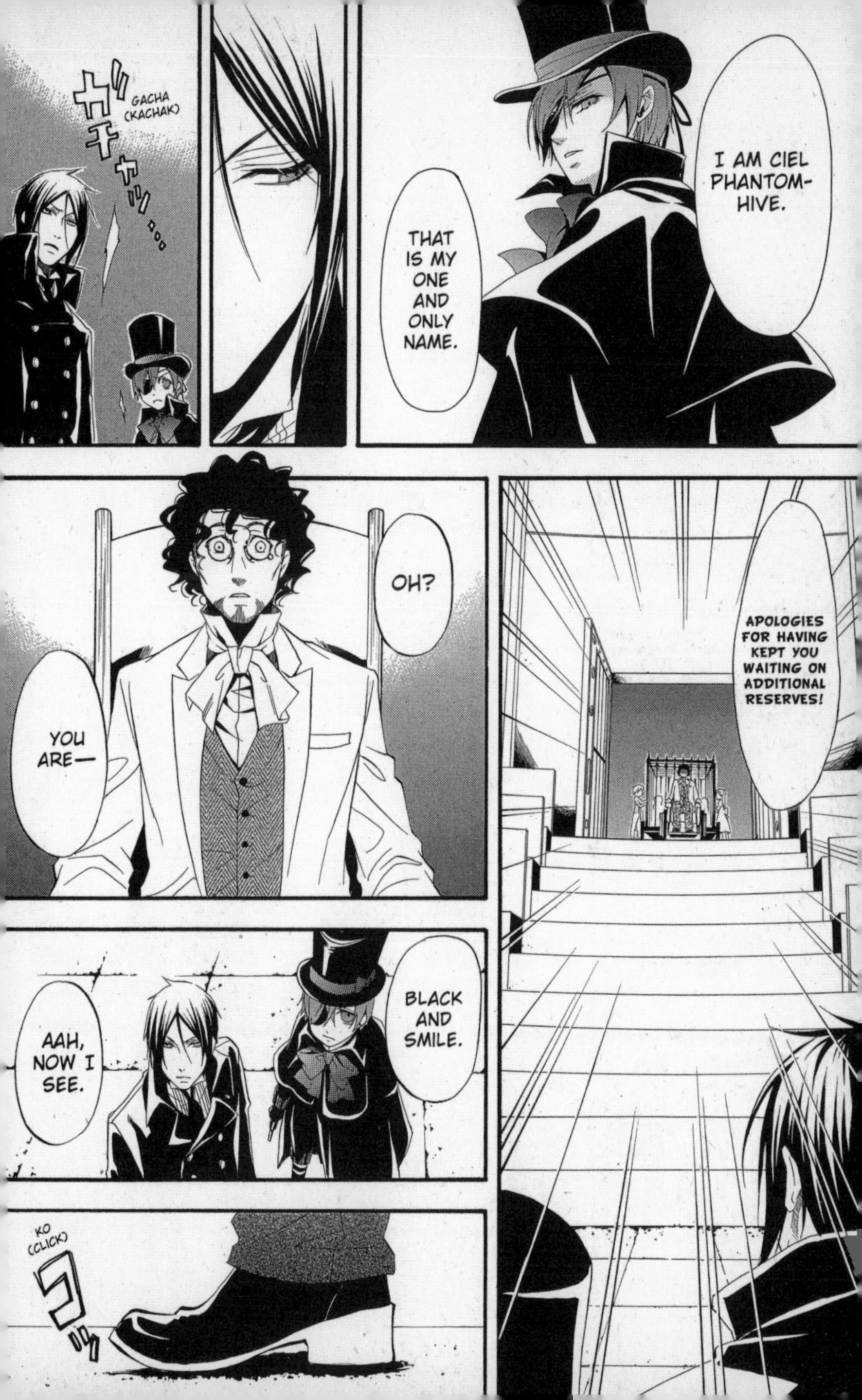
I AM CIEL PHANTOM-HIVE.
THAT IS MY ONE AND ONLY NAME.
GACHA (KACHAK)
APOLOGIES FOR HAVING KEPT YOU WAITING ON ADDITIONAL RESERVES!
OH?
YOU ARE—
BLACK AND SMILE.
AAH, NOW I SEE.
KO (CLICK)

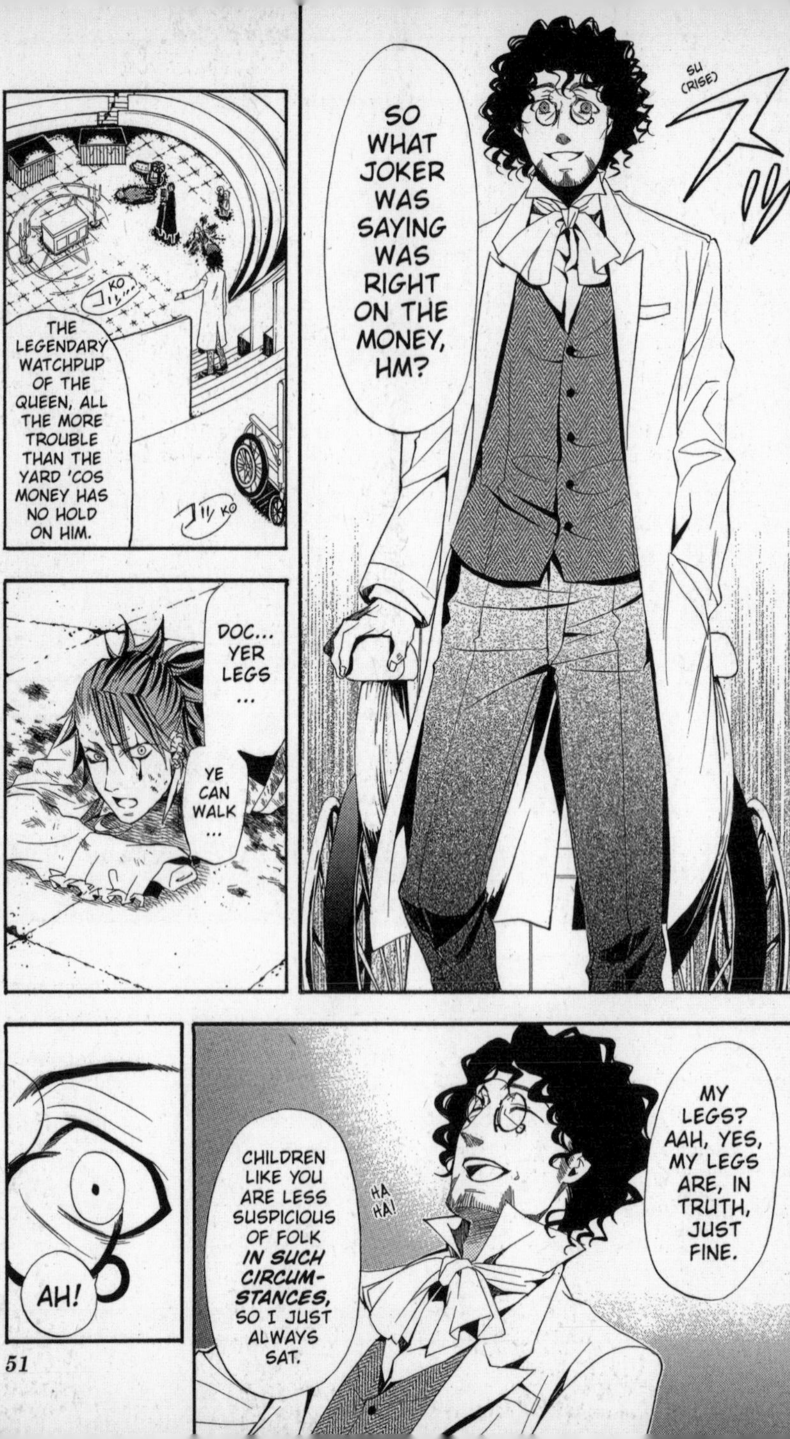
SU (RISE)
SO WHAT JOKER WAS SAYING WAS RIGHT ON THE MONEY, HM?
KO
THE LEGENDARY WATCHPUP OF THE QUEEN, ALL THE MORE TROUBLE THAN THE YARD 'COS MONEY HAS NO HOLD ON HIM.
KO
DOC... YER LEGS ...
YE CAN WALK ...
MY LEGS? AAH, YES, MY LEGS ARE, IN TRUTH, JUST FINE.
HA HA!
CHILDREN LIKE YOU ARE LESS SUSPICIOUS OF FOLK *IN SUCH CIRCUM-STANCES,* SO I JUST ALWAYS SAT.
AH!

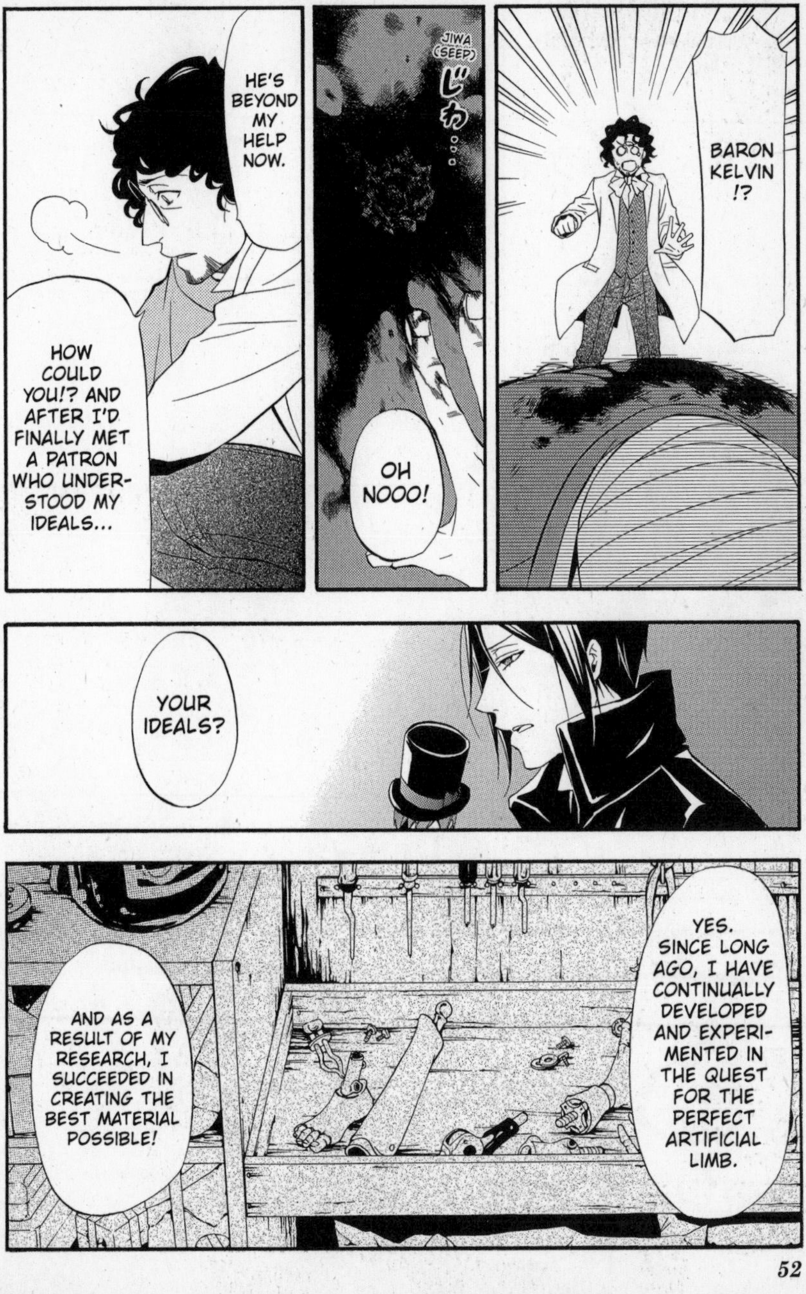
BARON KELVIN!?
JIWA (SEEP)
じわ…
OH NOOO!
HE'S BEYOND MY HELP NOW.
HOW COULD YOU!? AND AFTER I'D FINALLY MET A PATRON WHO UNDERSTOOD MY IDEALS...
YOUR IDEALS?
YES. SINCE LONG AGO, I HAVE CONTINUALLY DEVELOPED AND EXPERIMENTED IN THE QUEST FOR THE PERFECT ARTIFICIAL LIMB.
AND AS A RESULT OF MY RESEARCH, I SUCCEEDED IN CREATING THE BEST MATERIAL POSSIBLE!

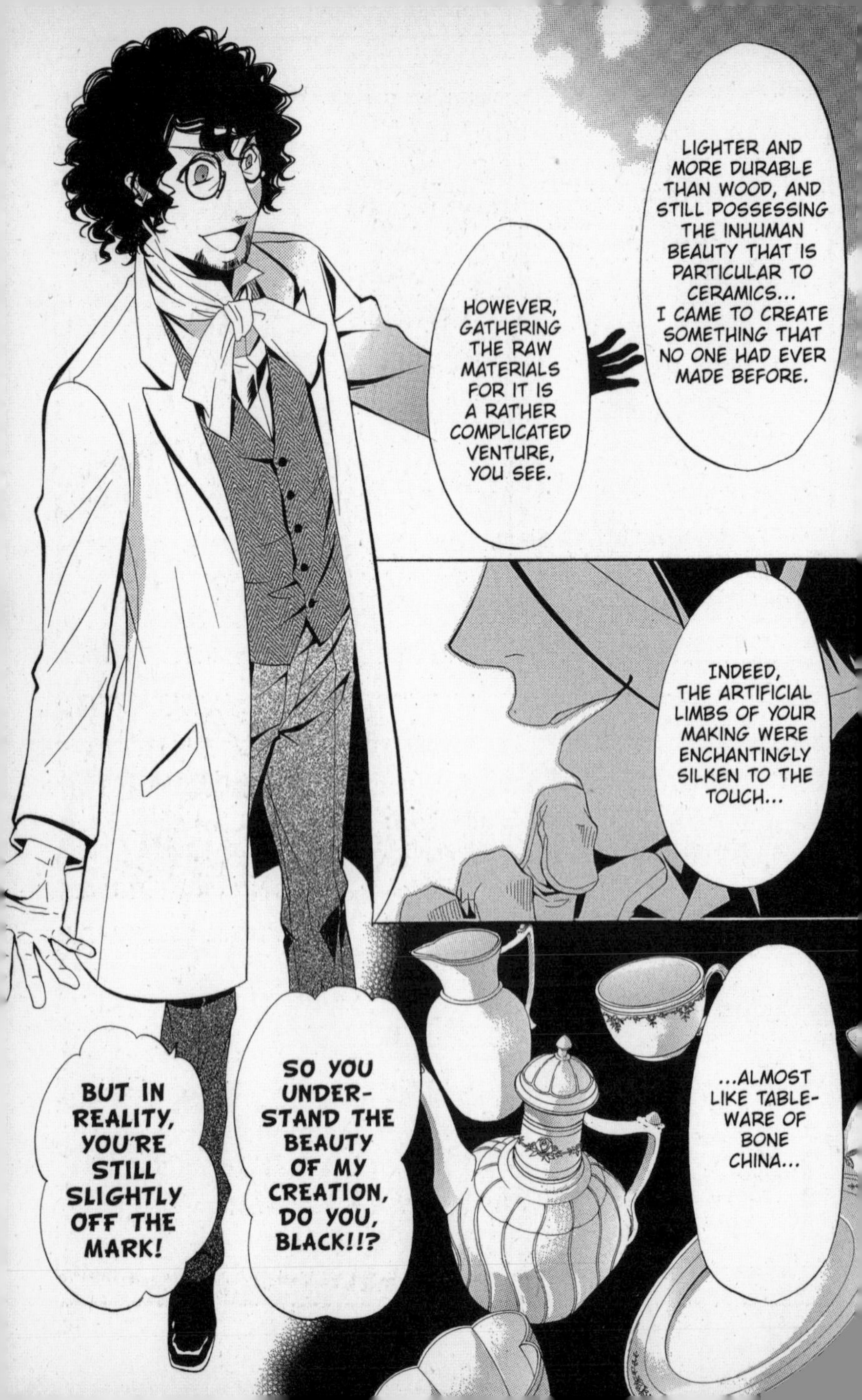
LIGHTER AND MORE DURABLE THAN WOOD, AND STILL POSSESSING THE INHUMAN BEAUTY THAT IS PARTICULAR TO CERAMICS... I CAME TO CREATE SOMETHING THAT NO ONE HAD EVER MADE BEFORE.
HOWEVER, GATHERING THE RAW MATERIALS FOR IT IS A RATHER COMPLICATED VENTURE, YOU SEE.
INDEED, THE ARTIFICIAL LIMBS OF YOUR MAKING WERE ENCHANTINGLY SILKEN TO THE TOUCH...
...ALMOST LIKE TABLE-WARE OF BONE CHINA...
SO YOU UNDER-STAND THE BEAUTY OF MY CREATION, DO YOU, BLACK!!?
BUT IN REALITY, YOU'RE STILL SLIGHTLY OFF THE MARK!

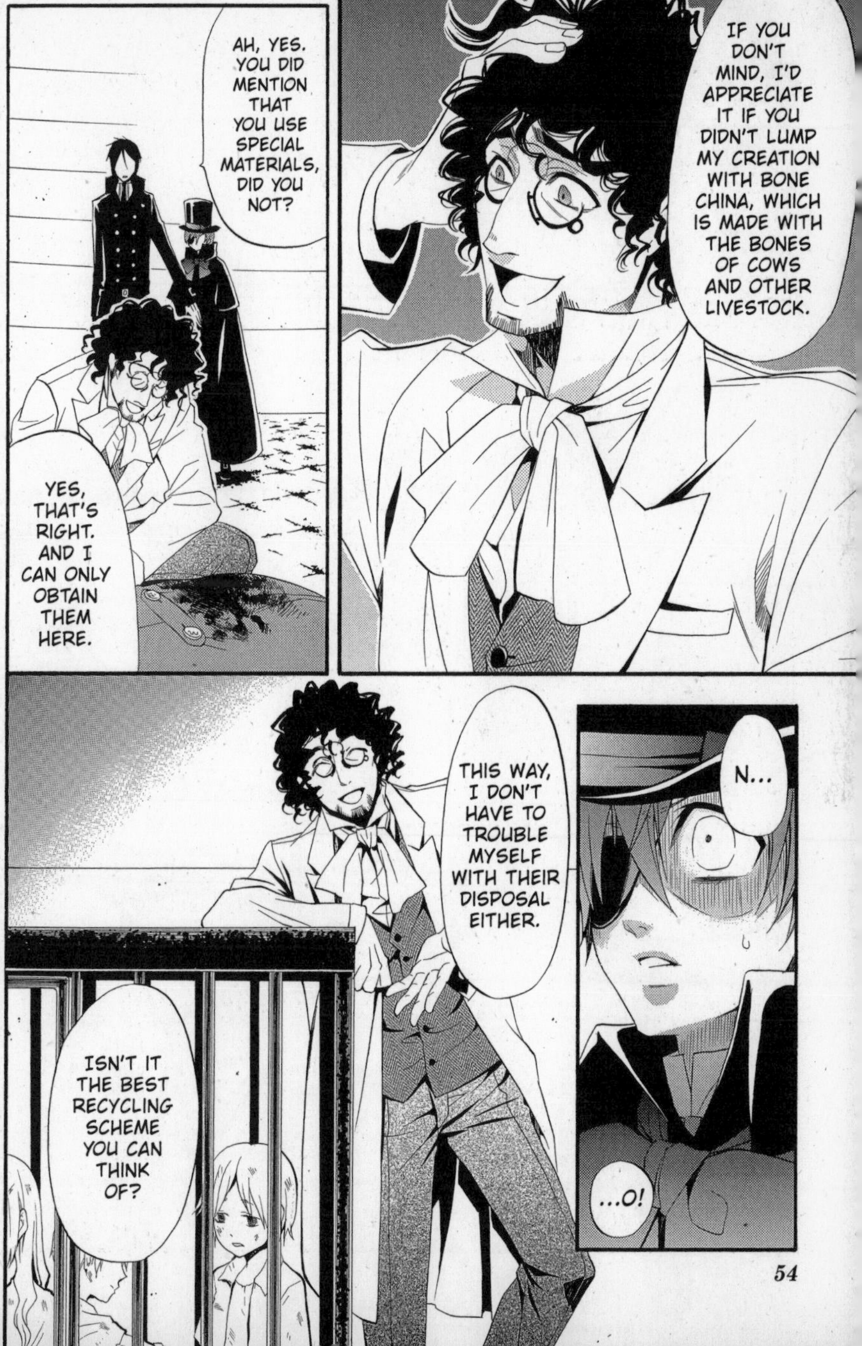
IF YOU DON'T MIND, I'D APPRECIATE IT IF YOU DIDN'T LUMP MY CREATION WITH BONE CHINA, WHICH IS MADE WITH THE BONES OF COWS AND OTHER LIVESTOCK.
AH, YES. YOU DID MENTION THAT YOU USE SPECIAL MATERIALS, DID YOU NOT?
YES, THAT'S RIGHT. AND I CAN ONLY OBTAIN THEM HERE.
THIS WAY, I DON'T HAVE TO TROUBLE MYSELF WITH THEIR DISPOSAL EITHER.
ISN'T IT THE BEST RECYCLING SCHEME YOU CAN THINK OF?
N...
...O!

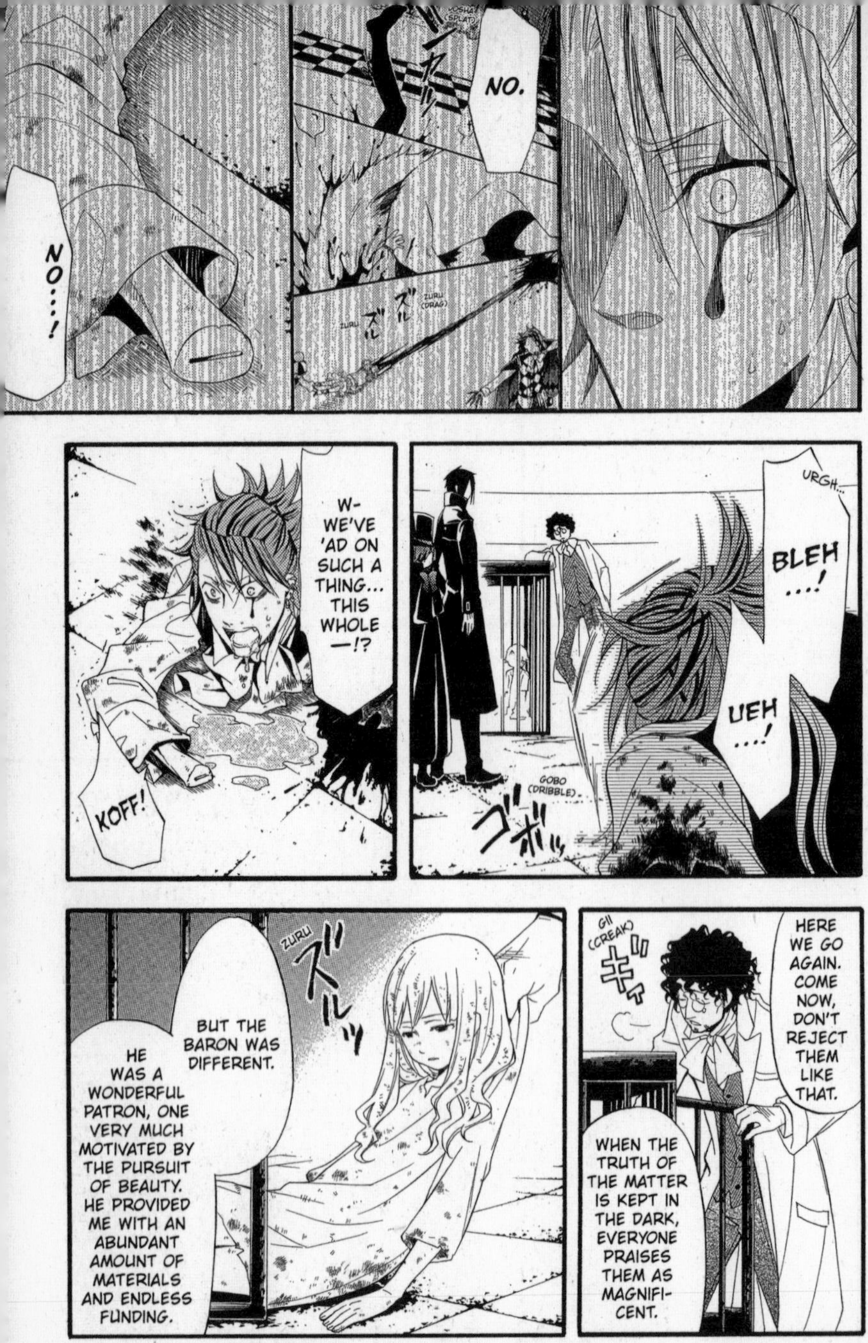
GOSHA (SPLAT)
NO.
ZURU (DRAG)
ZURU
NO...!
URGH...
BLEH...!
UEH...!
GOBO (DRIBBLE)
W-WE'VE 'AD ON SUCH A THING... THIS WHOLE—!?
KOFF!
GII (CREAK)
HERE WE GO AGAIN. COME NOW, DON'T REJECT THEM LIKE THAT.
WHEN THE TRUTH OF THE MATTER IS KEPT IN THE DARK, EVERYONE PRAISES THEM AS MAGNIFI-CENT.
ZURU
BUT THE BARON WAS DIFFERENT.
HE WAS A WONDERFUL PATRON, ONE VERY MUCH MOTIVATED BY THE PURSUIT OF BEAUTY. HE PROVIDED ME WITH AN ABUNDANT AMOUNT OF MATERIALS AND ENDLESS FUNDING.

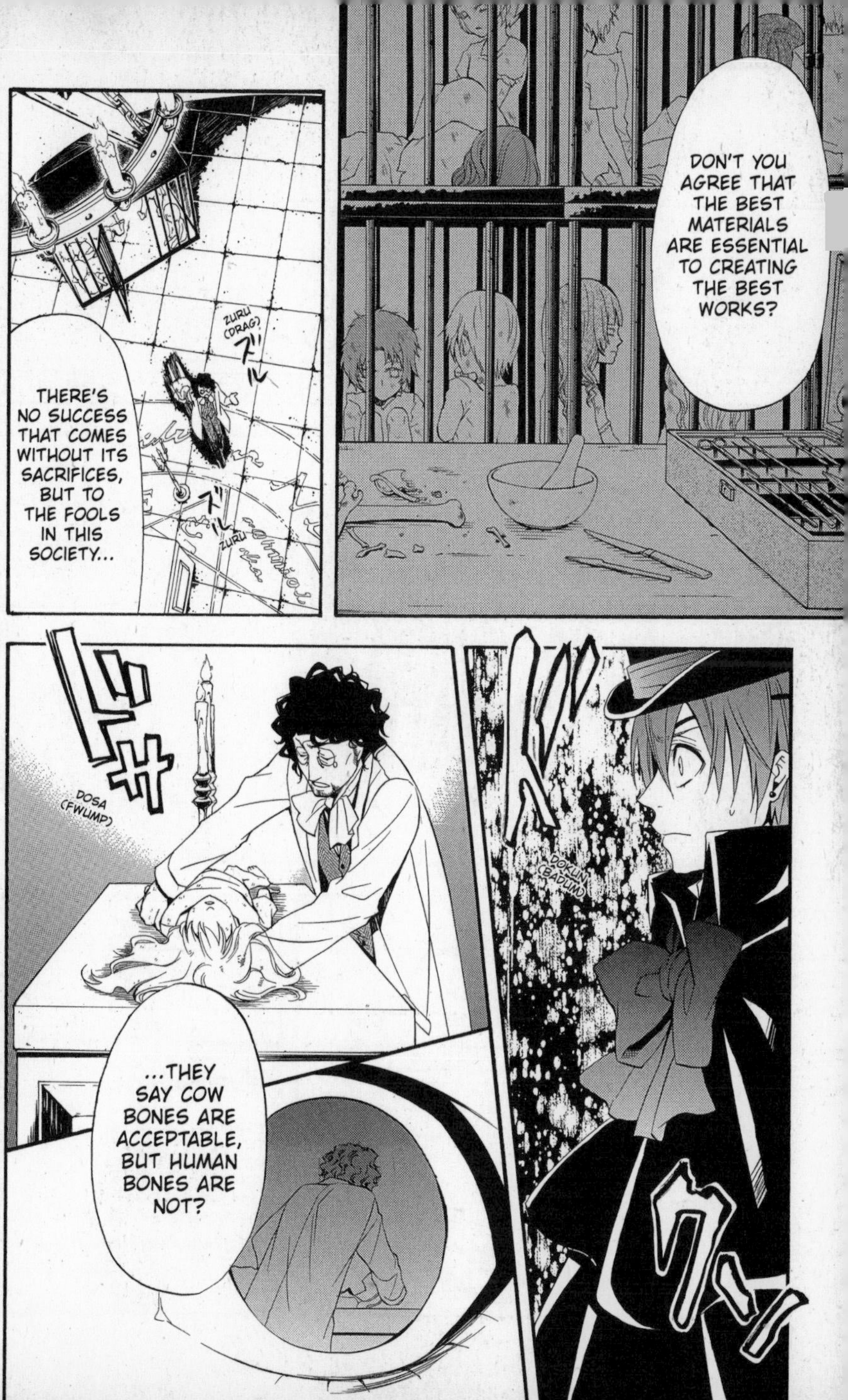
DON'T YOU AGREE THAT THE BEST MATERIALS ARE ESSENTIAL TO CREATING THE BEST WORKS?
ZURU (DRAG)
ZURU
THERE'S NO SUCCESS THAT COMES WITHOUT ITS SACRIFICES, BUT TO THE FOOLS IN THIS SOCIETY...
DOKUN (BADUMP)
DOSA (FWUMP)
...THEY SAY COW BONES ARE ACCEPTABLE, BUT HUMAN BONES ARE NOT?

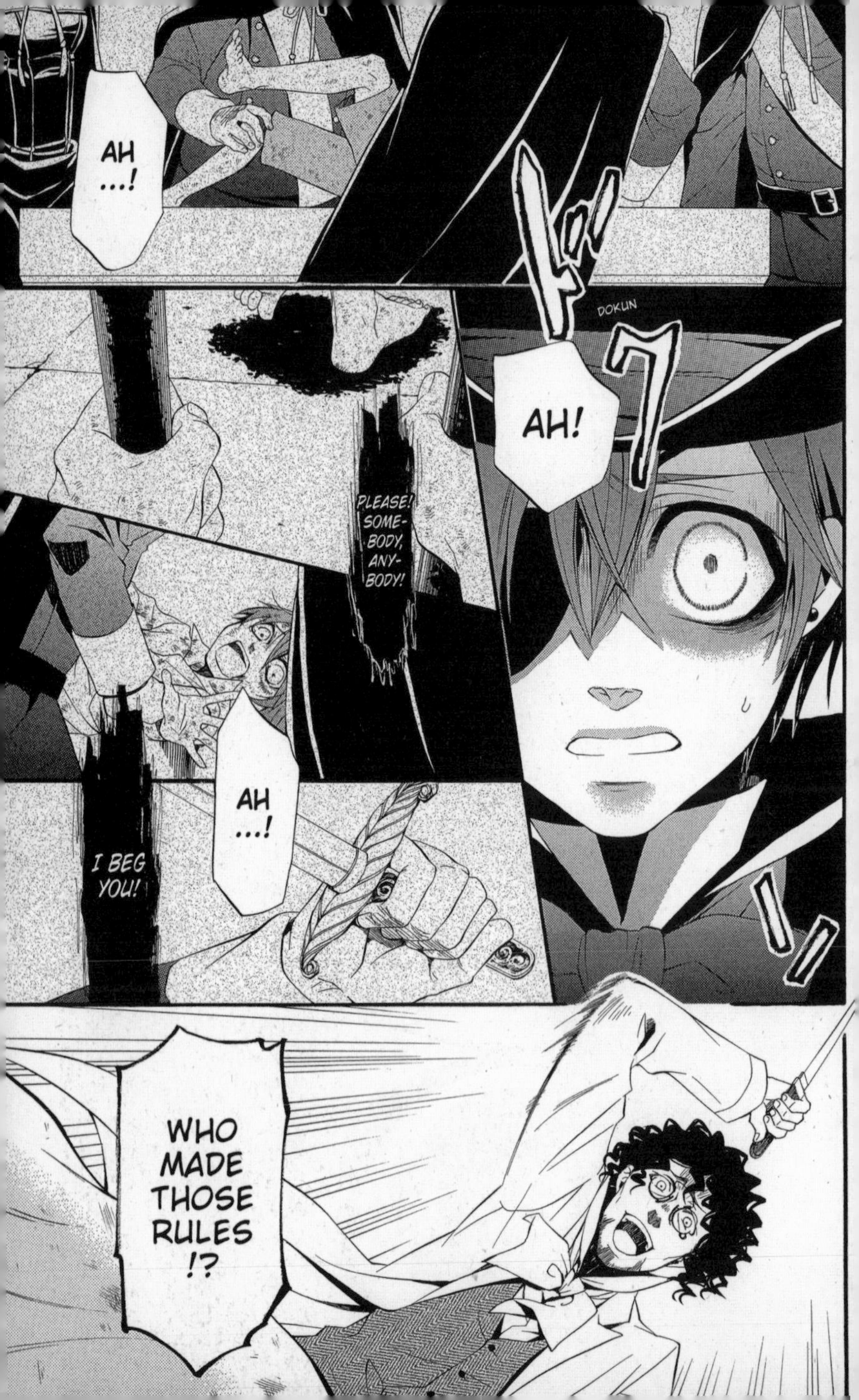
AH ...!
DOKUN
AH!
PLEASE! SOMEBODY, ANYBODY!
AH ...!
I BEG YOU!
WHO MADE THOSE RULES !?

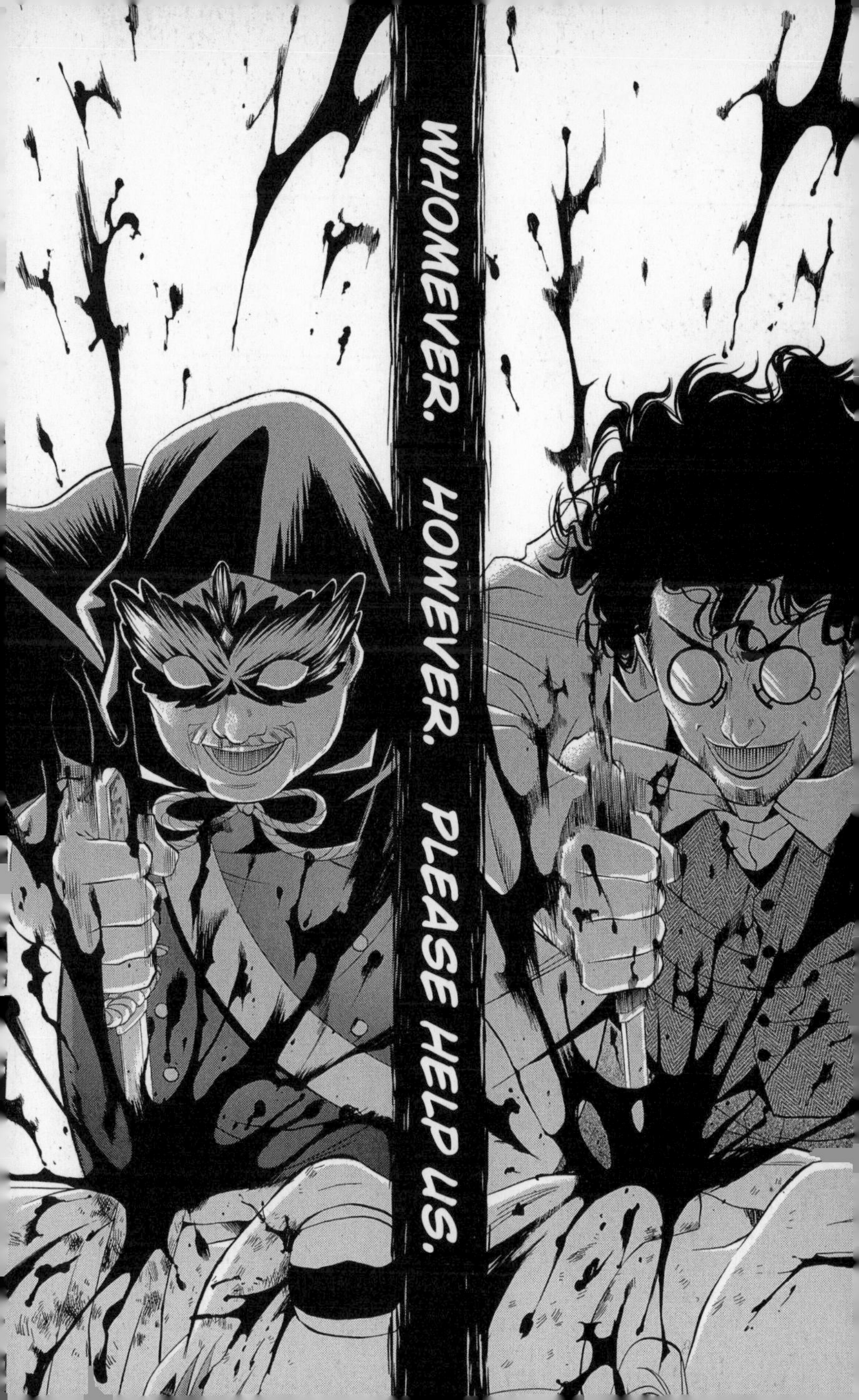
WHOMEVER. HOWEVER. PLEASE HELP US.

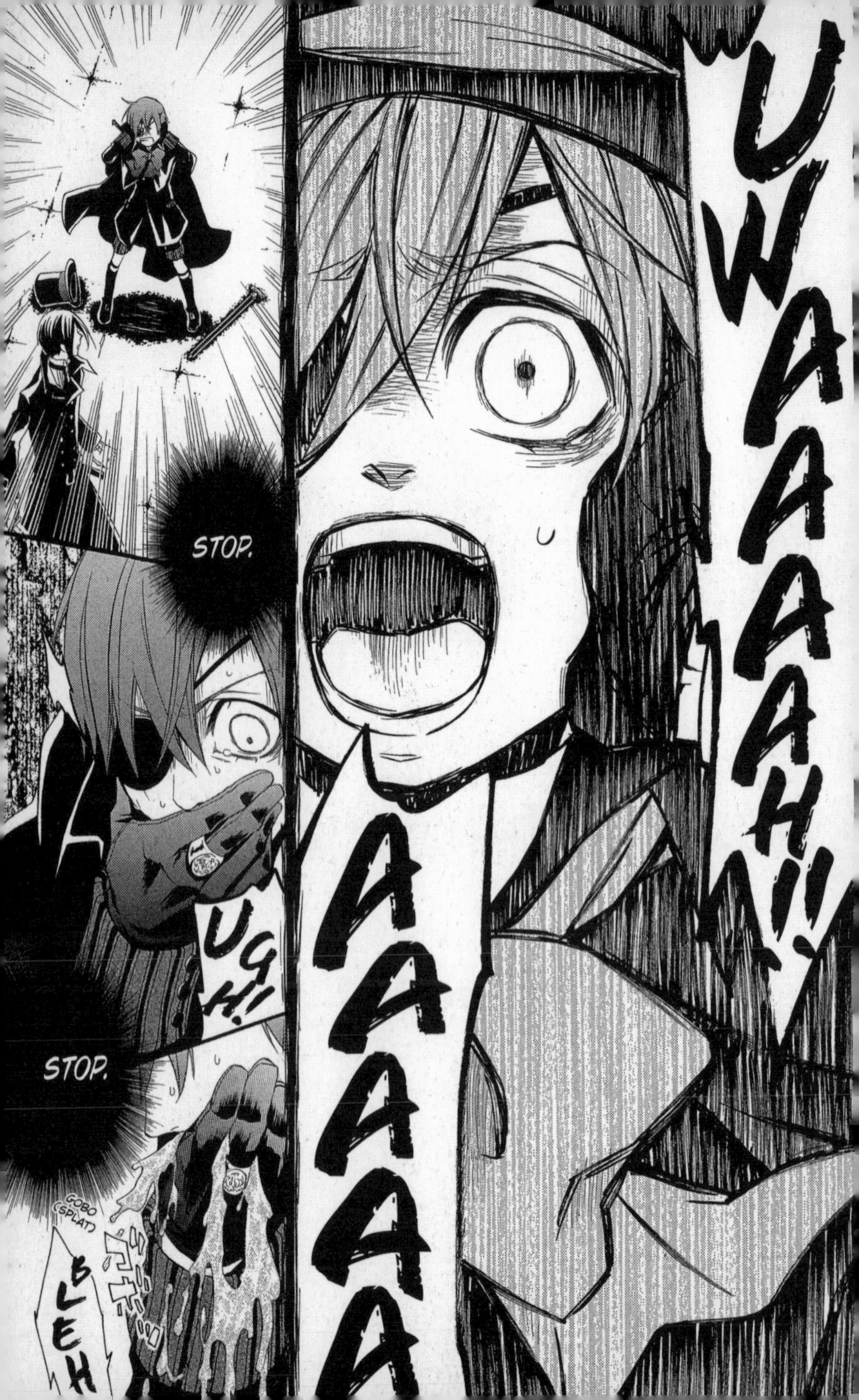
UWAAAAAH!!
AAAAAAAA
STOP.
UGH!
STOP.
GOBO (SPLAT)
BLEH

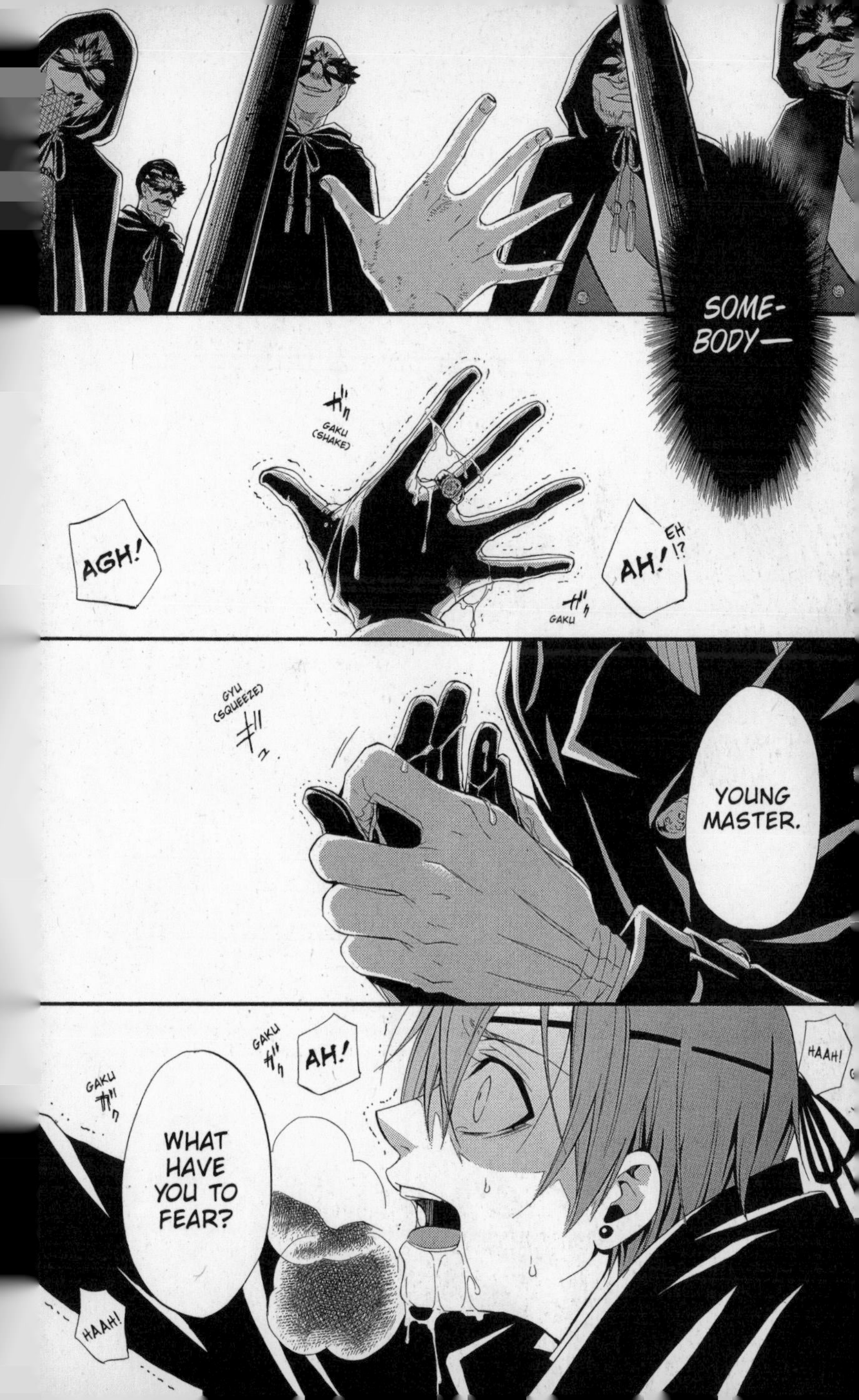
SOME-
BODY—
EH !?
AH!
GAKU (SHAKE)
AGH!
GAKU
YOUNG MASTER.
GYU (SQUEEZE)
HAAH!
AH!
GAKU
WHAT HAVE YOU TO FEAR?
GAKU
HAAH!

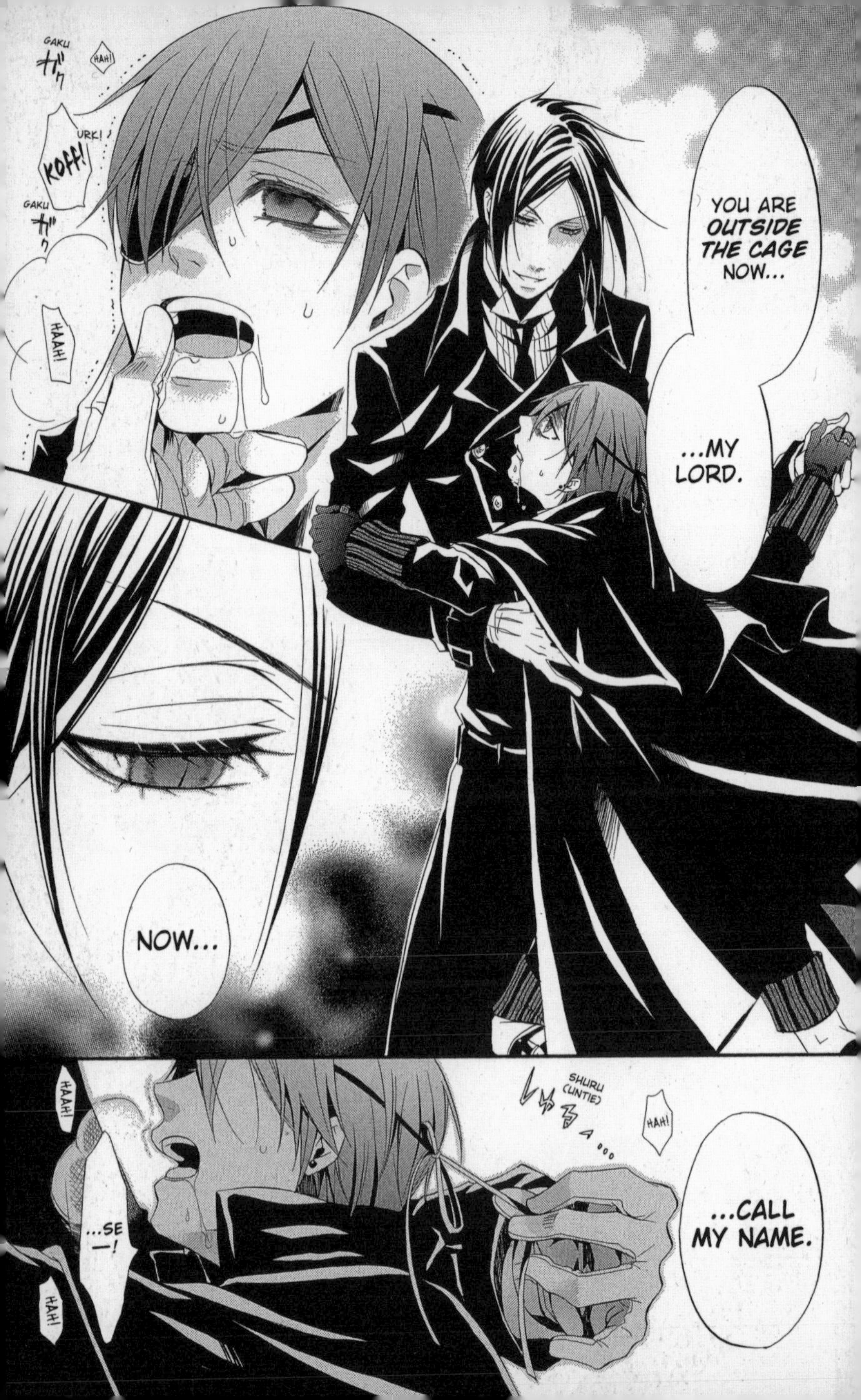
YOU ARE OUTSIDE THE CAGE NOW...
...MY LORD.
GAKU
HAH!
URK!
KOFF!
GAKU
HAAH!
NOW...
...CALL MY NAME.
HAH!
SHURU (UNTIE)
HAAH!
...SE—!
HAH!

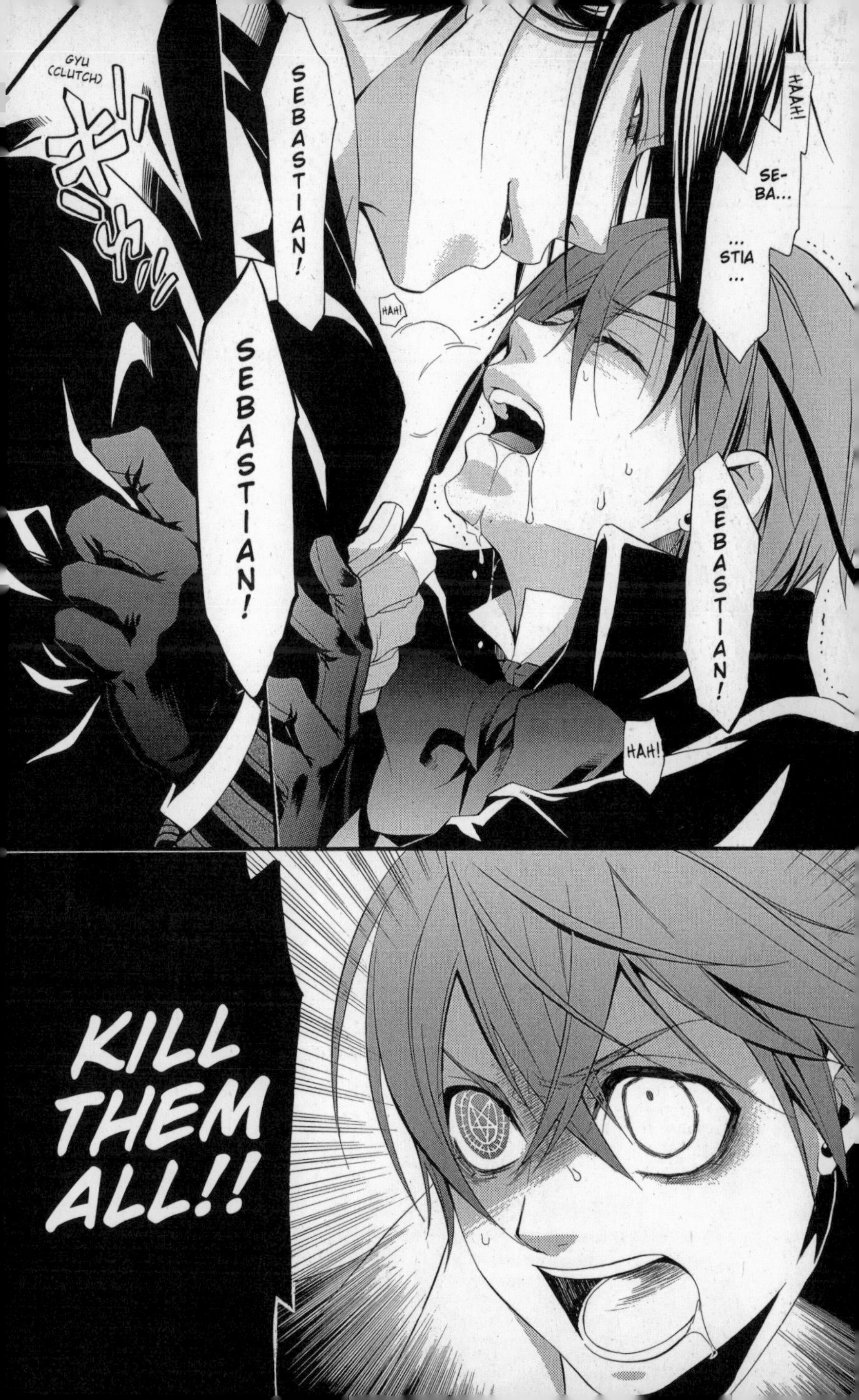
HAAH!
SE- BA...
... STIA ...
SEBASTIAN!
HAH!
SEBASTIAN!
HAH!
SEBASTIAN!
GYU (CLUTCH)
KILL THEM ALL!!

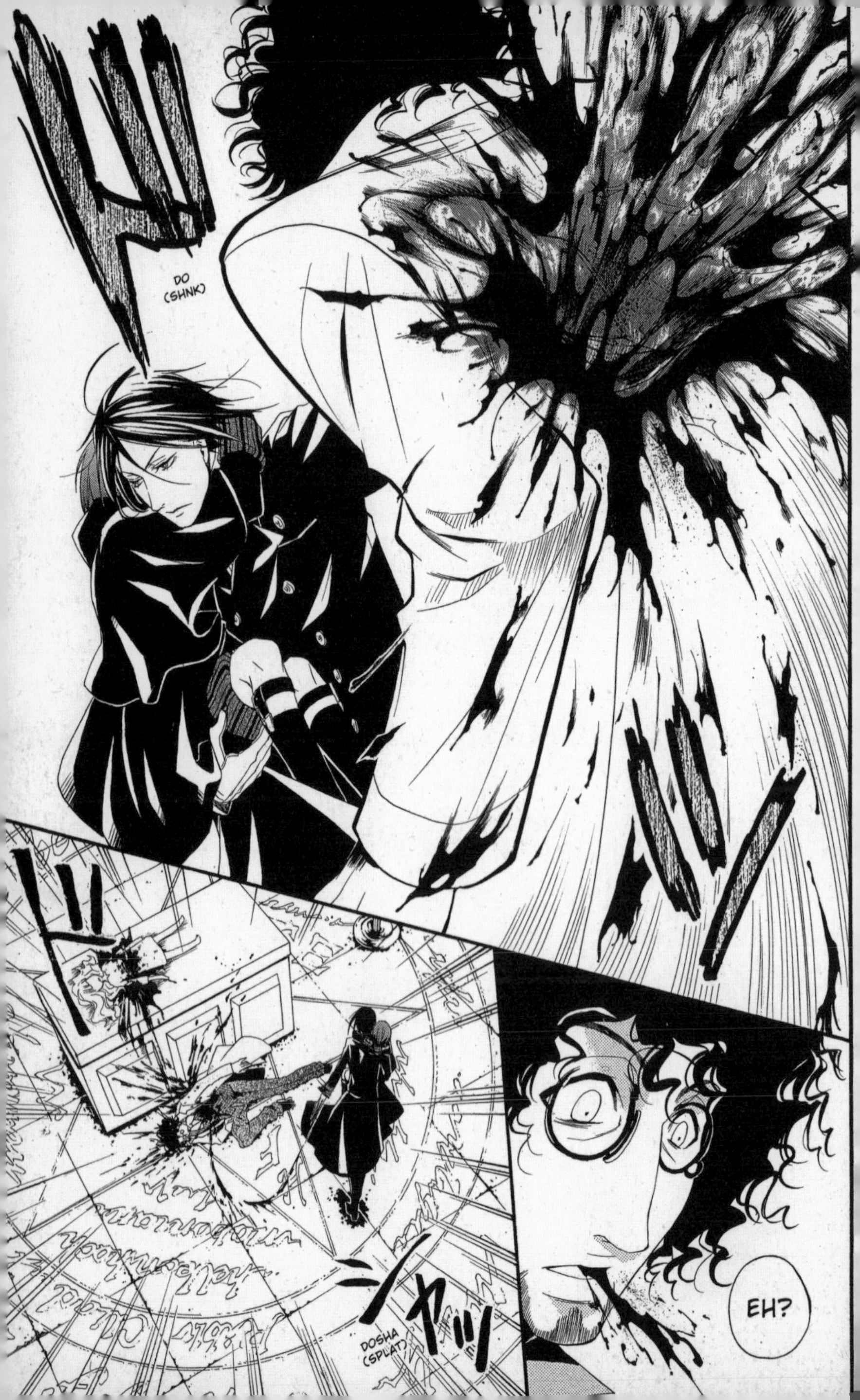
DO
(SHNK)
EH?
DOSHA
(SPLAT)

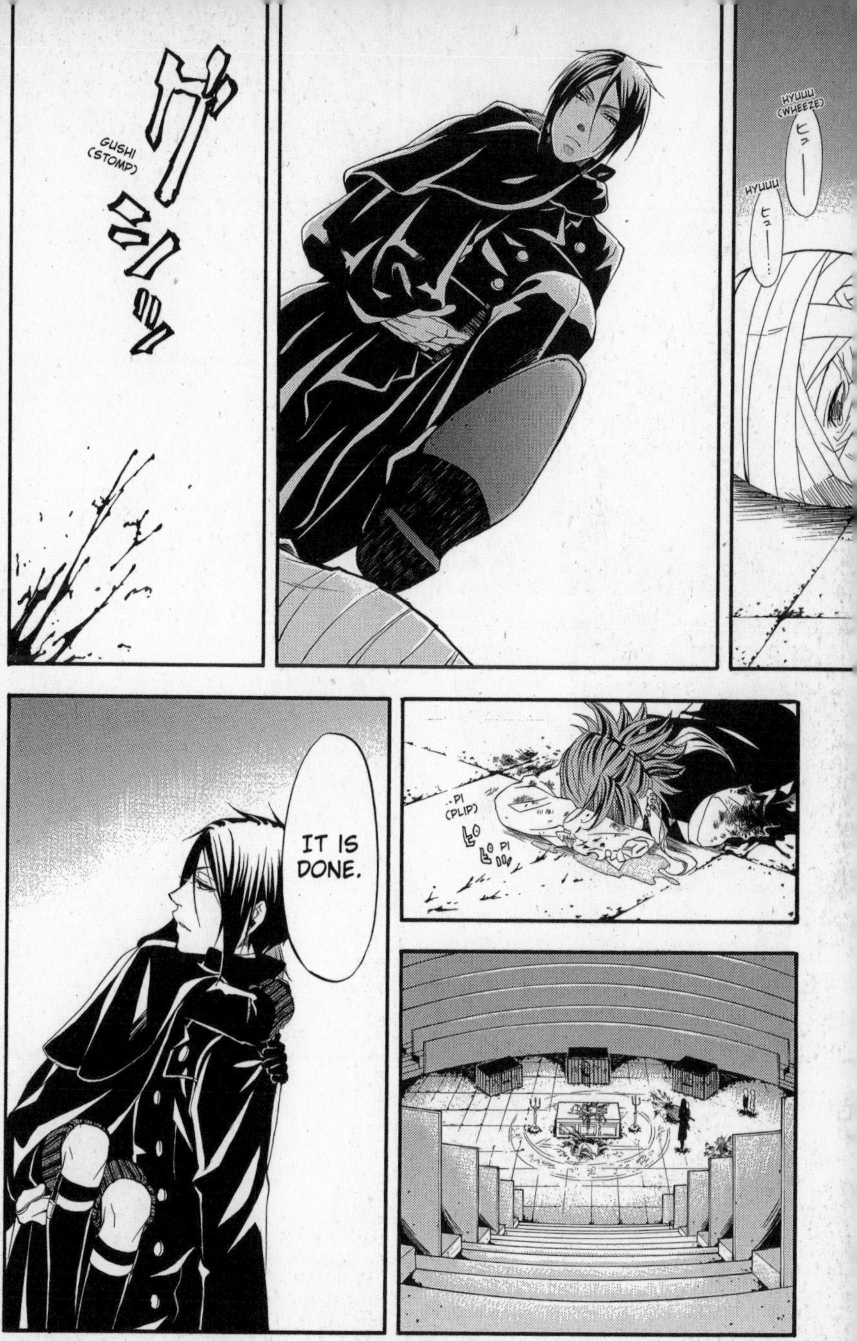
HYUUU (WHEEZE)
ヒュー
HYUUU
ヒュー……
GUSHI (STOMP)
..PI (PLIP)
PI
IT IS DONE.

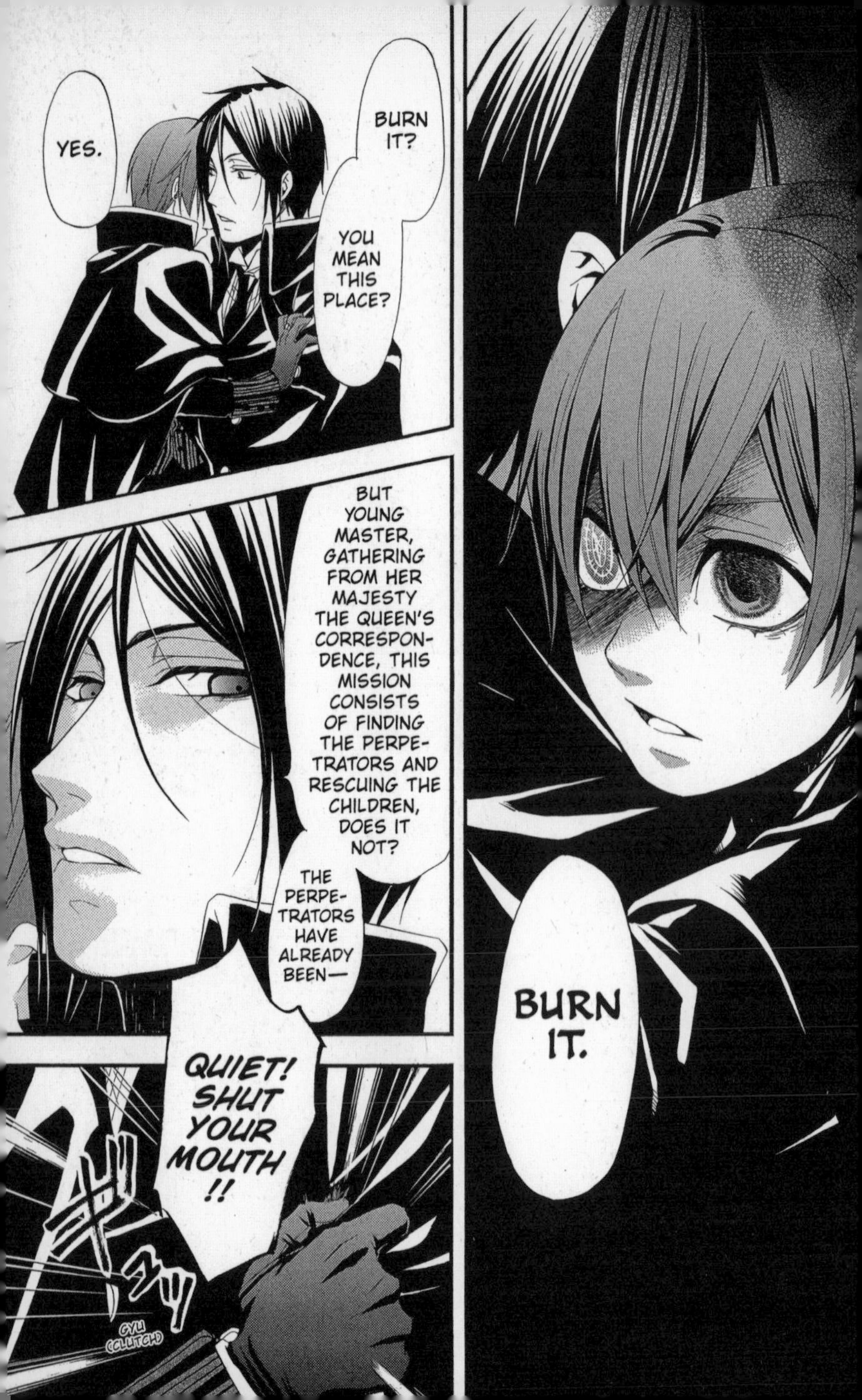
BURN IT.
BURN IT?
YOU MEAN THIS PLACE?
YES.
BUT YOUNG MASTER, GATHERING FROM HER MAJESTY THE QUEEN'S CORRESPONDENCE, THIS MISSION CONSISTS OF FINDING THE PERPETRATORS AND RESCUING THE CHILDREN, DOES IT NOT?
THE PERPETRATORS HAVE ALREADY BEEN—
QUIET! SHUT YOUR MOUTH!!
GYU (CLUTCH)

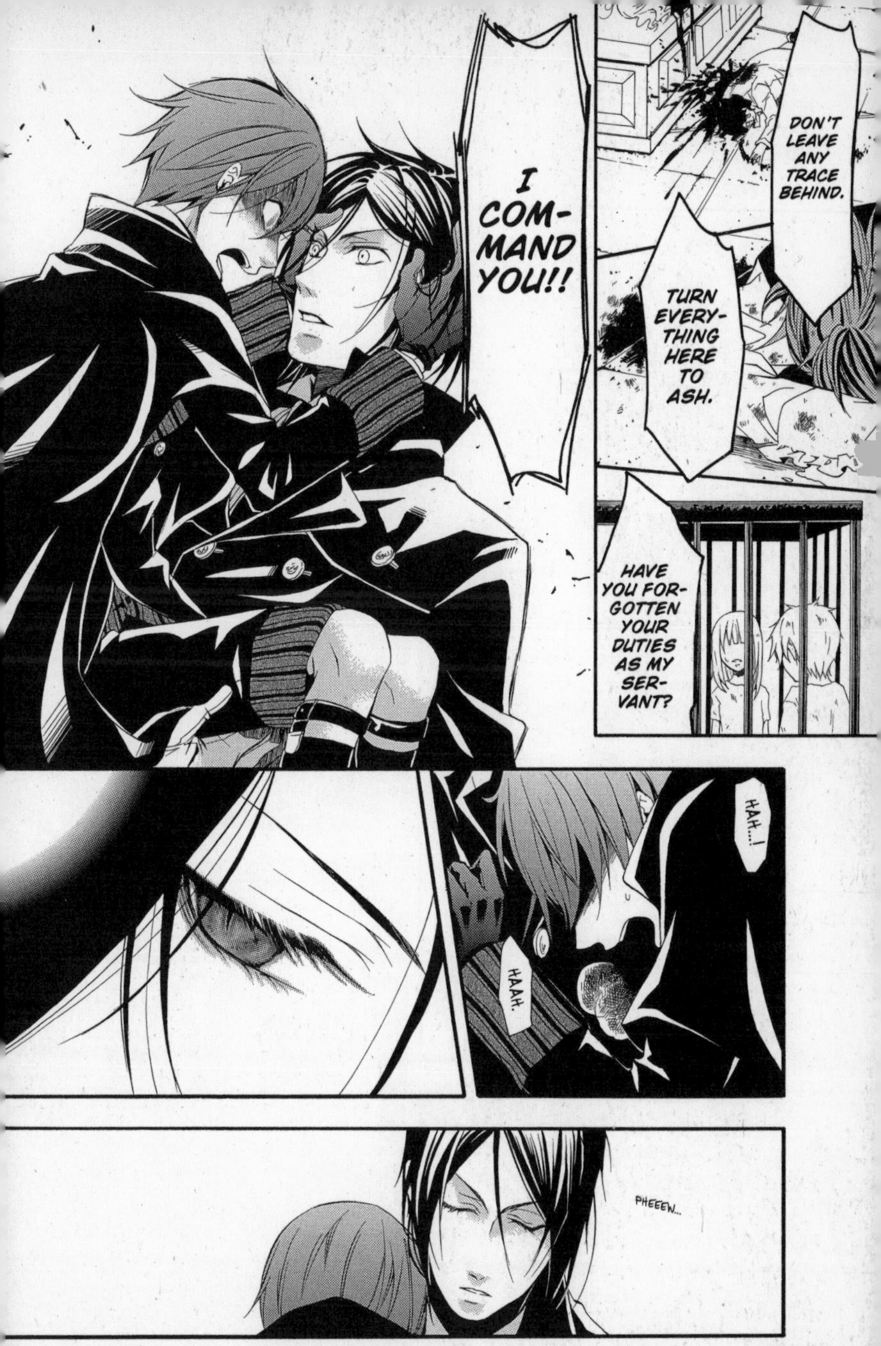
DON'T LEAVE ANY TRACE BEHIND.
TURN EVERY-THING HERE TO ASH.
HAVE YOU FOR-GOTTEN YOUR DUTIES AS MY SER-VANT?
I COM-MAND YOU!!
HAH...!
HAAH.
PHEEEW...

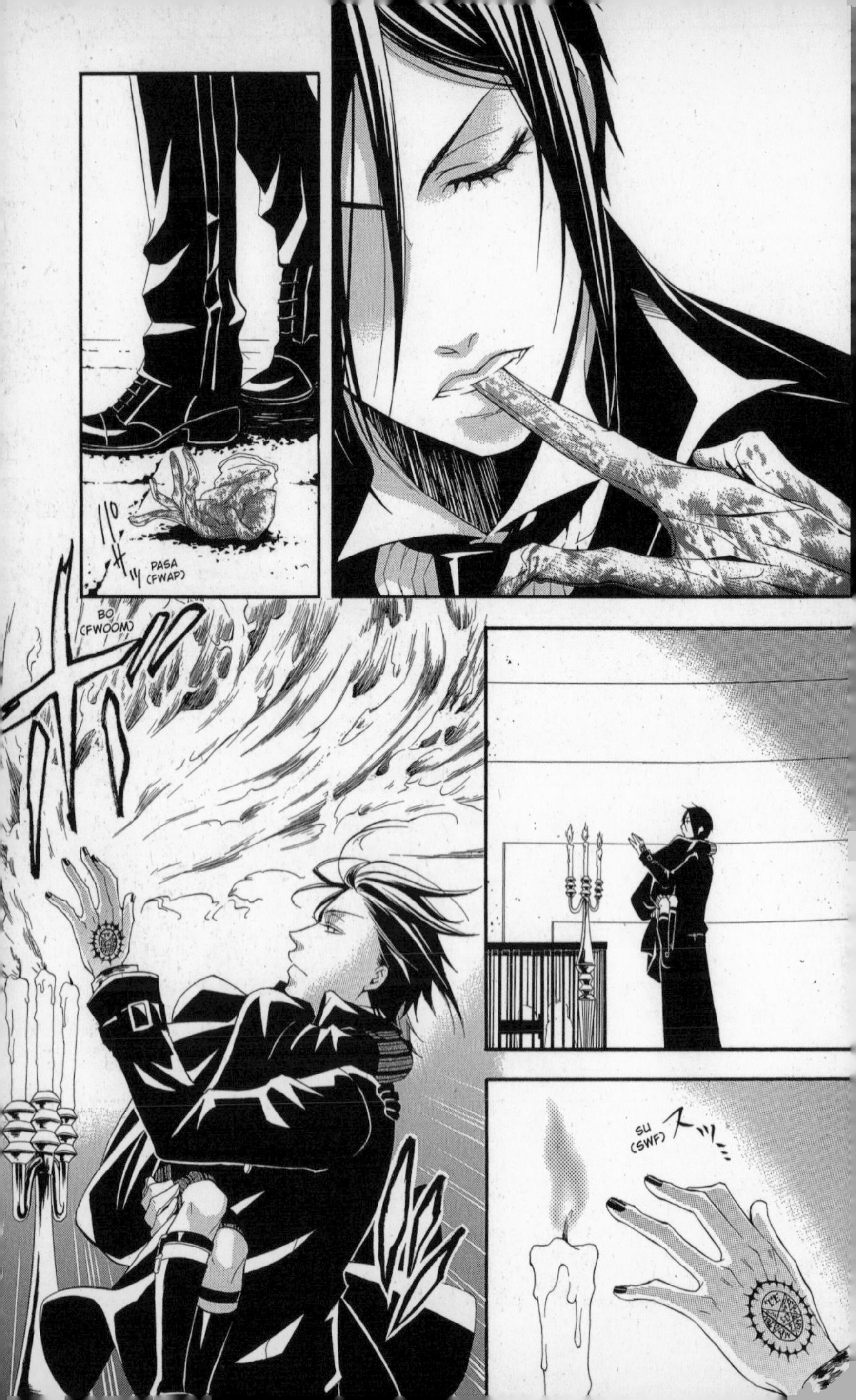
PASA
(FWAP)
SU
(SWF)
BO
(FWOOM)

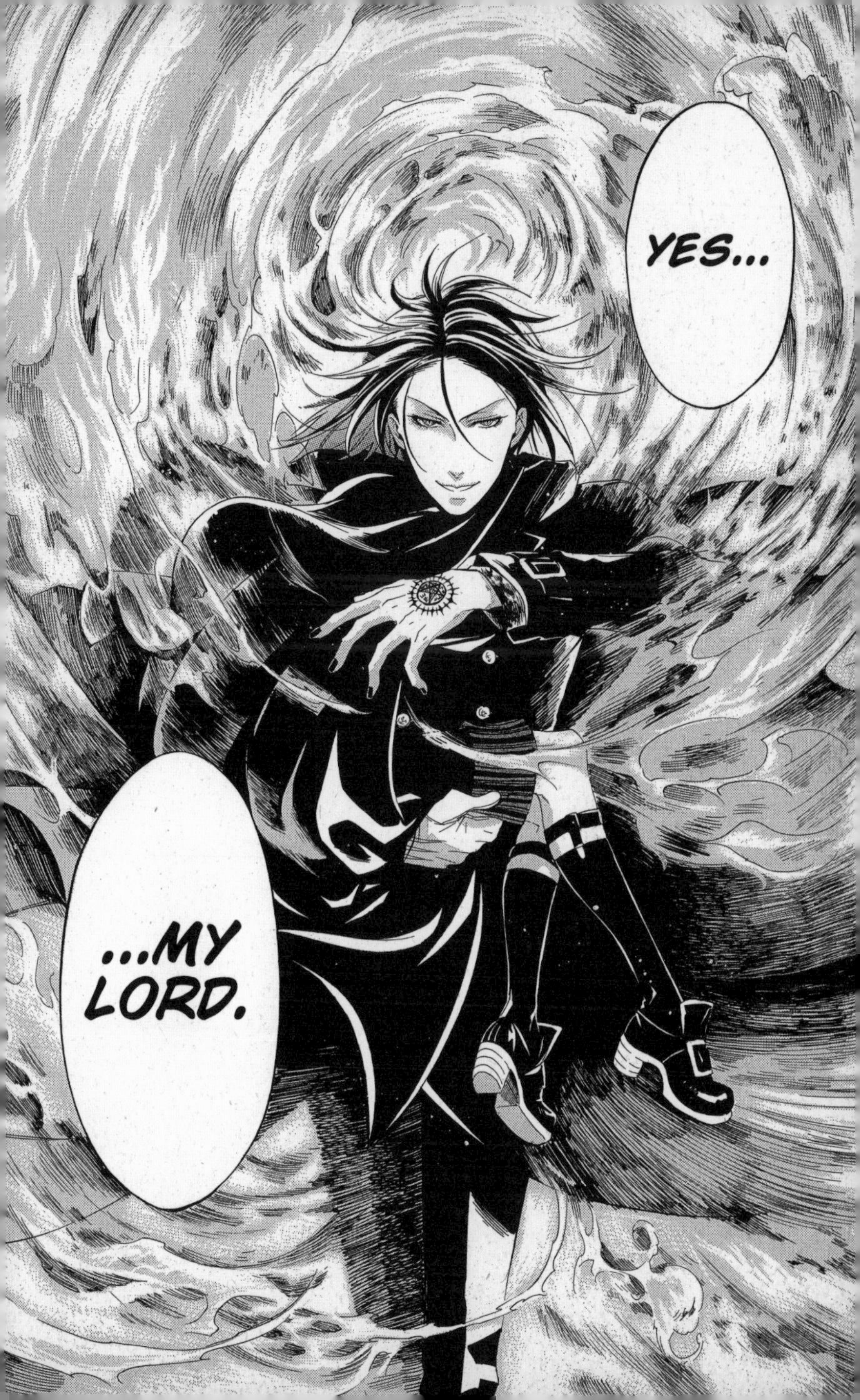
YES...
...MY LORD.

NOAH'S CIRCUS ARK

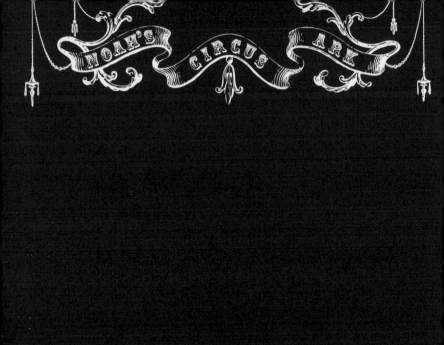

Black Butler

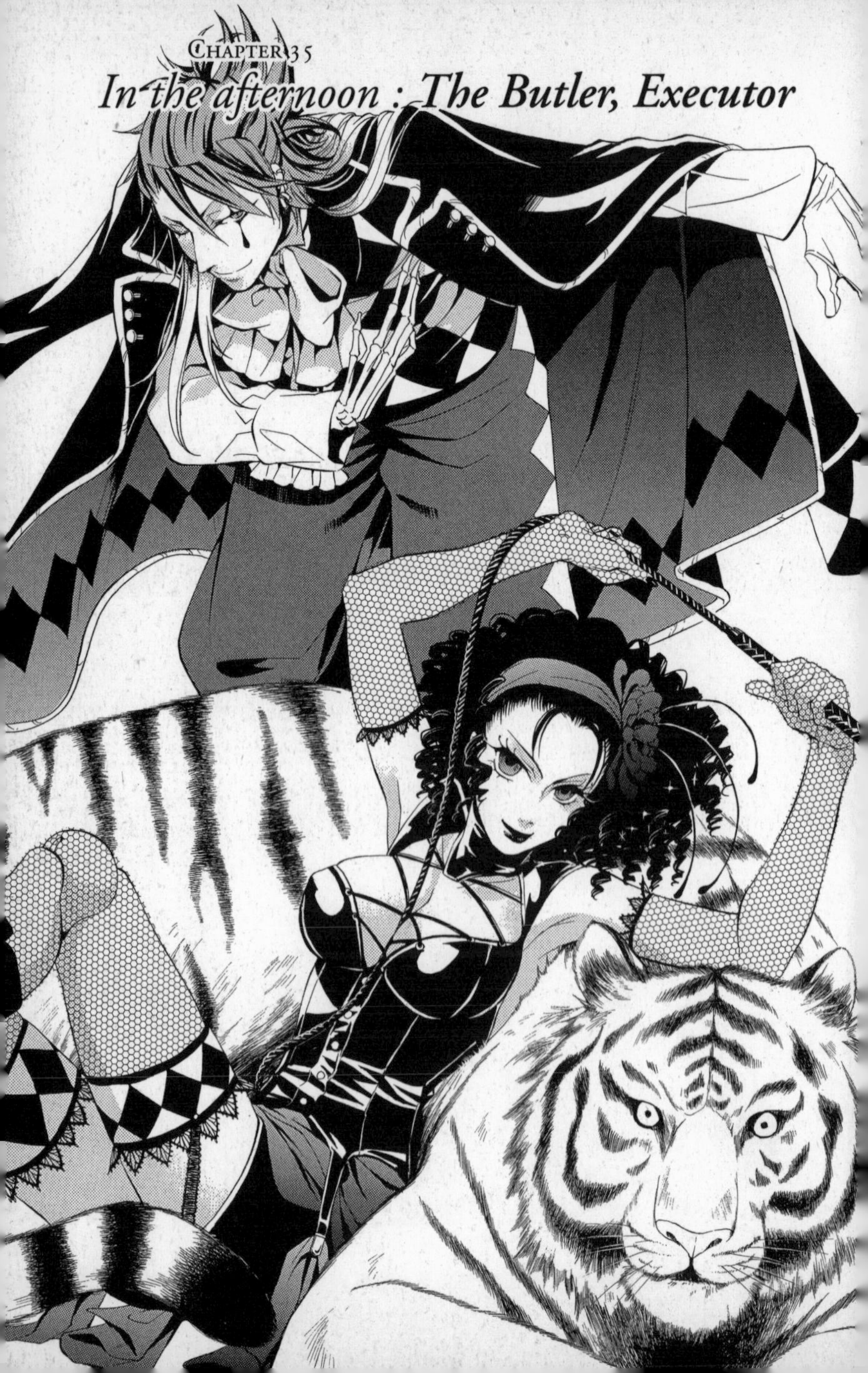
Chapter 35
In the afternoon : The Butler, Executor

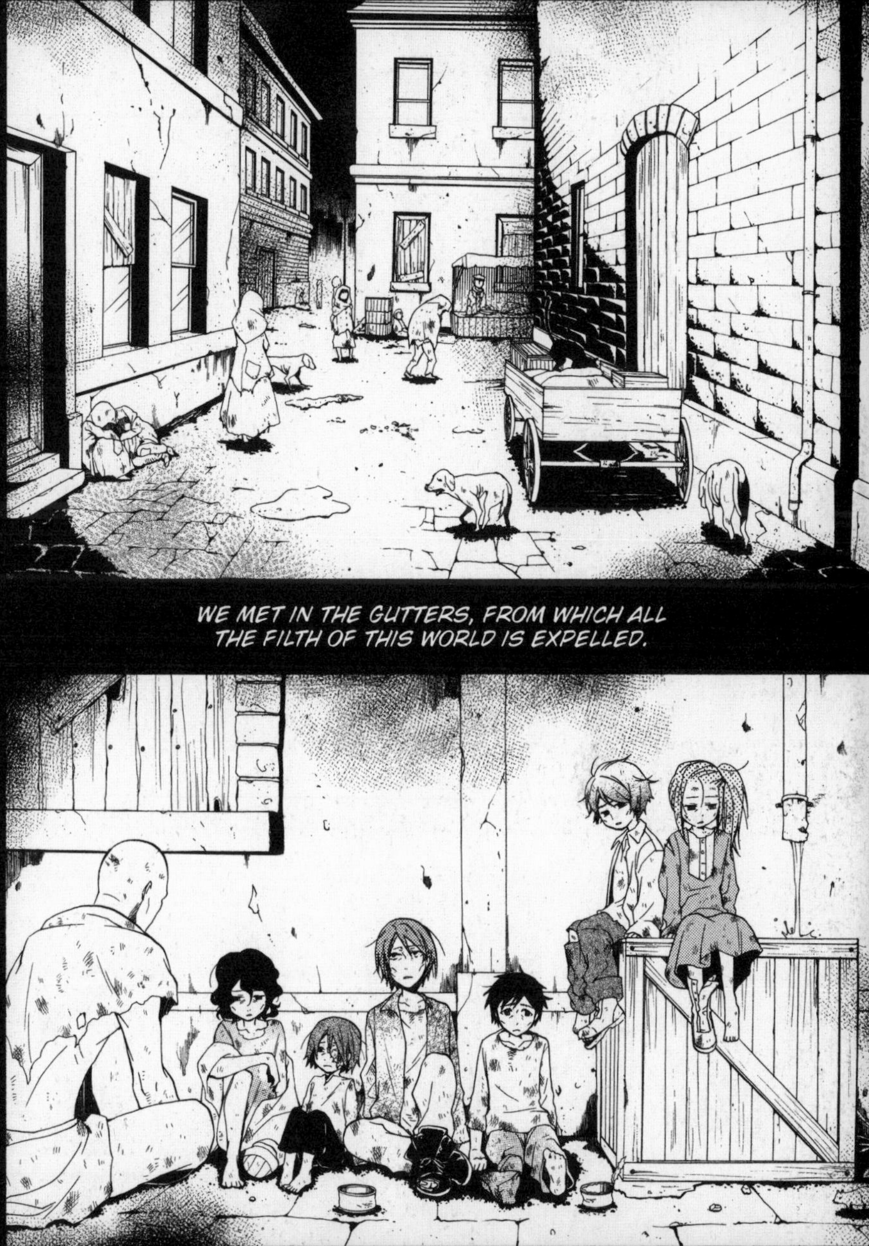
WE MET IN THE GUTTERS, FROM WHICH ALL THE FILTH OF THIS WORLD IS EXPELLED.

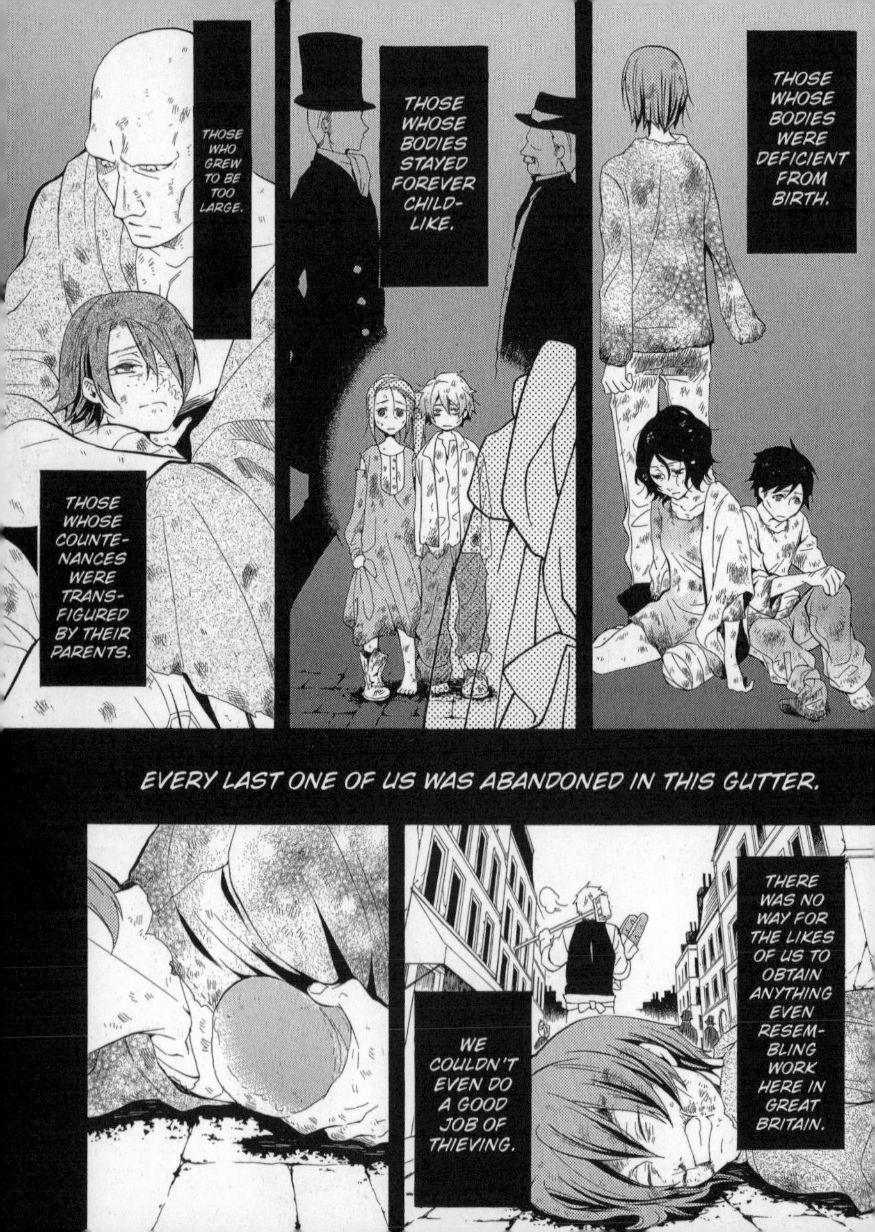
THOSE WHOSE BODIES WERE DEFICIENT FROM BIRTH.
THOSE WHOSE BODIES STAYED FOREVER CHILD-LIKE.
THOSE WHO GREW TO BE TOO LARGE.
THOSE WHOSE COUNTENANCES WERE TRANSFIGURED BY THEIR PARENTS.
EVERY LAST ONE OF US WAS ABANDONED IN THIS GUTTER.
THERE WAS NO WAY FOR THE LIKES OF US TO OBTAIN ANYTHING EVEN RESEMBLING WORK HERE IN GREAT BRITAIN.
WE COULDN'T EVEN DO A GOOD JOB OF THIEVING.

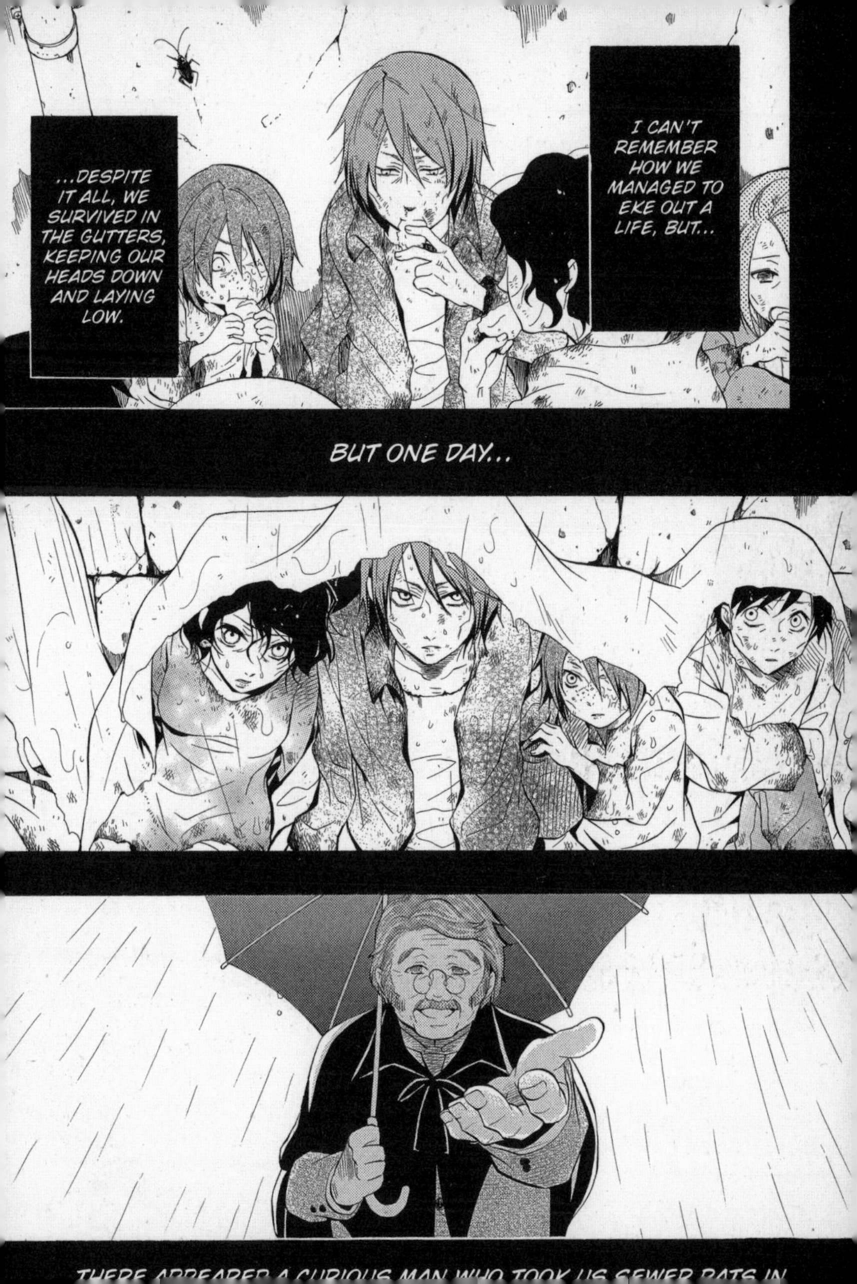
I CAN'T REMEMBER HOW WE MANAGED TO EKE OUT A LIFE, BUT...
...DESPITE IT ALL, WE SURVIVED IN THE GUTTERS, KEEPING OUR HEADS DOWN AND LAYING LOW.
BUT ONE DAY...
THERE APPEARED A CURIOUS MAN WHO TOOK US SEWER RATS IN.

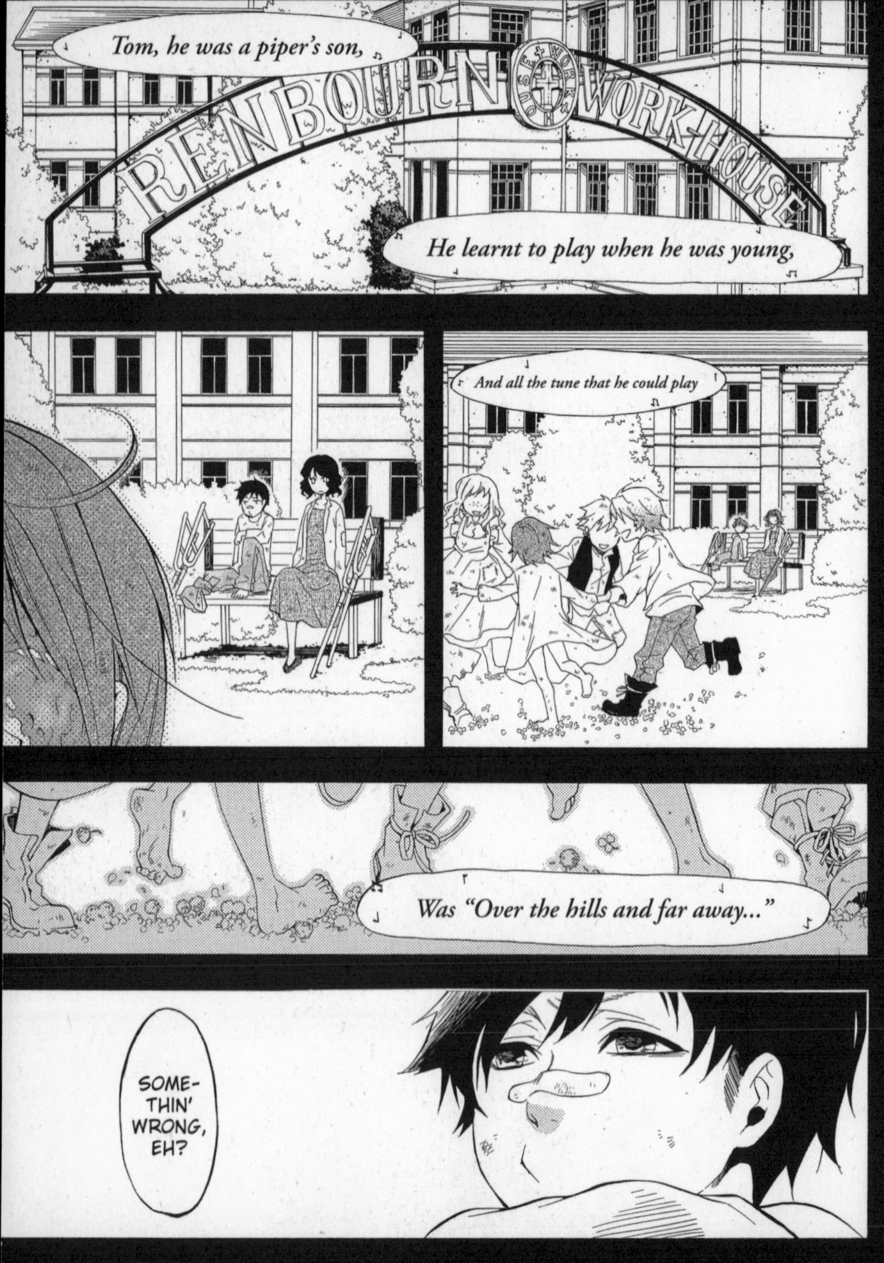
Tom, he was a piper's son,
RENBOURN WORKHOUSE
He learnt to play when he was young,
And all the tune that he could play
Was "Over the hills and far away..."
SOME-THIN' WRONG, EH?

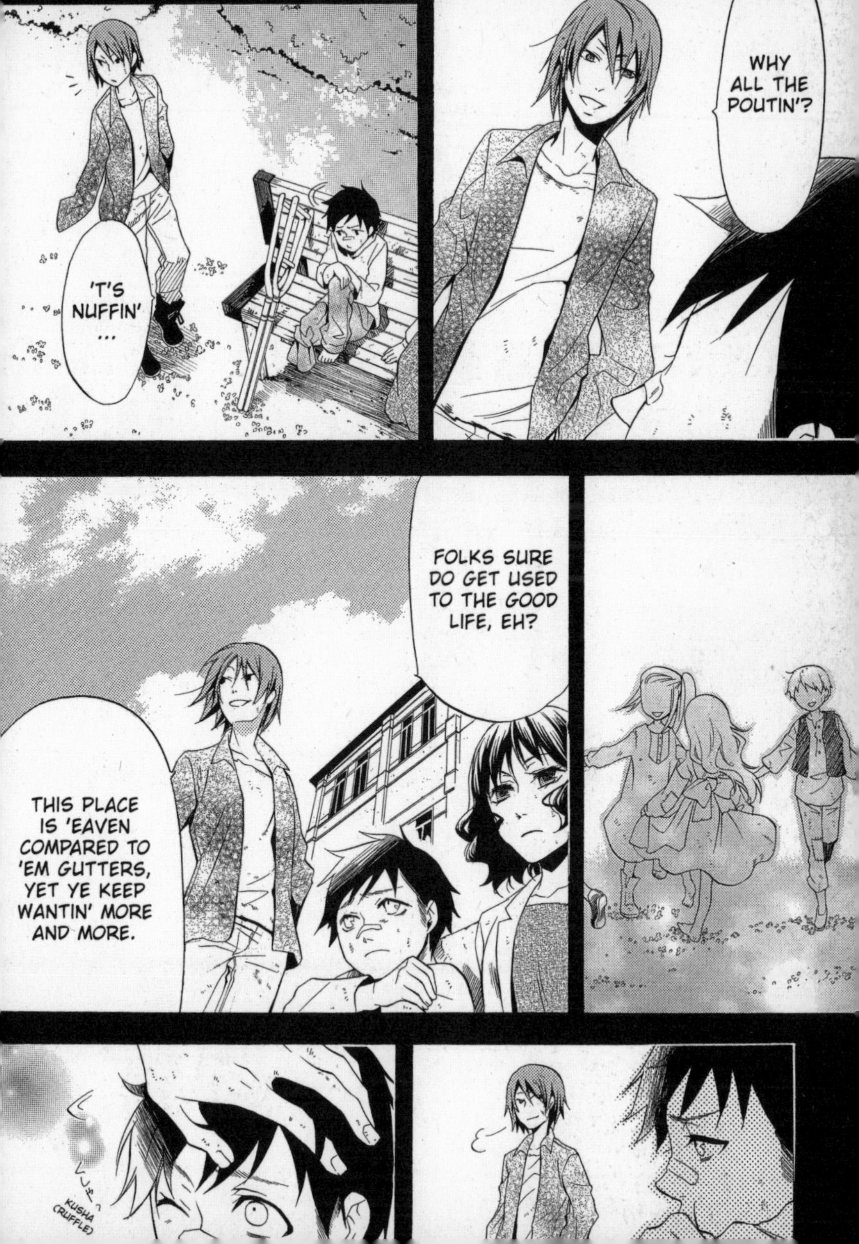
WHY ALL THE POUTIN'?
'T'S NUFFIN' ...
FOLKS SURE DO GET USED TO THE GOOD LIFE, EH?
THIS PLACE IS 'EAVEN COMPARED TO 'EM GUTTERS, YET YE KEEP WANTIN' MORE AND MORE.
KUSHA (RUFFLE)

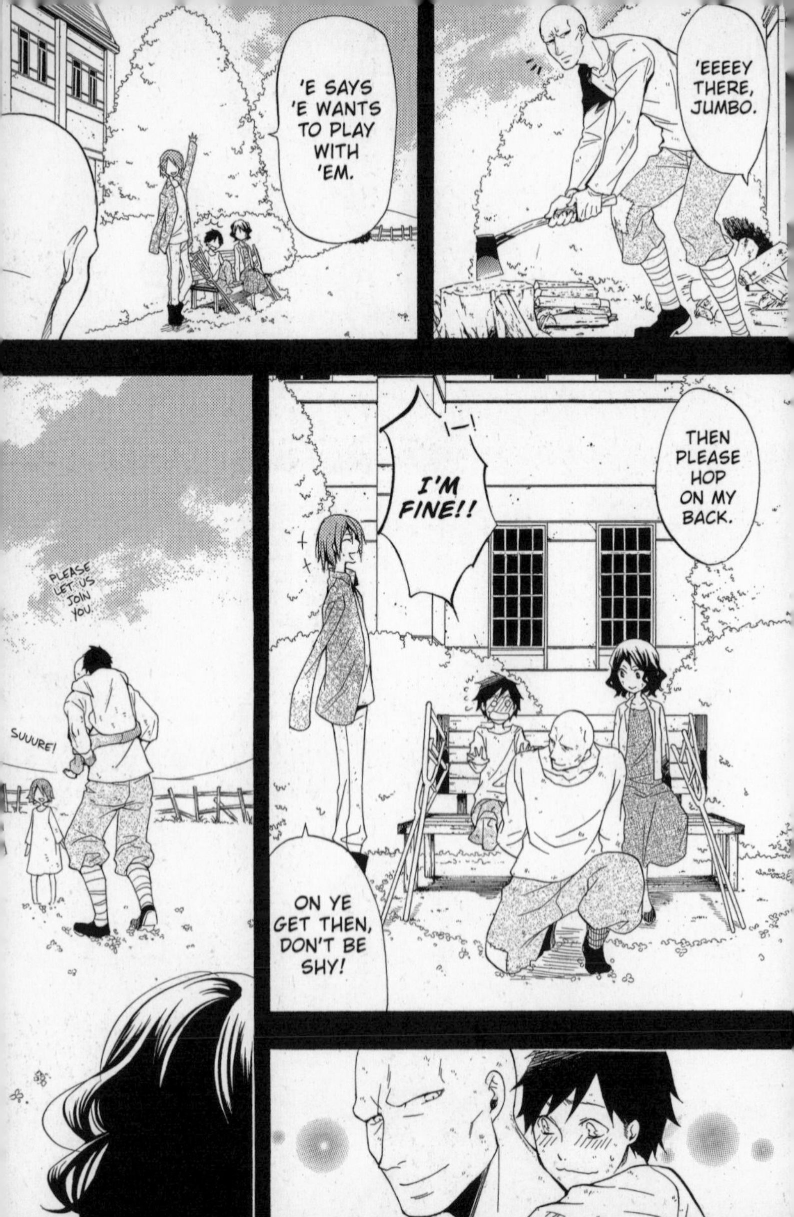
'EEEEY THERE, JUMBO.
'E SAYS 'E WANTS TO PLAY WITH 'EM.
THEN PLEASE HOP ON MY BACK.
I'M FINE!!
ON YE GET THEN, DON'T BE SHY!
PLEASE LET US JOIN YOU.
SUUURE!

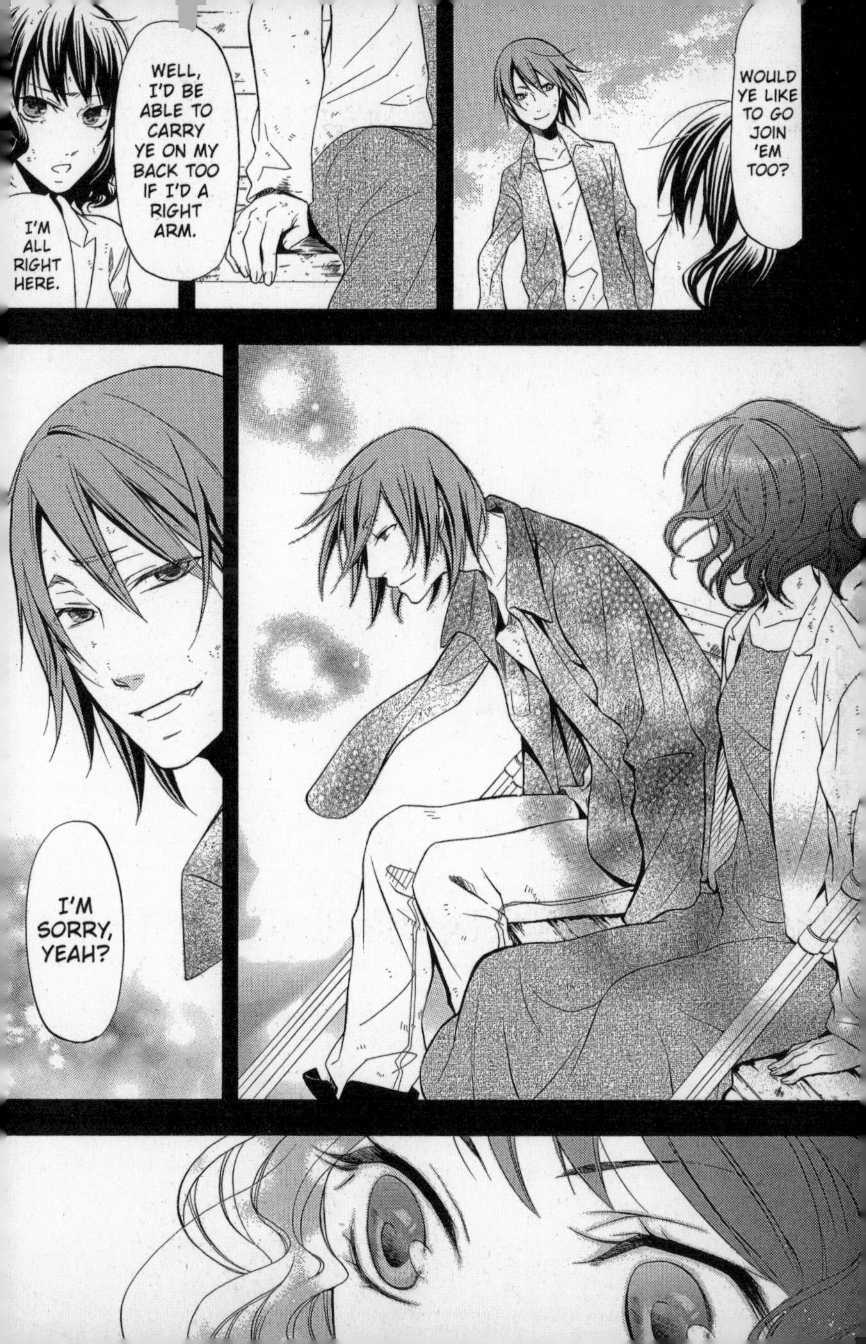
WOULD YE LIKE TO GO JOIN 'EM TOO?
I'M ALL RIGHT HERE.
WELL, I'D BE ABLE TO CARRY YE ON MY BACK TOO IF I'D A RIGHT ARM.
I'M SORRY, YEAH?

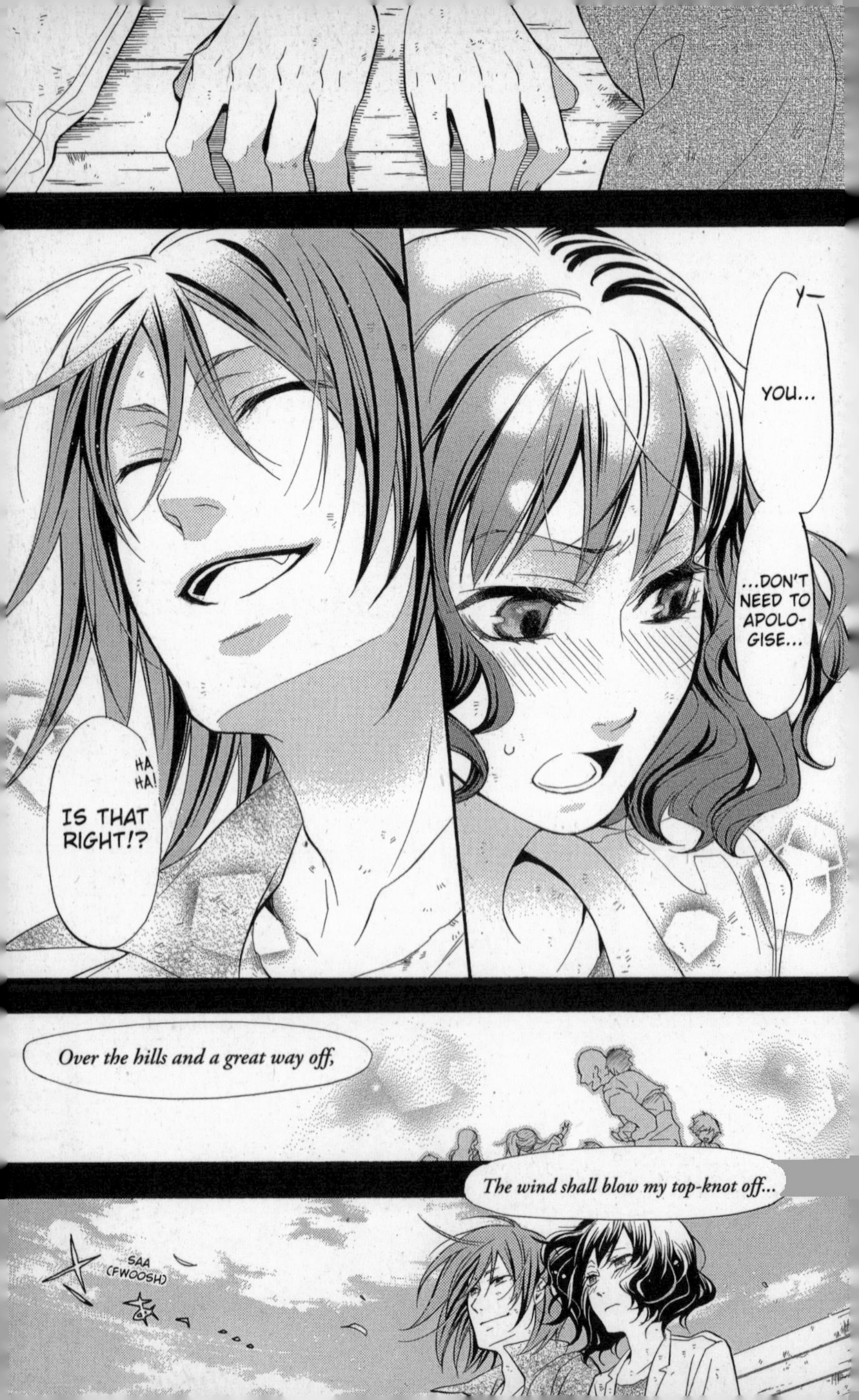
Y–
YOU...
...DON'T NEED TO APOLOGISE...
HA HA!
IS THAT RIGHT!?
Over the hills and a great way off,
The wind shall blow my top-knot off...
SAA (FWOOSH)

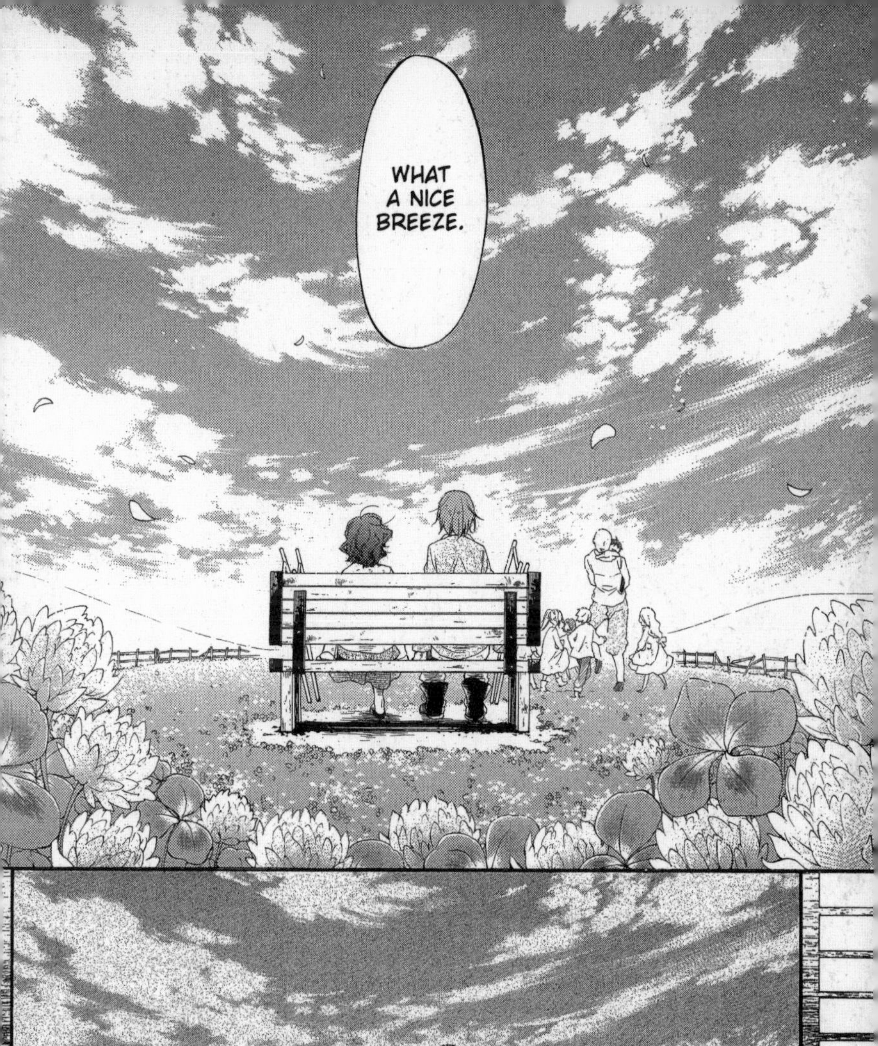
WHAT A NICE BREEZE.
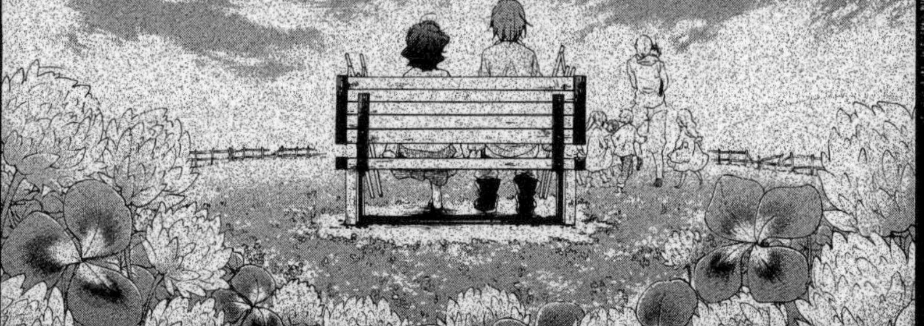
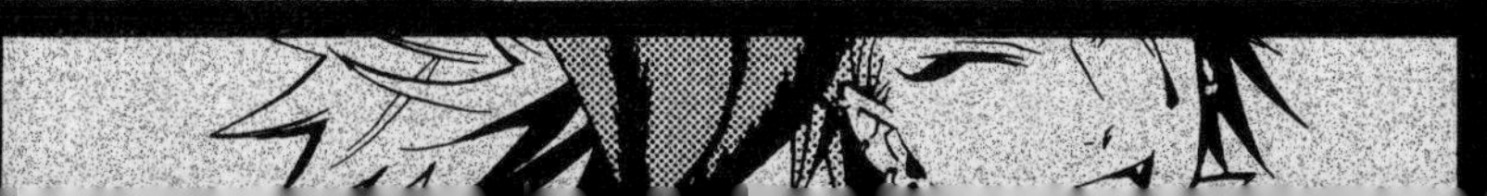

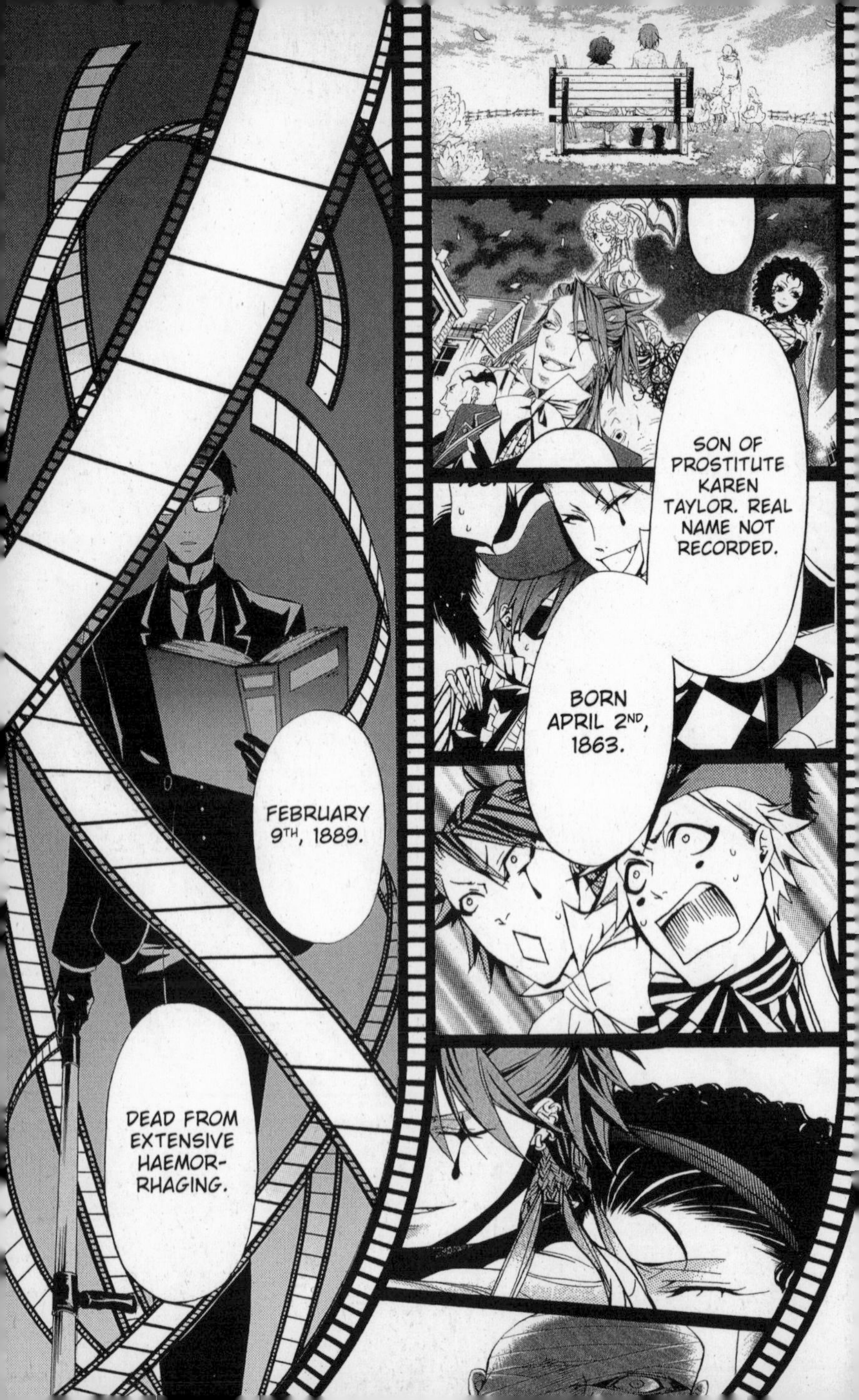
SON OF PROSTITUTE KAREN TAYLOR. REAL NAME NOT RECORDED.
BORN APRIL 2ND, 1863.
FEBRUARY 9TH, 1889.
DEAD FROM EXTENSIVE HAEMOR-RHAGING.

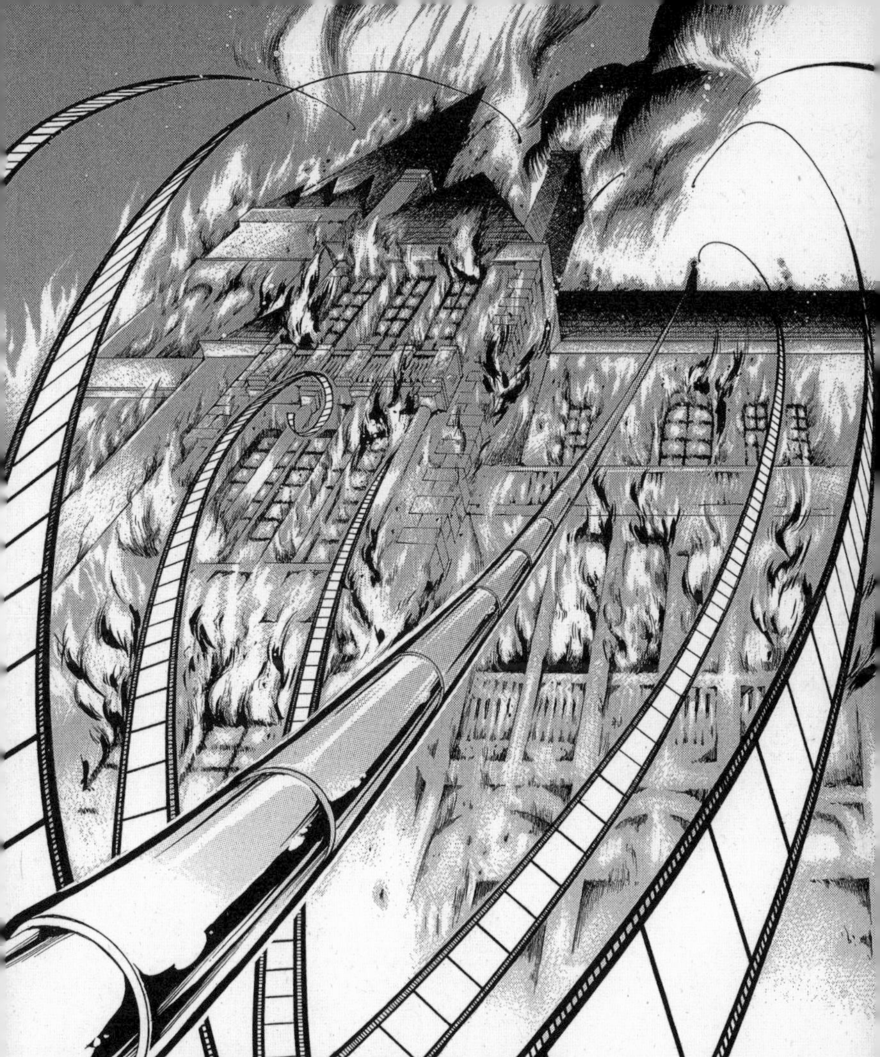

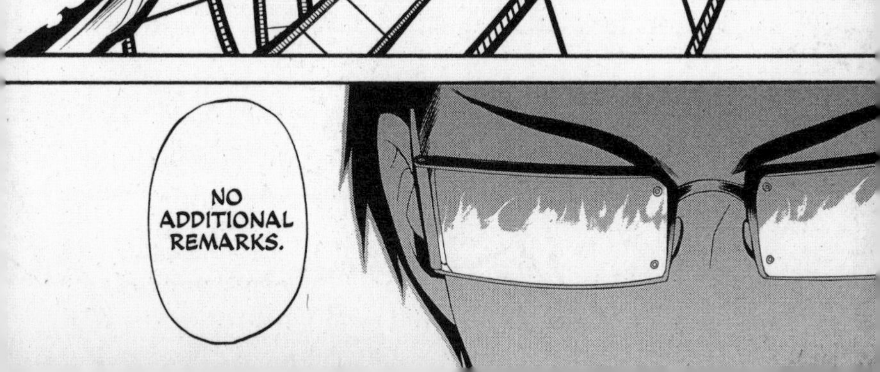

NO ADDITIONAL REMARKS.

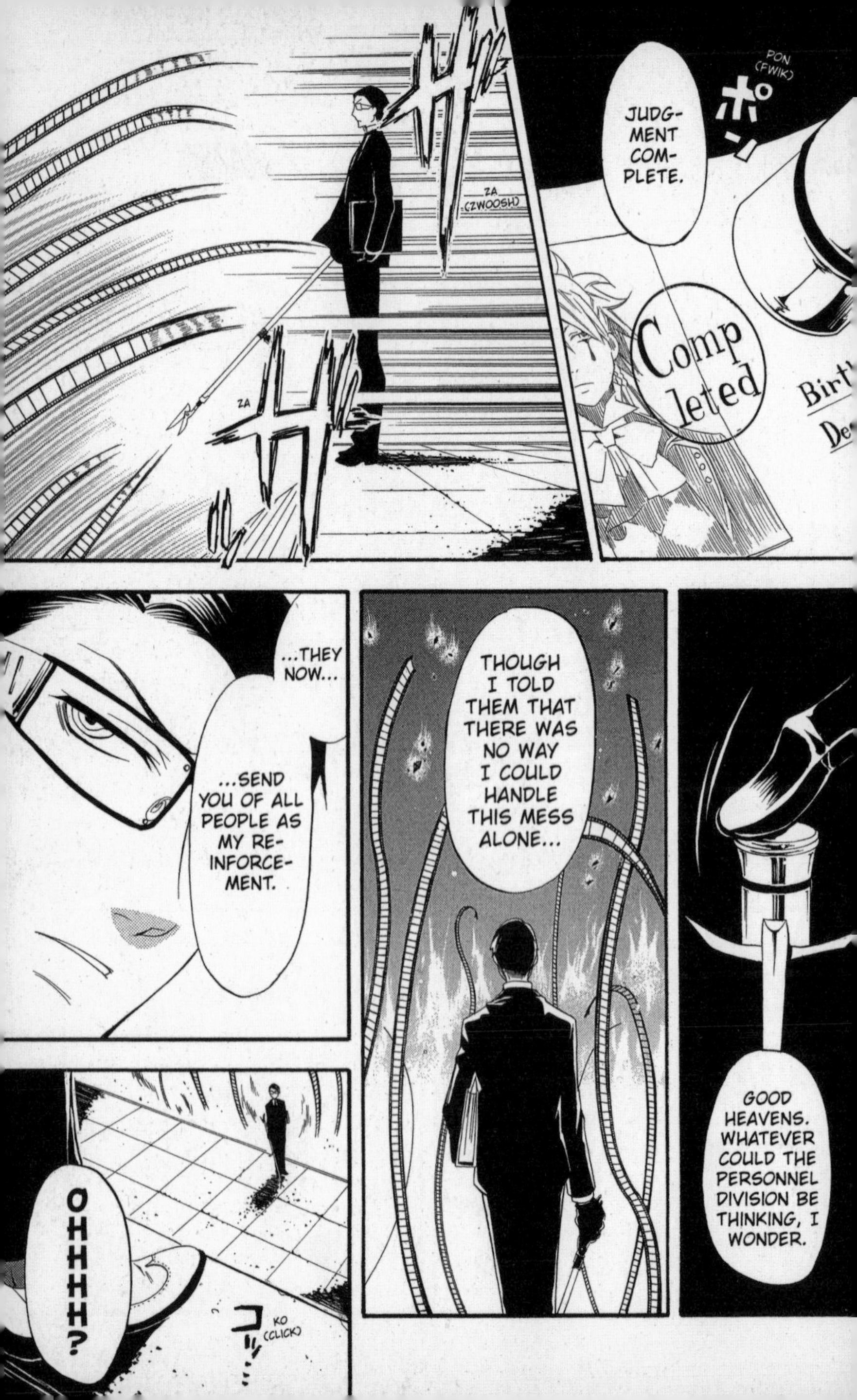
PON (FWIK)
JUDGMENT COMPLETE.
Completed
ZA (ZWOOSH)
ZA
GOOD HEAVENS. WHATEVER COULD THE PERSONNEL DIVISION BE THINKING, I WONDER.
THOUGH I TOLD THEM THAT THERE WAS NO WAY I COULD HANDLE THIS MESS ALONE...
...THEY NOW...
...SEND YOU OF ALL PEOPLE AS MY REINFORCEMENT.
OHHHH?
KO (CLICK)

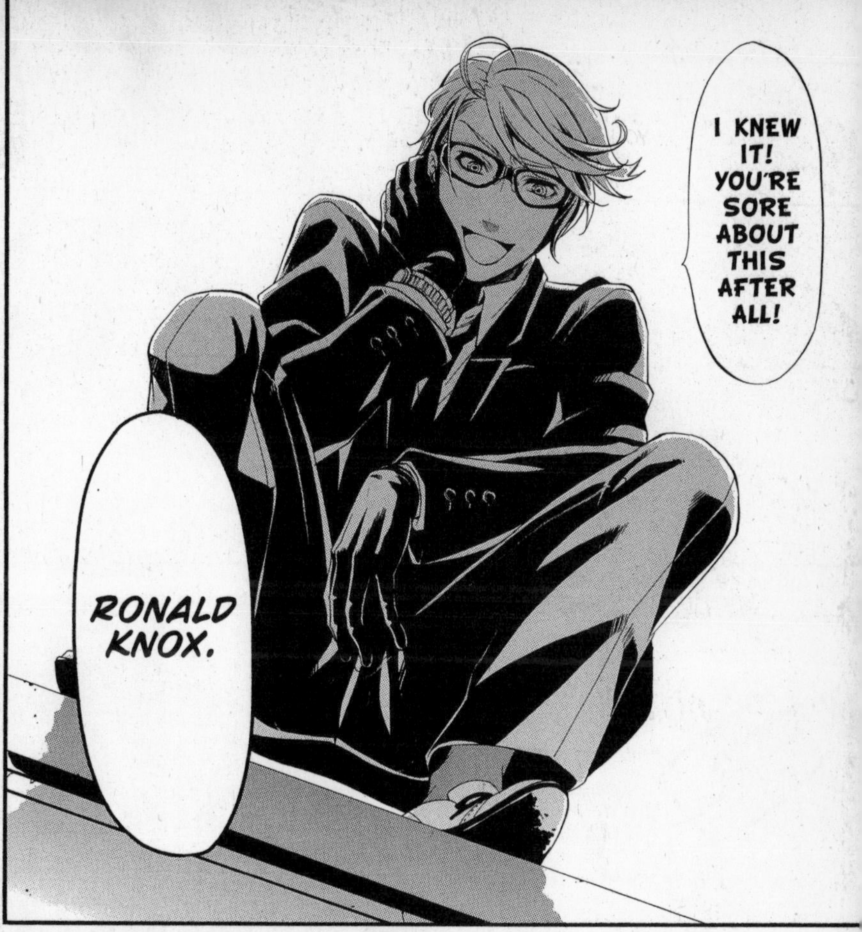
I KNEW IT! YOU'RE SORE ABOUT THIS AFTER ALL!
RONALD KNOX.

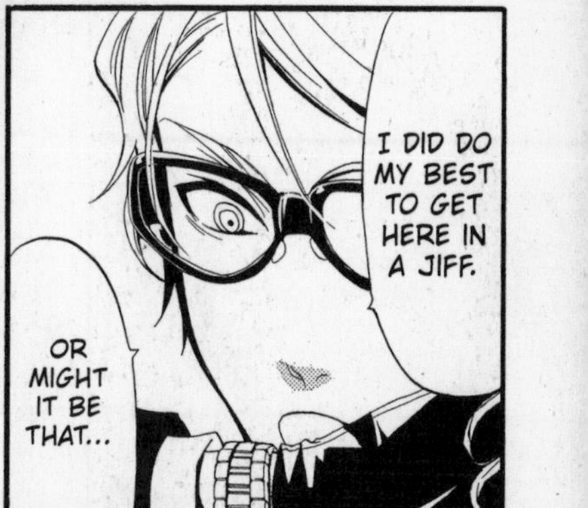
I DID DO MY BEST TO GET HERE IN A JIFF.
OR MIGHT IT BE THAT...

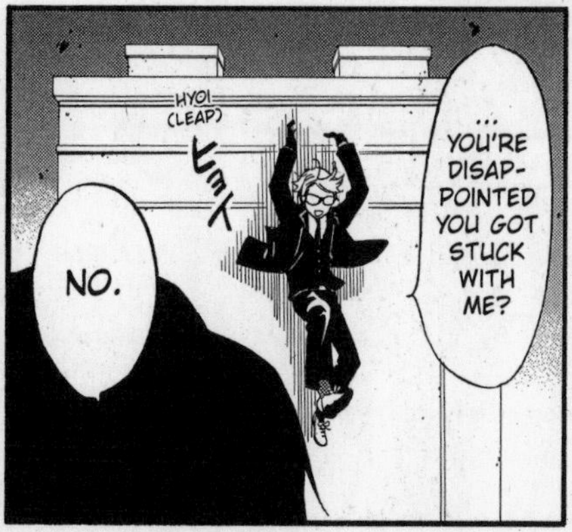
... YOU'RE DISAP-POINTED YOU GOT STUCK WITH ME?
HYOI (LEAP)
NO.

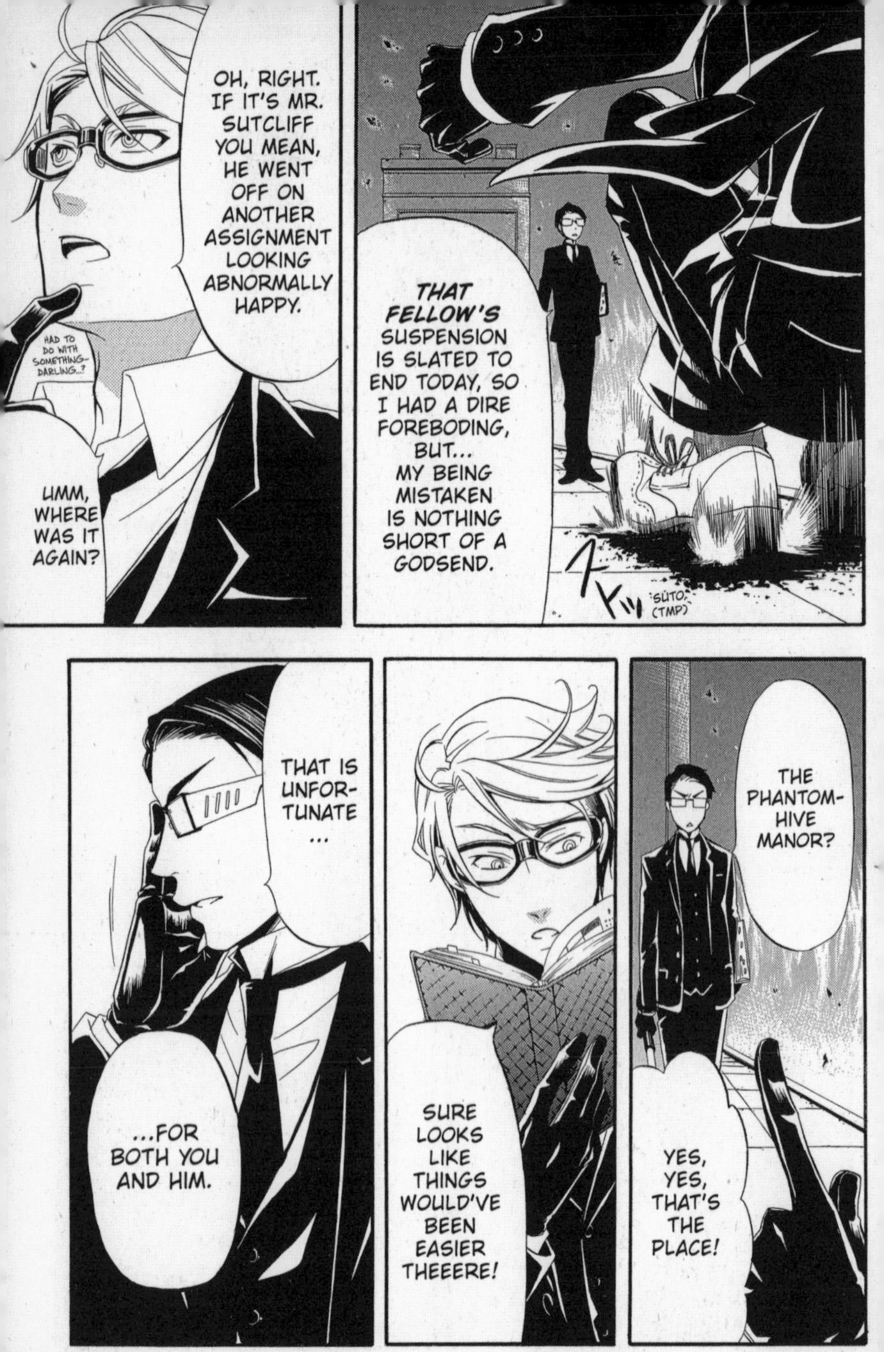
THAT FELLOW'S SUSPENSION IS SLATED TO END TODAY, SO I HAD A DIRE FOREBODING, BUT... MY BEING MISTAKEN IS NOTHING SHORT OF A GODSEND.
SUTO (TMP)
OH, RIGHT. IF IT'S MR. SUTCLIFF YOU MEAN, HE WENT OFF ON ANOTHER ASSIGNMENT LOOKING ABNORMALLY HAPPY.
HAD TO DO WITH SOMETHING-DARLING...?
UMM, WHERE WAS IT AGAIN?
THE PHANTOM-HIVE MANOR?
YES, YES, THAT'S THE PLACE!
SURE LOOKS LIKE THINGS WOULD'VE BEEN EASIER THEEERE!
THAT IS UNFOR-TUNATE...
...FOR BOTH YOU AND HIM.

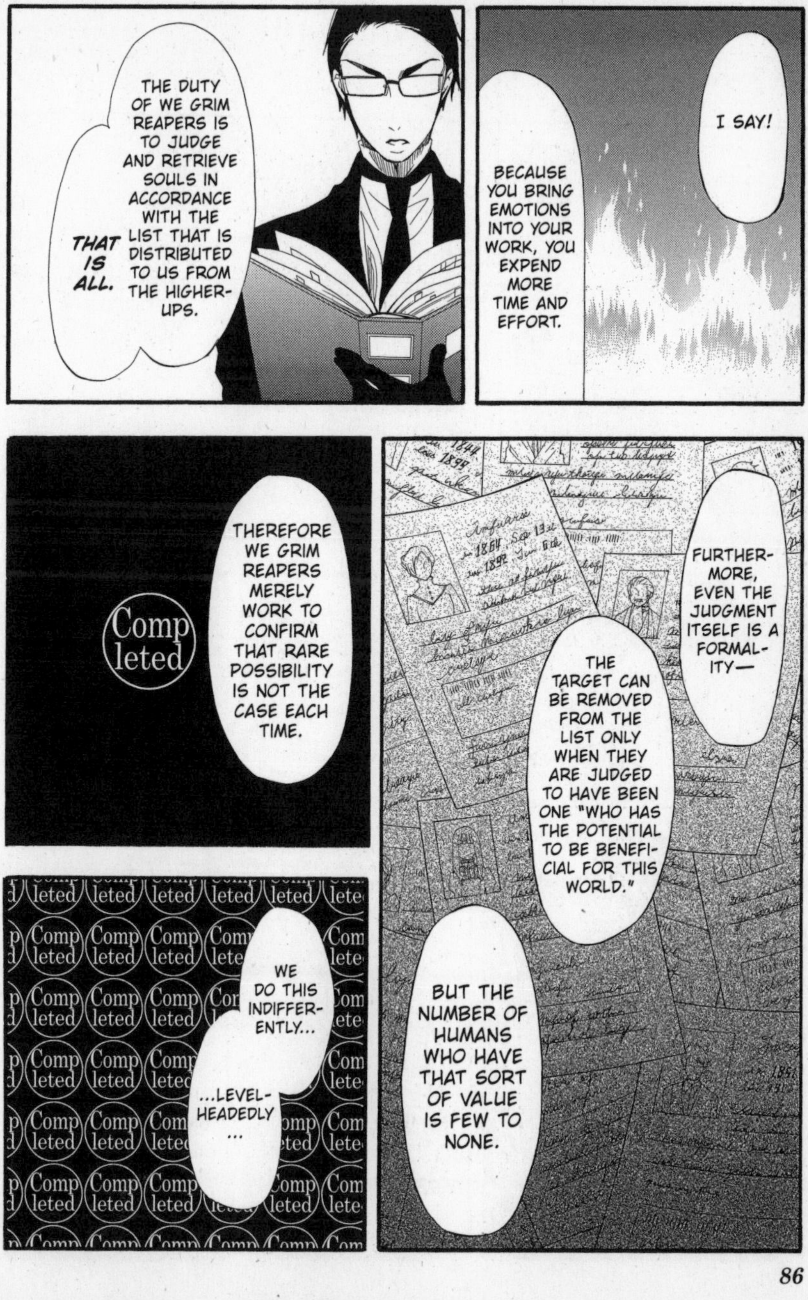
I SAY!
BECAUSE YOU BRING EMOTIONS INTO YOUR WORK, YOU EXPEND MORE TIME AND EFFORT.
THE DUTY OF WE GRIM REAPERS IS TO JUDGE AND RETRIEVE SOULS IN ACCORDANCE WITH THE LIST THAT IS DISTRIBUTED TO US FROM THE HIGHER-UPS.
THAT IS ALL.
FURTHERMORE, EVEN THE JUDGMENT ITSELF IS A FORMALITY—
THE TARGET CAN BE REMOVED FROM THE LIST ONLY WHEN THEY ARE JUDGED TO HAVE BEEN ONE "WHO HAS THE POTENTIAL TO BE BENEFICIAL FOR THIS WORLD."
BUT THE NUMBER OF HUMANS WHO HAVE THAT SORT OF VALUE IS FEW TO NONE.
THEREFORE WE GRIM REAPERS MERELY WORK TO CONFIRM THAT RARE POSSIBILITY IS NOT THE CASE EACH TIME.
Completed
WE DO THIS INDIFFERENTLY...
...LEVELHEADEDLY...

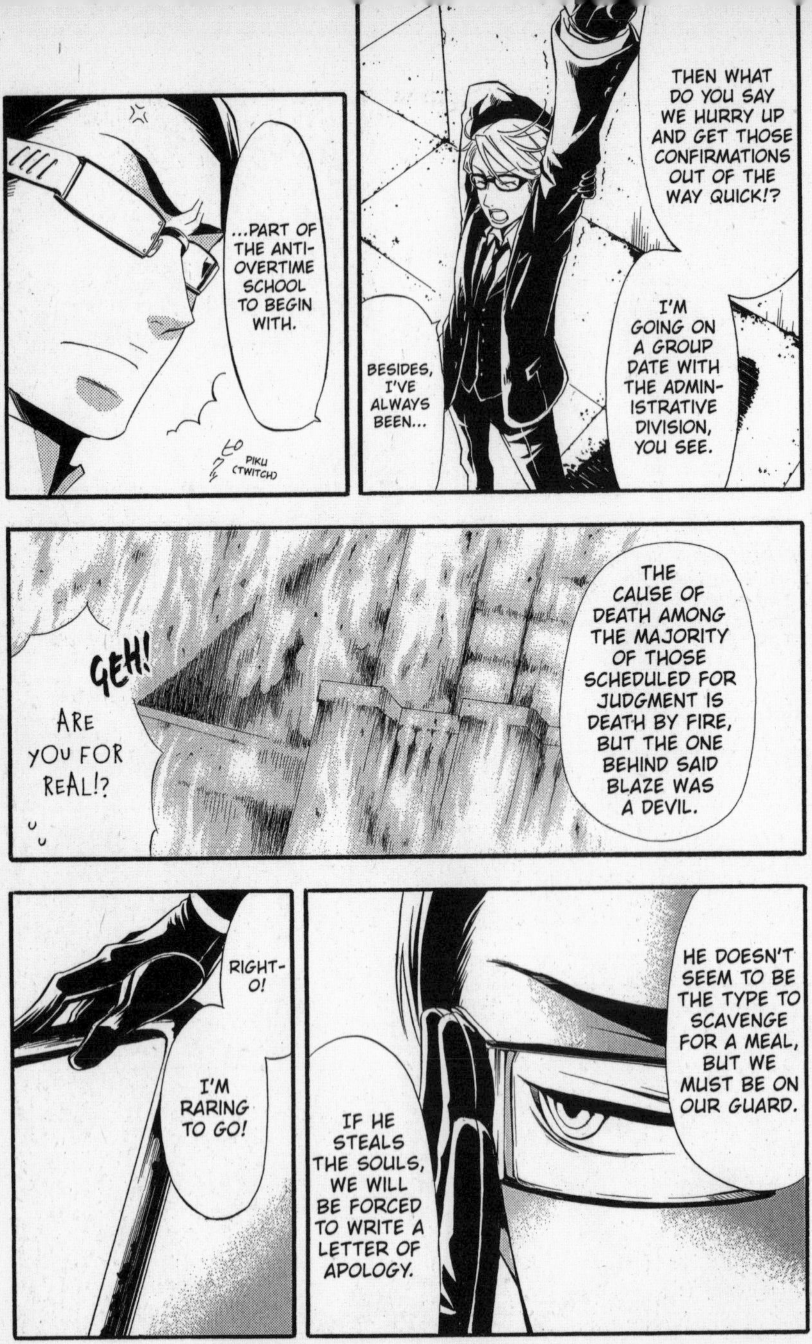
THEN WHAT DO YOU SAY WE HURRY UP AND GET THOSE CONFIRMATIONS OUT OF THE WAY QUICK!?
I'M GOING ON A GROUP DATE WITH THE ADMIN-ISTRATIVE DIVISION, YOU SEE.
BESIDES, I'VE ALWAYS BEEN...
...PART OF THE ANTI-OVERTIME SCHOOL TO BEGIN WITH.
PIKU (TWITCH)
THE CAUSE OF DEATH AMONG THE MAJORITY OF THOSE SCHEDULED FOR JUDGMENT IS DEATH BY FIRE, BUT THE ONE BEHIND SAID BLAZE WAS A DEVIL.
GEH!
ARE YOU FOR REAL!?
HE DOESN'T SEEM TO BE THE TYPE TO SCAVENGE FOR A MEAL, BUT WE MUST BE ON OUR GUARD.
IF HE STEALS THE SOULS, WE WILL BE FORCED TO WRITE A LETTER OF APOLOGY.
RIGHT-O!
I'M RARING TO GO!

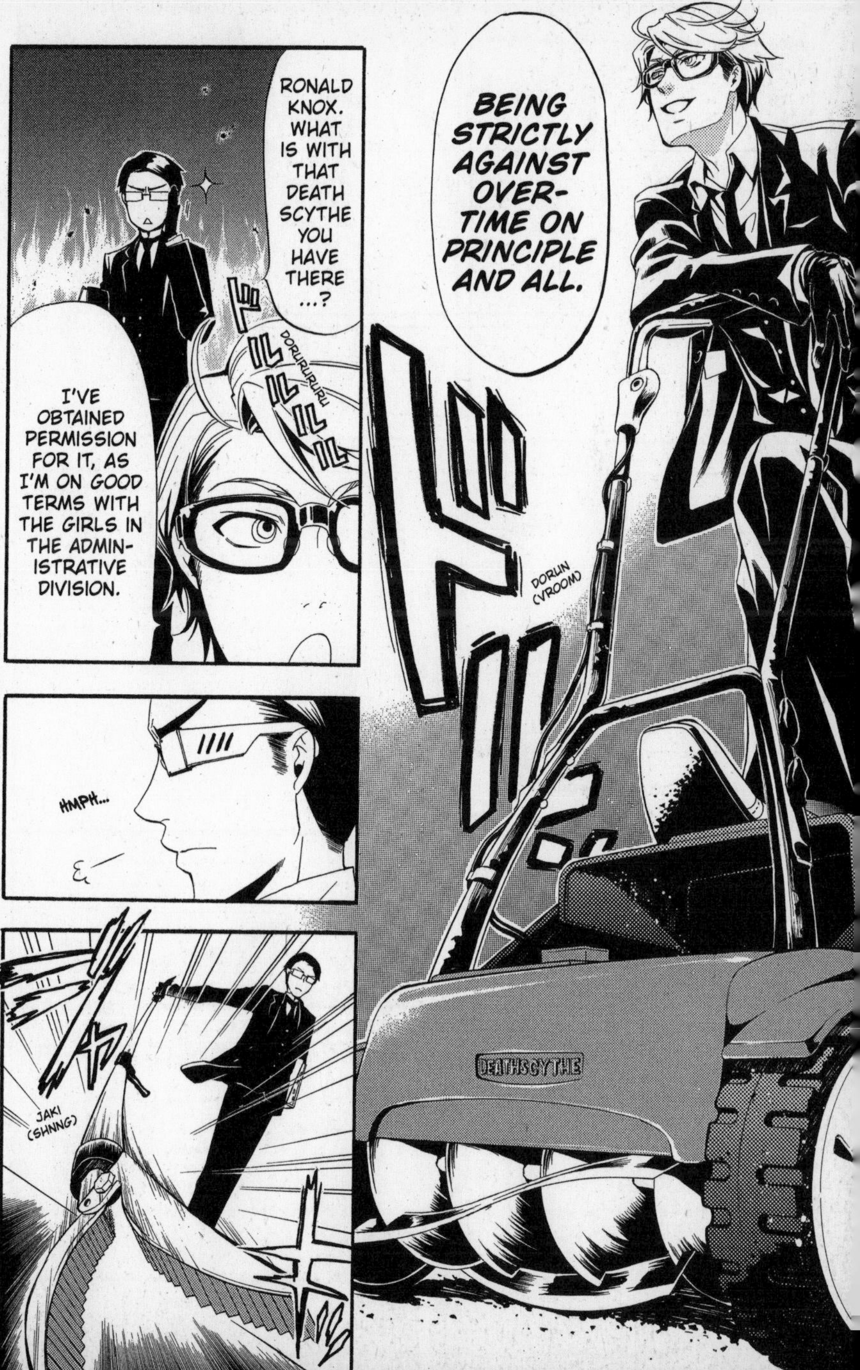
BEING STRICTLY AGAINST OVER-TIME ON PRINCIPLE AND ALL.
DORUN (VROOM)
DEATHSCYTHE
RONALD KNOX. WHAT IS WITH THAT DEATH SCYTHE YOU HAVE THERE ...?
DORURURURU
I'VE OBTAINED PERMISSION FOR IT, AS I'M ON GOOD TERMS WITH THE GIRLS IN THE ADMIN-ISTRATIVE DIVISION.
HMPH...
JAKI (SHNNG)

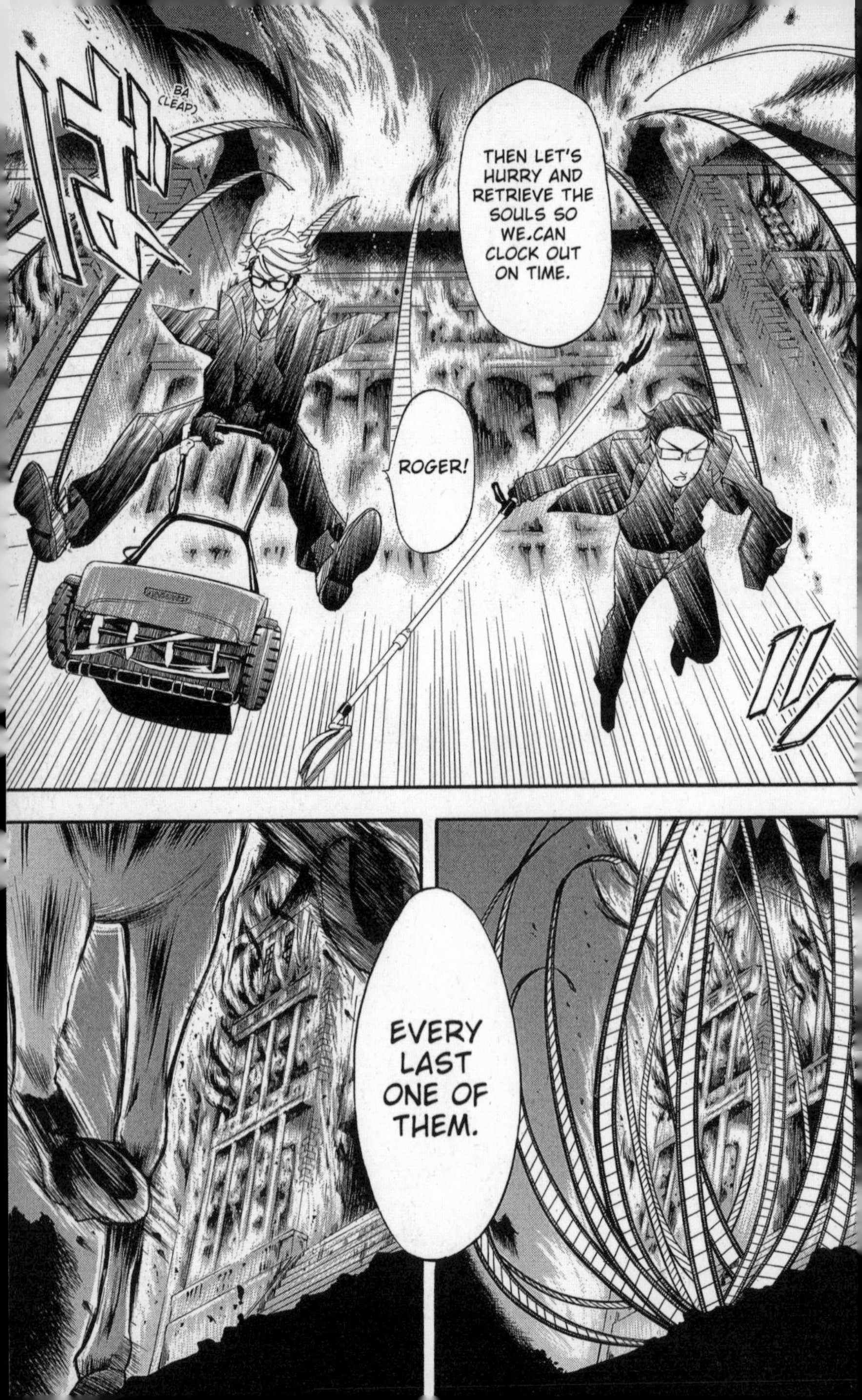
THEN LET'S HURRY AND RETRIEVE THE SOULS SO WE CAN CLOCK OUT ON TIME.
BA (LEAP)
ROGER!
EVERY LAST ONE OF THEM.

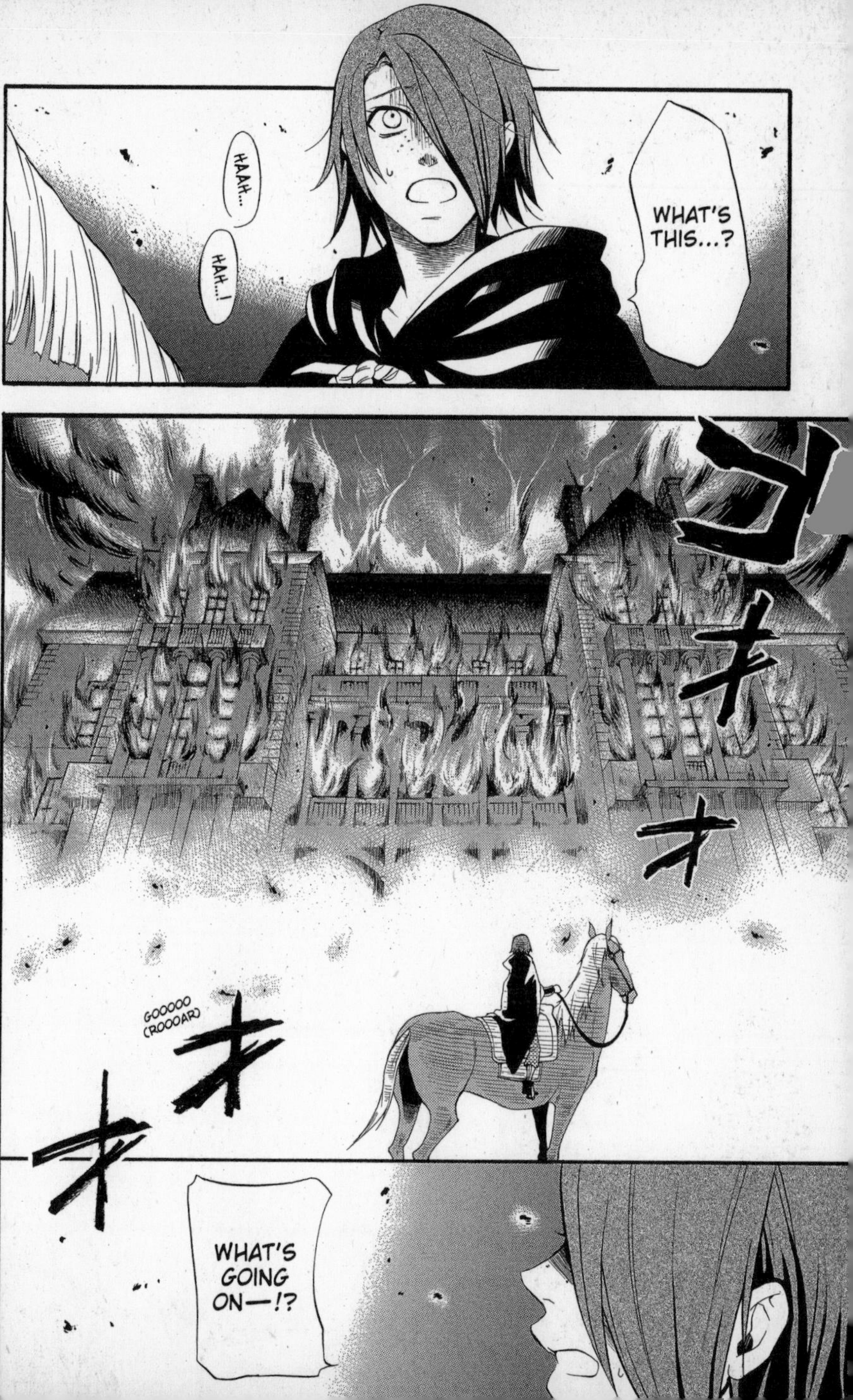
WHAT'S THIS...?
HAAH... HAH...!
GOOOOO (ROOOAR)
WHAT'S GOING ON—!?

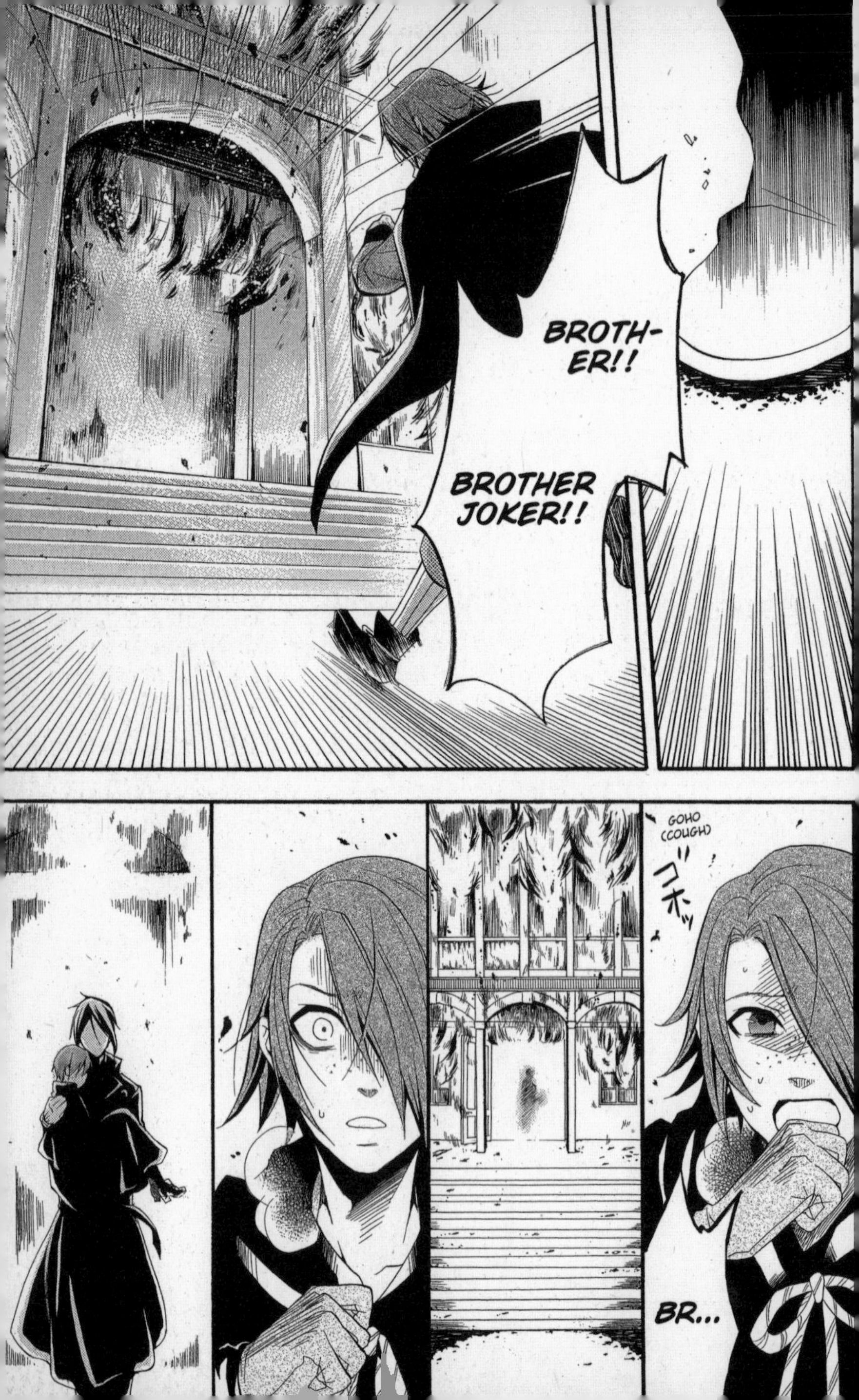
BROTH-
ER!!
BROTHER
JOKER!!
GOHO
(COUGH)
ゴホッ
BR...

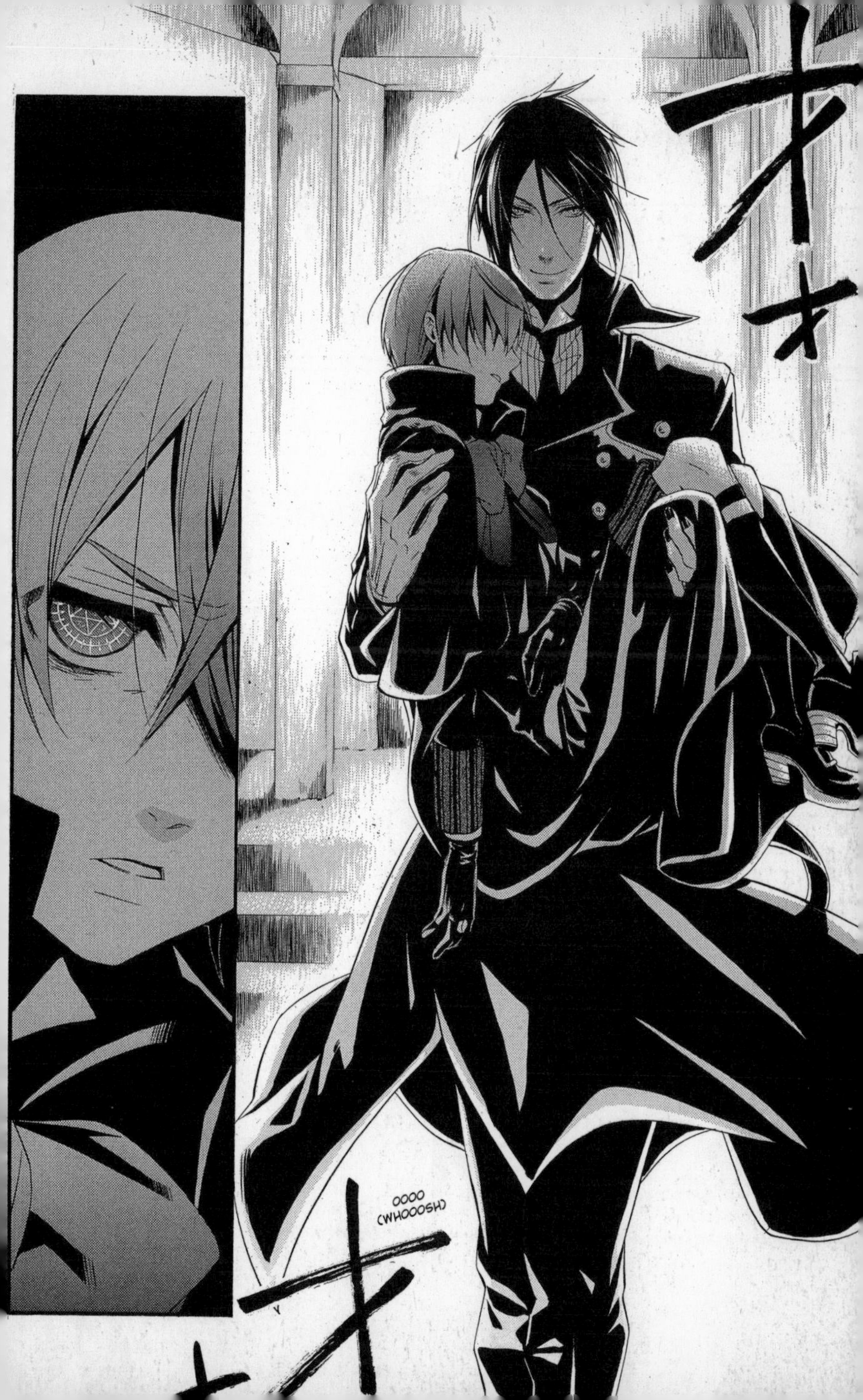
OOOO
(WHOOOSH)

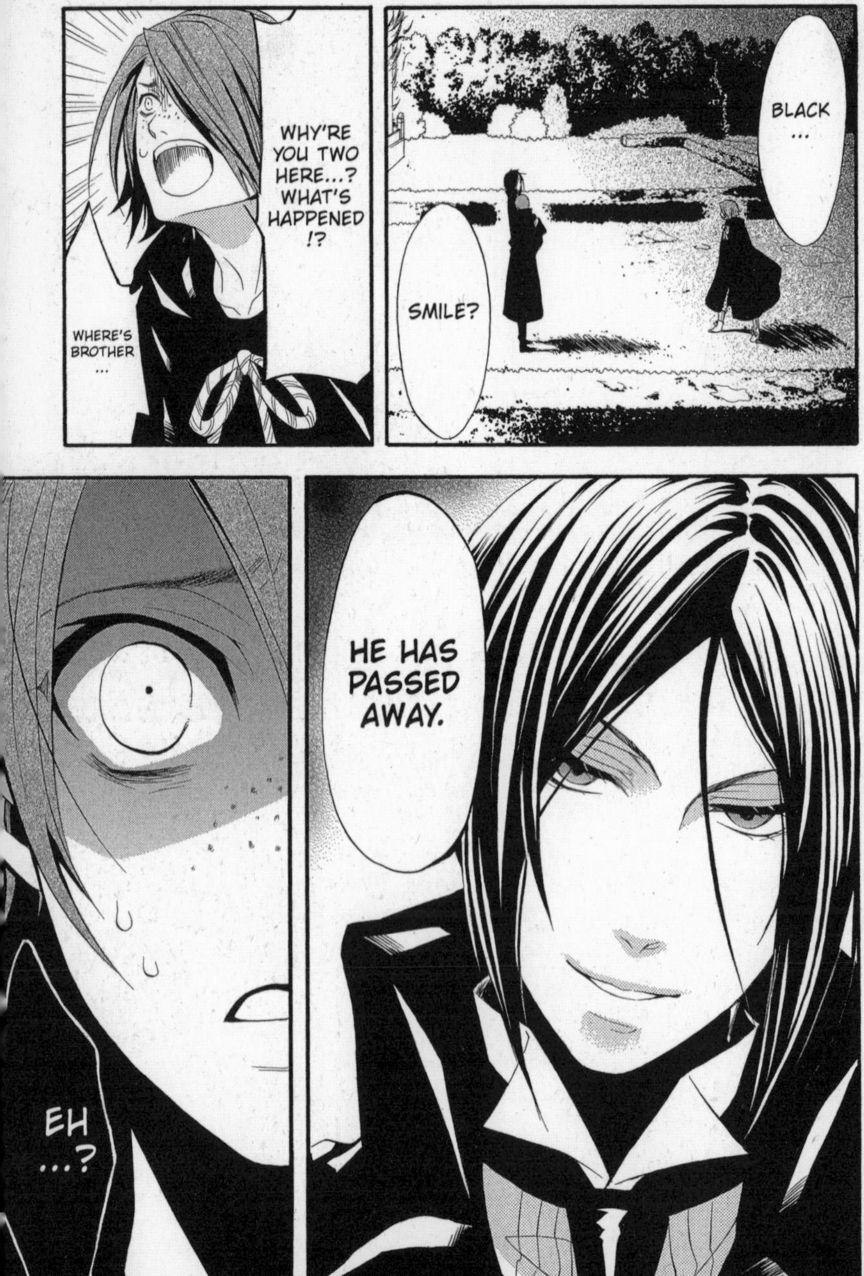
BLACK ...
SMILE?
WHY'RE YOU TWO HERE...? WHAT'S HAPPENED !?
WHERE'S BROTHER ...
HE HAS PASSED AWAY.
EH ...?

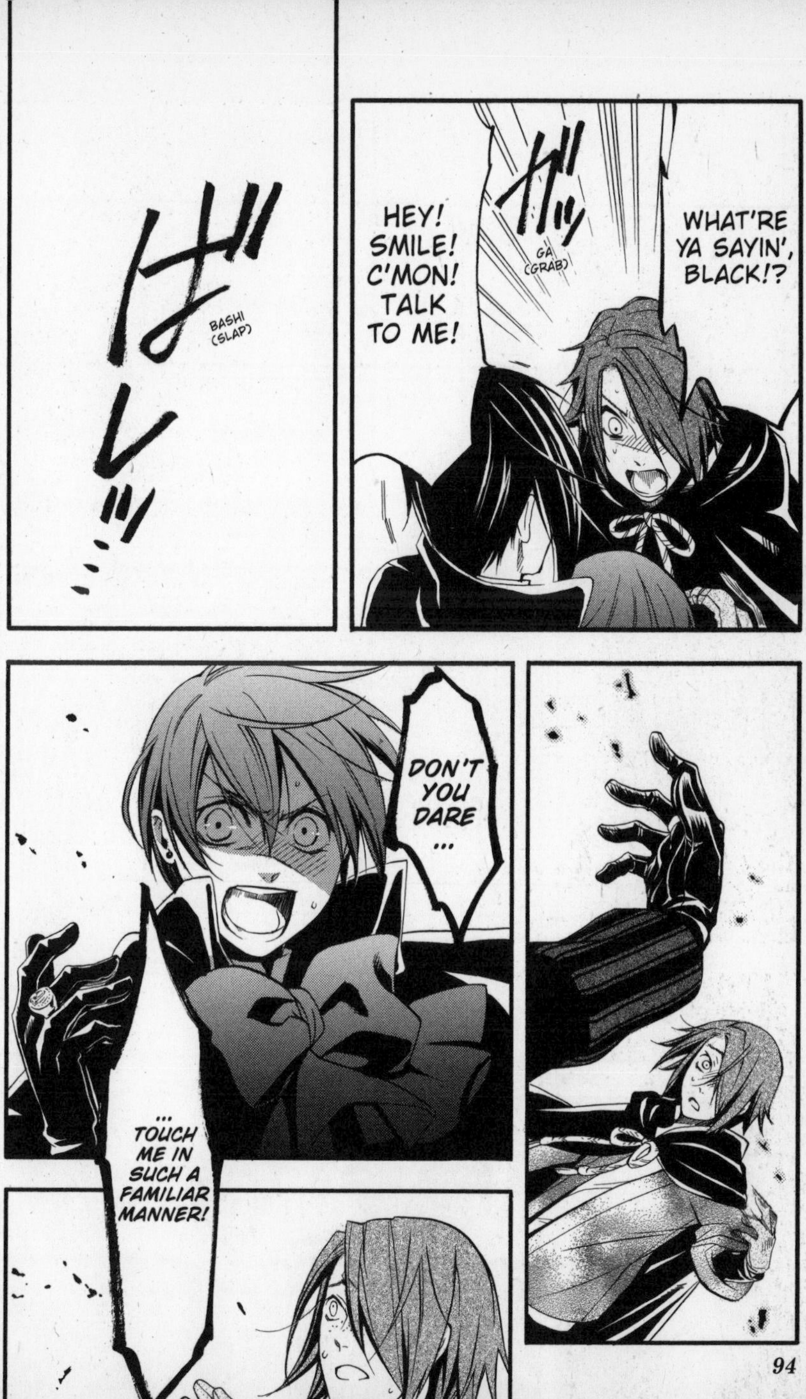
WHAT'RE YA SAYIN', BLACK!?
GA (GRAB)
HEY! SMILE! C'MON! TALK TO ME!
BASHI (SLAP)
DON'T YOU DARE ...
... TOUCH ME IN SUCH A FAMILIAR MANNER!

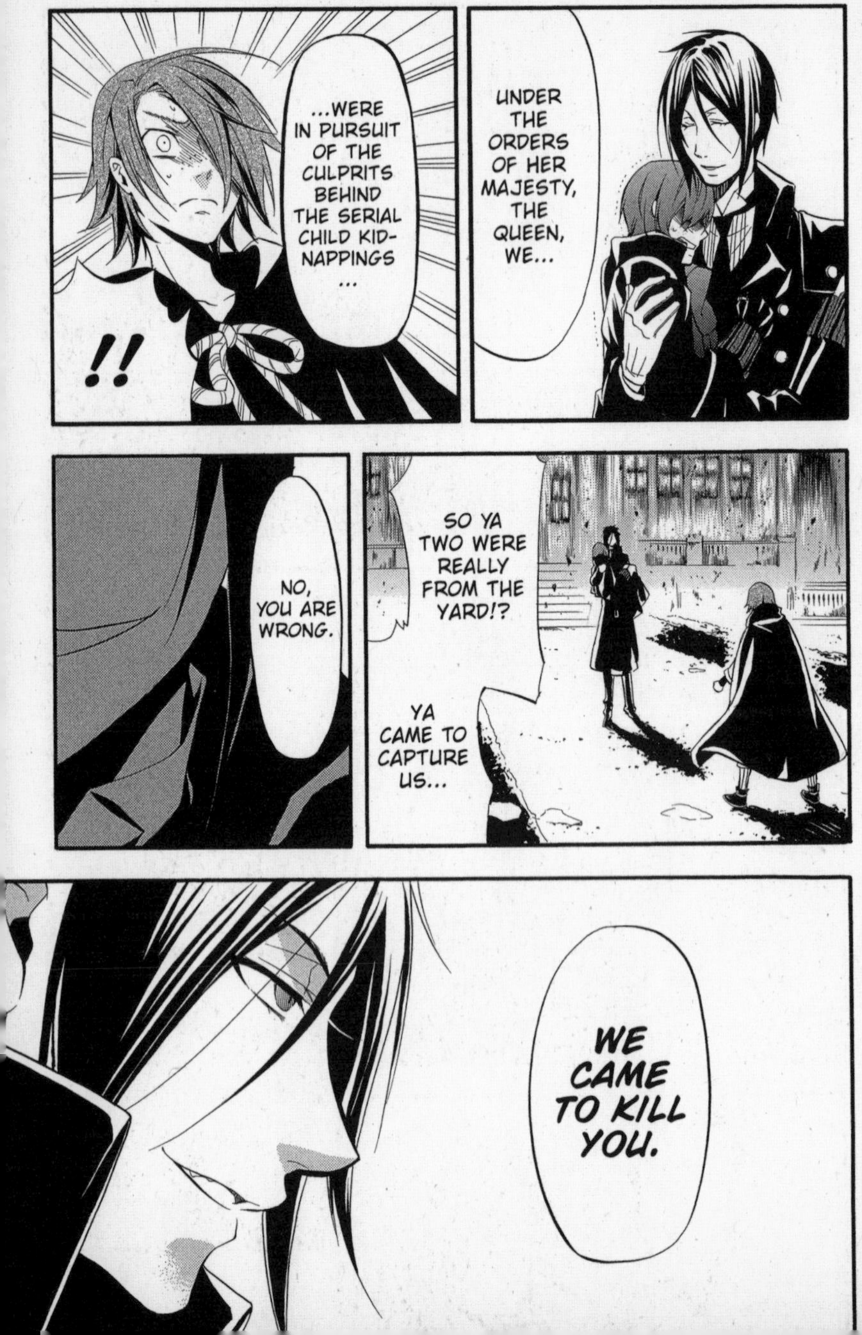
UNDER THE ORDERS OF HER MAJESTY, THE QUEEN, WE...
...WERE IN PURSUIT OF THE CULPRITS BEHIND THE SERIAL CHILD KID-NAPPINGS...
!!
SO YA TWO WERE REALLY FROM THE YARD!?
YA CAME TO CAPTURE US...
NO, YOU ARE WRONG.
WE CAME TO KILL YOU.

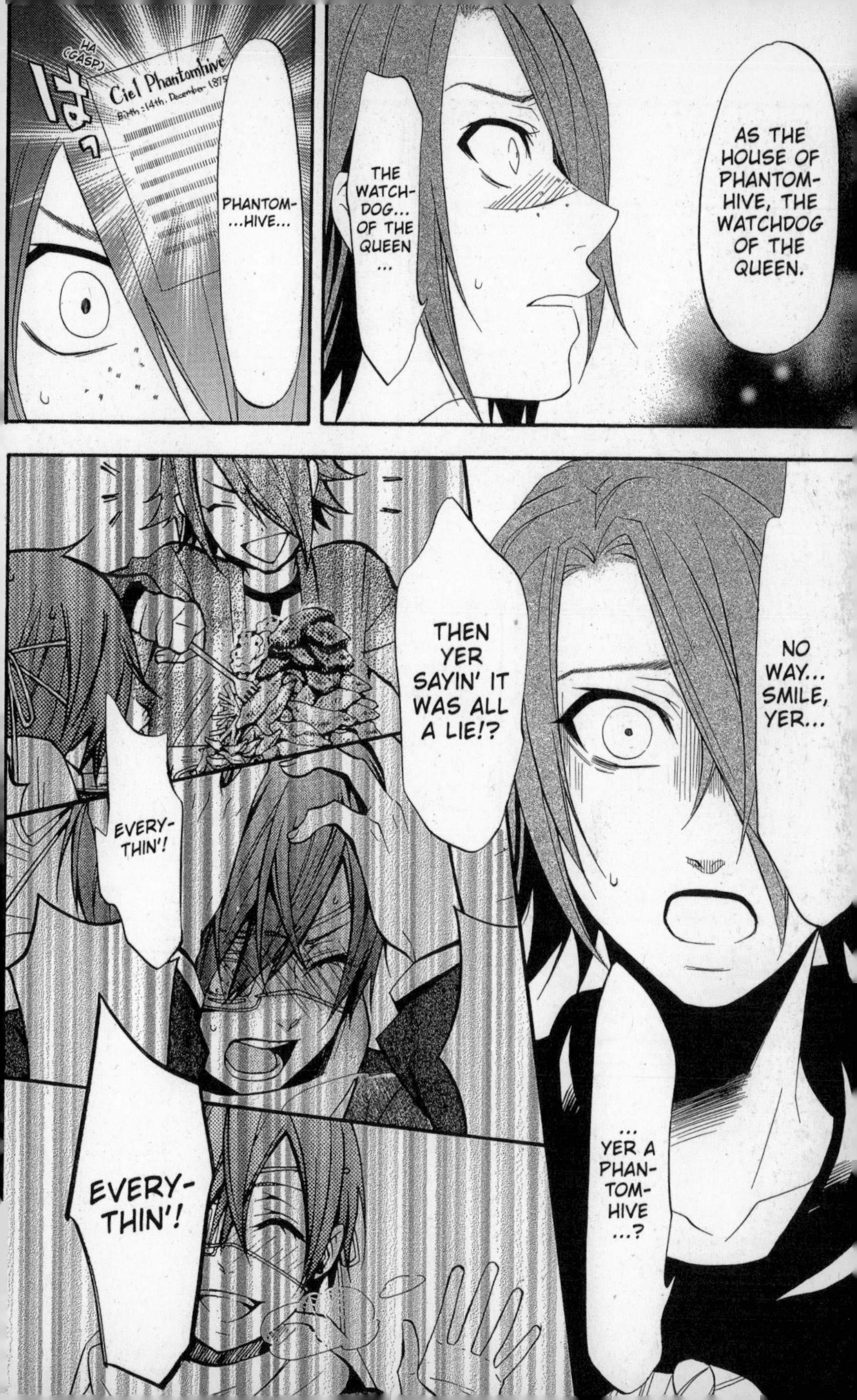
AS THE HOUSE OF PHANTOMHIVE, THE WATCHDOG OF THE QUEEN.
THE WATCHDOG... OF THE QUEEN ...
HA (GASP)
はっ
Ciel Phantomhive
Birth : 14th, December, 1875
PHANTOM- ...HIVE...
NO WAY... SMILE, YER...
... YER A PHANTOMHIVE ...?
THEN YER SAYIN' IT WAS ALL A LIE!?
EVERYTHIN'!
EVERYTHIN'!

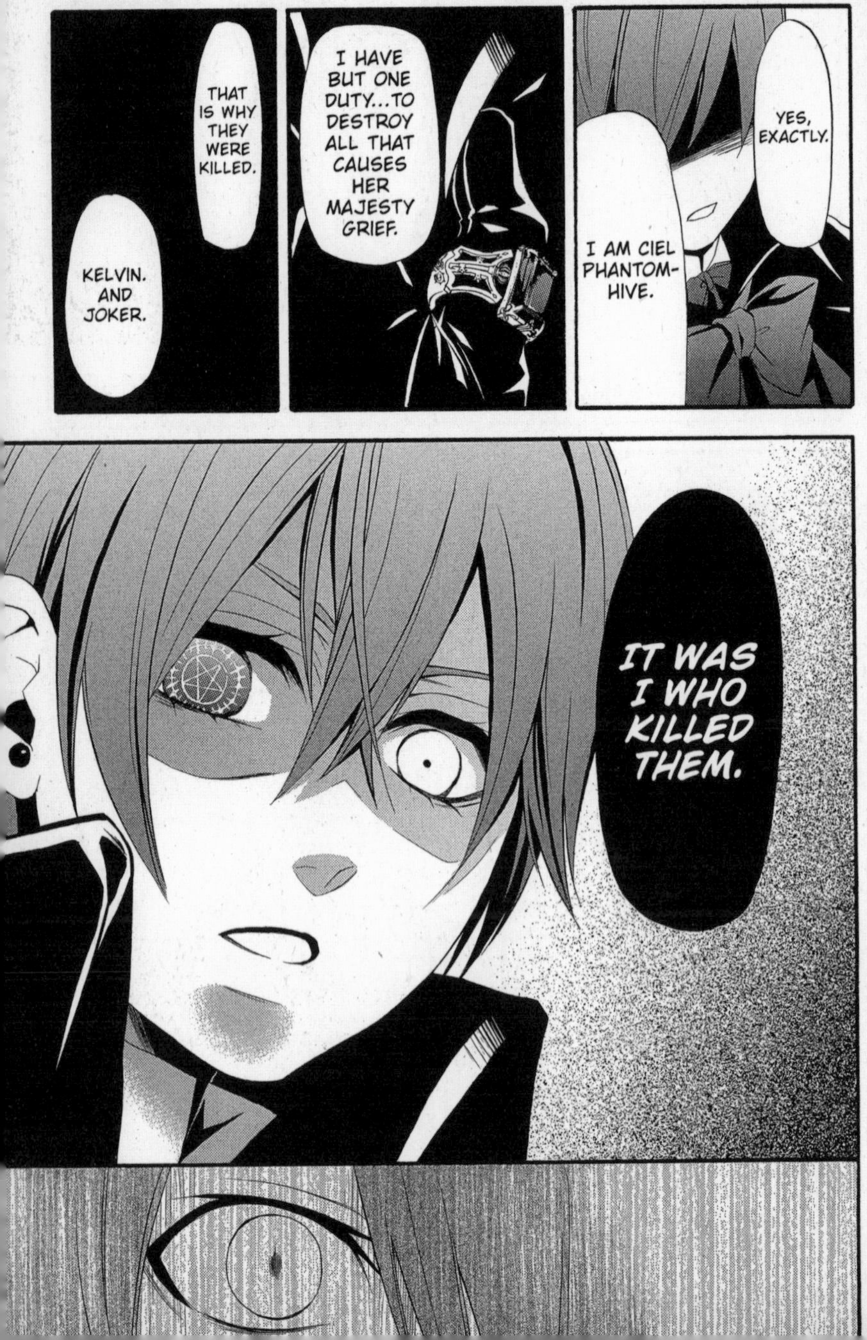
YES, EXACTLY.
I AM CIEL PHANTOM-HIVE.
I HAVE BUT ONE DUTY...TO DESTROY ALL THAT CAUSES HER MAJESTY GRIEF.
THAT IS WHY THEY WERE KILLED.
KELVIN. AND JOKER.
IT WAS I WHO KILLED THEM.

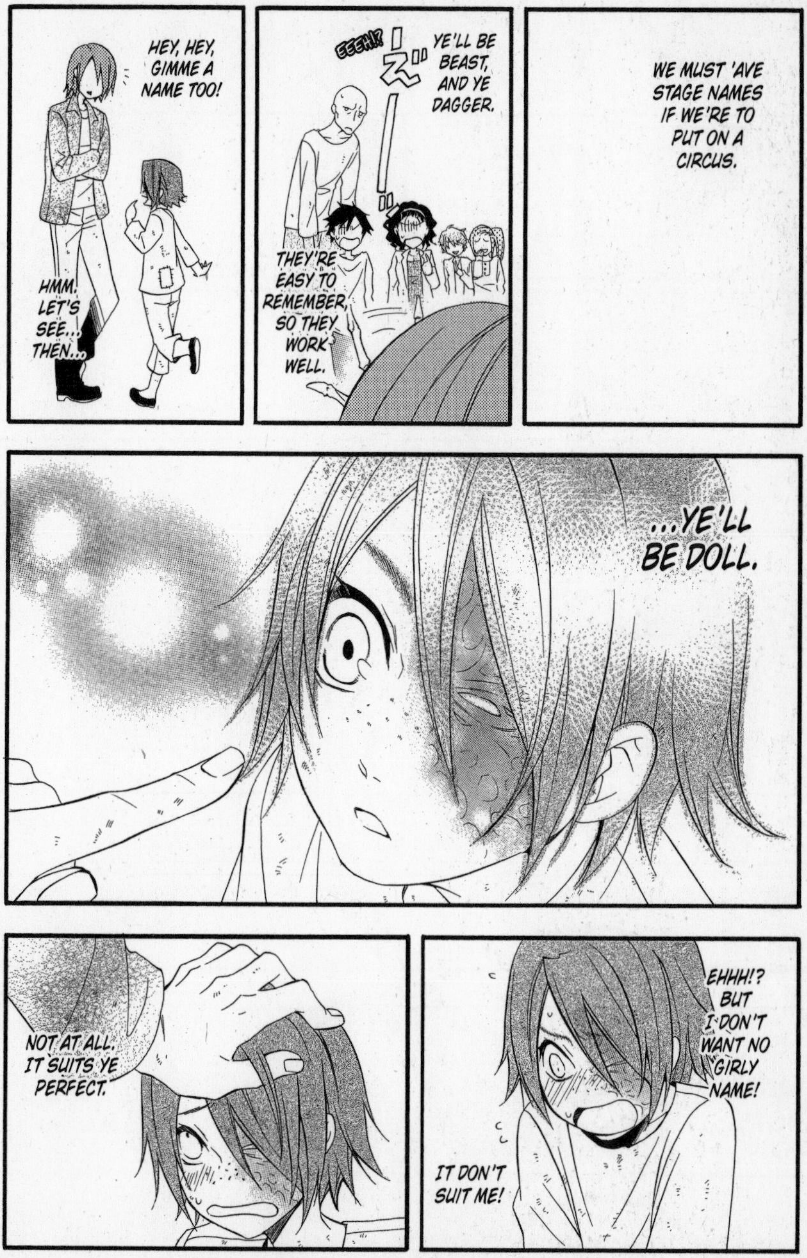
WE MUST 'AVE STAGE NAMES IF WE'RE TO PUT ON A CIRCUS.
YE'LL BE BEAST, AND YE DAGGER.
EEEH!?
え!
THEY'RE EASY TO REMEMBER, SO THEY WORK WELL.
HEY, HEY, GIMME A NAME TOO!
HMM. LET'S SEE... THEN...
...YE'LL BE DOLL.
EHHH!? BUT I DON'T WANT NO GIRLY NAME!
IT DON'T SUIT ME!
NOT AT ALL. IT SUITS YE PERFECT.

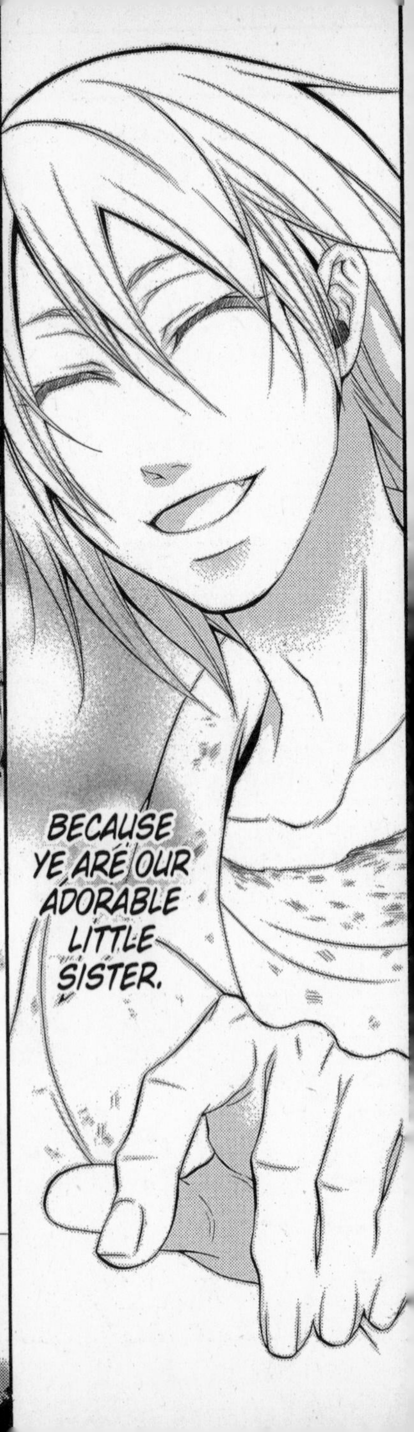
BECAUSE YE ARE OUR ADORABLE LITTLE SISTER.

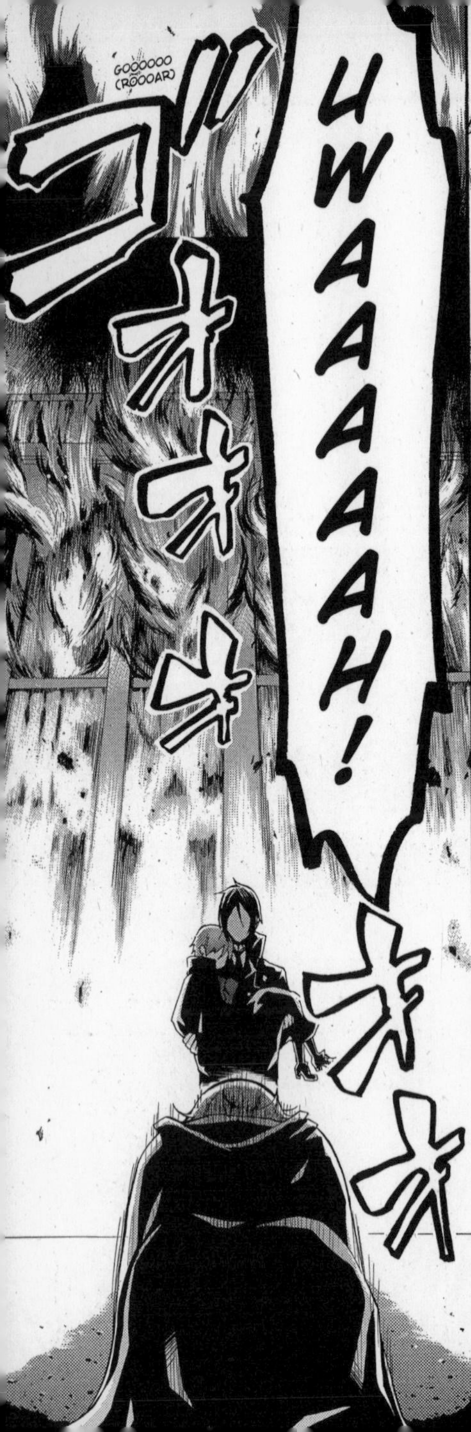
GOOOOOO (ROOOAR)
UWAAAAAH!

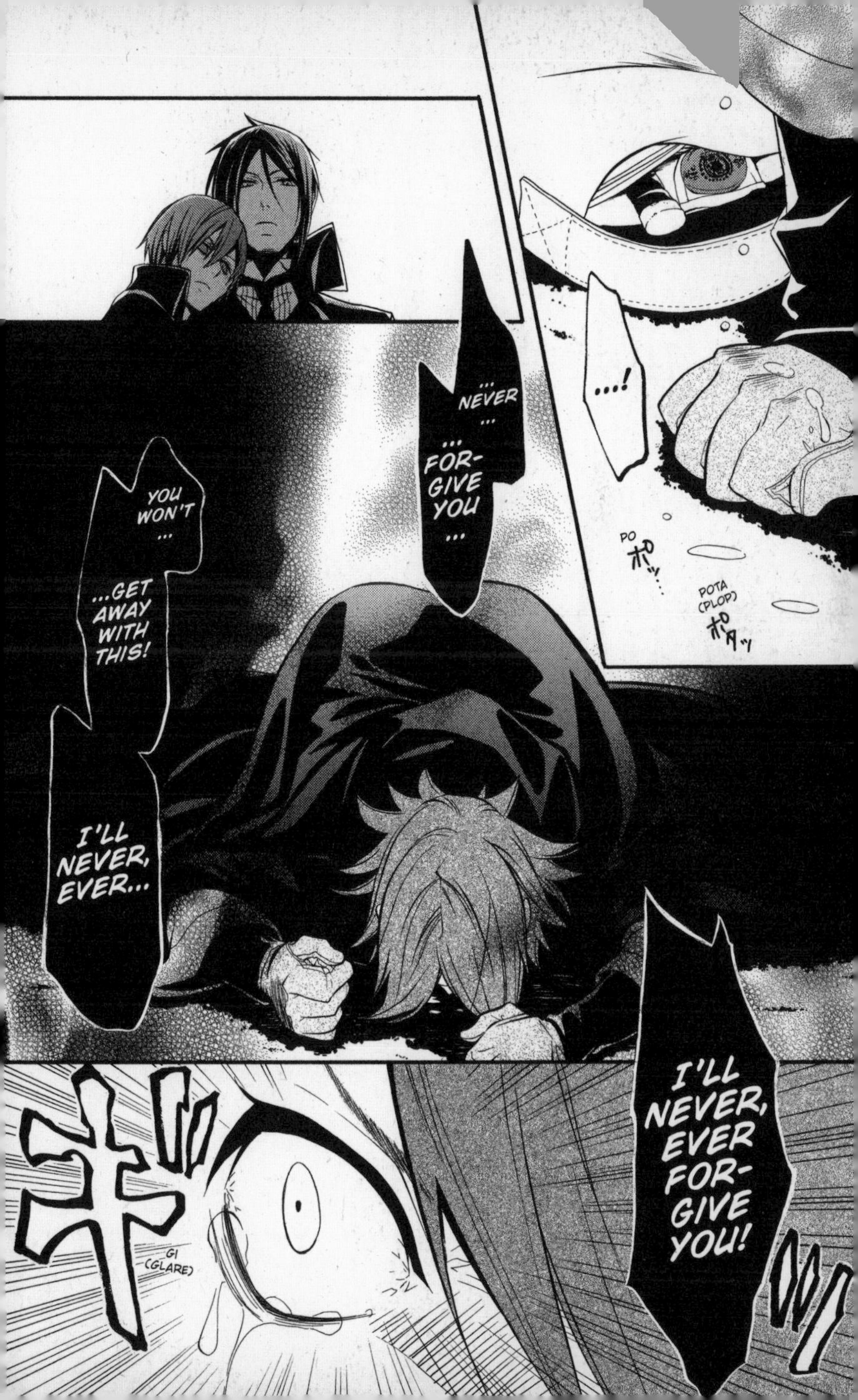
...!
PO
ポッ...
POTA
(PLOP)
ポタッ
...NEVER... ...FOR-GIVE YOU...
YOU WON'T... ...GET AWAY WITH THIS!
I'LL NEVER, EVER...
I'LL NEVER, EVER FOR-GIVE YOU!
GI
(GLARE)

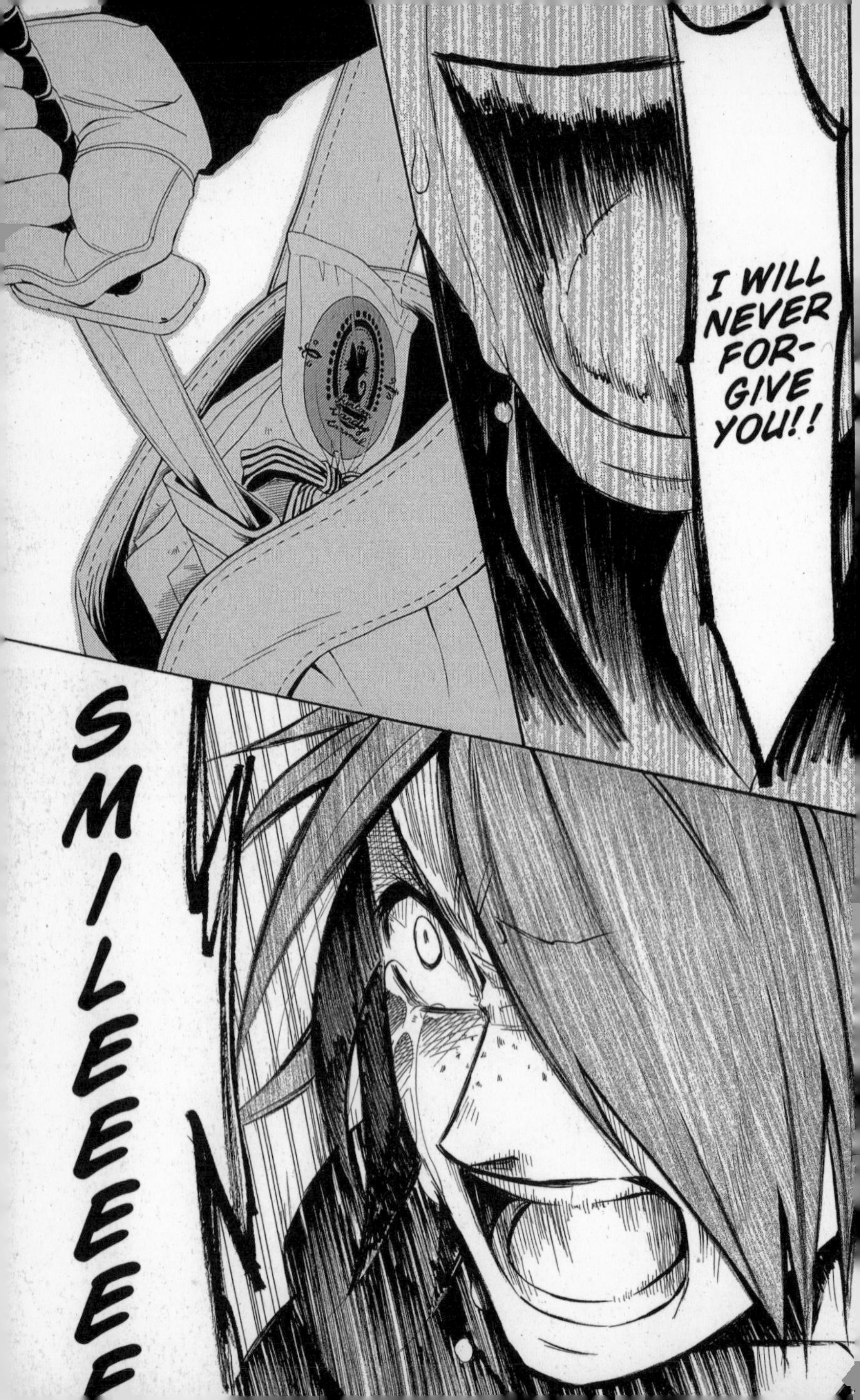
I WILL NEVER FOR-GIVE YOU!!
SMILEEEEE

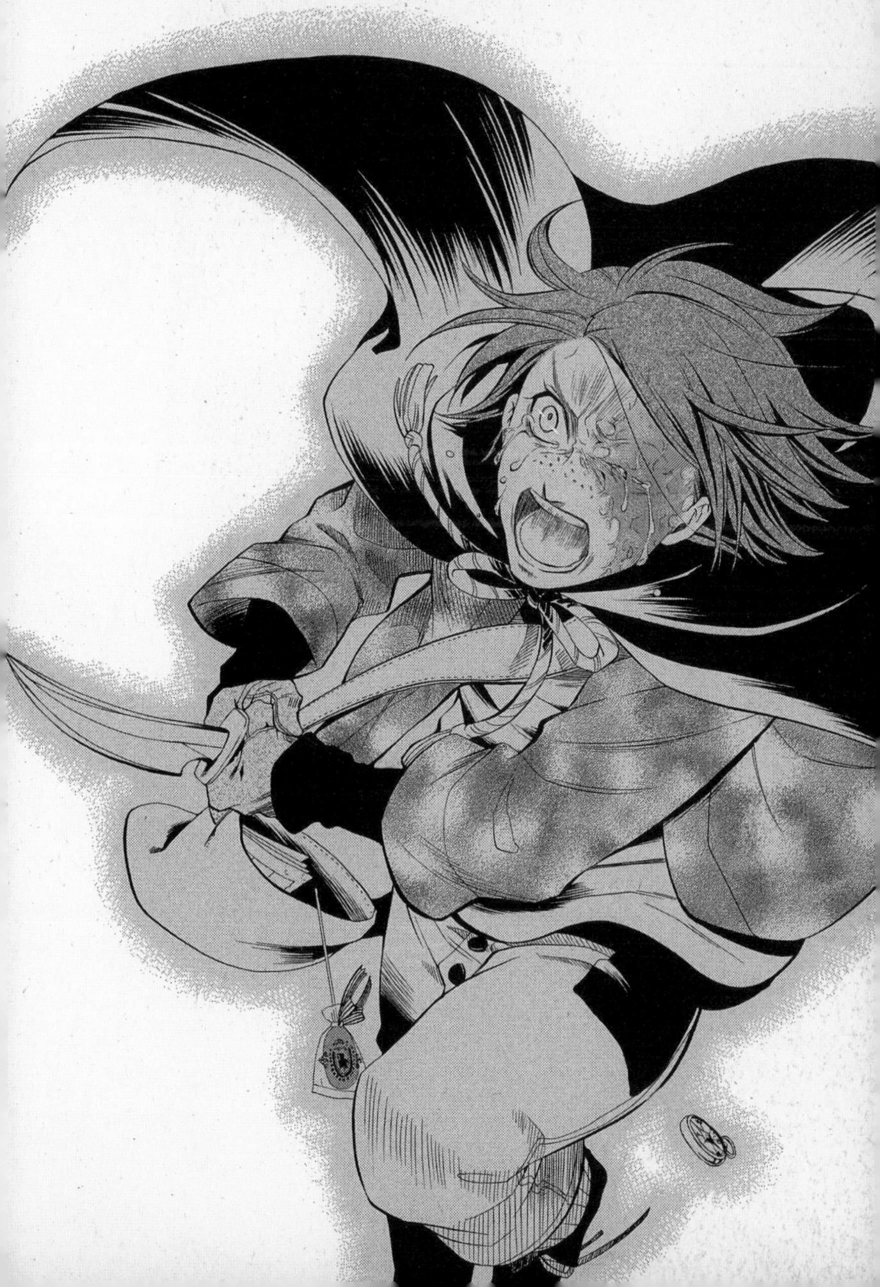

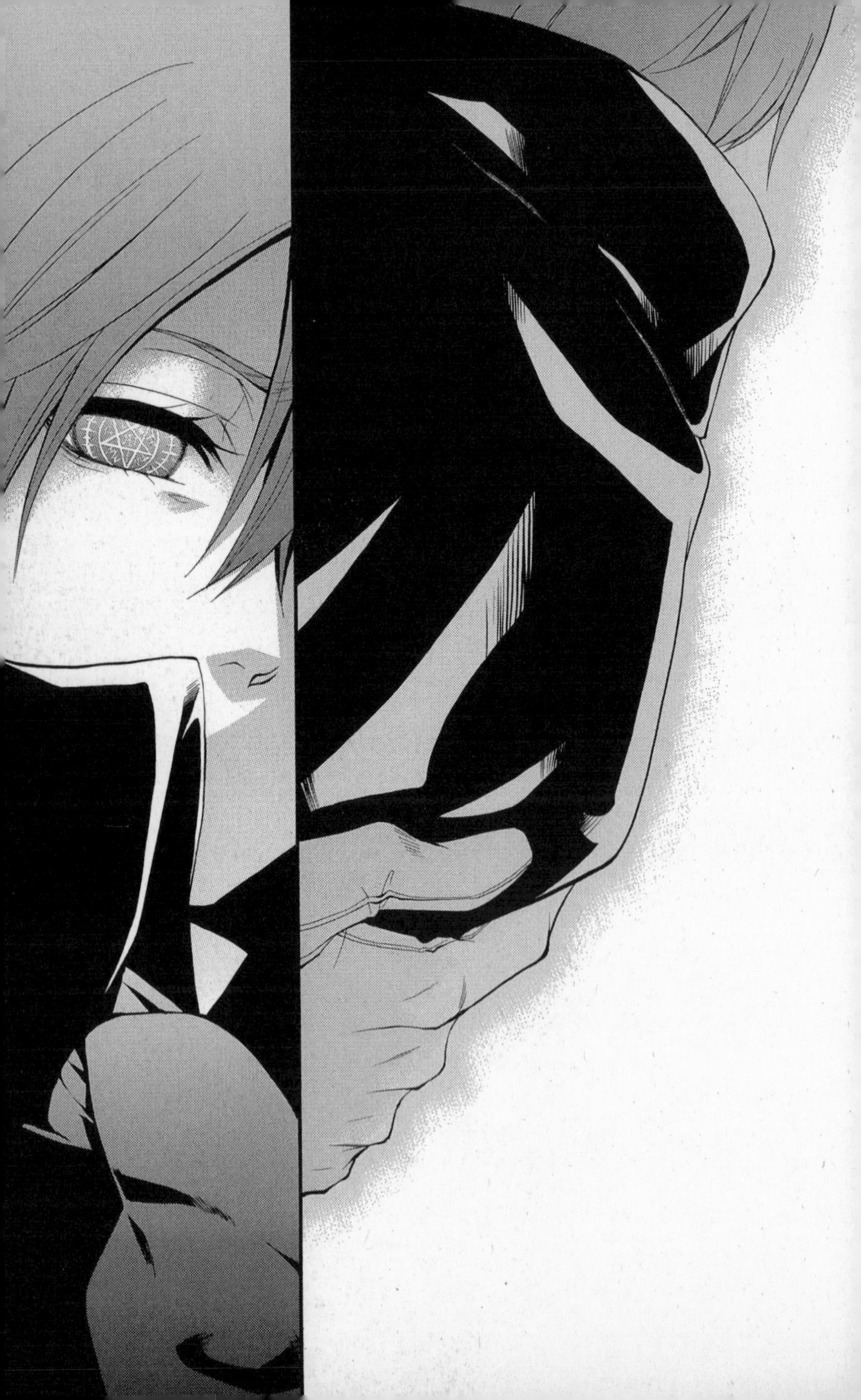

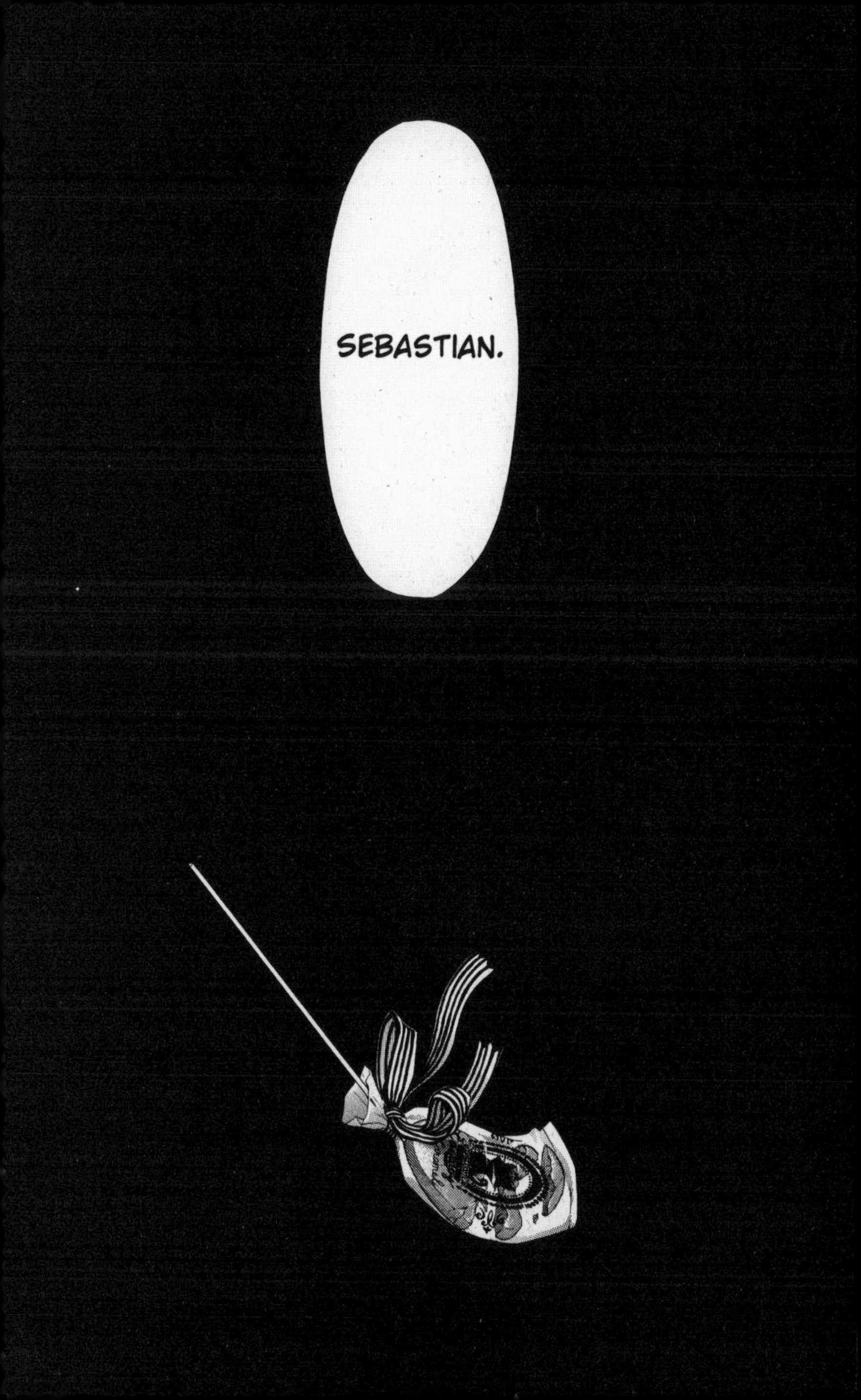
SEBASTIAN.

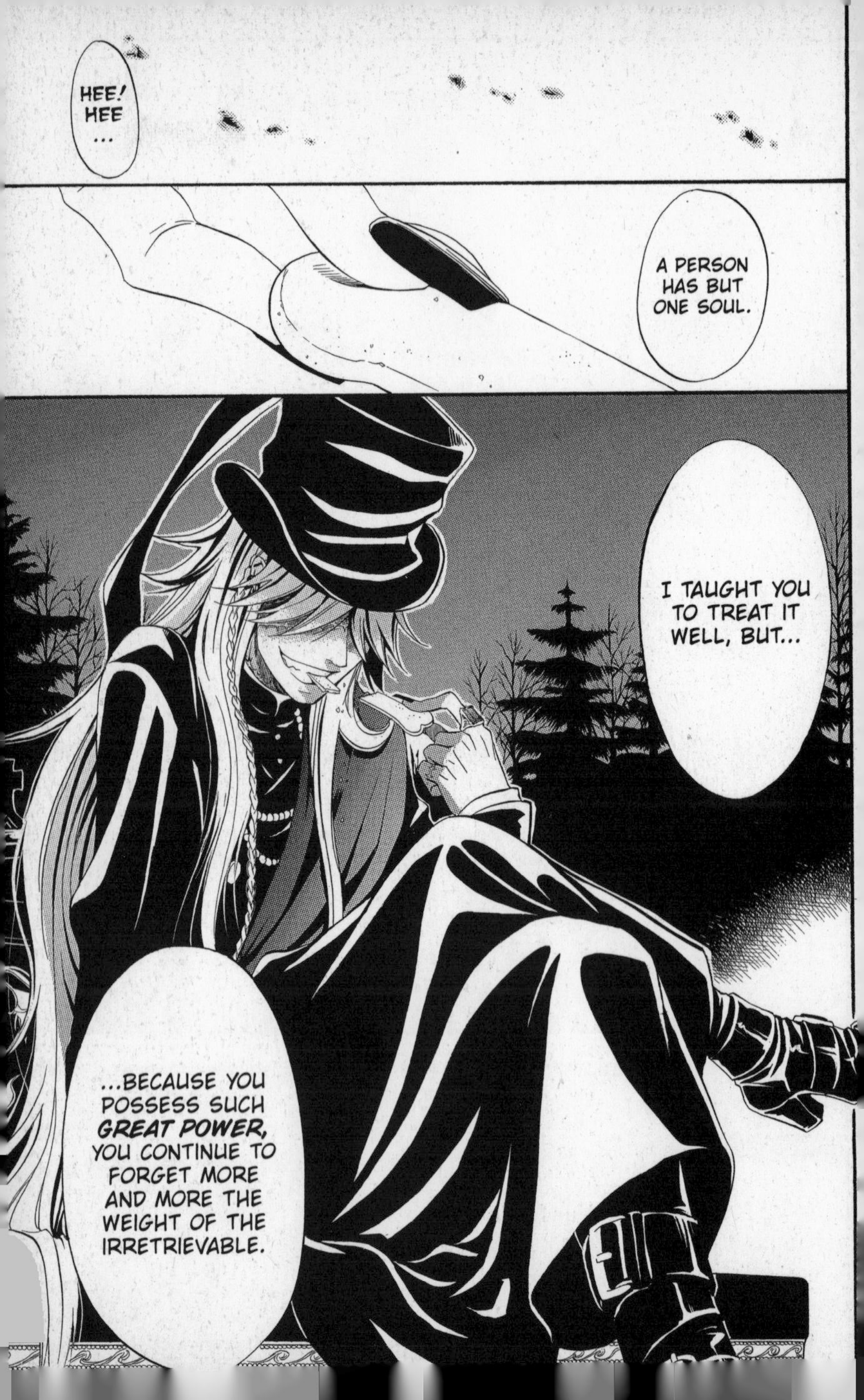
HEE! HEE ...
A PERSON HAS BUT ONE SOUL.
I TAUGHT YOU TO TREAT IT WELL, BUT...
...BECAUSE YOU POSSESS SUCH ***GREAT POWER,*** YOU CONTINUE TO FORGET MORE AND MORE THE WEIGHT OF THE IRRETRIEVABLE.

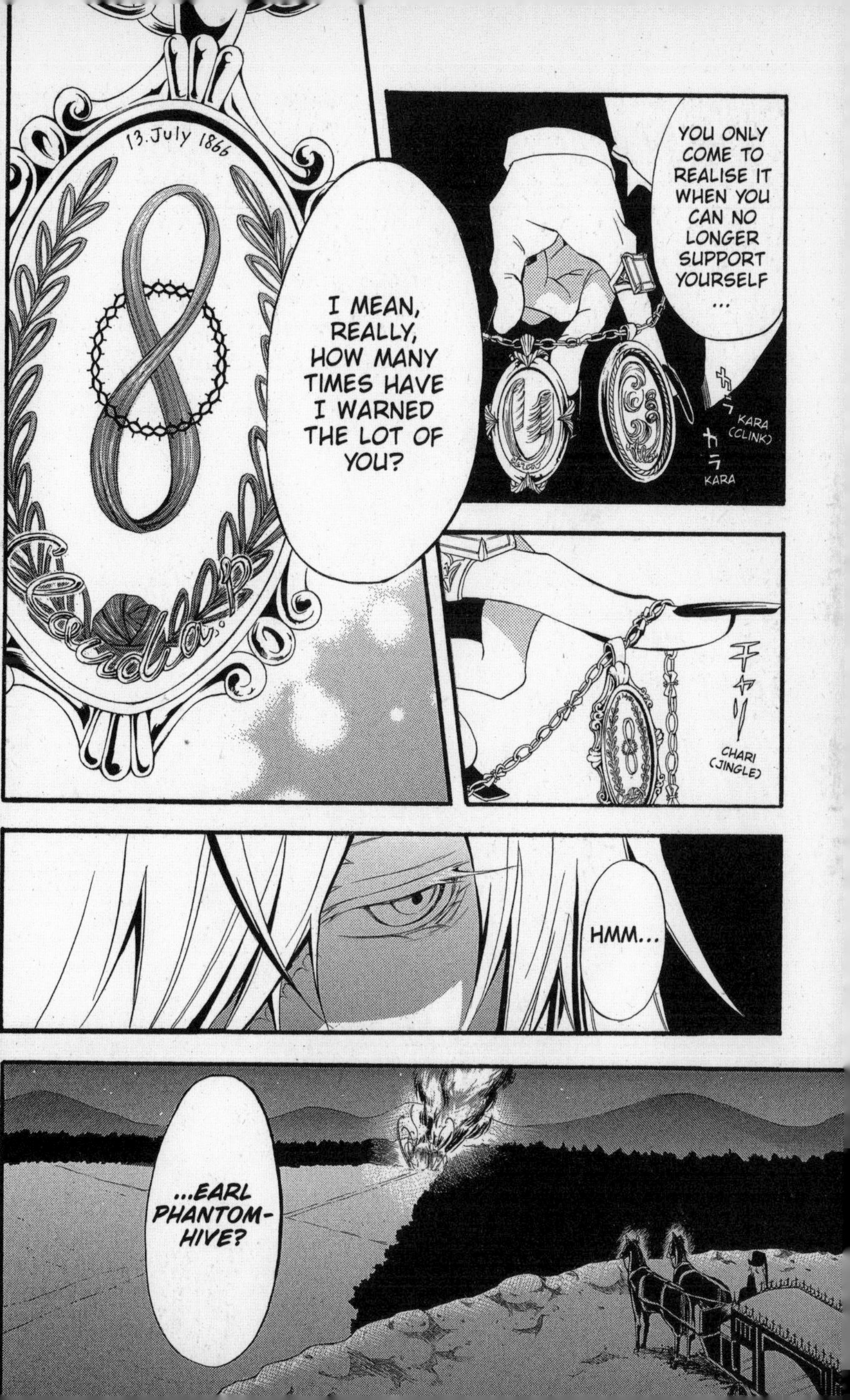
YOU ONLY COME TO REALISE IT WHEN YOU CAN NO LONGER SUPPORT YOURSELF ...
カラ KARA (CLINK)
カラ KARA
チャリ CHARI (JINGLE)
13.July 1866
I MEAN, REALLY, HOW MANY TIMES HAVE I WARNED THE LOT OF YOU?
HMM...
...EARL PHANTOM-HIVE?

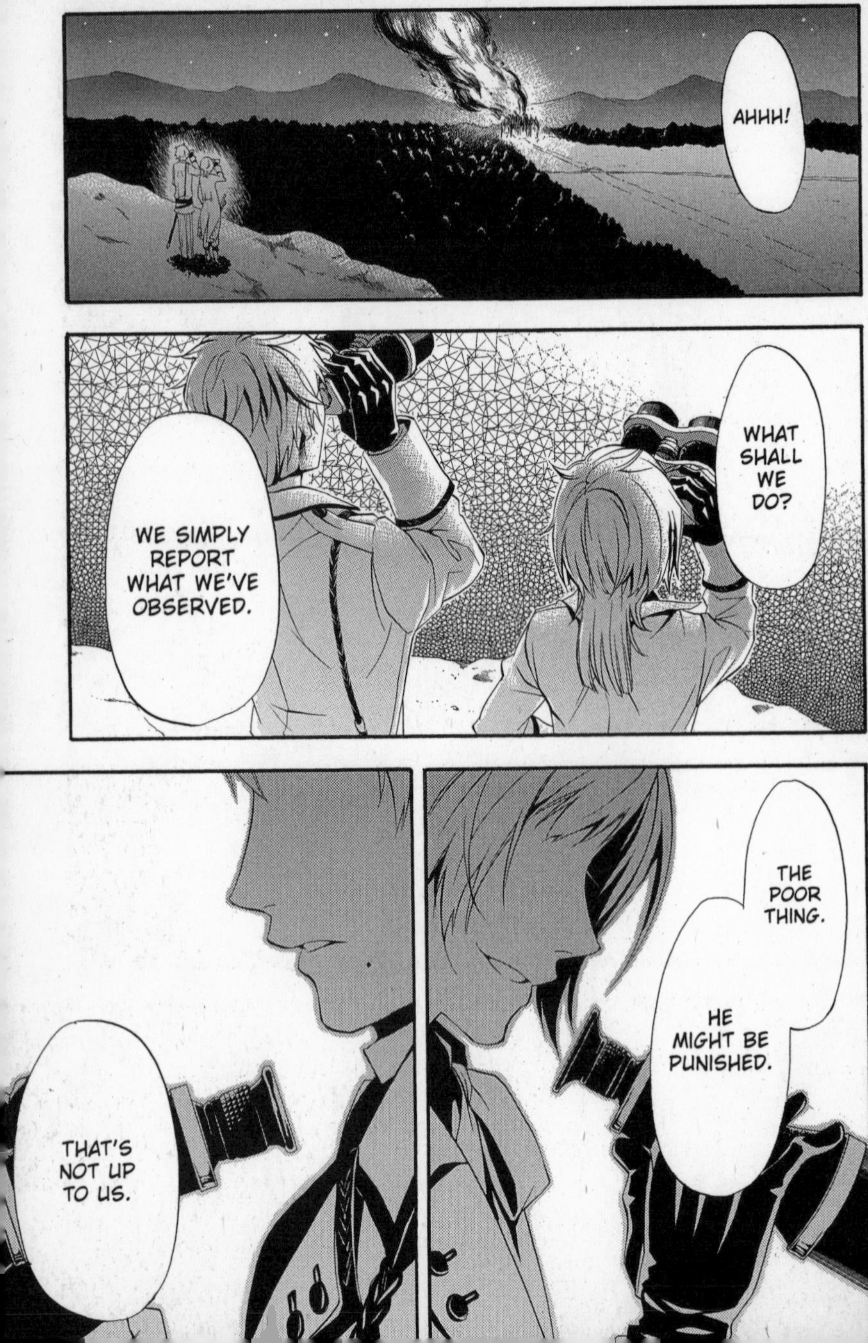
AHHH!
WHAT SHALL WE DO?
WE SIMPLY REPORT WHAT WE'VE OBSERVED.
THE POOR THING.
HE MIGHT BE PUNISHED.
THAT'S NOT UP TO US.

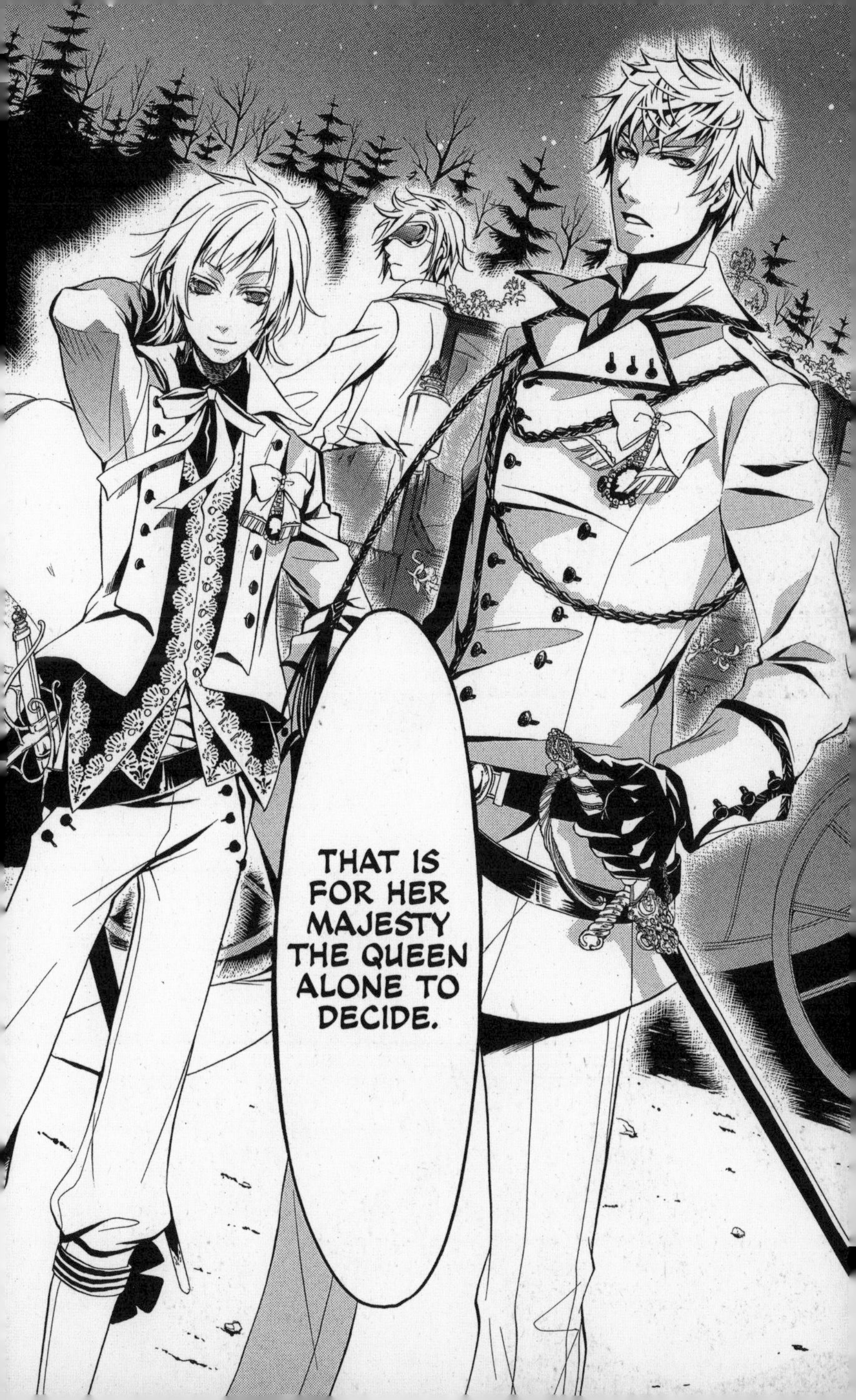
THAT IS FOR HER MAJESTY THE QUEEN ALONE TO DECIDE.

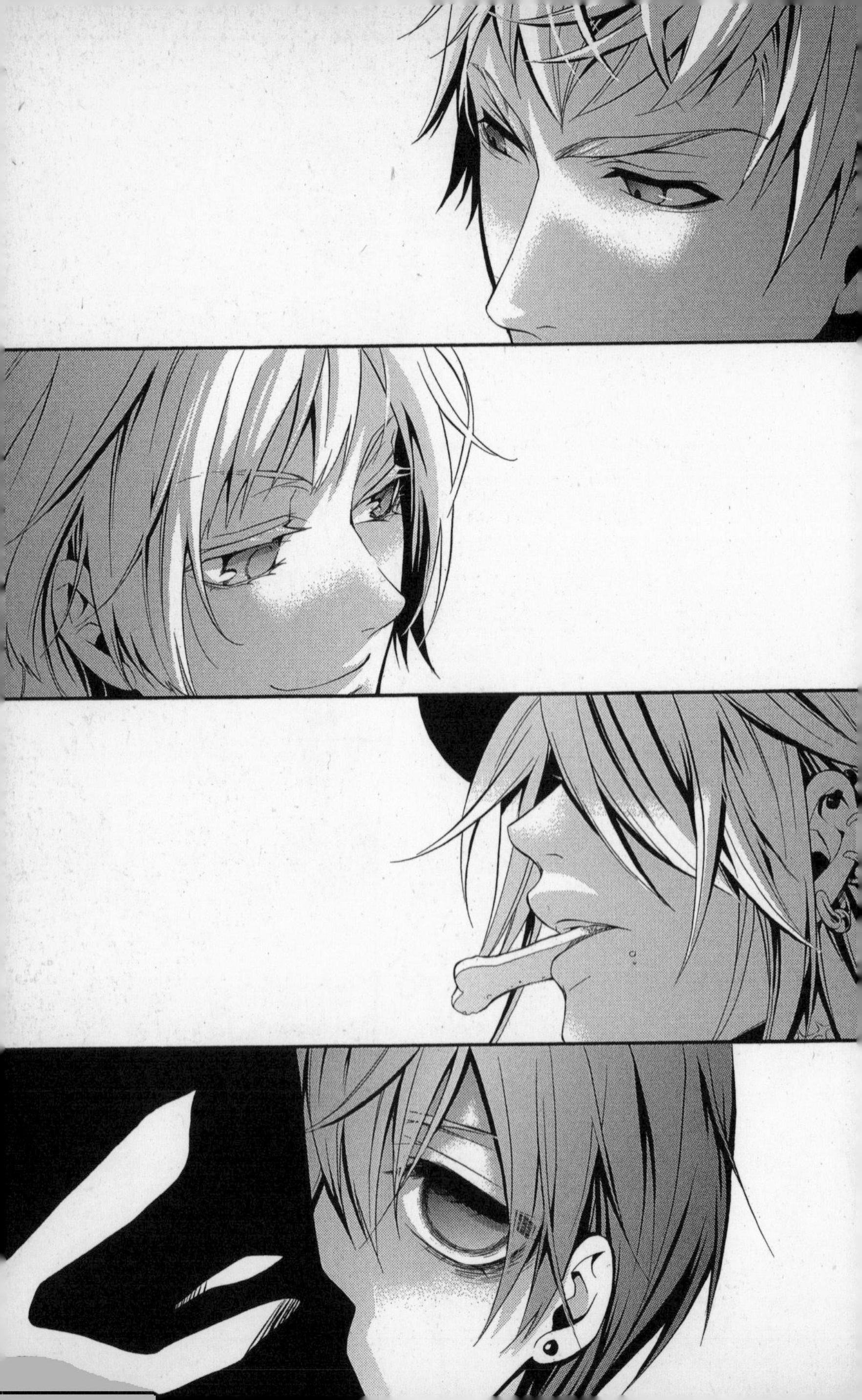

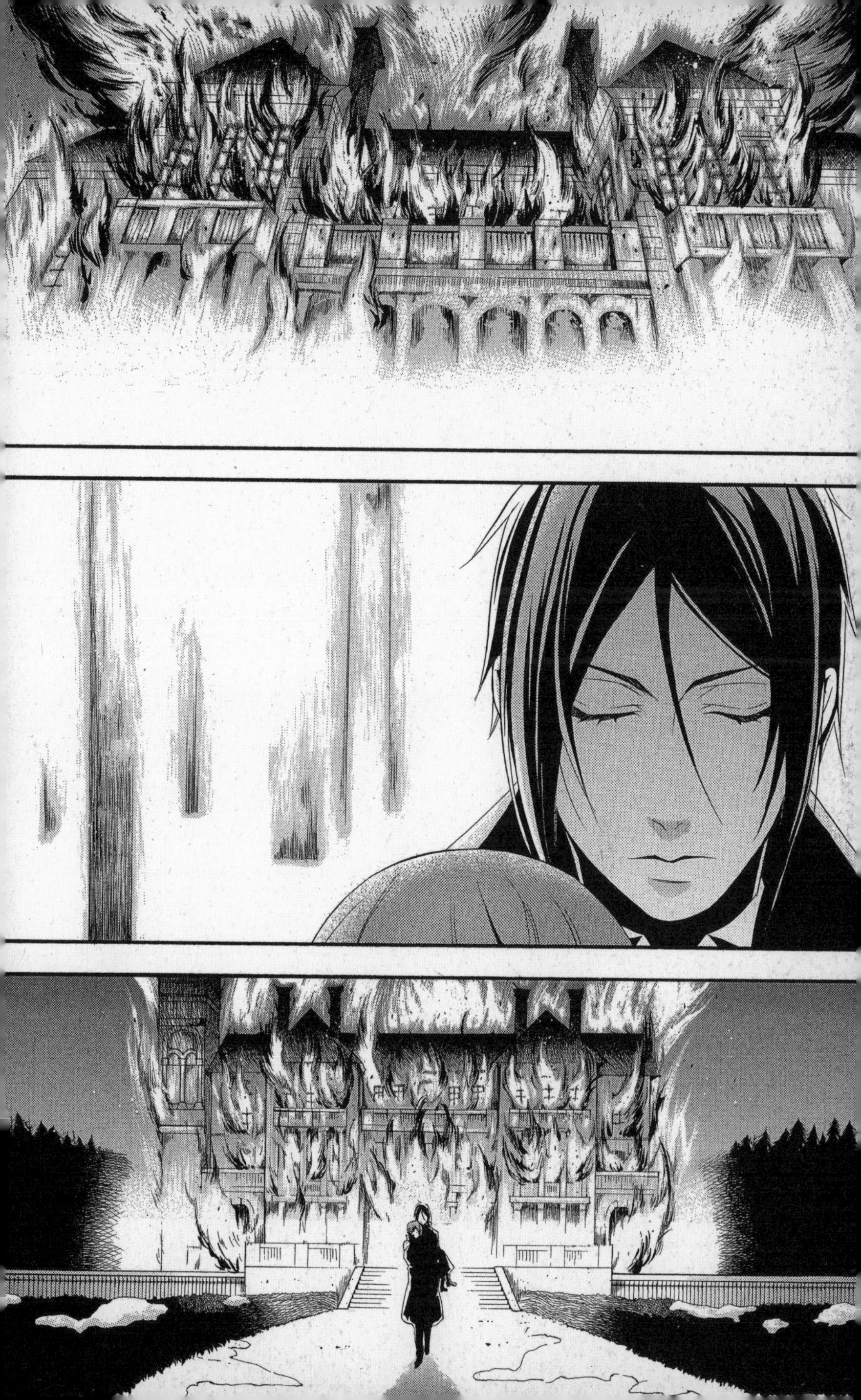

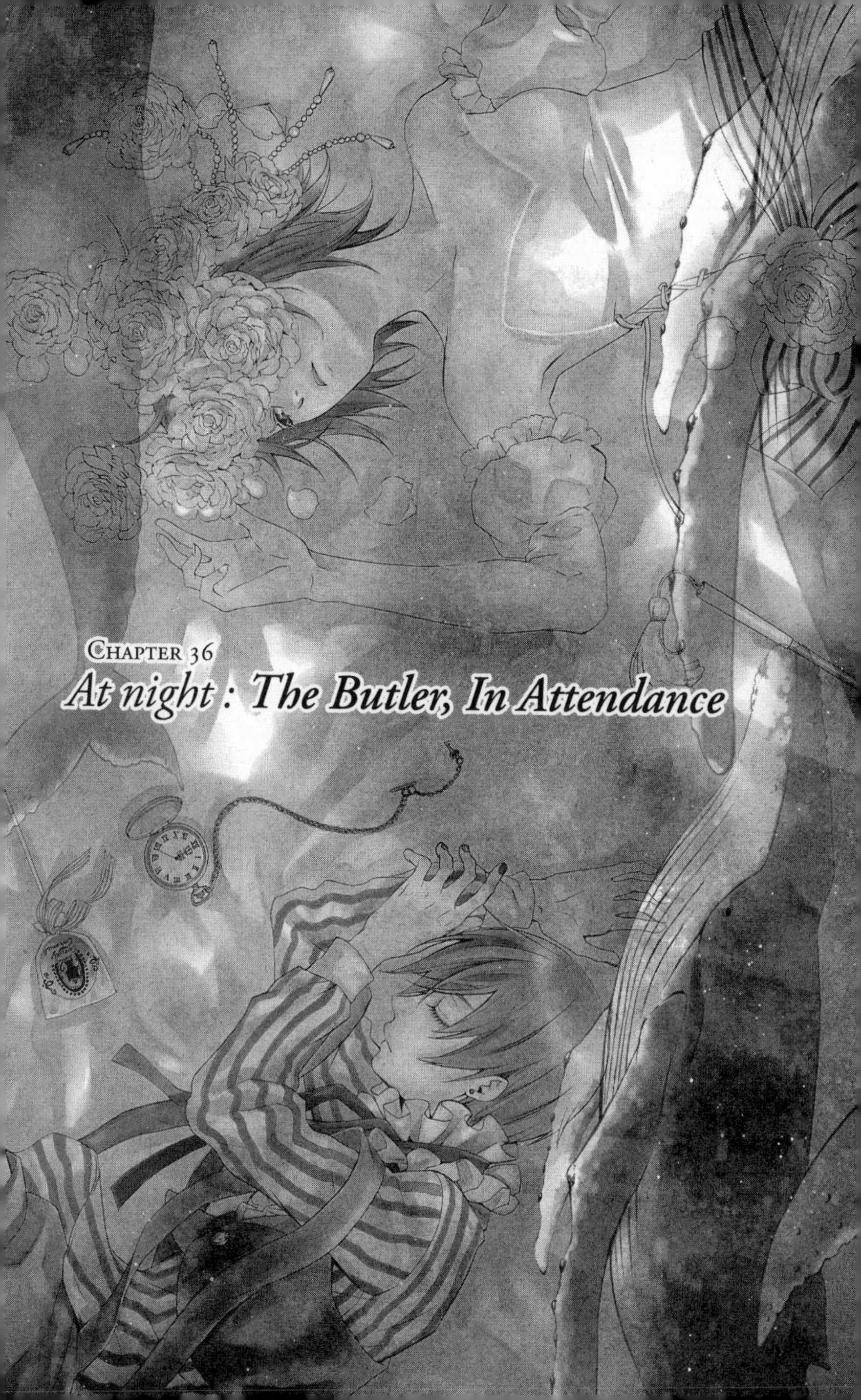
CHAPTER 36
At night : The Butler, In Attendance

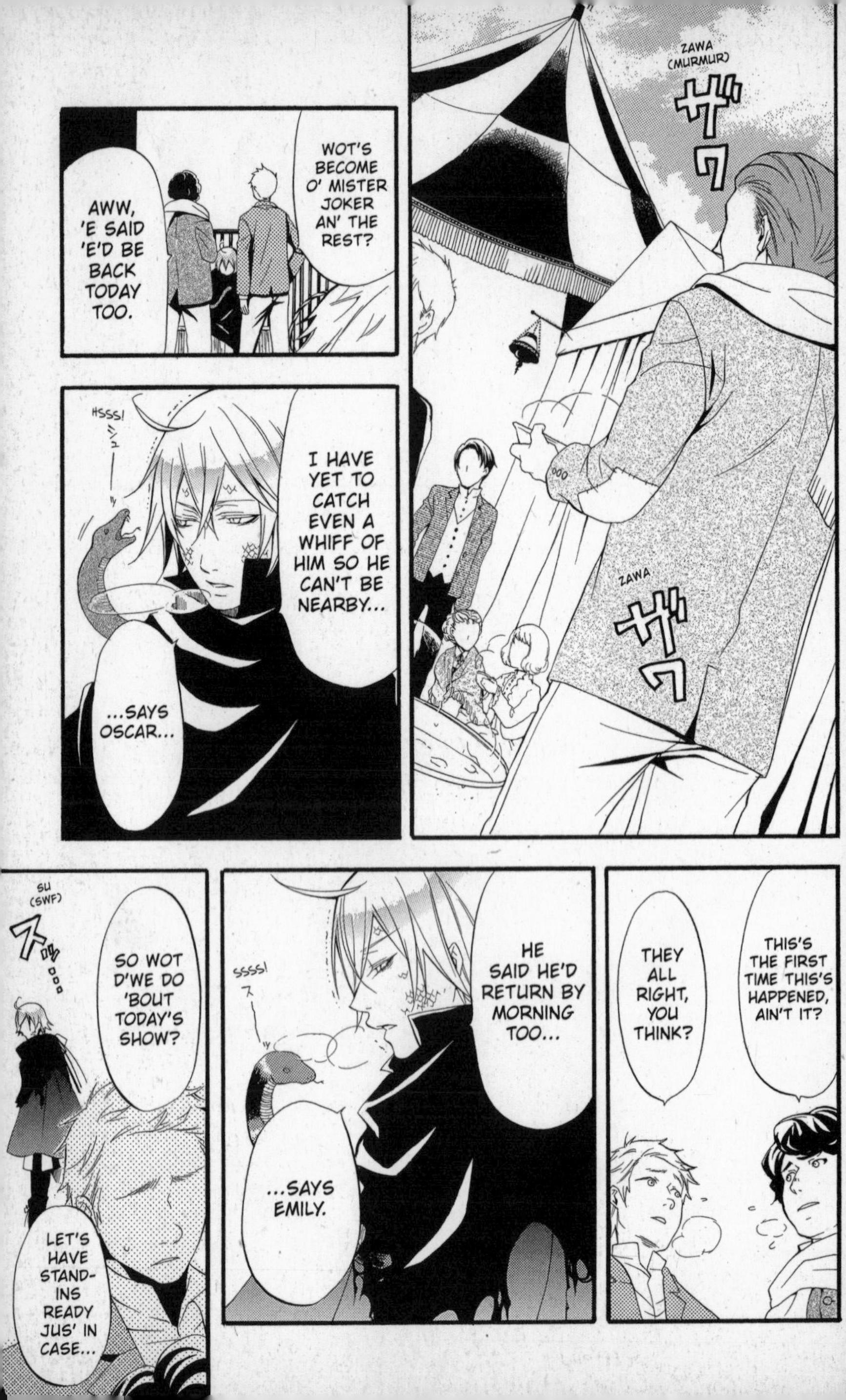
ZAWA (MURMUR)
ZAWA
WOT'S BECOME O' MISTER JOKER AN' THE REST?
AWW, 'E SAID 'E'D BE BACK TODAY TOO.
HSSS!
I HAVE YET TO CATCH EVEN A WHIFF OF HIM SO HE CAN'T BE NEARBY...
...SAYS OSCAR...
THIS'S THE FIRST TIME THIS'S HAPPENED, AIN'T IT?
THEY ALL RIGHT, YOU THINK?
HE SAID HE'D RETURN BY MORNING TOO...
SSSS!
...SAYS EMILY.
SU (SWF)
SO WOT D'WE DO 'BOUT TODAY'S SHOW?
LET'S HAVE STAND-INS READY JUS' IN CASE...

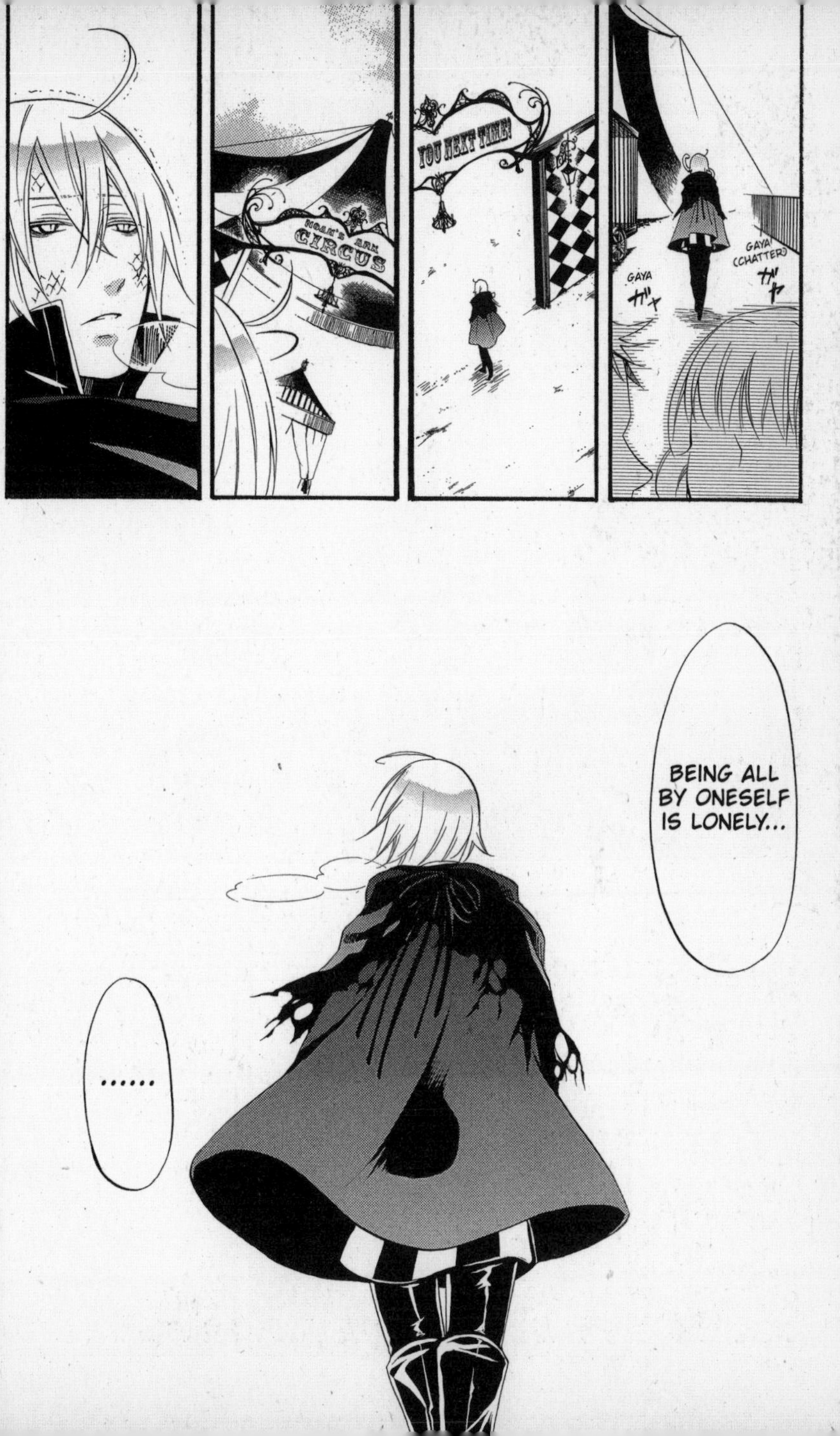
GAYA (CHATTER)
ガヤ
GAYA
ガヤ
YOU NEXT TIME!
NOAH'S ARK CIRCUS
BEING ALL BY ONESELF IS LONELY...
......

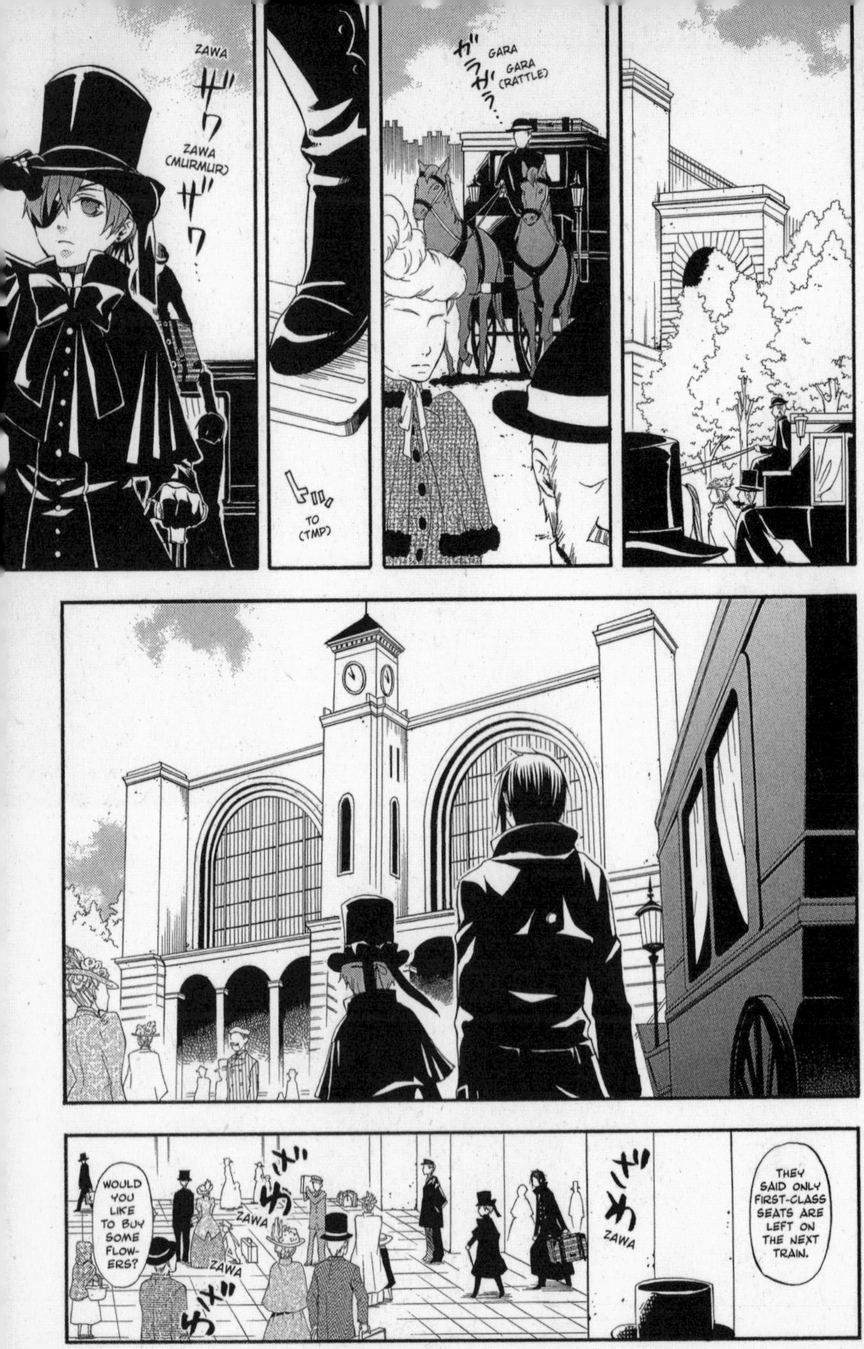
ガラガラ…
GARA
GARA
(RATTLE)
トッ
TO
(TMP)
ZAWA
ザワ
ZAWA
(MURMUR)
ザワ…
THEY SAID ONLY FIRST-CLASS SEATS ARE LEFT ON THE NEXT TRAIN.
ざわ
ZAWA
ざわ
ZAWA
ZAWA
ざわ
WOULD YOU LIKE TO BUY SOME FLOWERS?

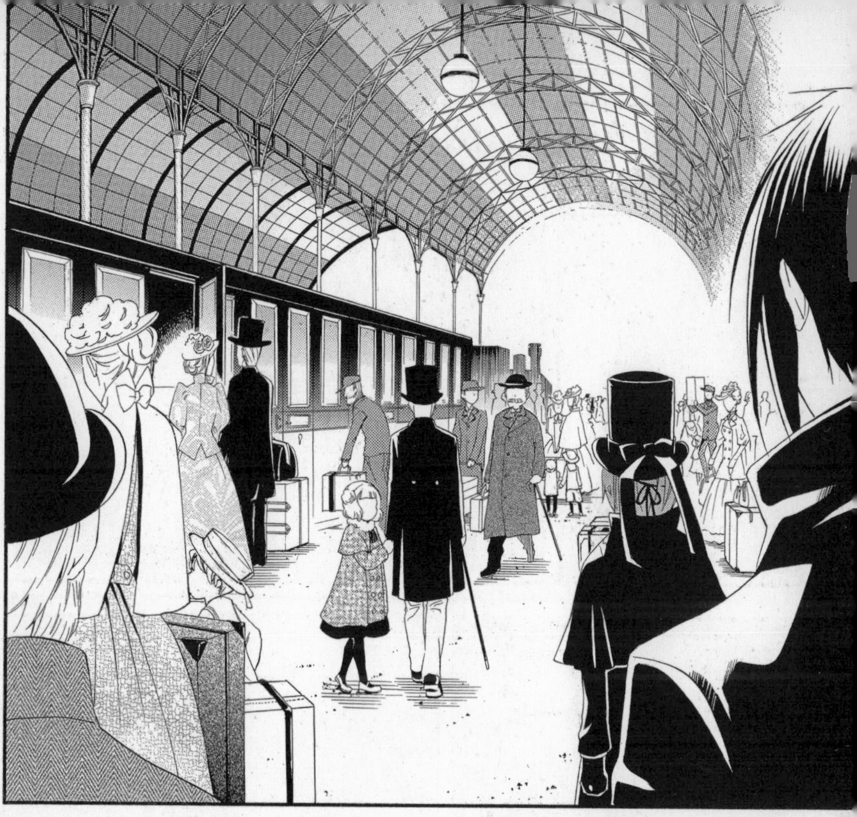

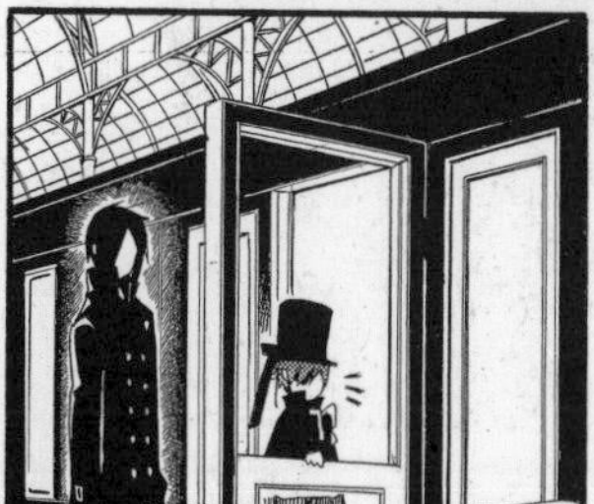
FIRST CLASS
GOOD SIR.

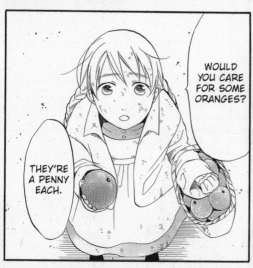

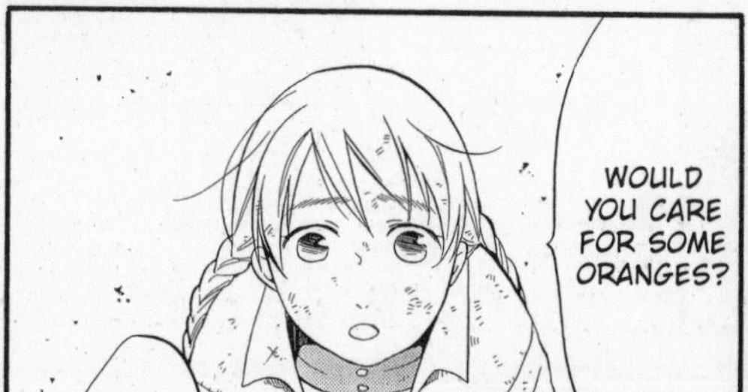
WOULD YOU CARE FOR SOME ORANGES?
THEY'RE A PENNY EACH.

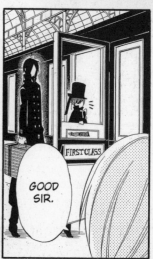

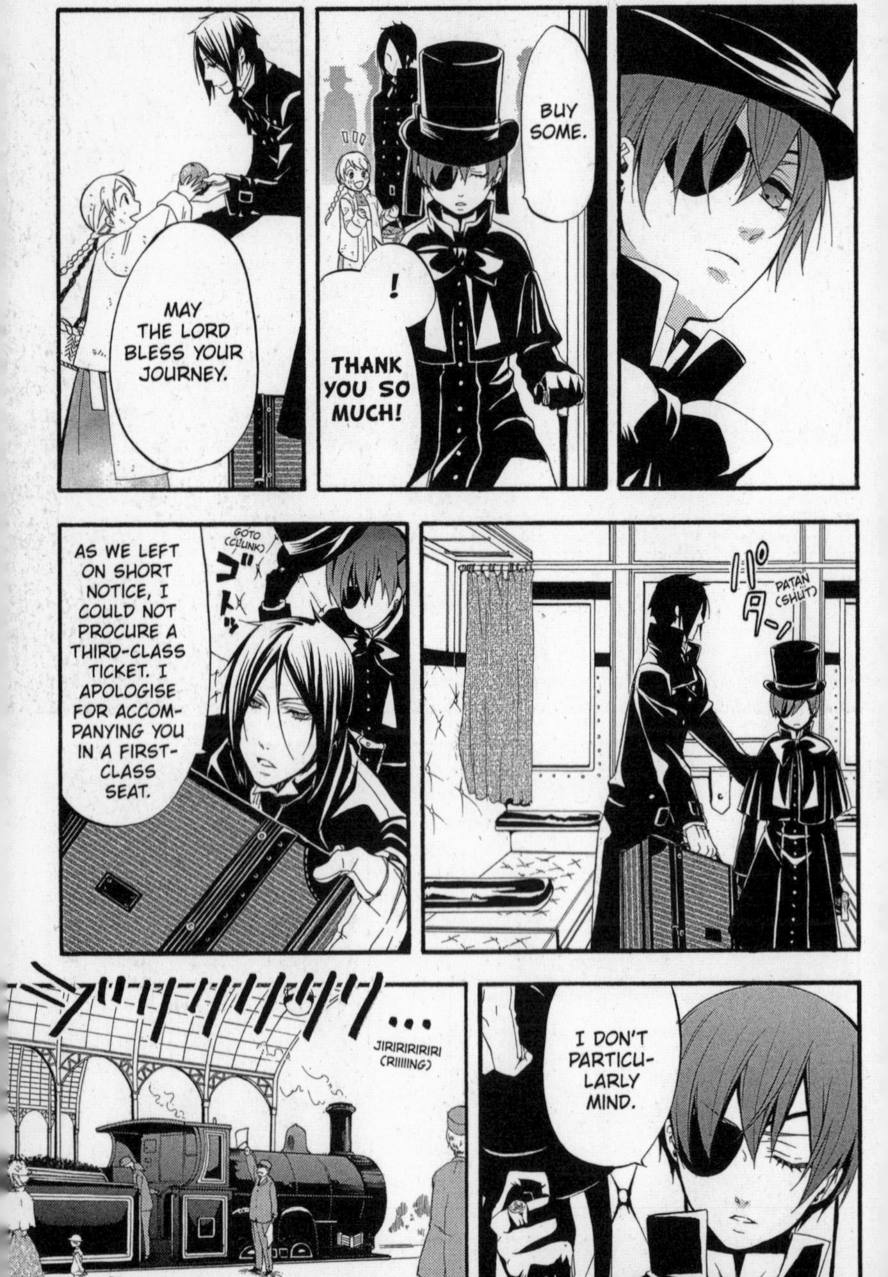
BUY SOME.
!
THANK YOU SO MUCH!
MAY THE LORD BLESS YOUR JOURNEY.
PATAN (SHUT)
GOTO (CLUNK)
AS WE LEFT ON SHORT NOTICE, I COULD NOT PROCURE A THIRD-CLASS TICKET. I APOLOGISE FOR ACCOMPANYING YOU IN A FIRST-CLASS SEAT.
I DON'T PARTICULARLY MIND.
...
JIRIRIRIRIRI (RIIIIING)

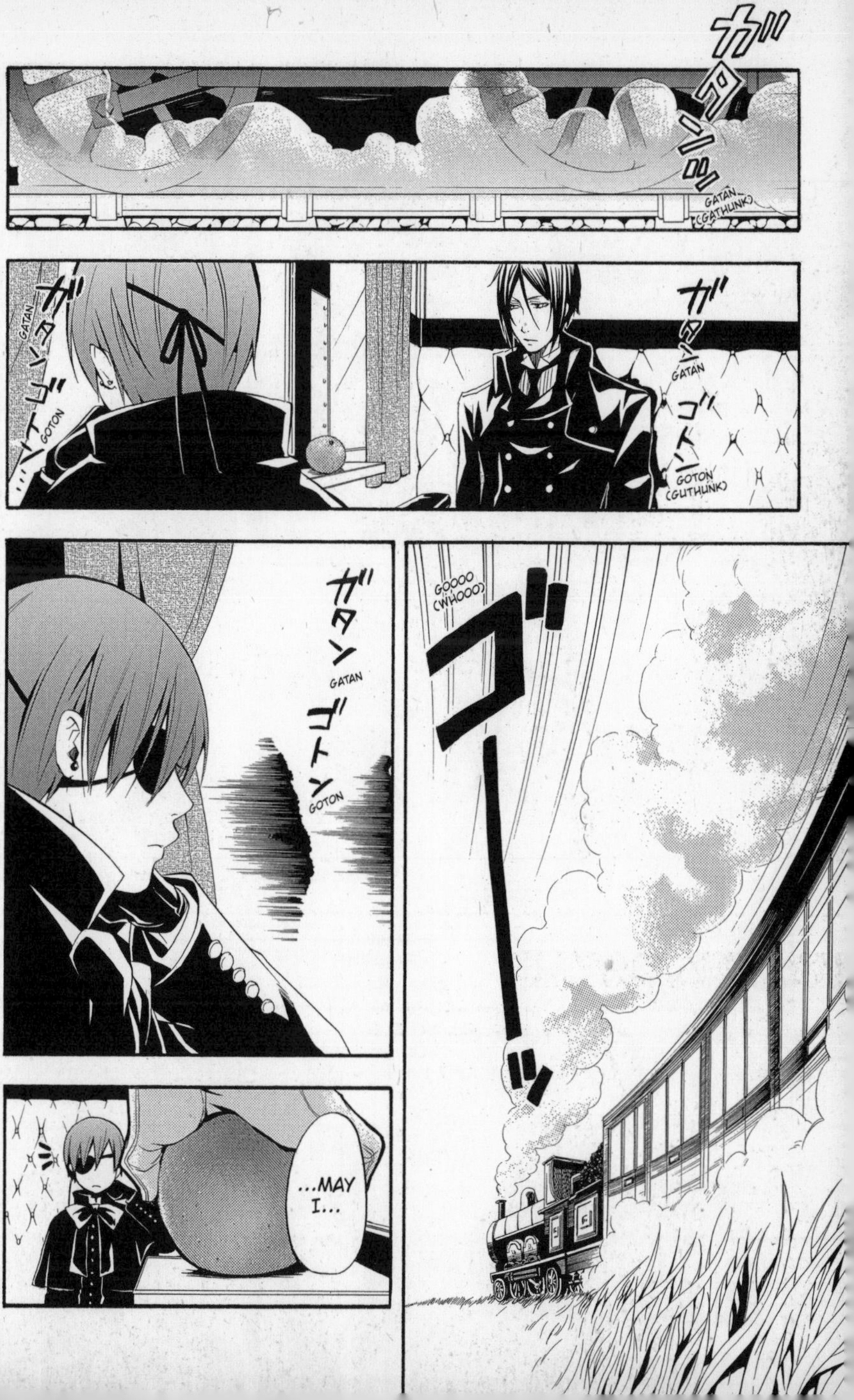
ガタン
GATAN (GATHUNK)
ガタン
GATAN
ゴトン
GOTON (GUTHUNK)
ガタン
GATAN
ゴトン
GOTON
ゴーッ
GOOOO (WHOOO)
ガタン
GATAN
ゴトン
GOTON
...MAY I...

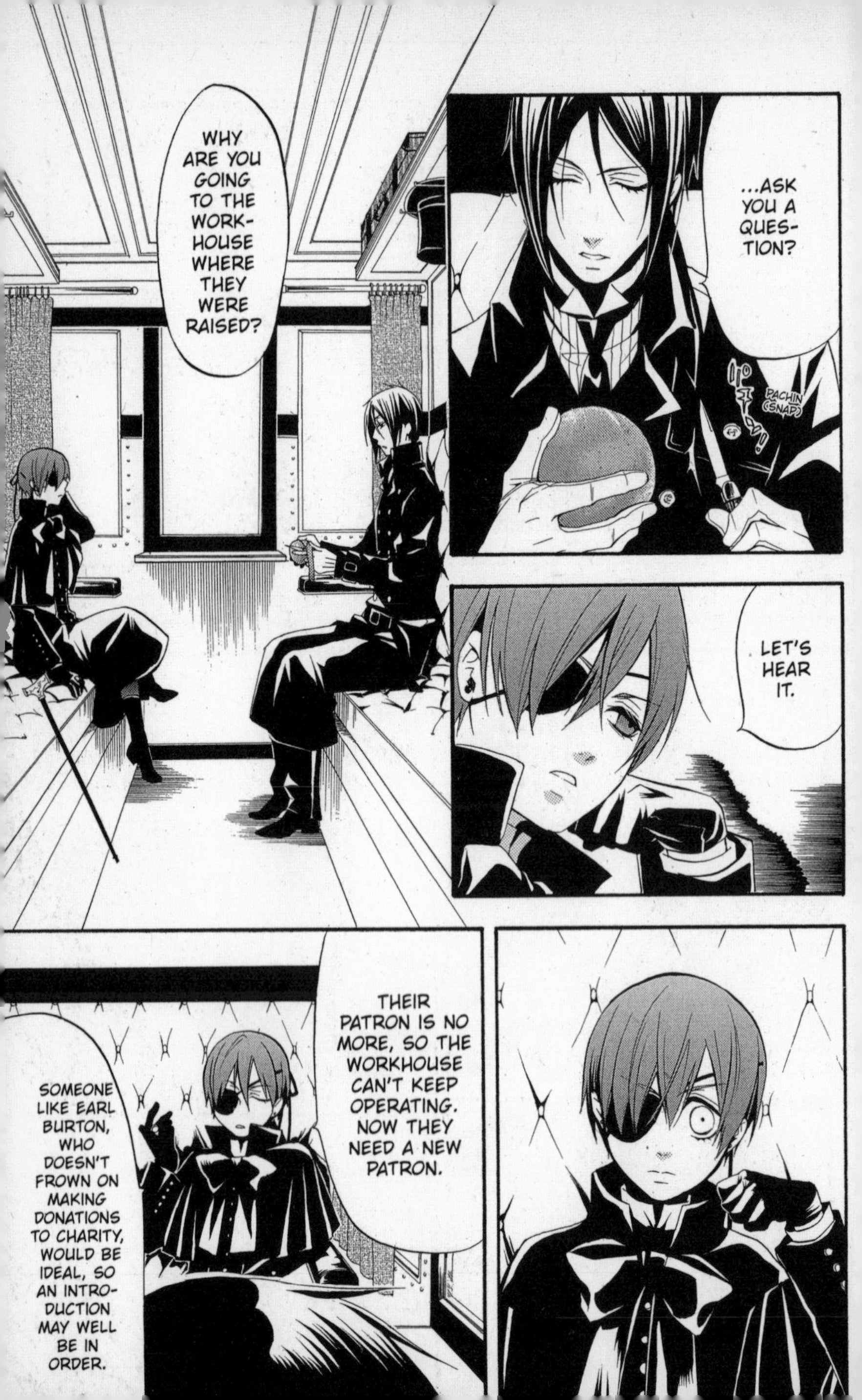
...ASK YOU A QUESTION?
PACHIN (SNAP)
LET'S HEAR IT.
WHY ARE YOU GOING TO THE WORKHOUSE WHERE THEY WERE RAISED?
THEIR PATRON IS NO MORE, SO THE WORKHOUSE CAN'T KEEP OPERATING. NOW THEY NEED A NEW PATRON.
SOMEONE LIKE EARL BURTON, WHO DOESN'T FROWN ON MAKING DONATIONS TO CHARITY, WOULD BE IDEAL, SO AN INTRODUCTION MAY WELL BE IN ORDER.

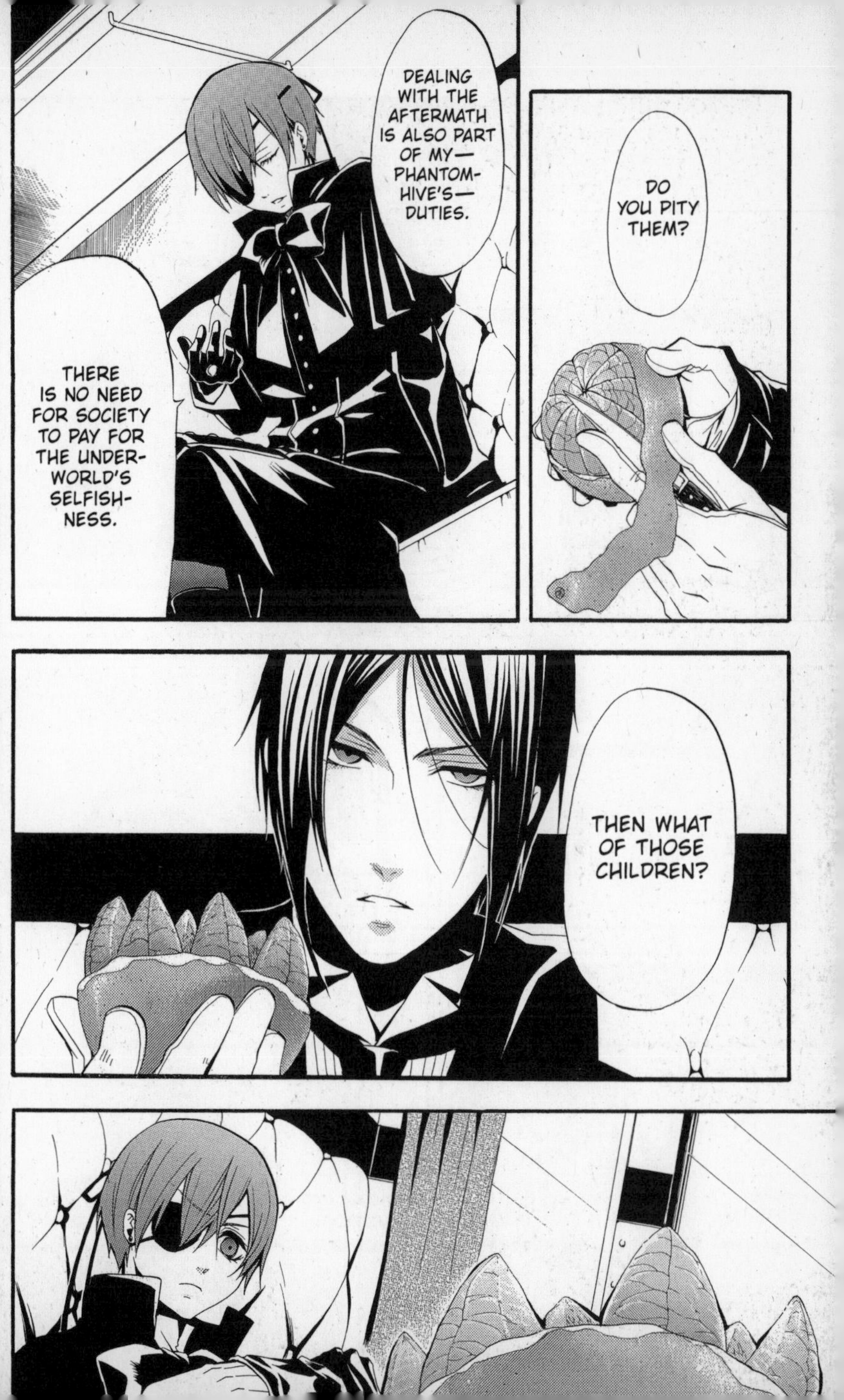
DO YOU PITY THEM?
DEALING WITH THE AFTERMATH IS ALSO PART OF MY—PHANTOMHIVE'S—DUTIES.
THERE IS NO NEED FOR SOCIETY TO PAY FOR THE UNDERWORLD'S SELFISHNESS.
THEN WHAT OF THOSE CHILDREN?

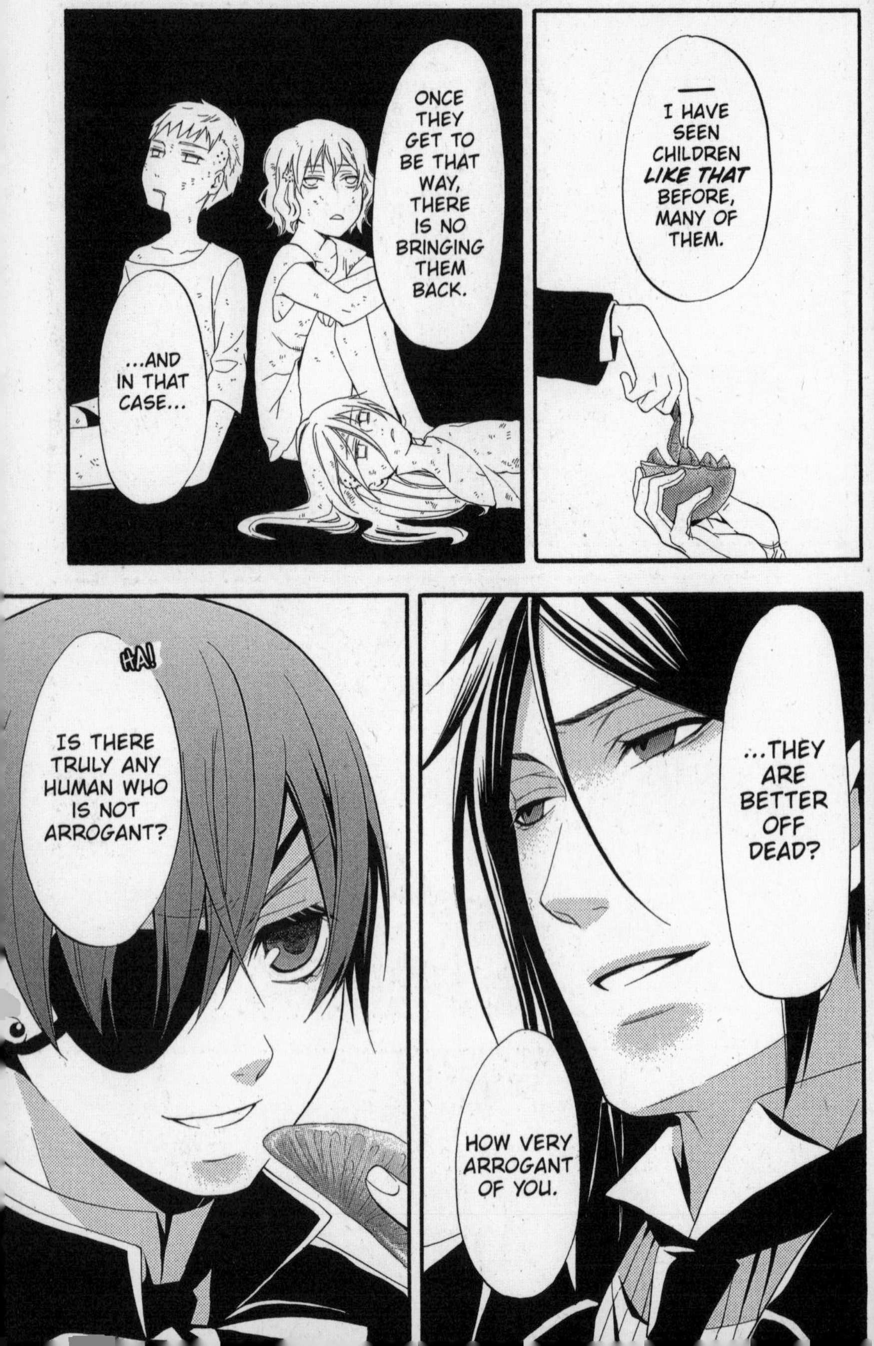
— I HAVE SEEN CHILDREN LIKE THAT BEFORE, MANY OF THEM.
ONCE THEY GET TO BE THAT WAY, THERE IS NO BRINGING THEM BACK.
...AND IN THAT CASE...
...THEY ARE BETTER OFF DEAD?
HOW VERY ARROGANT OF YOU.
HA!
IS THERE TRULY ANY HUMAN WHO IS NOT ARROGANT?

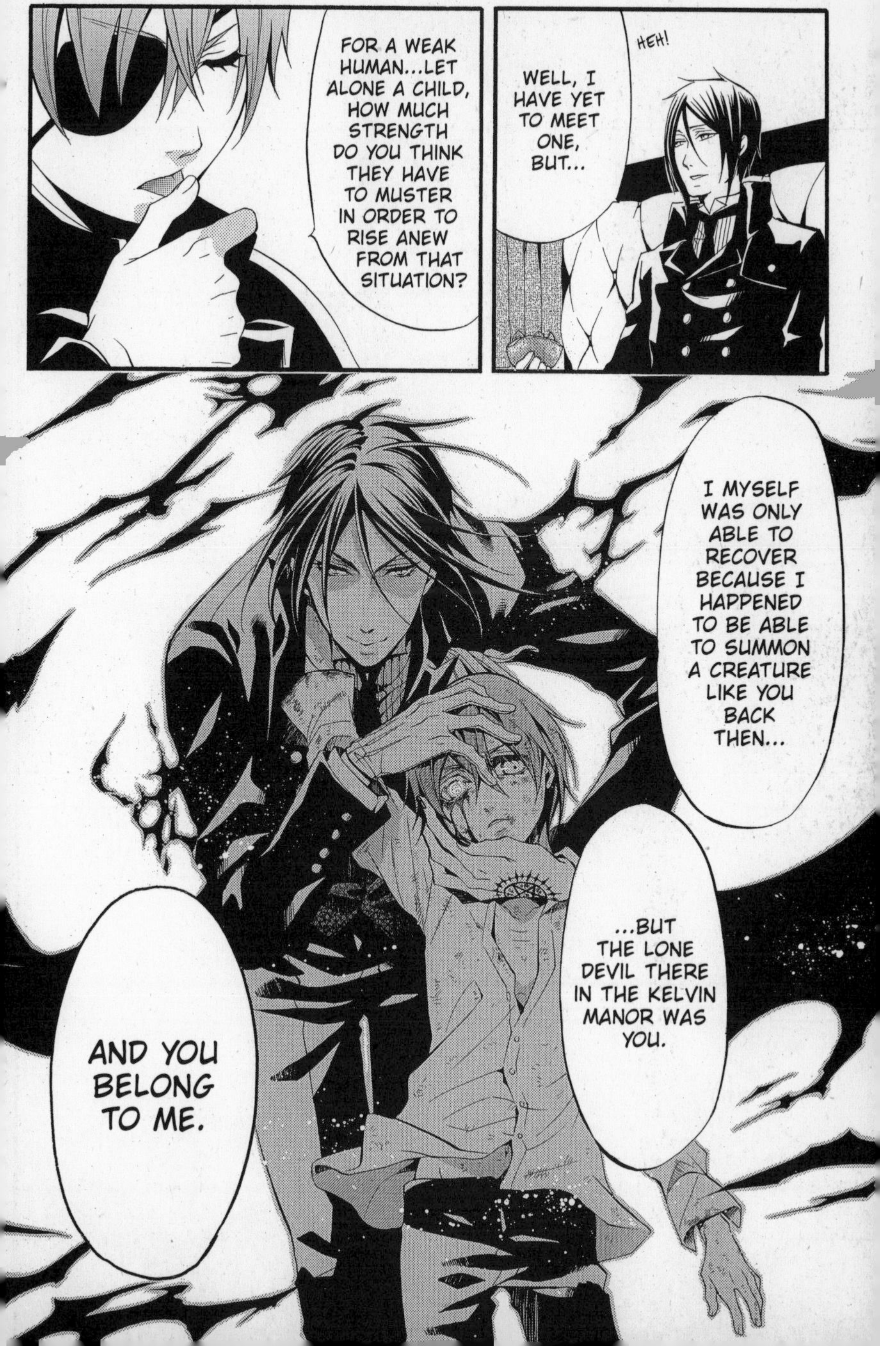
HEH!
WELL, I HAVE YET TO MEET ONE, BUT...
FOR A WEAK HUMAN...LET ALONE A CHILD, HOW MUCH STRENGTH DO YOU THINK THEY HAVE TO MUSTER IN ORDER TO RISE ANEW FROM THAT SITUATION?
I MYSELF WAS ONLY ABLE TO RECOVER BECAUSE I HAPPENED TO BE ABLE TO SUMMON A CREATURE LIKE YOU BACK THEN...
...BUT THE LONE DEVIL THERE IN THE KELVIN MANOR WAS YOU.
AND YOU BELONG TO ME.

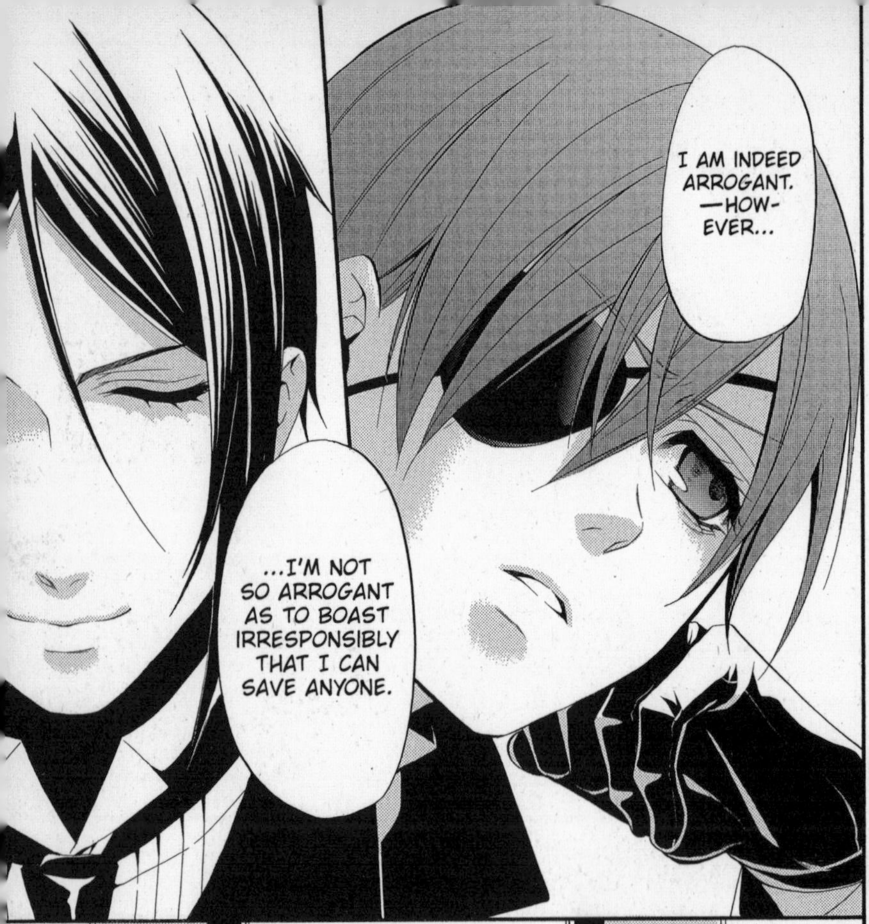
I AM INDEED ARROGANT. —HOW-EVER...
...I'M NOT SO ARROGANT AS TO BOAST IRRESPONSIBLY THAT I CAN SAVE ANYONE.
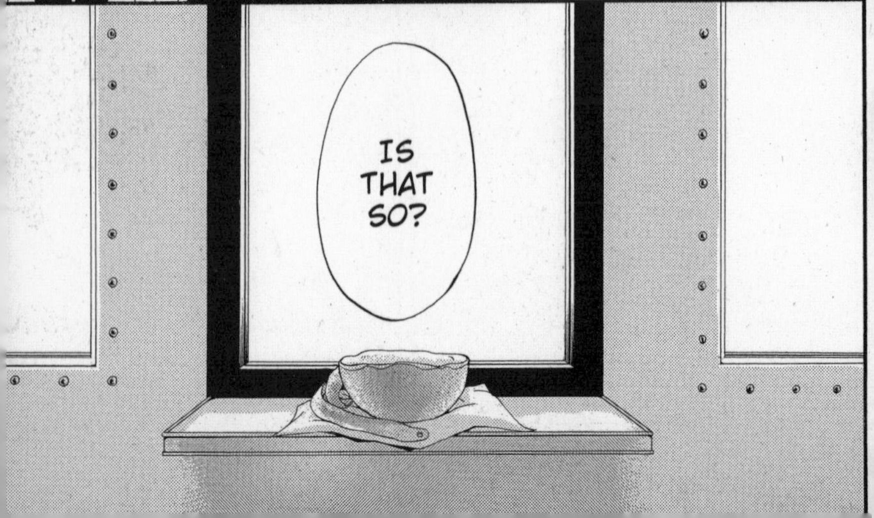
IS THAT SO?

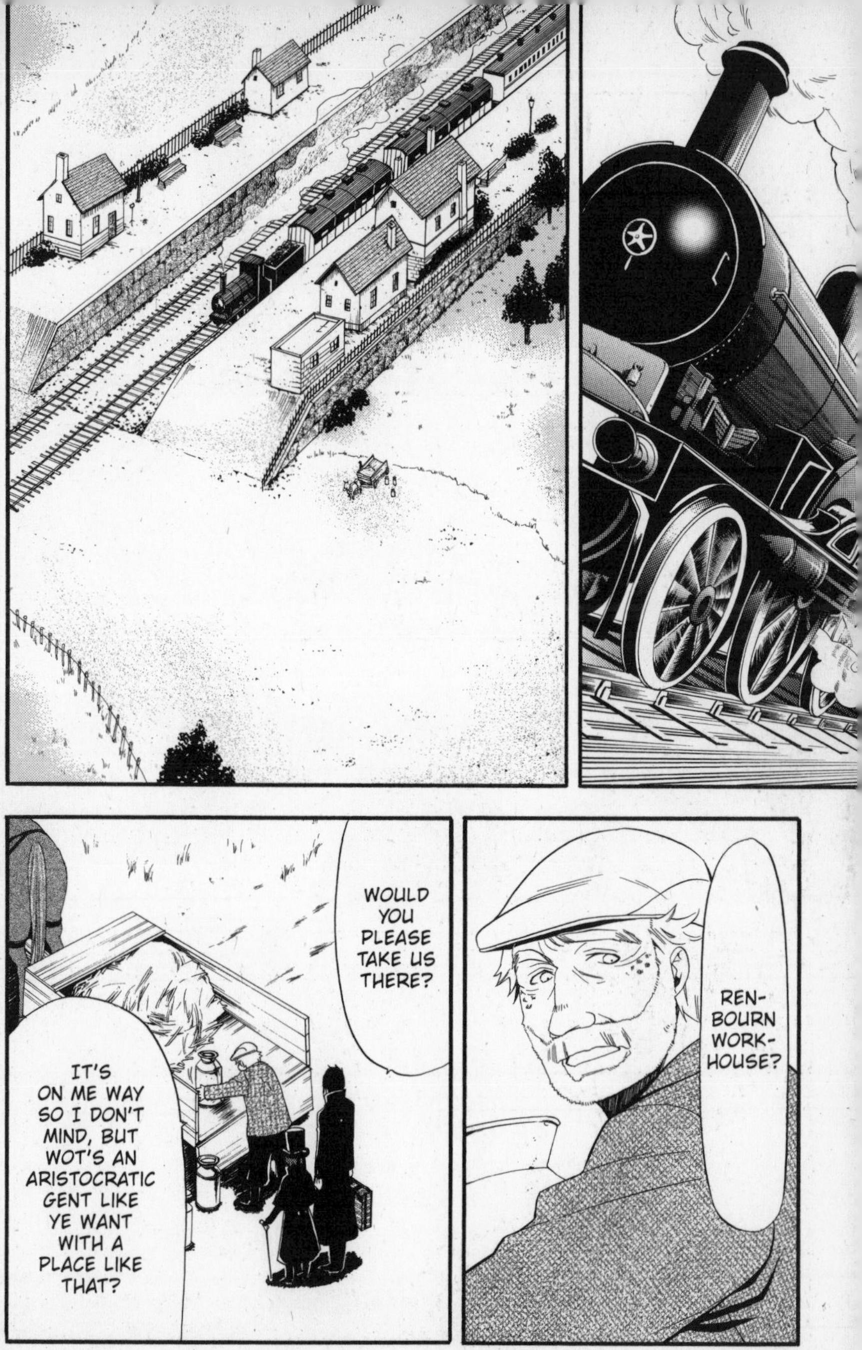
REN-BOURN WORK-HOUSE?
WOULD YOU PLEASE TAKE US THERE?
IT'S ON ME WAY SO I DON'T MIND, BUT WOT'S AN ARISTOCRATIC GENT LIKE YE WANT WITH A PLACE LIKE THAT?

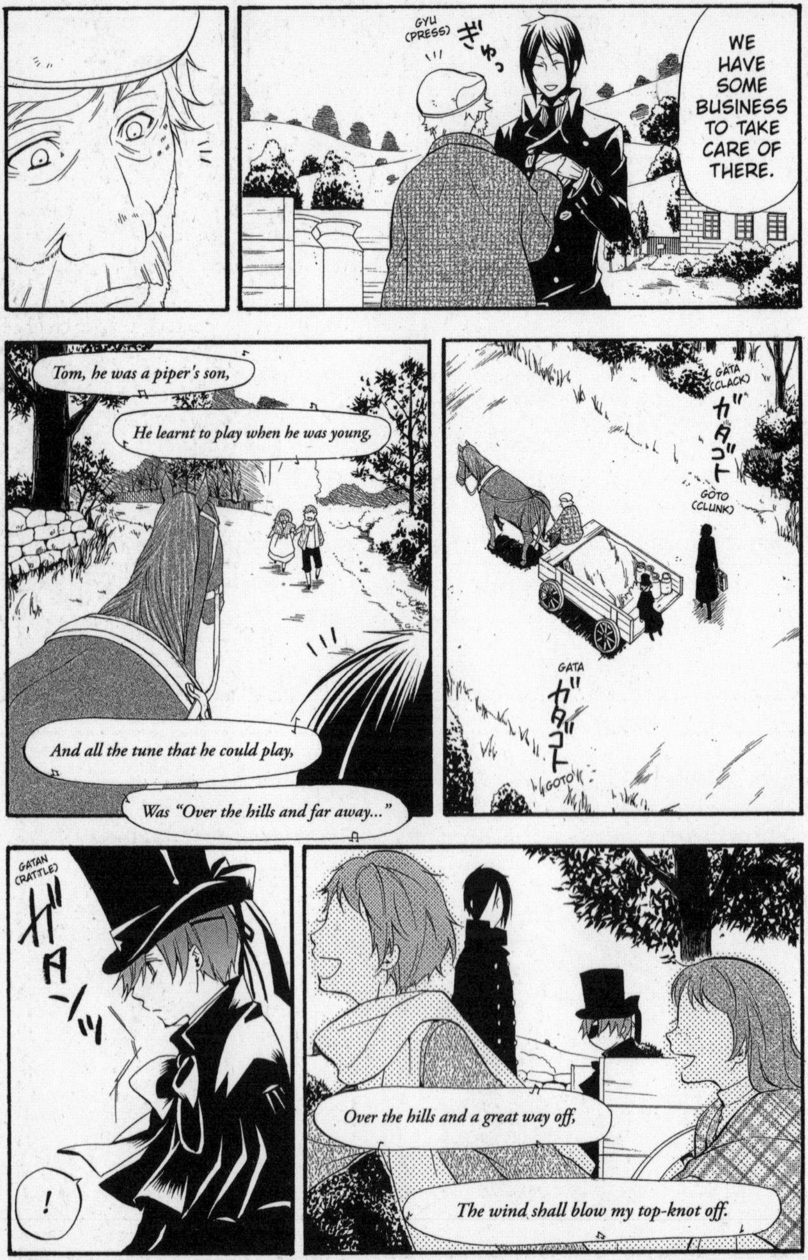
WE HAVE SOME BUSINESS TO TAKE CARE OF THERE.
GYU (PRESS)
ぎゅっ
GATA (CLACK)
ガタ
GOTO (CLUNK)
ゴト
GATA
ガタ
ゴト
GOTO
Tom, he was a piper's son,
He learnt to play when he was young,
And all the tune that he could play,
Was "Over the hills and far away..."
Over the hills and a great way off,
The wind shall blow my top-knot off.
GATAN (RATTLE)
ガターンッ
!

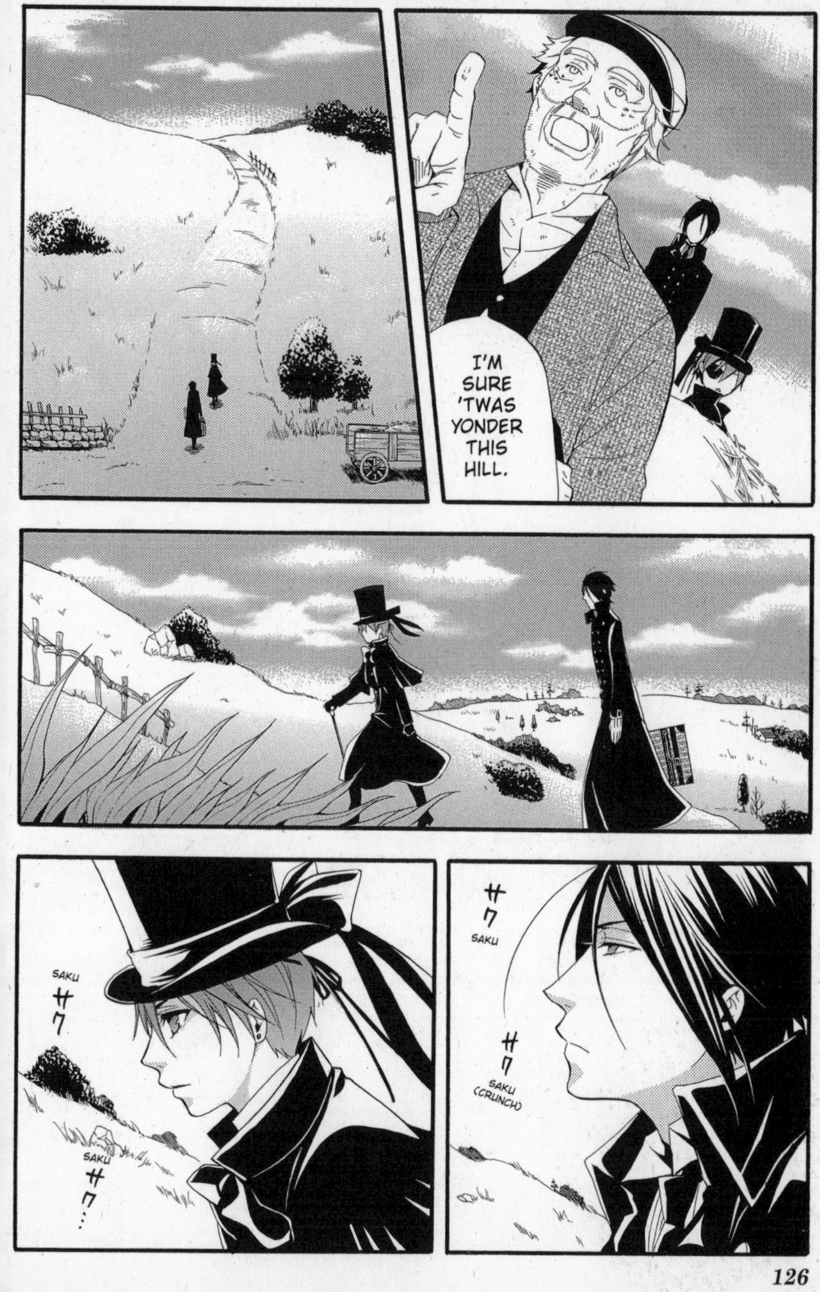
I'M SURE 'TWAS YONDER THIS HILL.
サク
SAKU
サク
SAKU (CRUNCH)
SAKU
サク
SAKU
サク...

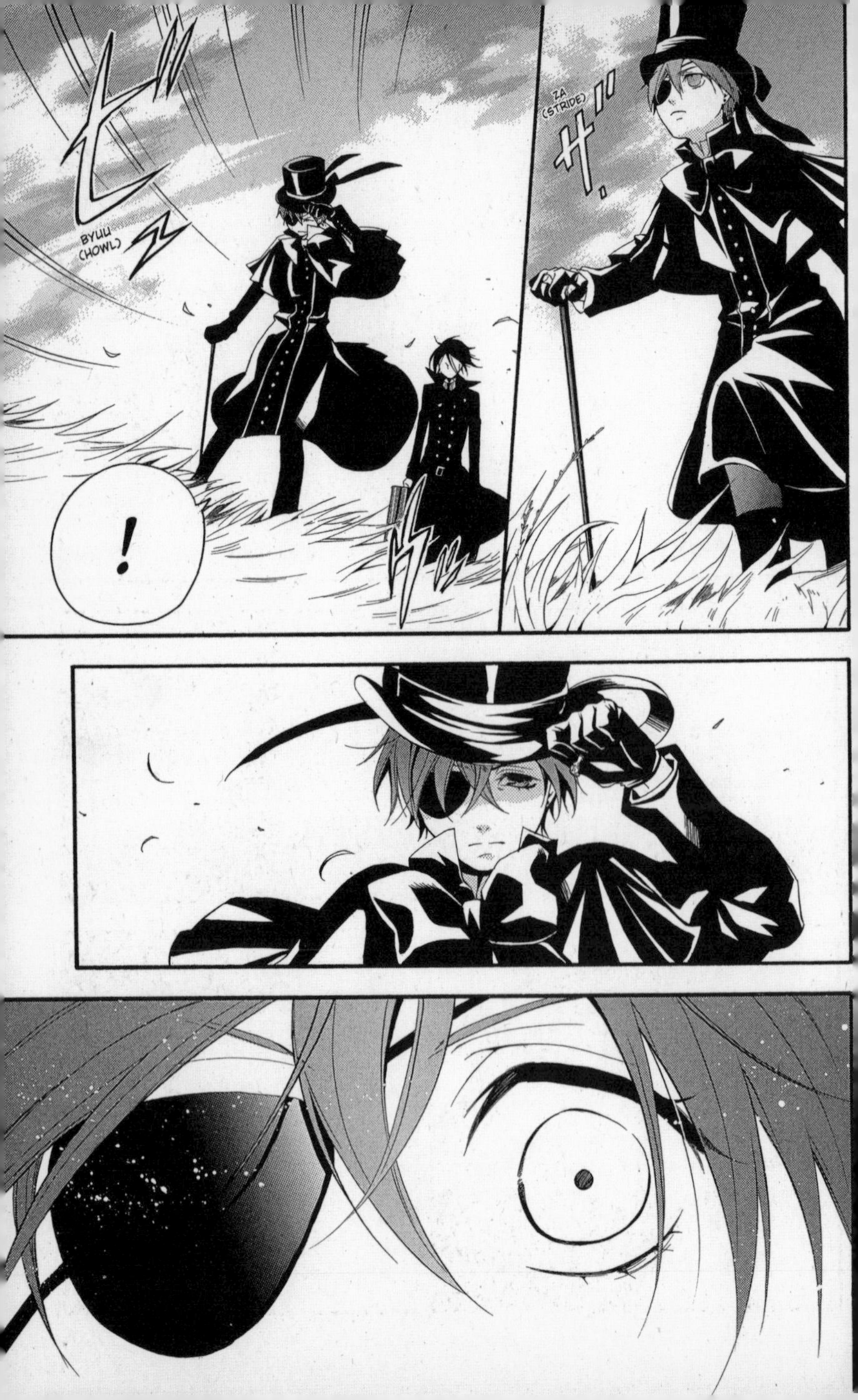
ZA
(STRIDE)
BYUU
(HOWL)
!

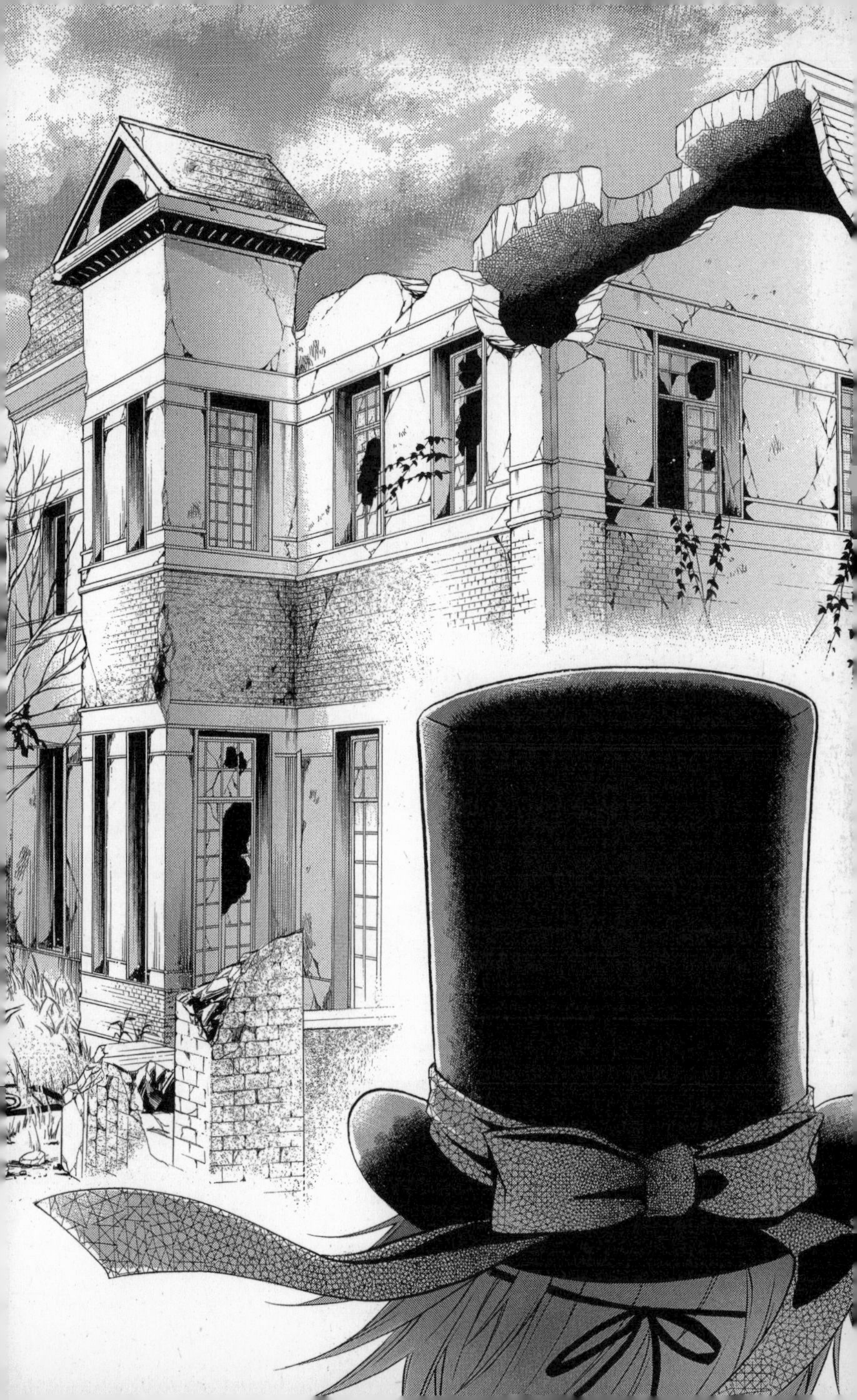

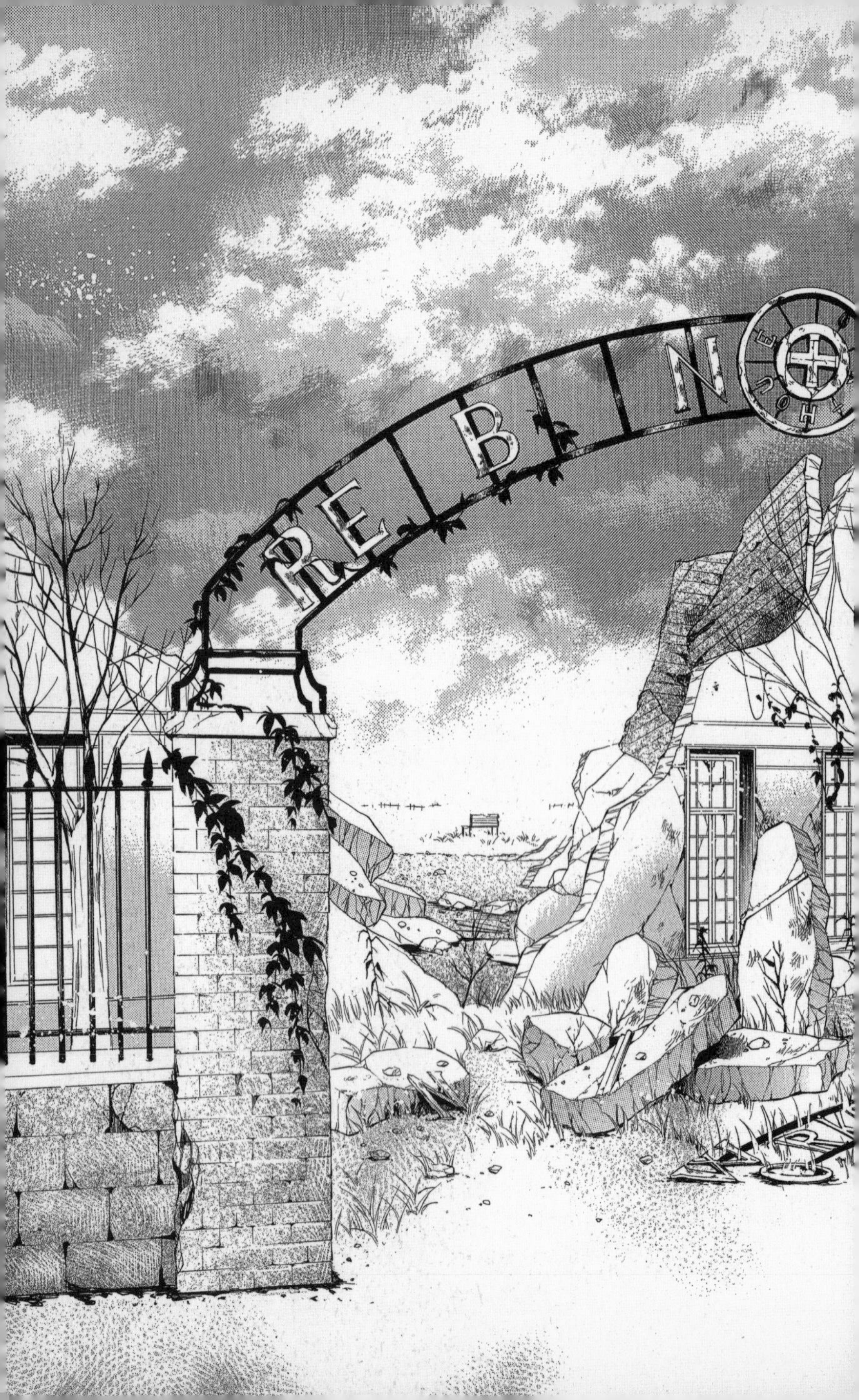
RE B N

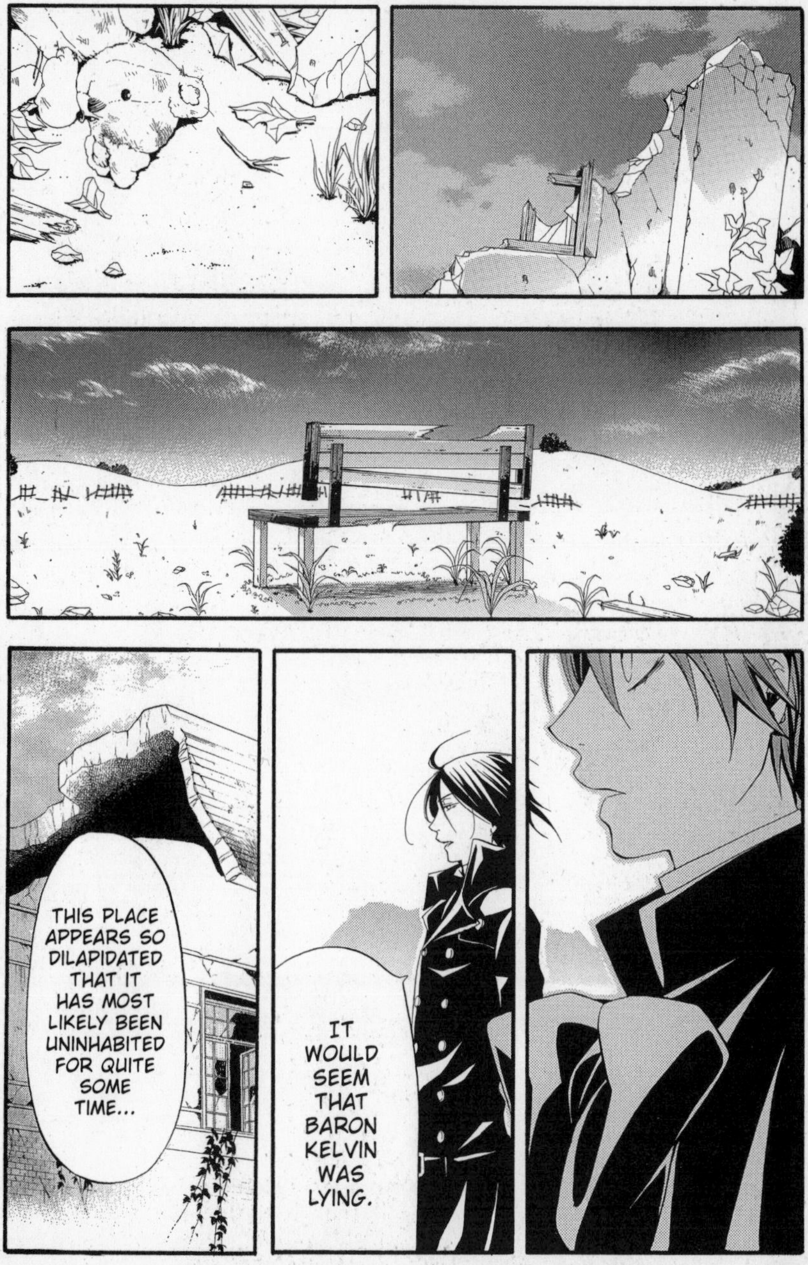
IT WOULD SEEM THAT BARON KELVIN WAS LYING.
THIS PLACE APPEARS SO DILAPIDATED THAT IT HAS MOST LIKELY BEEN UNINHABITED FOR QUITE SOME TIME...

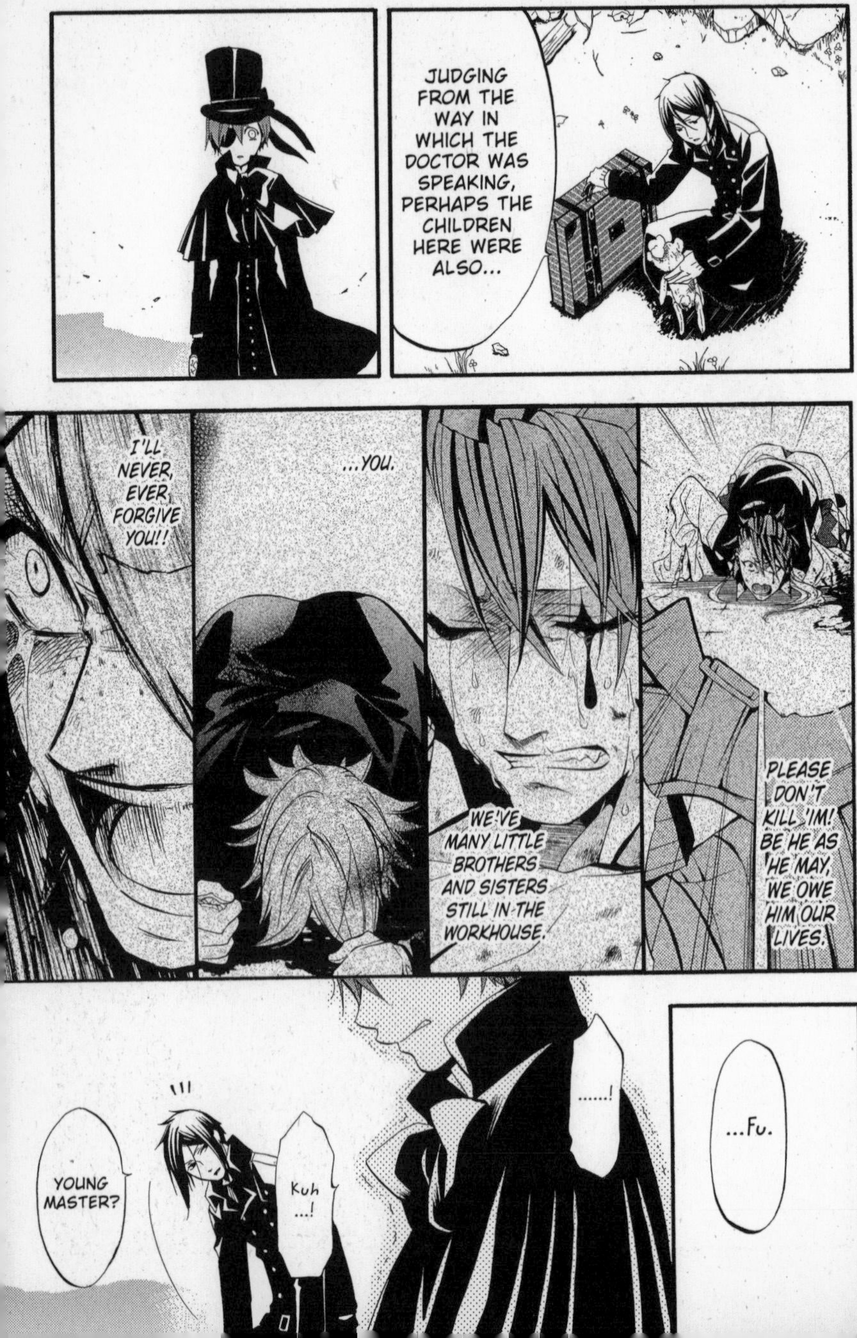
JUDGING FROM THE WAY IN WHICH THE DOCTOR WAS SPEAKING, PERHAPS THE CHILDREN HERE WERE ALSO...
PLEASE DON'T KILL 'IM! BE HE AS HE MAY, WE OWE HIM OUR LIVES.
WE'VE MANY LITTLE BROTHERS AND SISTERS STILL IN THE WORKHOUSE.
...YOU.
I'LL NEVER, EVER FORGIVE YOU!!
...Fu.
......!
Kuh ...!
YOUNG MASTER?

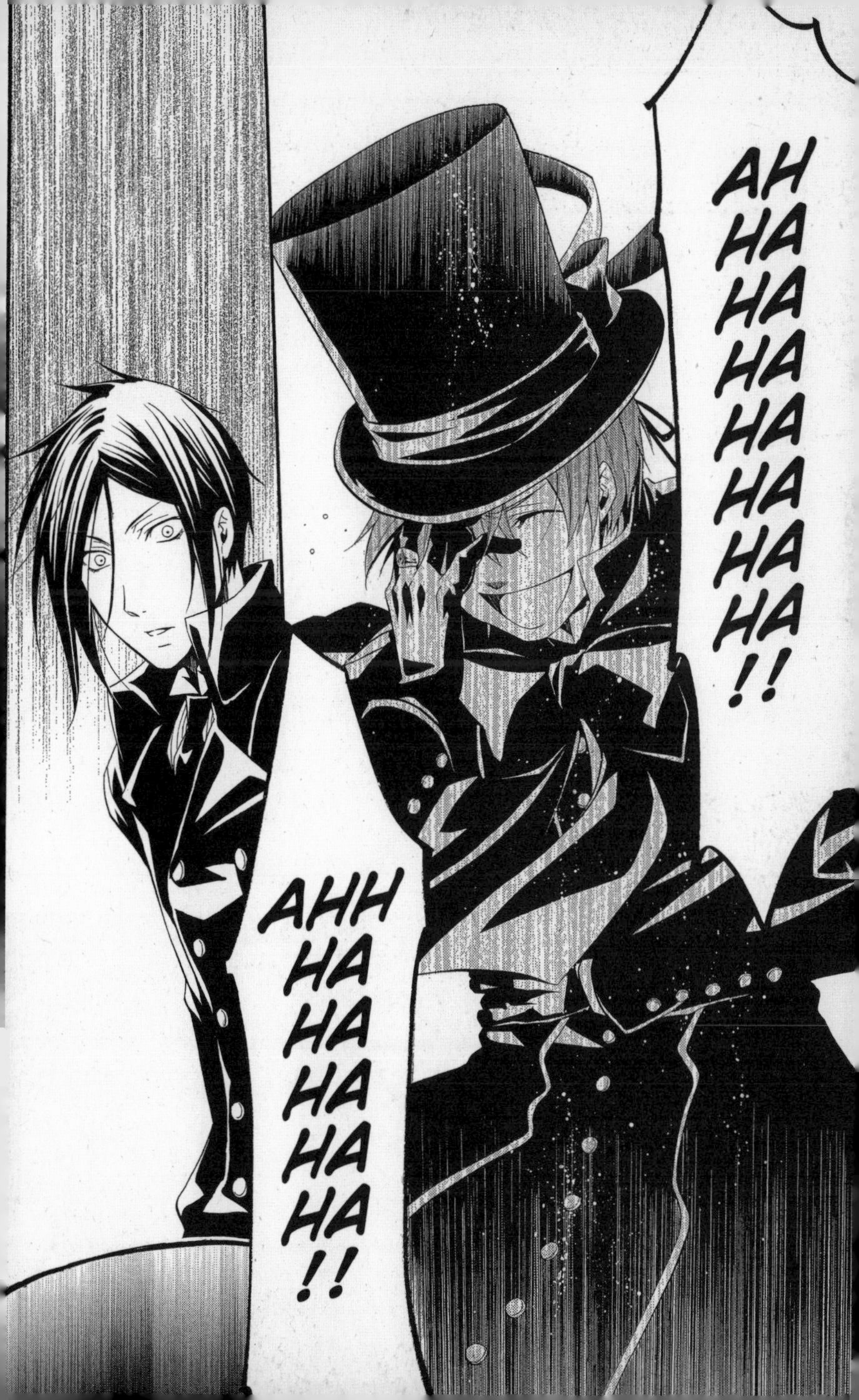
AH HA HA HA HA HA HA HA HA HA!!
AHH HA HA HA HA HA HA HA!!

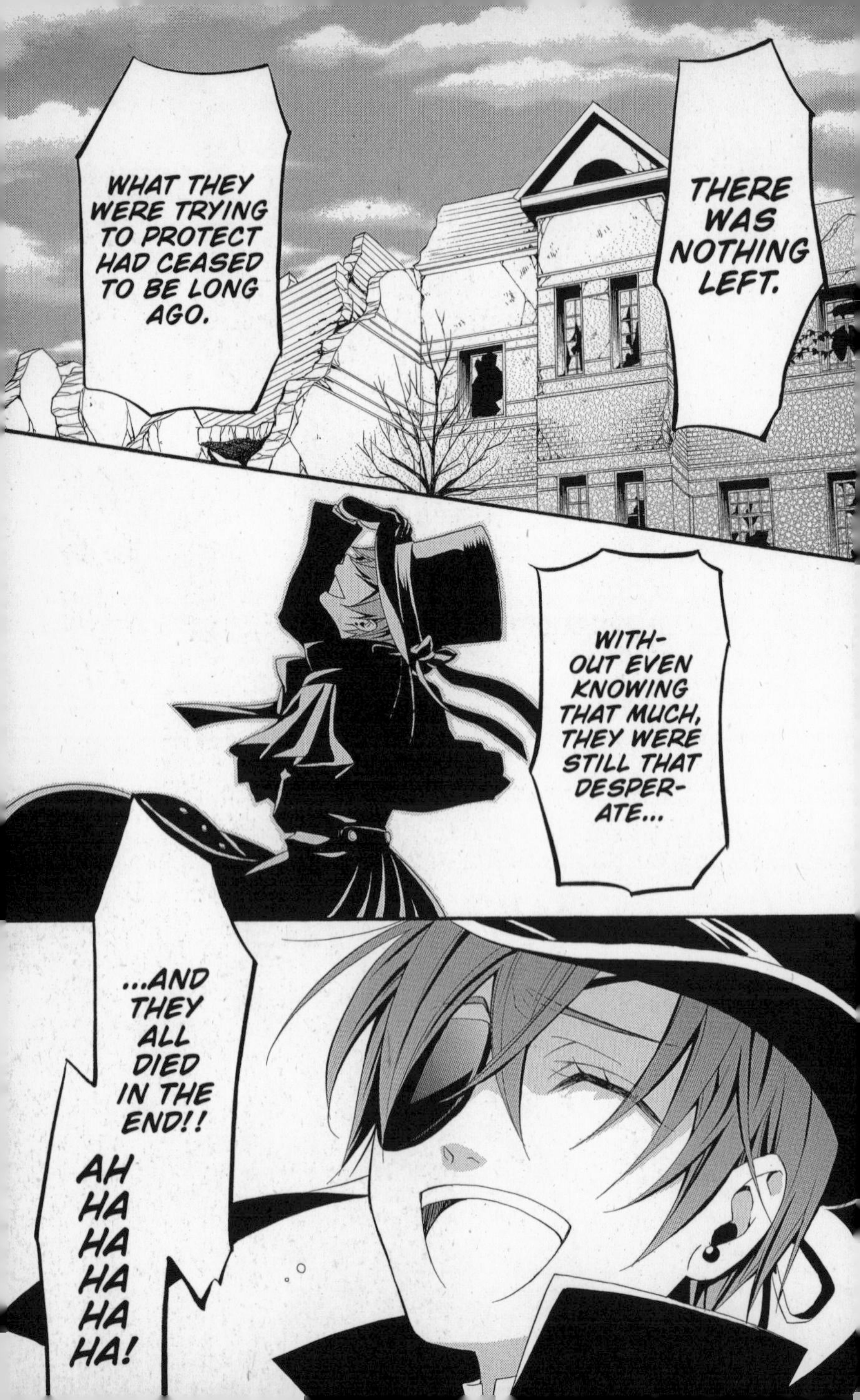
THERE WAS NOTHING LEFT.
WHAT THEY WERE TRYING TO PROTECT HAD CEASED TO BE LONG AGO.
WITH-OUT EVEN KNOWING THAT MUCH, THEY WERE STILL THAT DESPER-ATE...
...AND THEY ALL DIED IN THE END!!
AH HA HA HA HA HA HA!

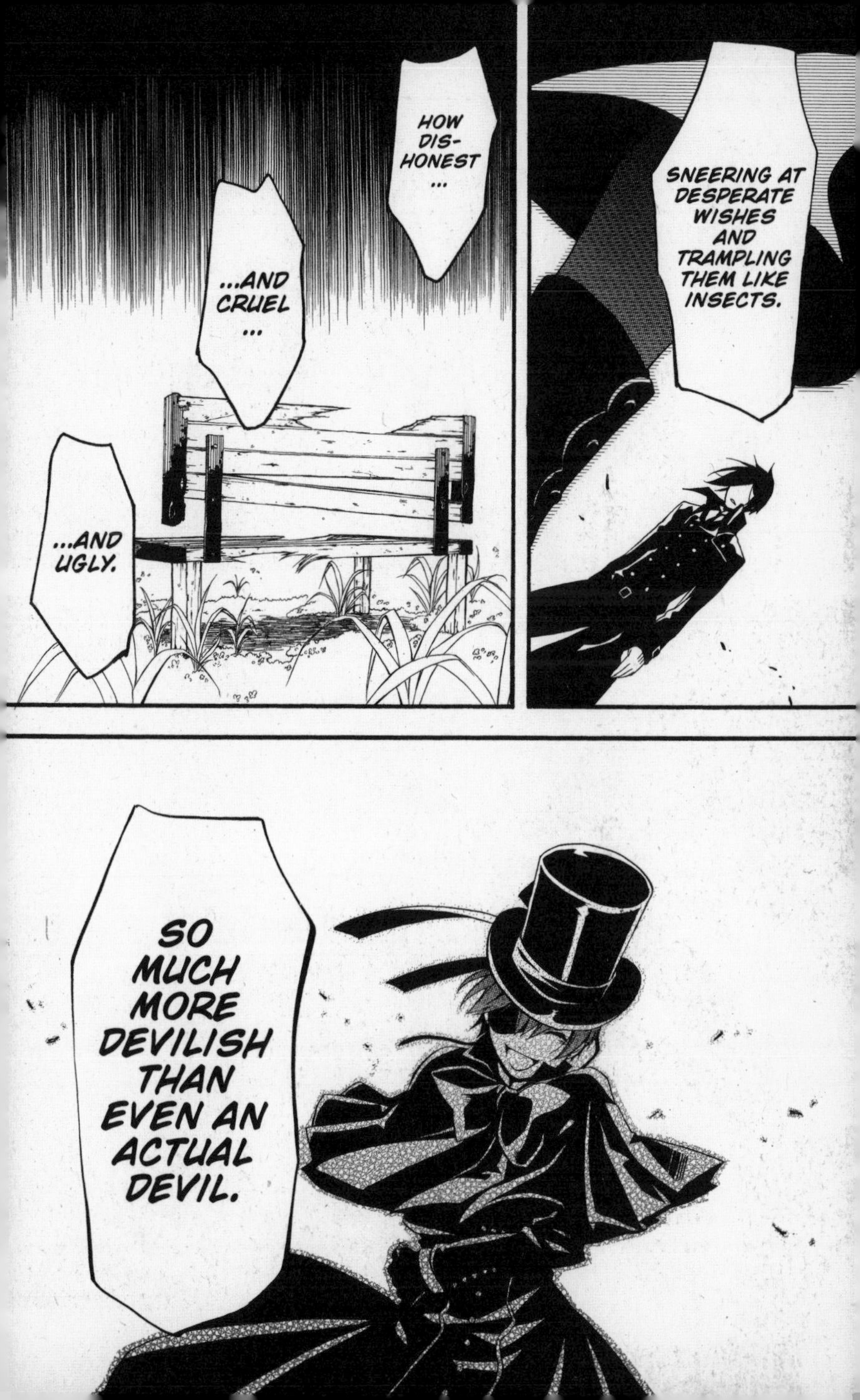
SNEERING AT DESPERATE WISHES AND TRAMPLING THEM LIKE INSECTS.
HOW DIS-HONEST ...
...AND CRUEL ...
...AND UGLY.
SO MUCH MORE DEVILISH THAN EVEN AN ACTUAL DEVIL.

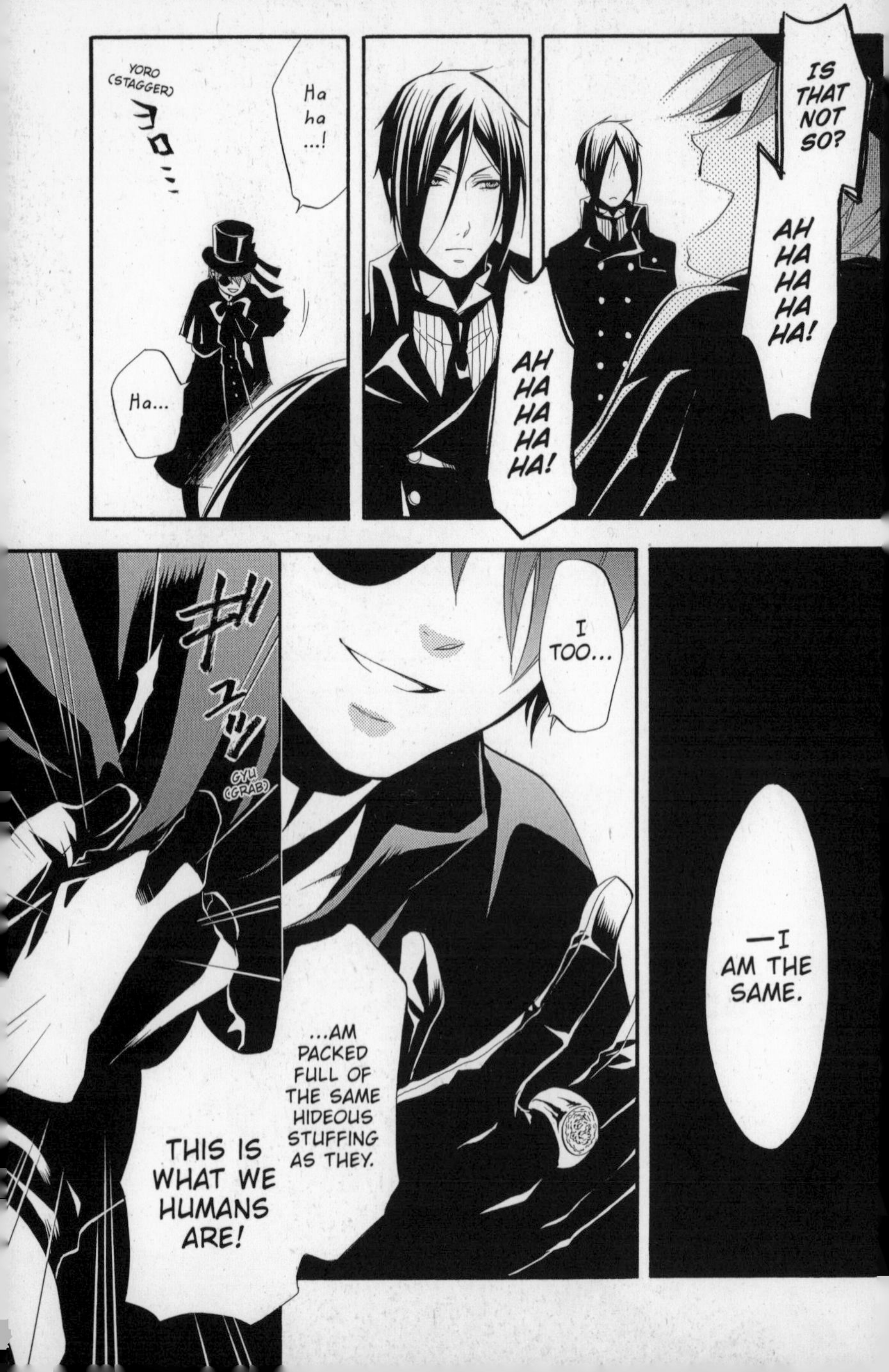
IS THAT NOT SO?
AH HA HA HA HA!
AH HA HA HA HA!
Ha ha ...!
ヨロ
YORO (STAGGER)
Ha...
—I AM THE SAME.
I TOO...
...AM PACKED FULL OF THE SAME HIDEOUS STUFFING AS THEY.
ギュッ
GYU (GRAB)
THIS IS WHAT WE HUMANS ARE!

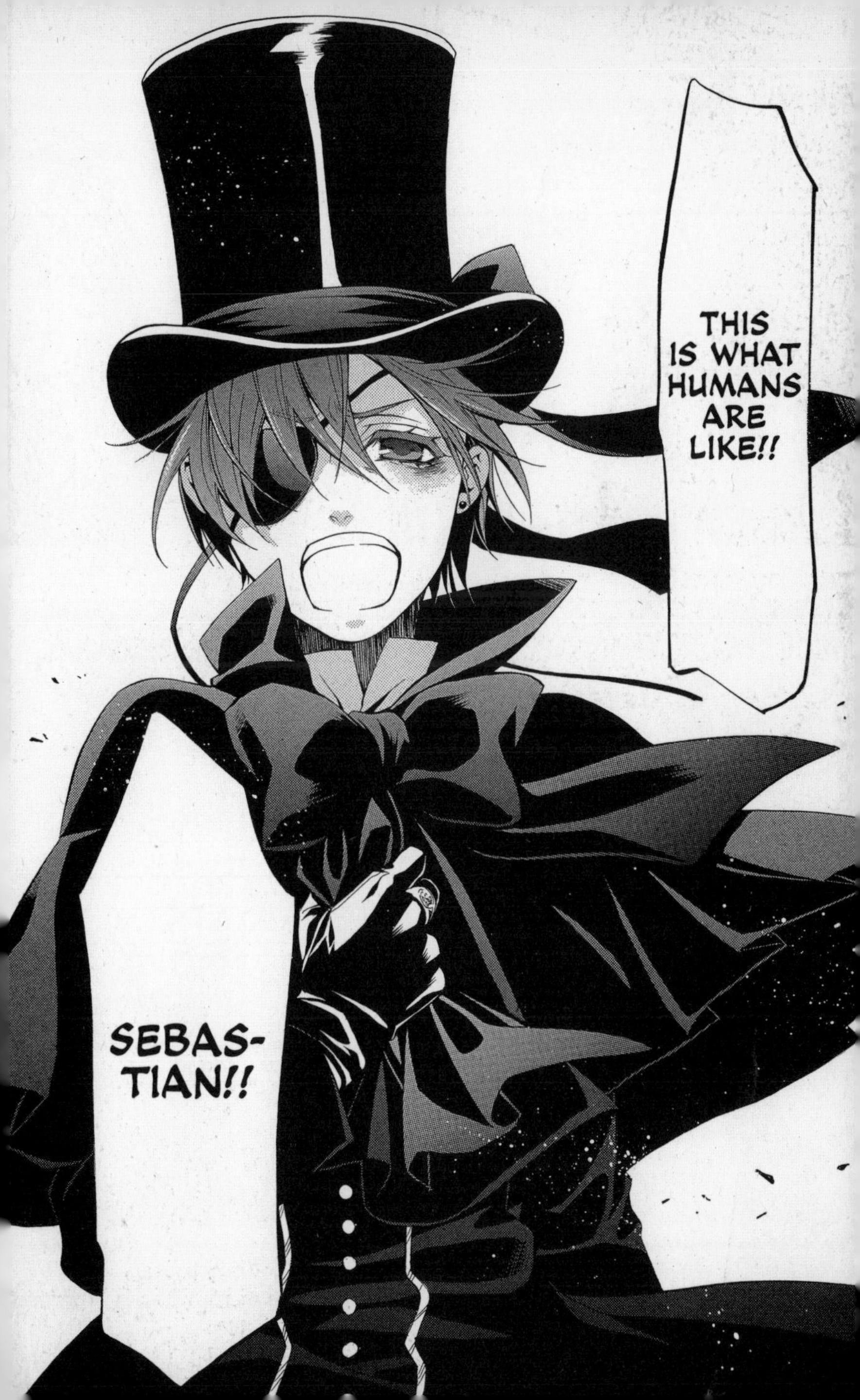
THIS IS WHAT HUMANS ARE LIKE!!
SEBAS-TIAN!!

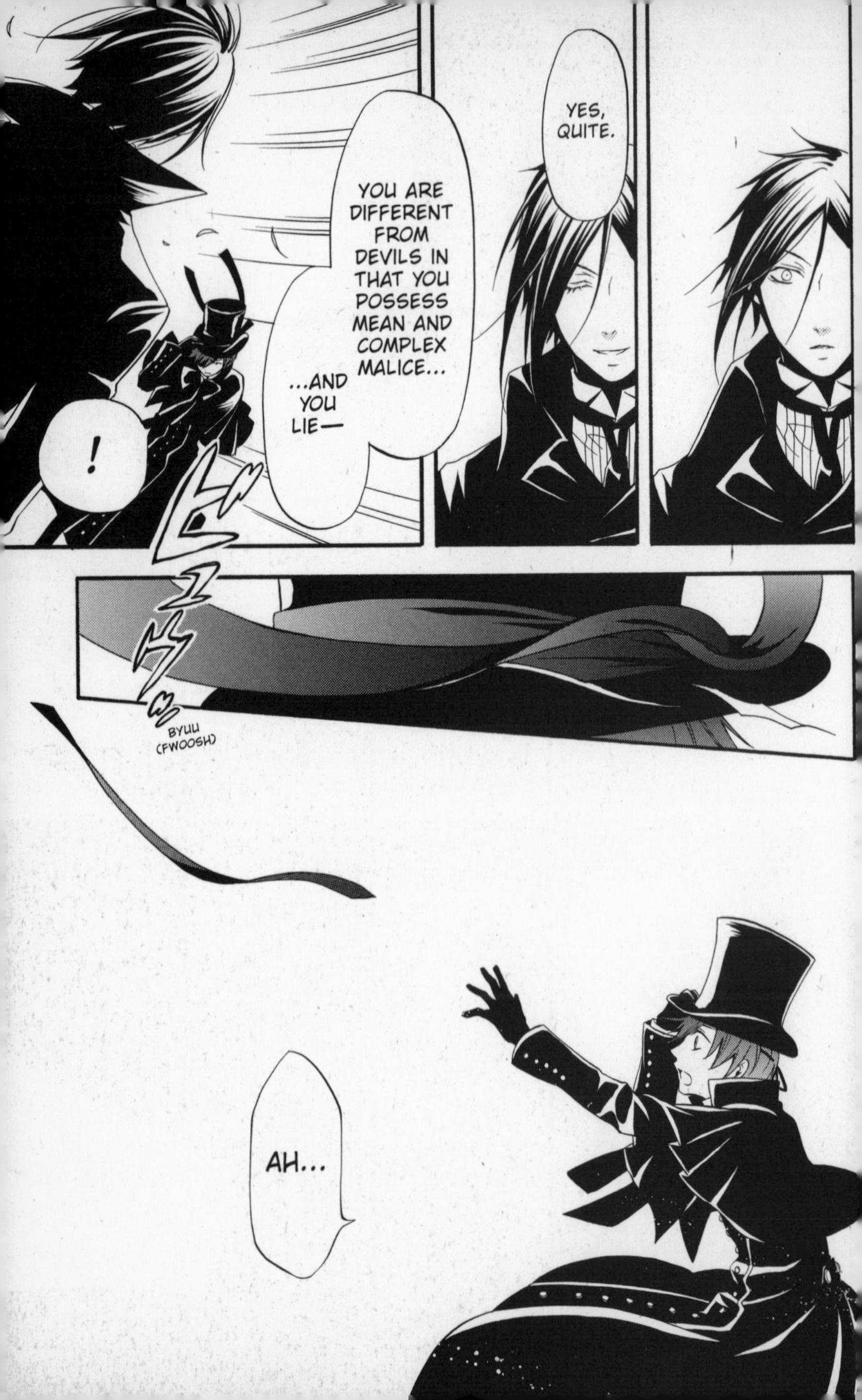
YES, QUITE.
YOU ARE DIFFERENT FROM DEVILS IN THAT YOU POSSESS MEAN AND COMPLEX MALICE...
...AND YOU LIE—
!
BYUU (FWOOSH)
AH...

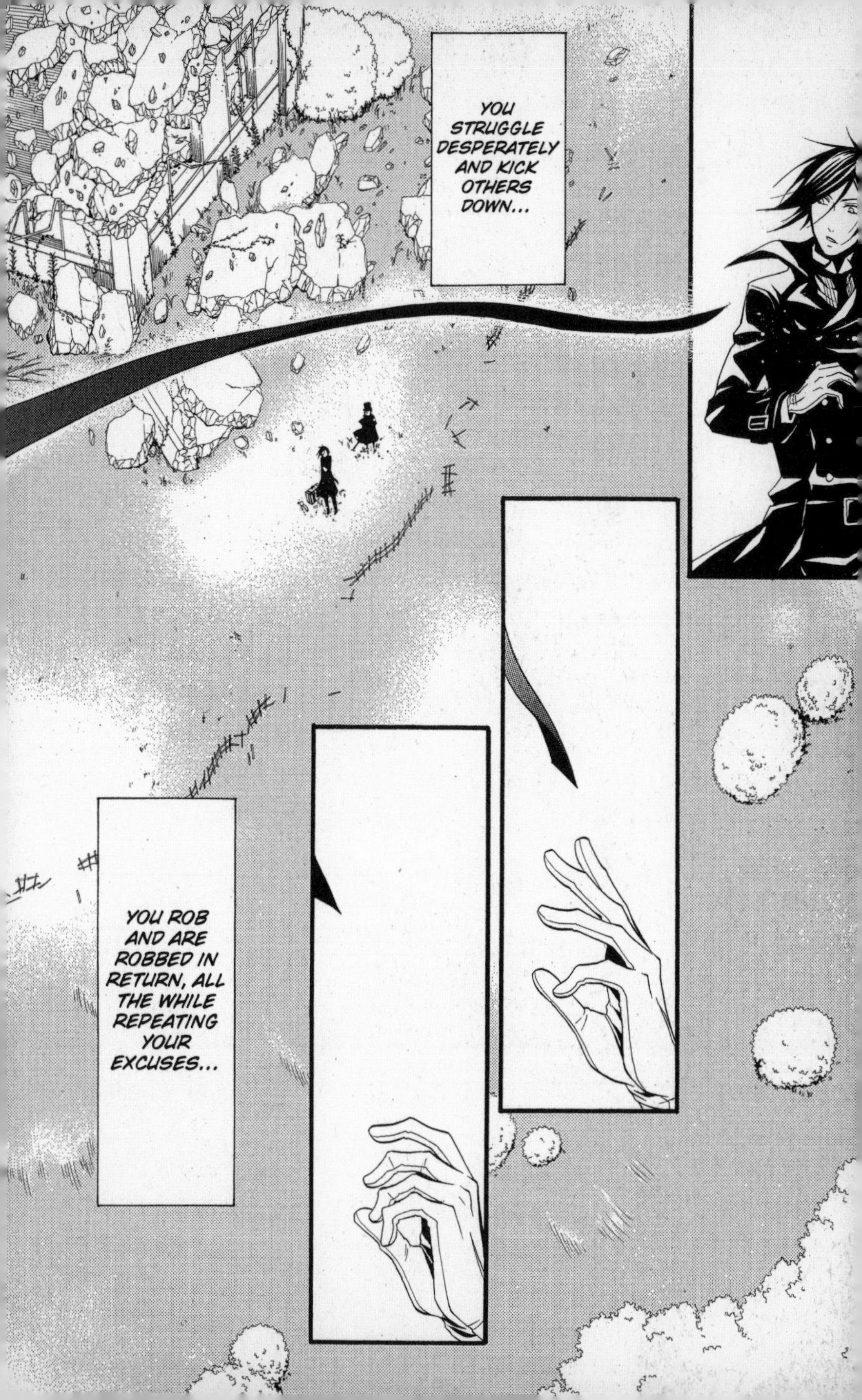
YOU STRUGGLE DESPERATELY AND KICK OTHERS DOWN...
YOU ROB AND ARE ROBBED IN RETURN, ALL THE WHILE REPEATING YOUR EXCUSES...

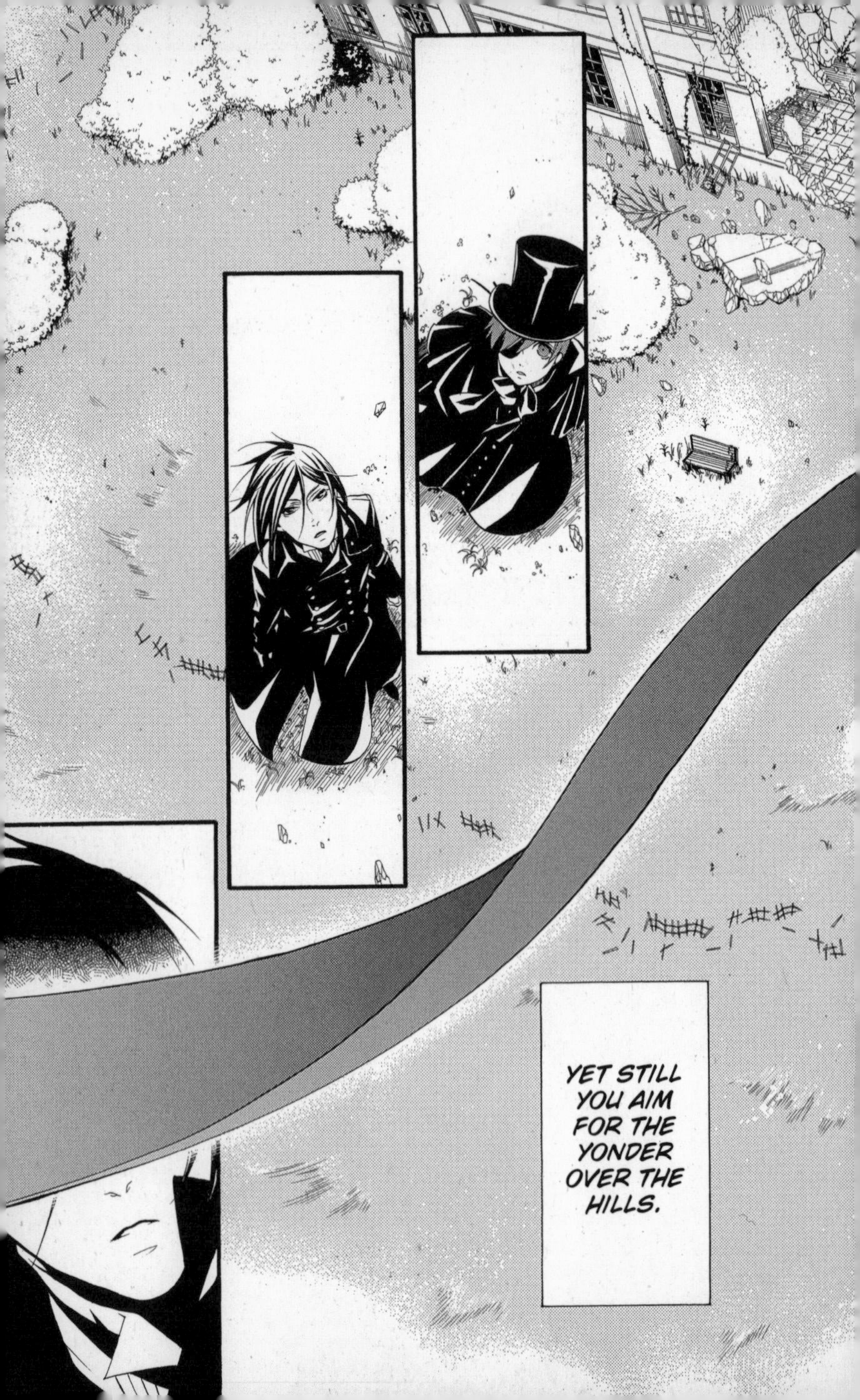
YET STILL YOU AIM FOR THE YONDER OVER THE HILLS.

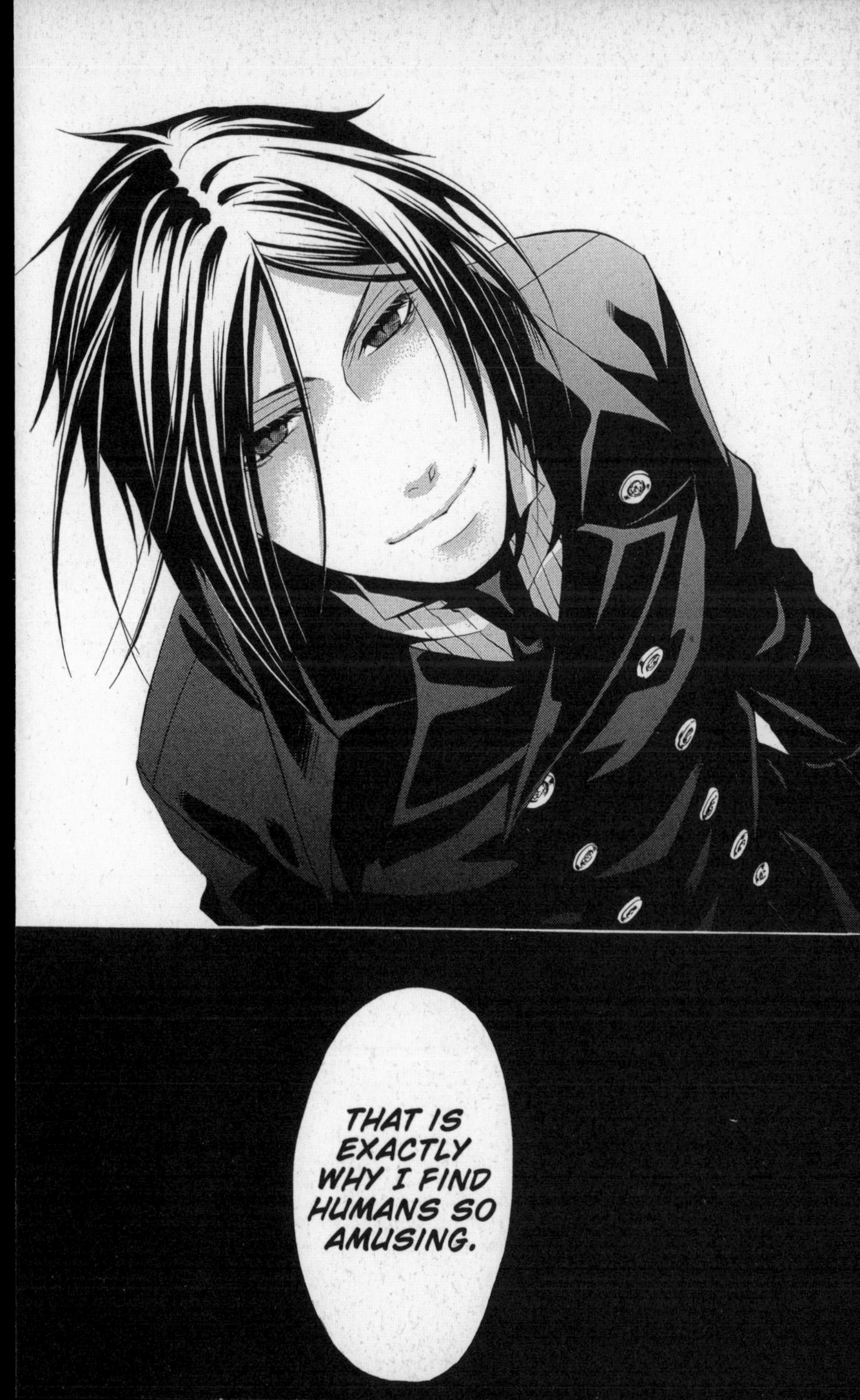
THAT IS EXACTLY WHY I FIND HUMANS SO AMUSING.

Black Butler

Black Butler

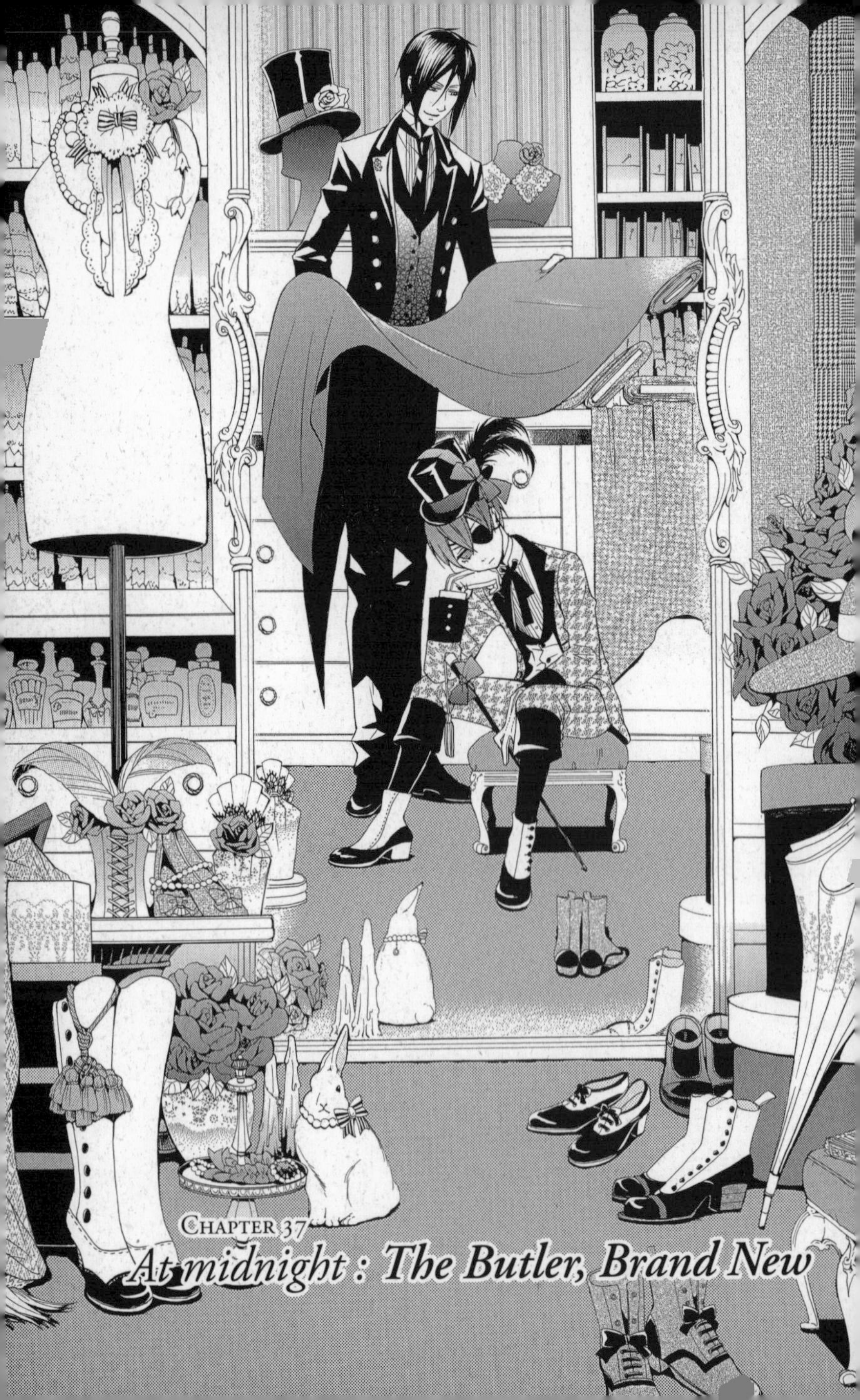
Chapter 37
At midnight : The Butler, Brand New

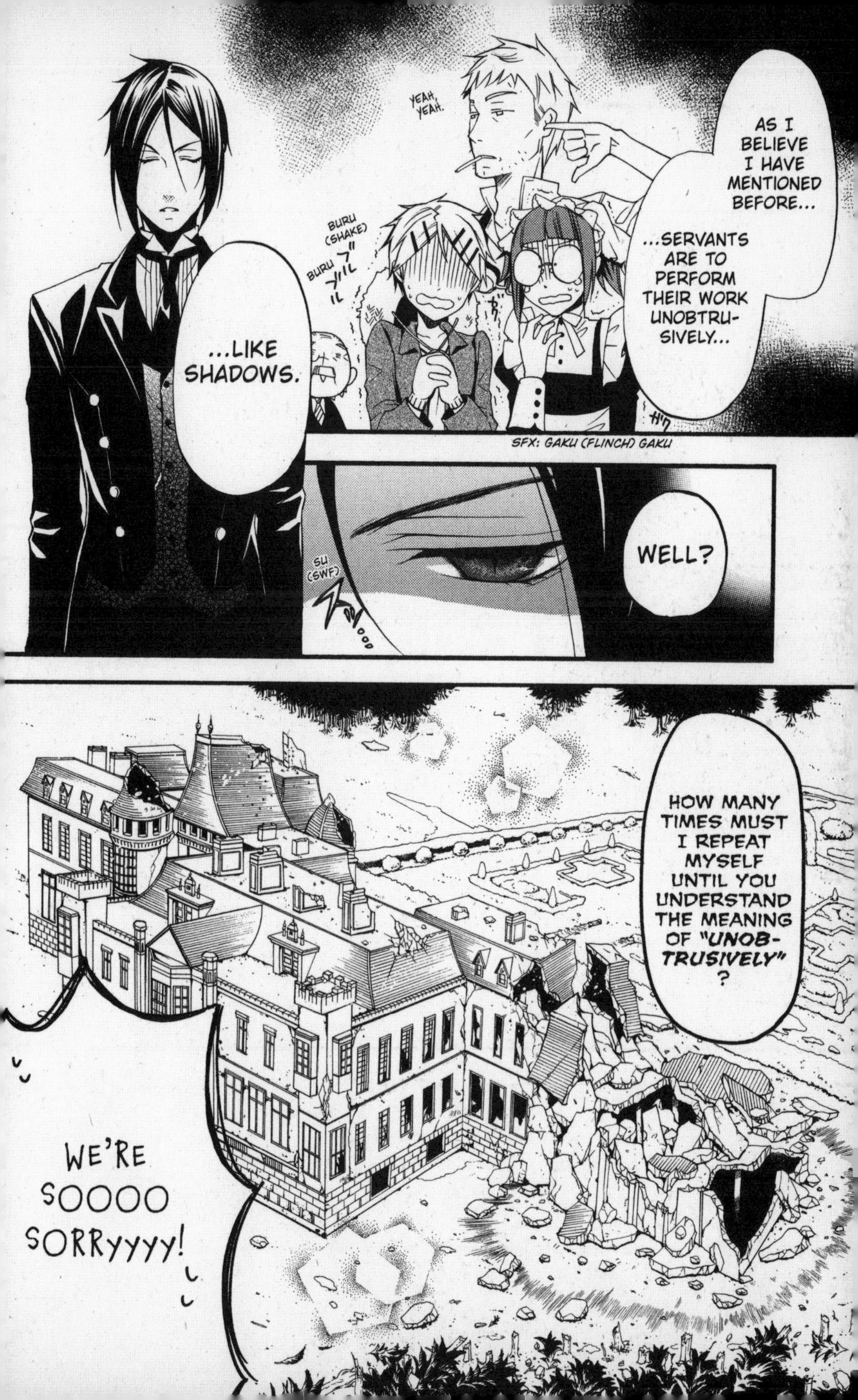
AS I BELIEVE I HAVE MENTIONED BEFORE...
YEAH, YEAH.
...SERVANTS ARE TO PERFORM THEIR WORK UNOBTRU-SIVELY...
BURU (SHAKE) BURU
...LIKE SHADOWS.
SFX: GAKU (FLINCH) GAKU
WELL?
SU (SWF)
HOW MANY TIMES MUST I REPEAT MYSELF UNTIL YOU UNDERSTAND THE MEANING OF "UNOB-TRUSIVELY"?
WE'RE SOOOO SORRYYYY!

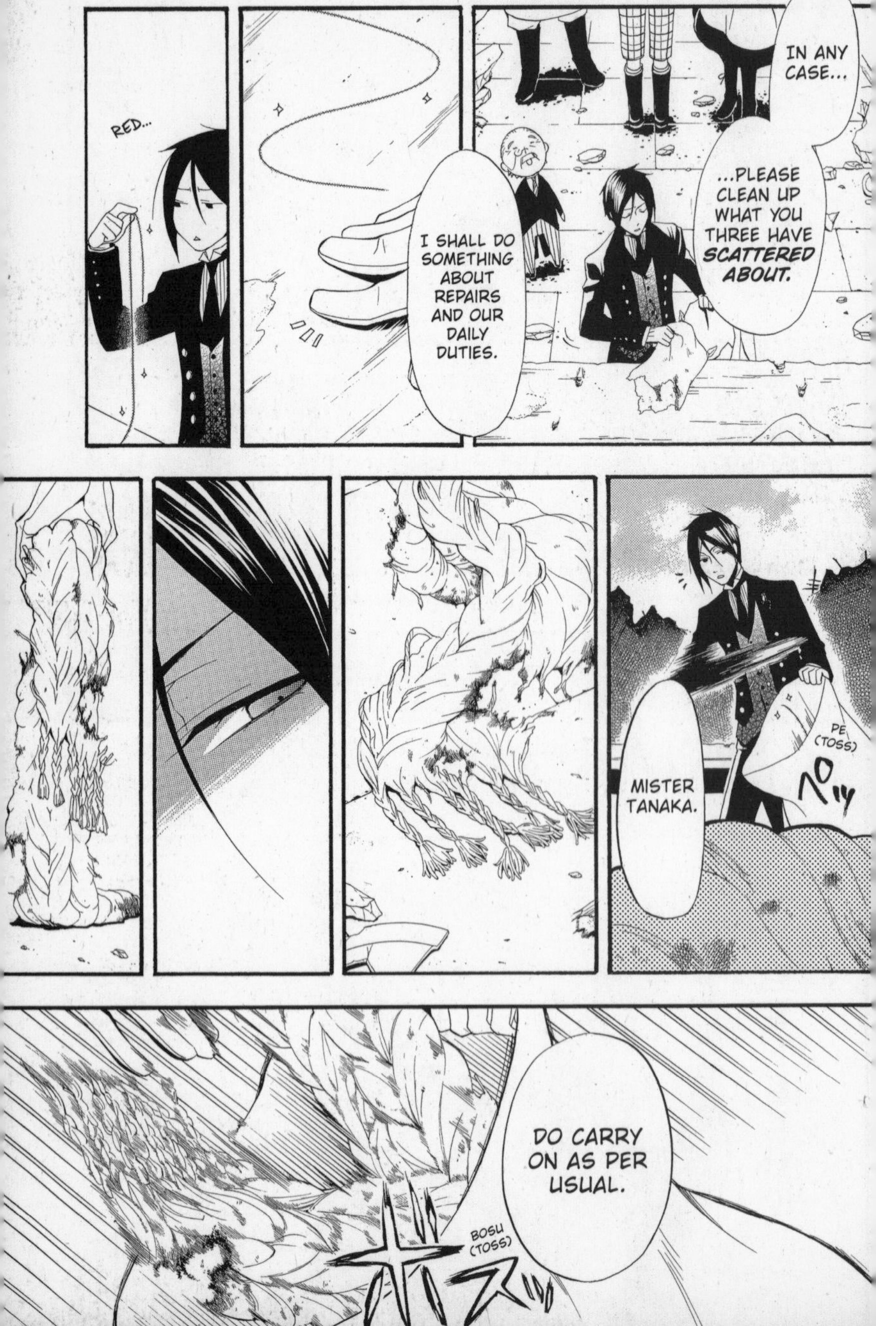
IN ANY CASE...
...PLEASE CLEAN UP WHAT YOU THREE HAVE SCATTERED ABOUT.
I SHALL DO SOMETHING ABOUT REPAIRS AND OUR DAILY DUTIES.
RED...
MISTER TANAKA.
PE (TOSS)
ペッ
DO CARRY ON AS PER USUAL.
BOSU (TOSS)
ボスッ

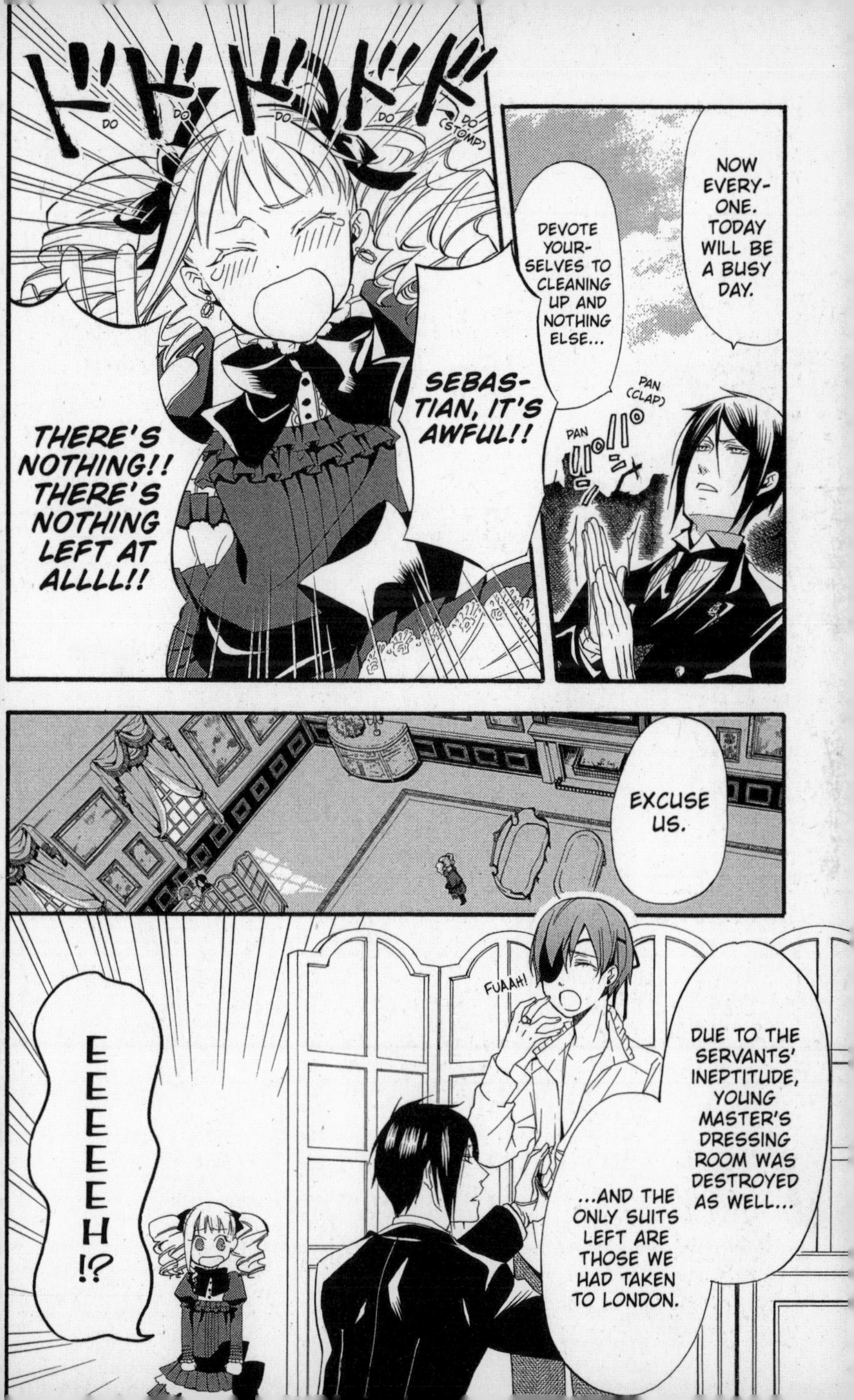
NOW EVERY-ONE. TODAY WILL BE A BUSY DAY.
DEVOTE YOUR-SELVES TO CLEANING UP AND NOTHING ELSE...
PAN (CLAP)
PAN
DO DO DO DO DO (STOMP)
SEBAS-TIAN, IT'S AWFUL!!
THERE'S NOTHING!! THERE'S NOTHING LEFT AT ALLLL!!
EXCUSE US.
FUAAH!
DUE TO THE SERVANTS' INEPTITUDE, YOUNG MASTER'S DRESSING ROOM WAS DESTROYED AS WELL...
...AND THE ONLY SUITS LEFT ARE THOSE WE HAD TAKEN TO LONDON.
EEEEEH!?

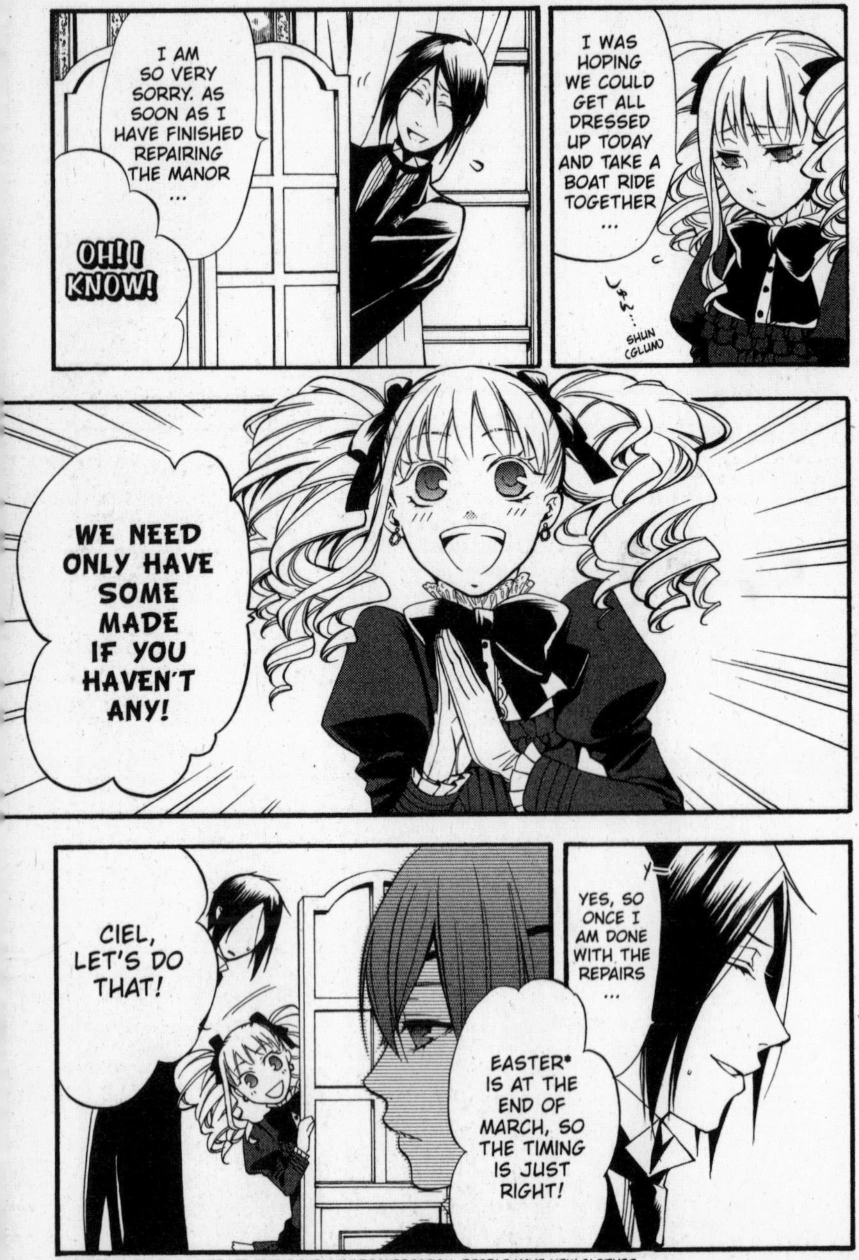
I WAS HOPING WE COULD GET ALL DRESSED UP TODAY AND TAKE A BOAT RIDE TOGETHER ...
しゅん…
SHUN (GLUM)
I AM SO VERY SORRY. AS SOON AS I HAVE FINISHED REPAIRING THE MANOR ...
OH! I KNOW!
WE NEED ONLY HAVE SOME MADE IF YOU HAVEN'T ANY!
YES, SO ONCE I AM DONE WITH THE REPAIRS ...
CIEL, LET'S DO THAT!
EASTER* IS AT THE END OF MARCH, SO THE TIMING IS JUST RIGHT!

*EASTER: A DAY TO CELEBRATE JESUS CHRIST'S RESURRECTION. PEOPLE HAVE NEW CLOTHES MADE AND GO OUT WITH THEIR FANCY BONNETS AND FLOWERS IN THEIR BUTTONHOLES.

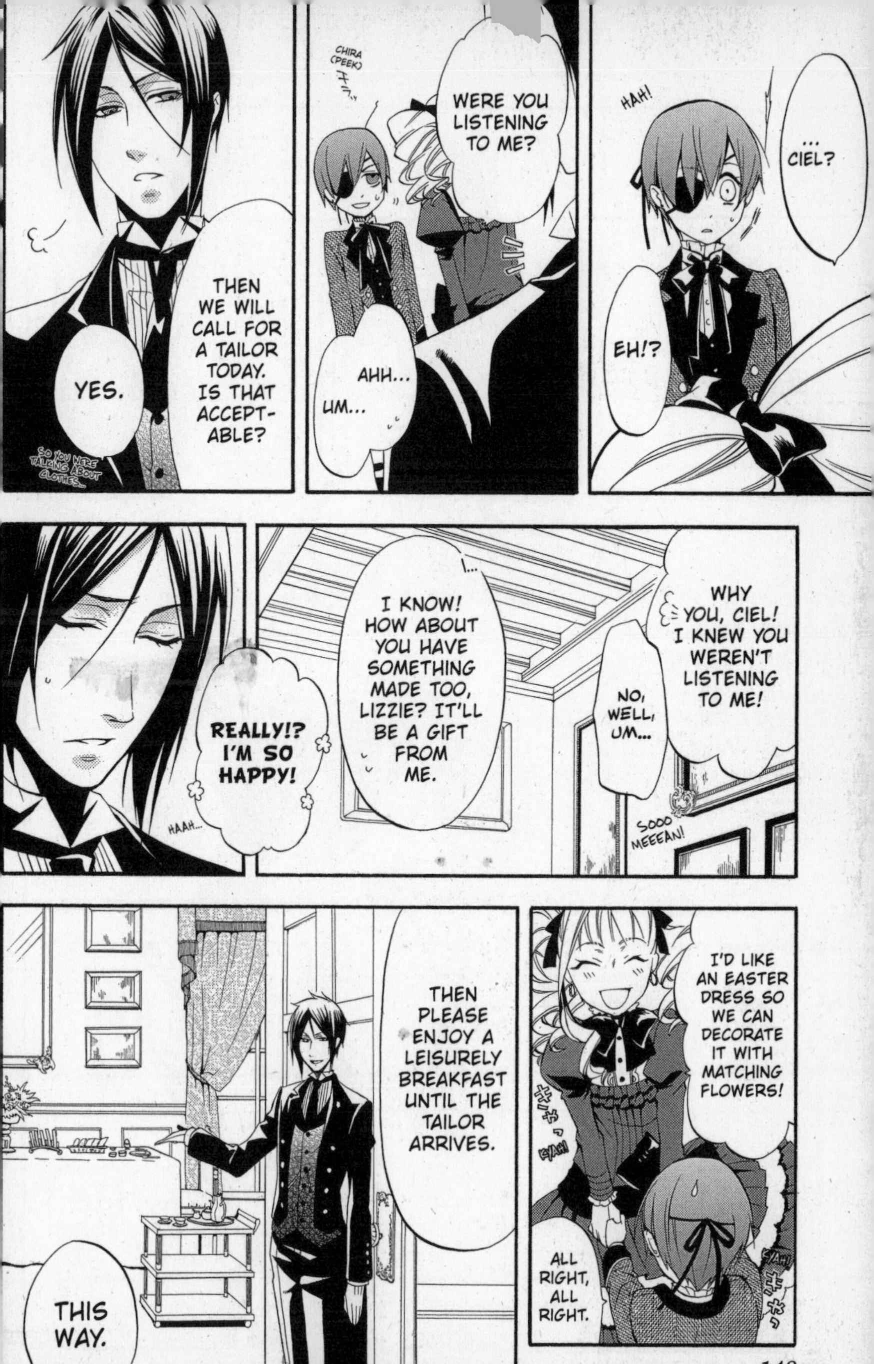
HAH!
... CIEL?
EH!?
CHIRA (PEEK)
WERE YOU LISTENING TO ME?
AHH... UM...
THEN WE WILL CALL FOR A TAILOR TODAY. IS THAT ACCEPT-ABLE?
YES.
SO YOU WERE TALKING ABOUT CLOTHES...
WHY YOU, CIEL! I KNEW YOU WEREN'T LISTENING TO ME!
NO, WELL, UM...
SOOO MEEEAN!
I...
I KNOW! HOW ABOUT YOU HAVE SOMETHING MADE TOO, LIZZIE? IT'LL BE A GIFT FROM ME.
REALLY!? I'M SO HAPPY!
HAAH...
I'D LIKE AN EASTER DRESS SO WE CAN DECORATE IT WITH MATCHING FLOWERS!
KYAH!
ALL RIGHT, ALL RIGHT.
KYAH!
THEN PLEASE ENJOY A LEISURELY BREAKFAST UNTIL THE TAILOR ARRIVES.
THIS WAY.

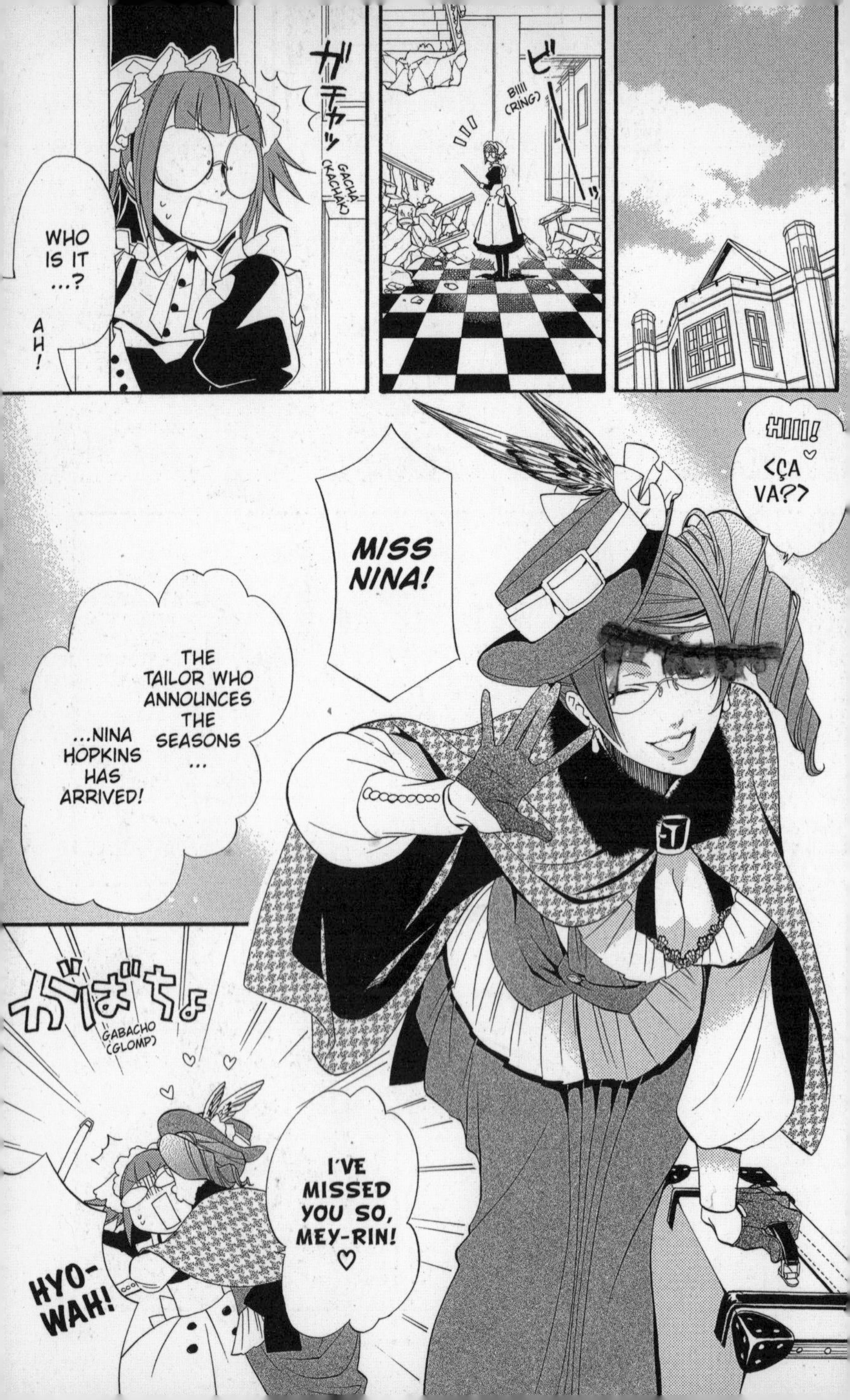
ビ
BIIII (RING)
!!!
ガチャッ
GACHA (KACHA)
WHO IS IT ...?
AH!
HIIII! <ÇA VA?> ♡
MISS NINA!
THE TAILOR WHO ANNOUNCES THE SEASONS ...
...NINA HOPKINS HAS ARRIVED!
がばちょ
GABACHO (GLOMP)
I'VE MISSED YOU SO, MEY-RIN! ♡
HYO-WAH!

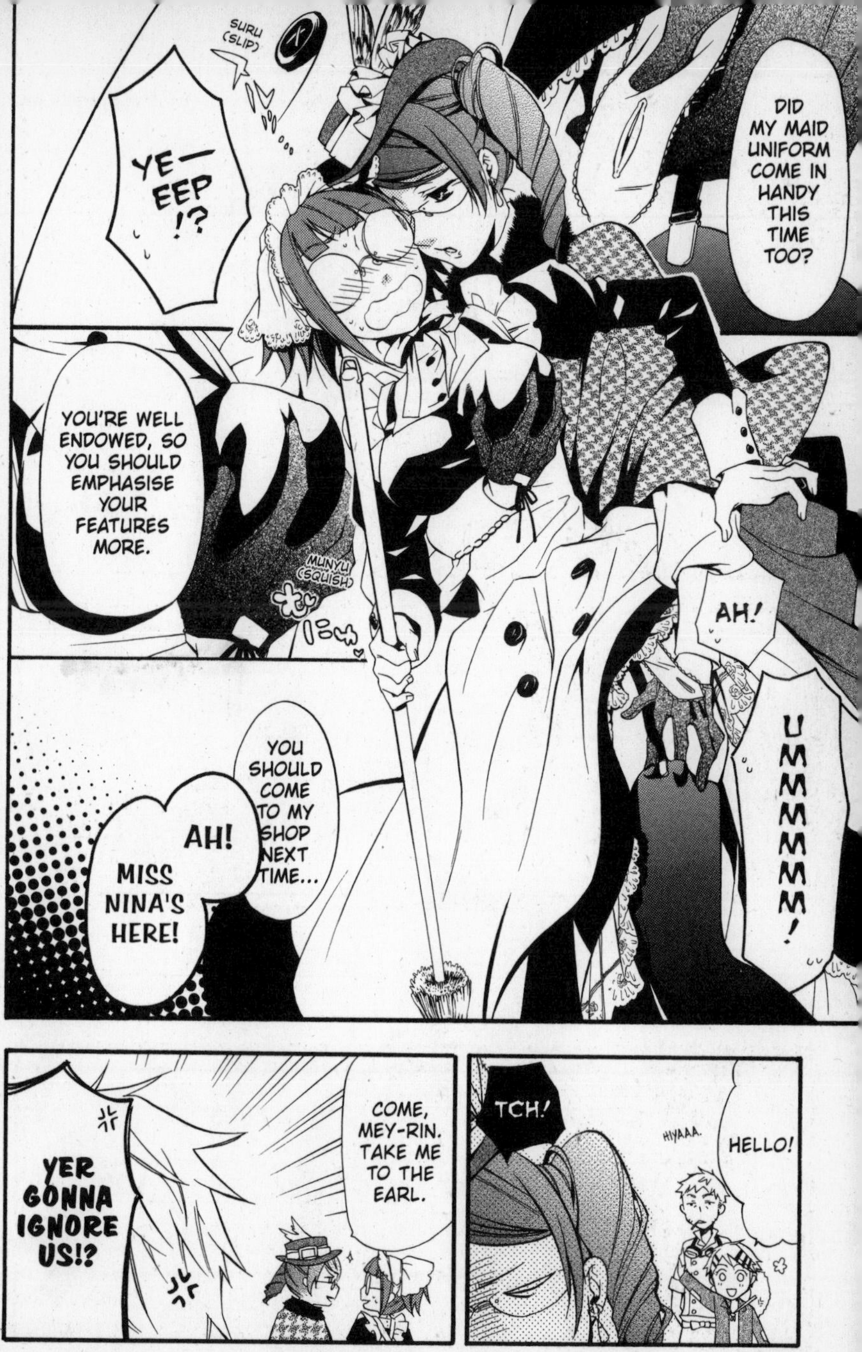
DID MY MAID UNIFORM COME IN HANDY THIS TIME TOO?
SURU (SLIP)
YE—EEP!?
YOU'RE WELL ENDOWED, SO YOU SHOULD EMPHASISE YOUR FEATURES MORE.
MUNYU (SQUISH)
AH!
UMMMMMMM!
YOU SHOULD COME TO MY SHOP NEXT TIME...
AH! MISS NINA'S HERE!
HELLO!
HIYAAA.
TCH!
COME, MEY-RIN. TAKE ME TO THE EARL.
YER GONNA IGNORE US!?

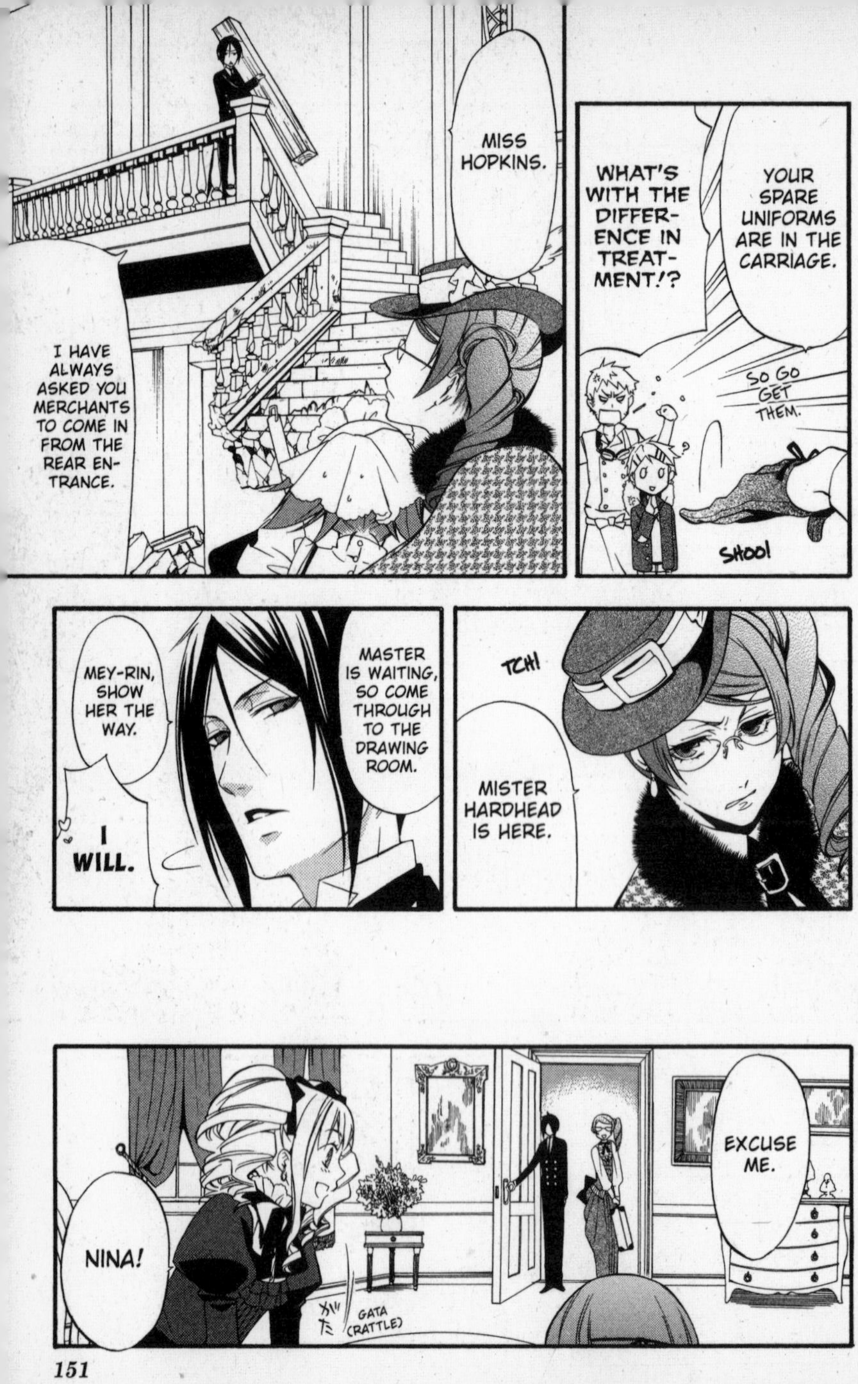
MISS HOPKINS.
I HAVE ALWAYS ASKED YOU MERCHANTS TO COME IN FROM THE REAR ENTRANCE.
YOUR SPARE UNIFORMS ARE IN THE CARRIAGE.
WHAT'S WITH THE DIFFERENCE IN TREATMENT!?
SO GO GET THEM.
SHOO!
TCH!
MISTER HARDHEAD IS HERE.
MASTER IS WAITING, SO COME THROUGH TO THE DRAWING ROOM.
MEY-RIN, SHOW HER THE WAY.
I WILL.
EXCUSE ME.
NINA!
GATA (RATTLE)

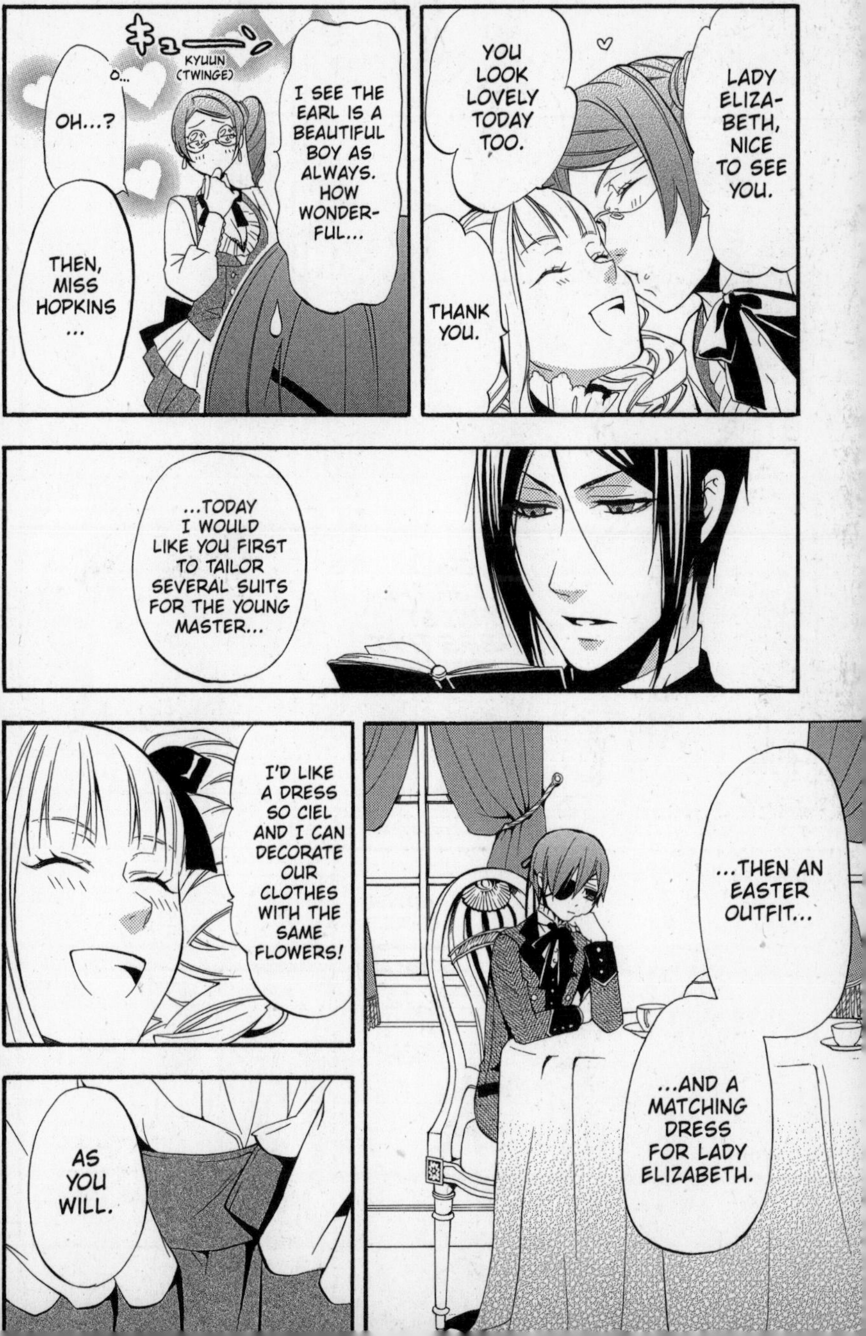
LADY ELIZA-BETH, NICE TO SEE YOU.
YOU LOOK LOVELY TODAY TOO.
THANK YOU.
I SEE THE EARL IS A BEAUTIFUL BOY AS ALWAYS. HOW WONDER-FUL...
KYUUN (TWINGE)
O...
OH...?
THEN, MISS HOPKINS...
...TODAY I WOULD LIKE YOU FIRST TO TAILOR SEVERAL SUITS FOR THE YOUNG MASTER...
...THEN AN EASTER OUTFIT...
...AND A MATCHING DRESS FOR LADY ELIZABETH.
I'D LIKE A DRESS SO CIEL AND I CAN DECORATE OUR CLOTHES WITH THE SAME FLOWERS!
AS YOU WILL.

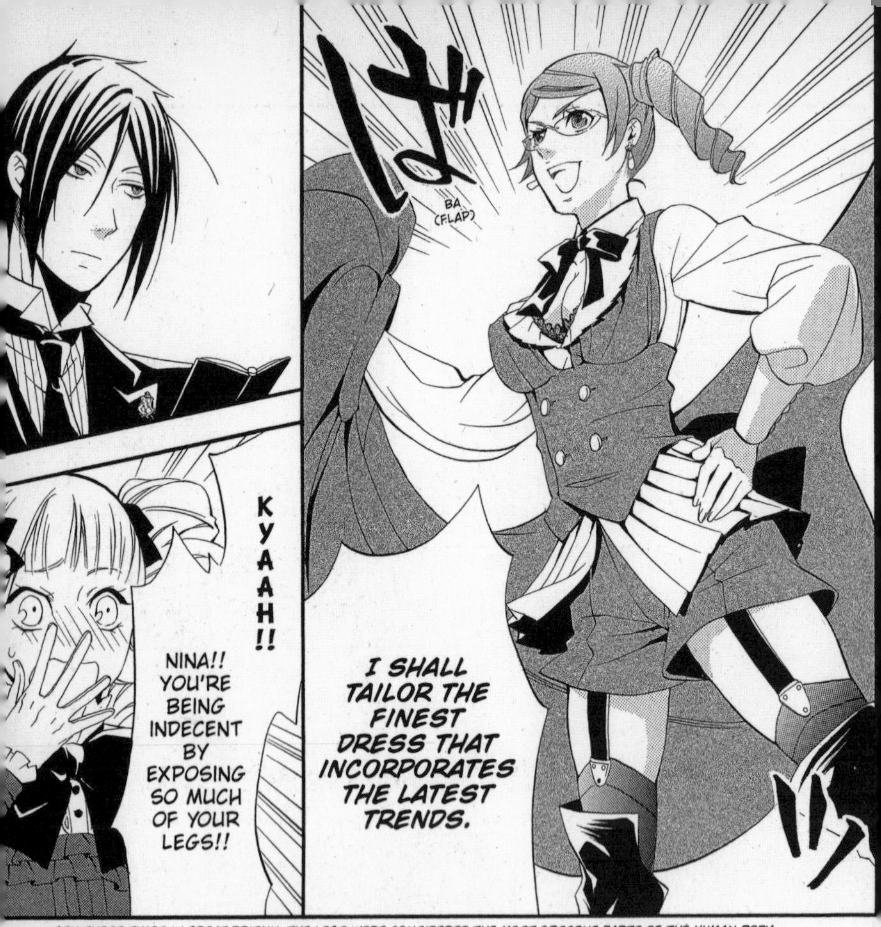
BA (FLAP)
I SHALL TAILOR THE FINEST DRESS THAT INCORPORATES THE LATEST TRENDS.
KYAAH!!
NINA!! YOU'RE BEING INDECENT BY EXPOSING SO MUCH OF YOUR LEGS!!

*IN THESE TIMES IN GREAT BRITAIN, THE LEGS WERE CONSIDERED THE MOST OBSCENE PARTS OF THE HUMAN BODY.

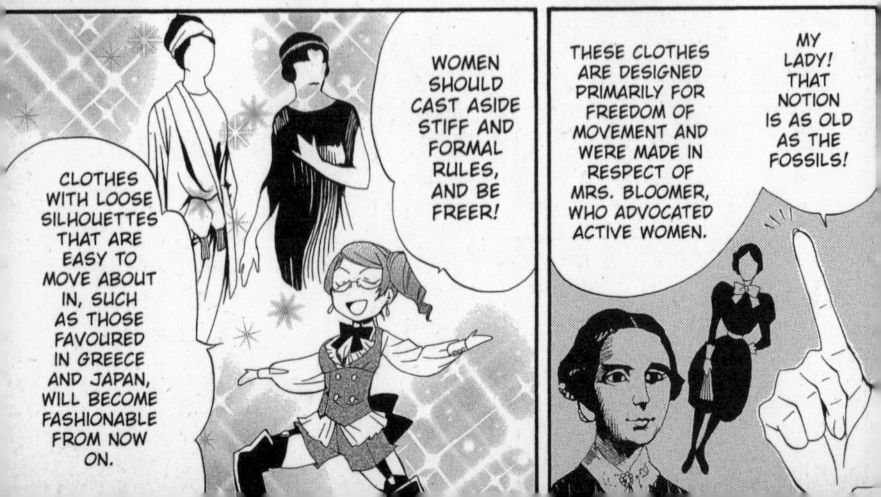
MY LADY! THAT NOTION IS AS OLD AS THE FOSSILS!
THESE CLOTHES ARE DESIGNED PRIMARILY FOR FREEDOM OF MOVEMENT AND WERE MADE IN RESPECT OF MRS. BLOOMER, WHO ADVOCATED ACTIVE WOMEN.
WOMEN SHOULD CAST ASIDE STIFF AND FORMAL RULES, AND BE FREER!
CLOTHES WITH LOOSE SILHOUETTES THAT ARE EASY TO MOVE ABOUT IN, SUCH AS THOSE FAVOURED IN GREECE AND JAPAN, WILL BECOME FASHIONABLE FROM NOW ON.

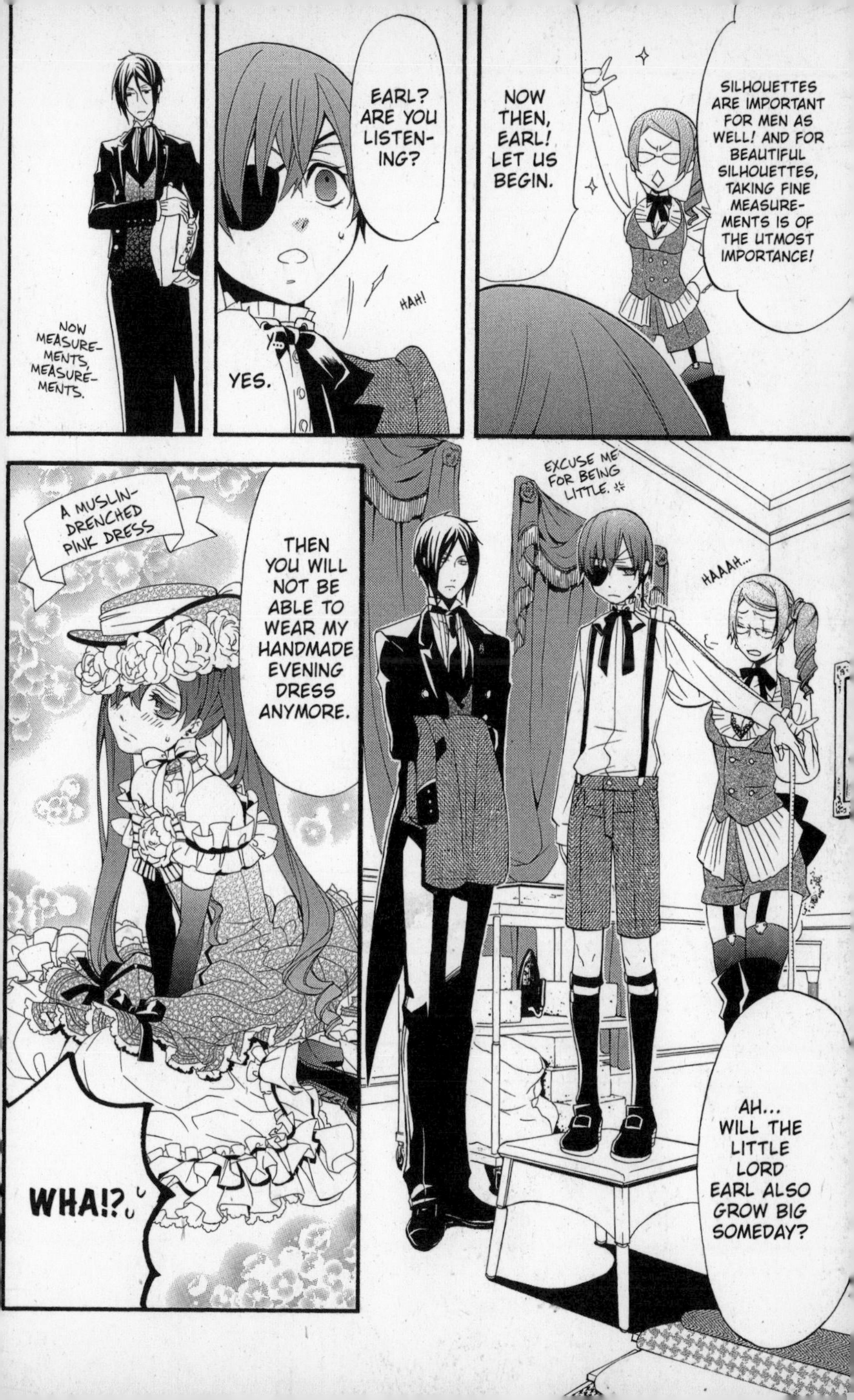
SILHOUETTES ARE IMPORTANT FOR MEN AS WELL! AND FOR BEAUTIFUL SILHOUETTES, TAKING FINE MEASUREMENTS IS OF THE UTMOST IMPORTANCE!
NOW THEN, EARL! LET US BEGIN.
EARL? ARE YOU LISTENING?
HAH!
YES.
NOW MEASUREMENTS, MEASUREMENTS.
HAAAH...
EXCUSE ME FOR BEING LITTLE.
AH... WILL THE LITTLE LORD EARL ALSO GROW BIG SOMEDAY?
THEN YOU WILL NOT BE ABLE TO WEAR MY HANDMADE EVENING DRESS ANYMORE.
A MUSLIN-DRENCHED PINK DRESS
WHA!?

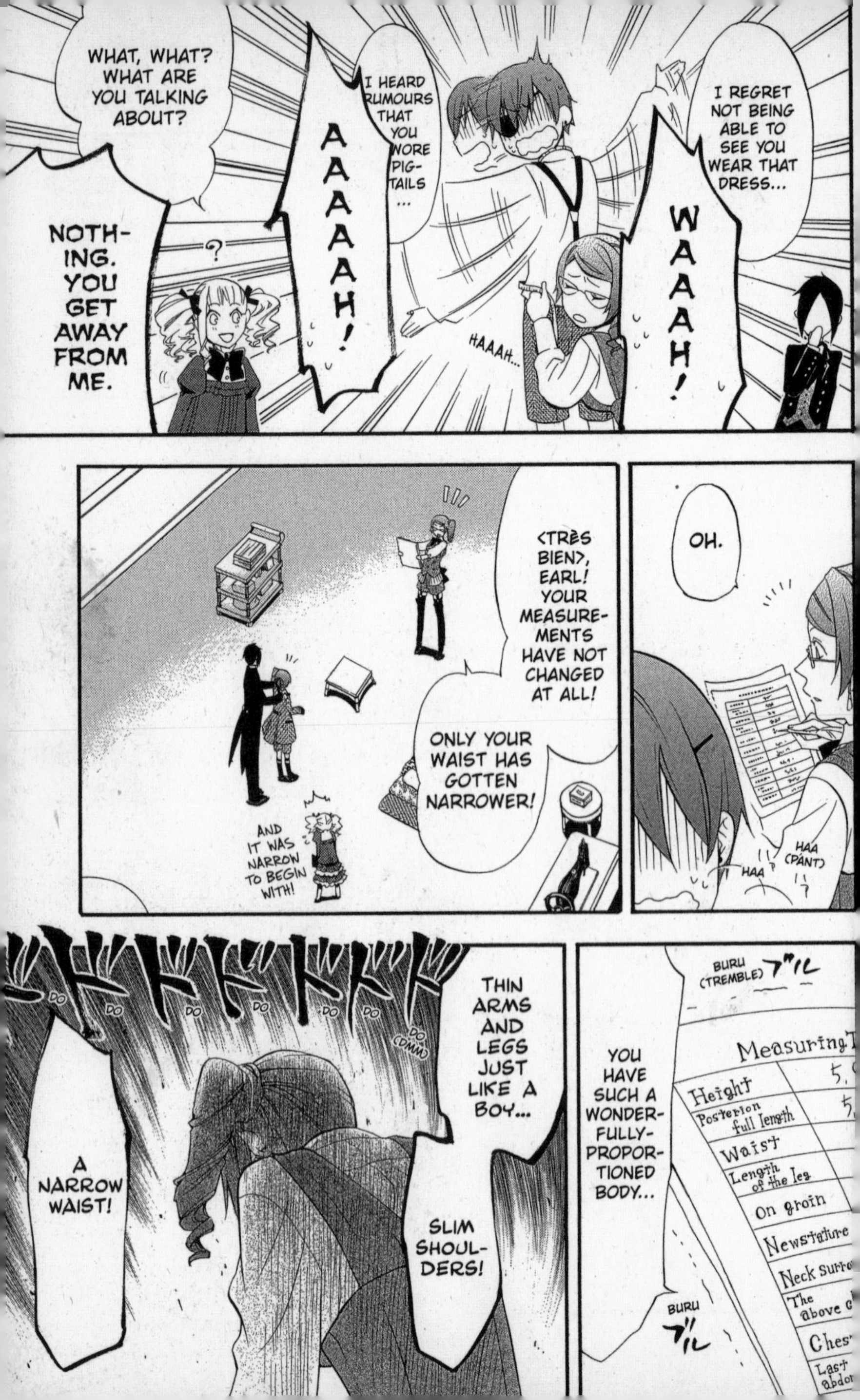
I REGRET NOT BEING ABLE TO SEE YOU WEAR THAT DRESS...
WAAAH!
I HEARD RUMOURS THAT YOU WORE PIG-TAILS...
AAAAAH!
HAAAH...
WHAT, WHAT? WHAT ARE YOU TALKING ABOUT?
?
NOTHING. YOU GET AWAY FROM ME.
OH.
HAA HAA (PANT)
<TRÈS BIEN>, EARL! YOUR MEASUREMENTS HAVE NOT CHANGED AT ALL!
ONLY YOUR WAIST HAS GOTTEN NARROWER!
AND IT WAS NARROW TO BEGIN WITH!
BURU (TREMBLE)
Height
Posterion full length
Waist
Length of the leg
On groin
Newstature
YOU HAVE SUCH A WONDERFULLY-PROPORTIONED BODY...
BURU
DO DO DO DO DO DO DO (DMM)
THIN ARMS AND LEGS JUST LIKE A BOY...
SLIM SHOULDERS!
A NARROW WAIST!

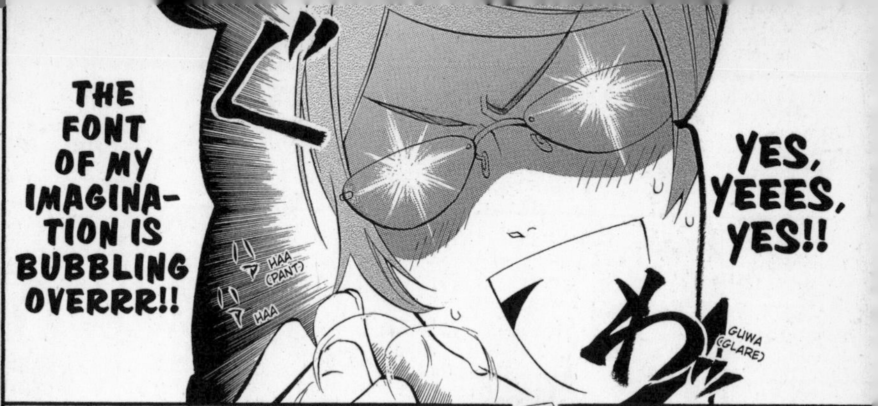
YES, YEEES, YES!!
GUWA (GLARE)
THE FONT OF MY IMAGINATION IS BUBBLING OVERRR!!
HAA (PANT)
HAA

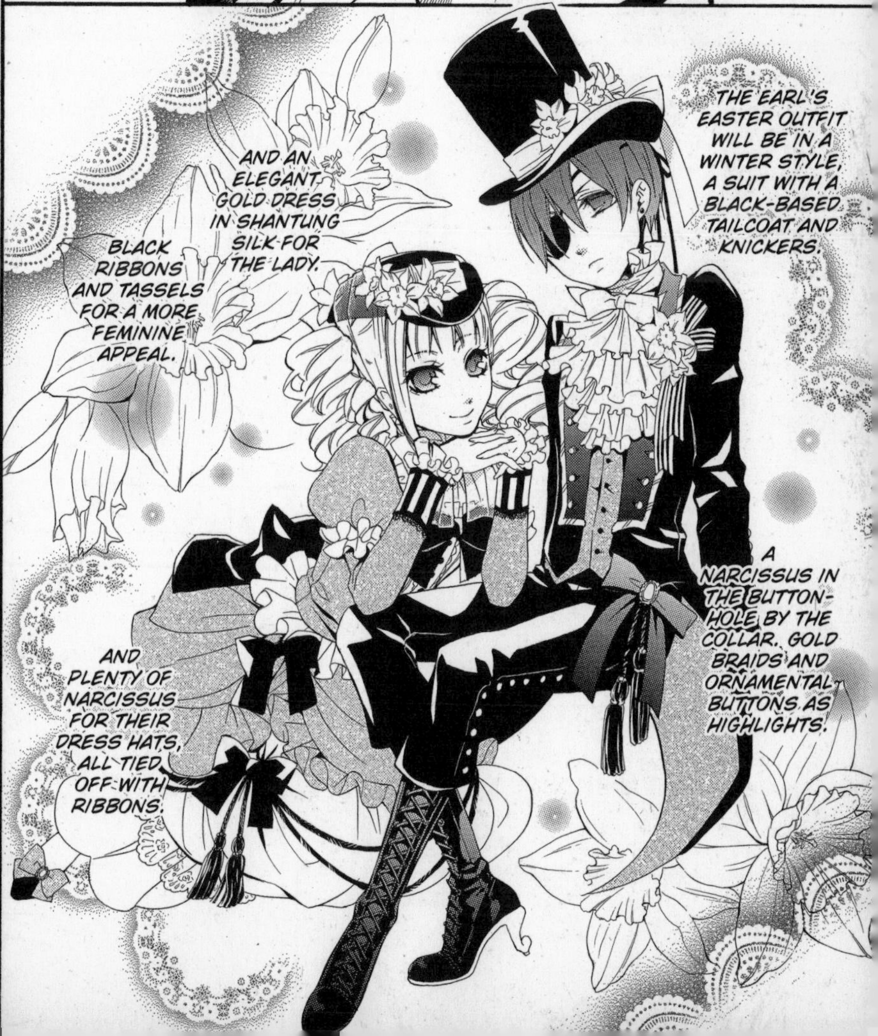
THE EARL'S EASTER OUTFIT WILL BE IN A WINTER STYLE, A SUIT WITH A BLACK-BASED TAILCOAT AND KNICKERS.
AND AN ELEGANT GOLD DRESS IN SHANTUNG SILK FOR THE LADY.
BLACK RIBBONS AND TASSELS FOR A MORE FEMININE APPEAL.
A NARCISSUS IN THE BUTTON-HOLE BY THE COLLAR. GOLD BRAIDS AND ORNAMENTAL BUTTONS AS HIGHLIGHTS.
AND PLENTY OF NARCISSUS FOR THEIR DRESS HATS, ALL TIED OFF WITH RIBBONS.

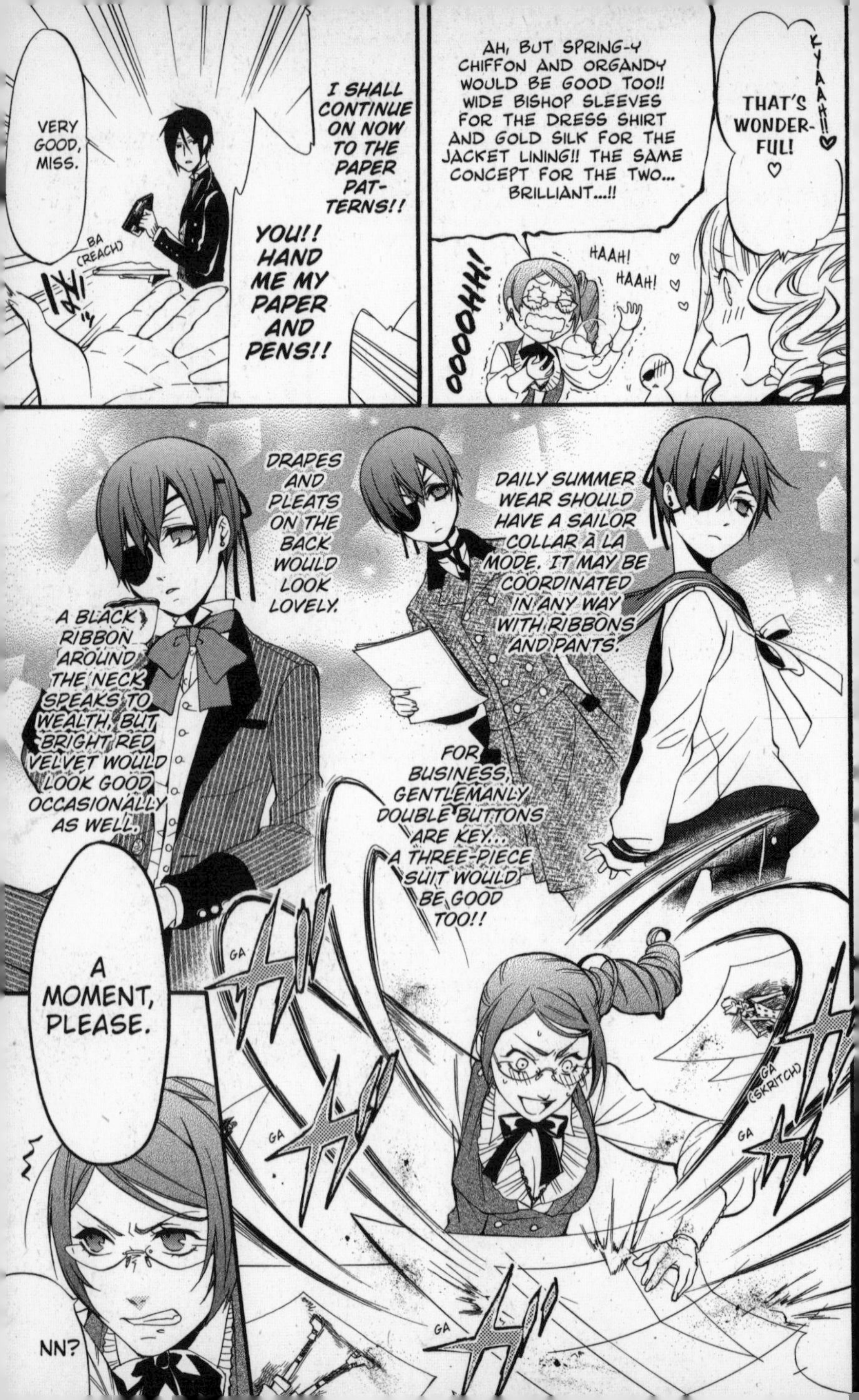
KYAAAH!!
THAT'S WONDER-FUL!
AH, BUT SPRING-Y CHIFFON AND ORGANDY WOULD BE GOOD TOO!! WIDE BISHOP SLEEVES FOR THE DRESS SHIRT AND GOLD SILK FOR THE JACKET LINING!! THE SAME CONCEPT FOR THE TWO... BRILLIANT...!!
HAAH! HAAH!
OOOOOHH!!
I SHALL CONTINUE ON NOW TO THE PAPER PAT-TERNS!!
YOU!! HAND ME MY PAPER AND PENS!!
VERY GOOD, MISS.
BA (REACH)
DAILY SUMMER WEAR SHOULD HAVE A SAILOR COLLAR À LA MODE. IT MAY BE COORDINATED IN ANY WAY WITH RIBBONS AND PANTS.
DRAPES AND PLEATS ON THE BACK WOULD LOOK LOVELY.
FOR BUSINESS, GENTLEMANLY DOUBLE BUTTONS ARE KEY... A THREE-PIECE SUIT WOULD BE GOOD TOO!!
A BLACK RIBBON AROUND THE NECK SPEAKS TO WEALTH, BUT BRIGHT RED VELVET WOULD LOOK GOOD OCCASIONALLY AS WELL.
GA (SKRITCH)
GA
GA
GA
GA
A MOMENT, PLEASE.
NN?

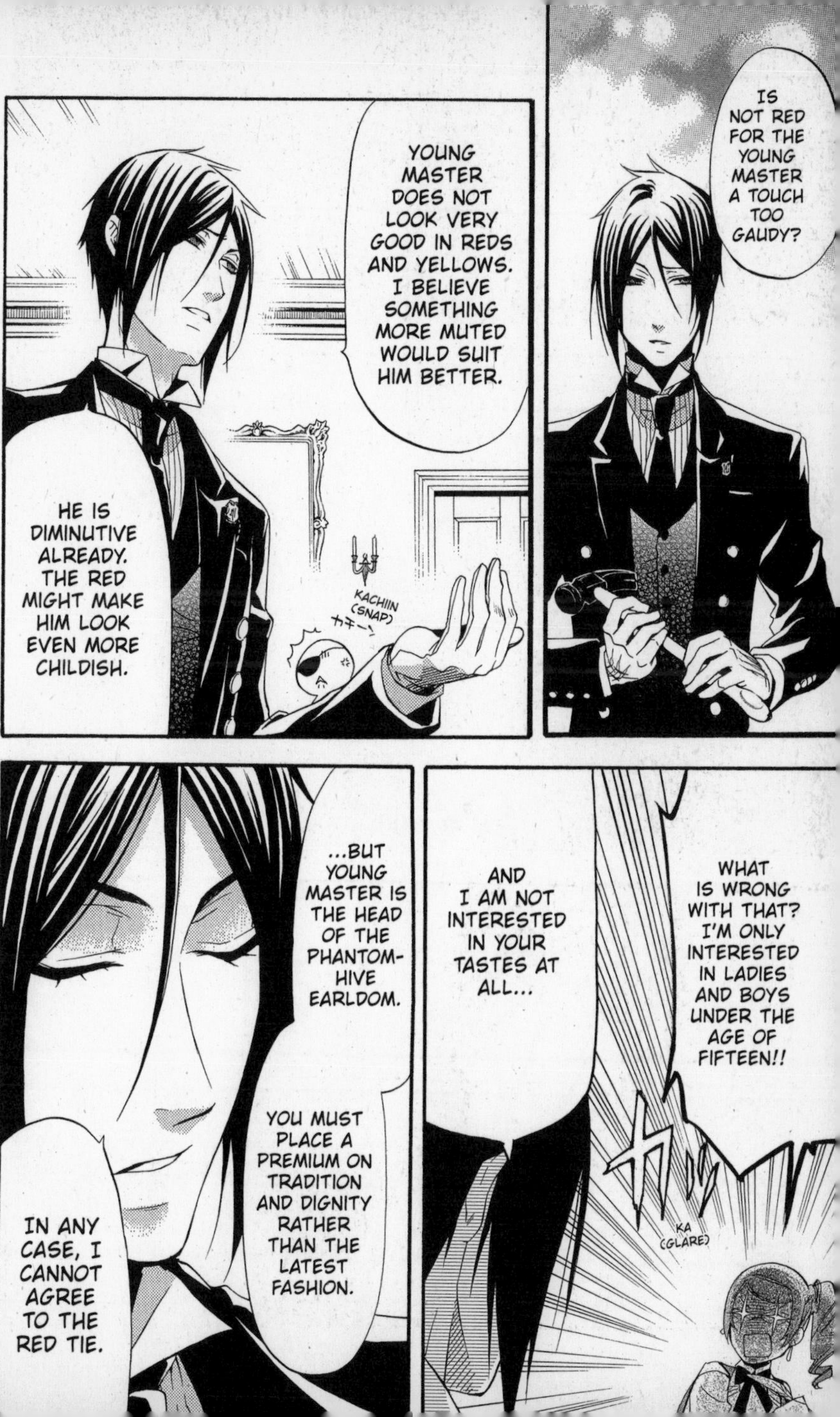
IS NOT RED FOR THE YOUNG MASTER A TOUCH TOO GAUDY?
YOUNG MASTER DOES NOT LOOK VERY GOOD IN REDS AND YELLOWS. I BELIEVE SOMETHING MORE MUTED WOULD SUIT HIM BETTER.
HE IS DIMINUTIVE ALREADY. THE RED MIGHT MAKE HIM LOOK EVEN MORE CHILDISH.
KACHIIN (SNAP)
WHAT IS WRONG WITH THAT? I'M ONLY INTERESTED IN LADIES AND BOYS UNDER THE AGE OF FIFTEEN!!
KA (GLARE)
AND I AM NOT INTERESTED IN YOUR TASTES AT ALL...
...BUT YOUNG MASTER IS THE HEAD OF THE PHANTOM-HIVE EARLDOM.
YOU MUST PLACE A PREMIUM ON TRADITION AND DIGNITY RATHER THAN THE LATEST FASHION.
IN ANY CASE, I CANNOT AGREE TO THE RED TIE.

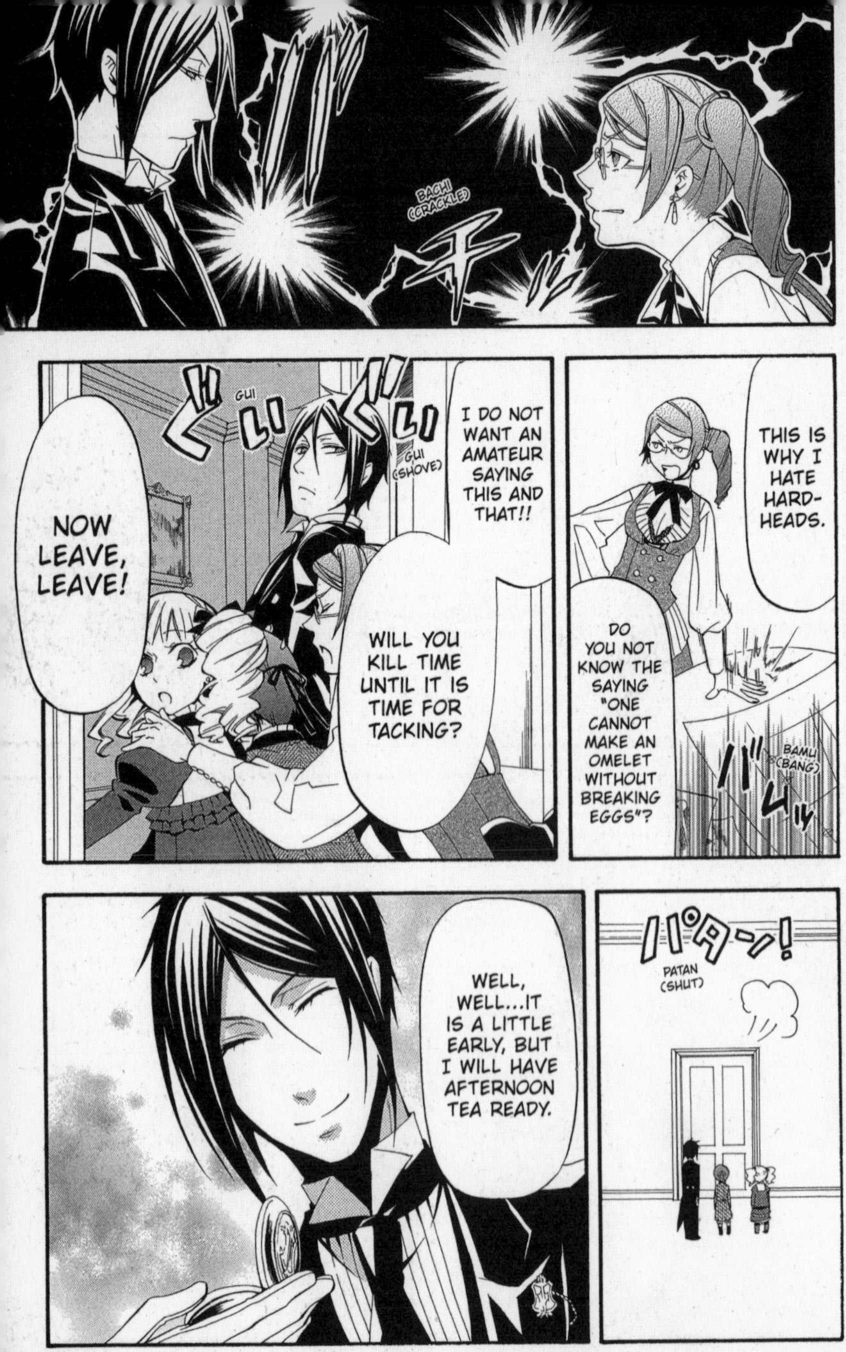
BACHI (CRACKLE)
THIS IS WHY I HATE HARD-HEADS.
DO YOU NOT KNOW THE SAYING "ONE CANNOT MAKE AN OMELET WITHOUT BREAKING EGGS"?
BAMU (BANG)
I DO NOT WANT AN AMATEUR SAYING THIS AND THAT!!
GUI
GUI (SHOVE)
WILL YOU KILL TIME UNTIL IT IS TIME FOR TACKING?
NOW LEAVE, LEAVE!
PATAN (SHUT)
WELL, WELL...IT IS A LITTLE EARLY, BUT I WILL HAVE AFTERNOON TEA READY.

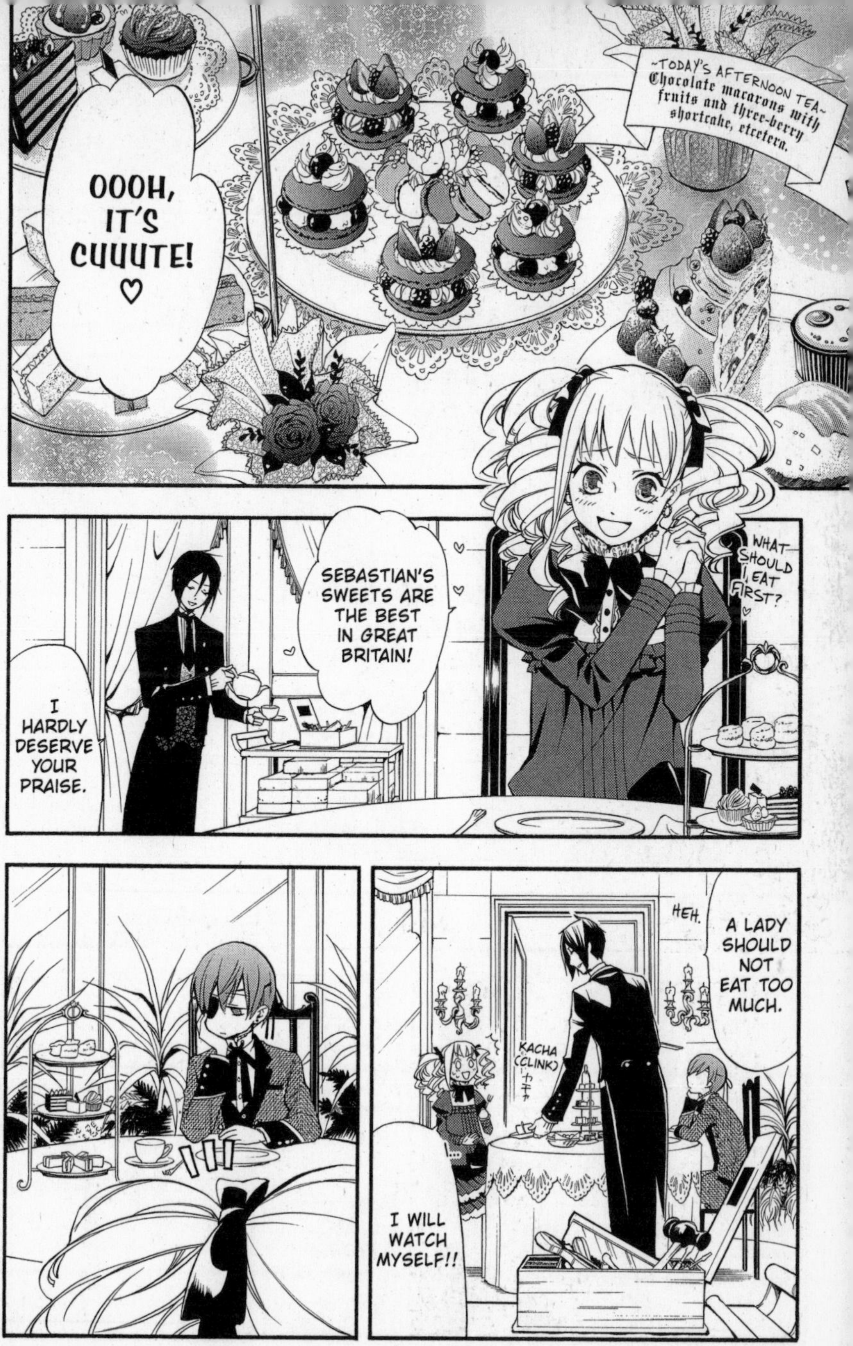
~TODAY'S AFTERNOON TEA~
Chocolate macarons with fruits and three-berry shortcake, etcetera.
OOOH, IT'S CUUUTE! ♡
WHAT SHOULD I EAT FIRST?
SEBASTIAN'S SWEETS ARE THE BEST IN GREAT BRITAIN!
I HARDLY DESERVE YOUR PRAISE.
A LADY SHOULD NOT EAT TOO MUCH.
HEH.
KACHA (CLINK)
I WILL WATCH MYSELF!!

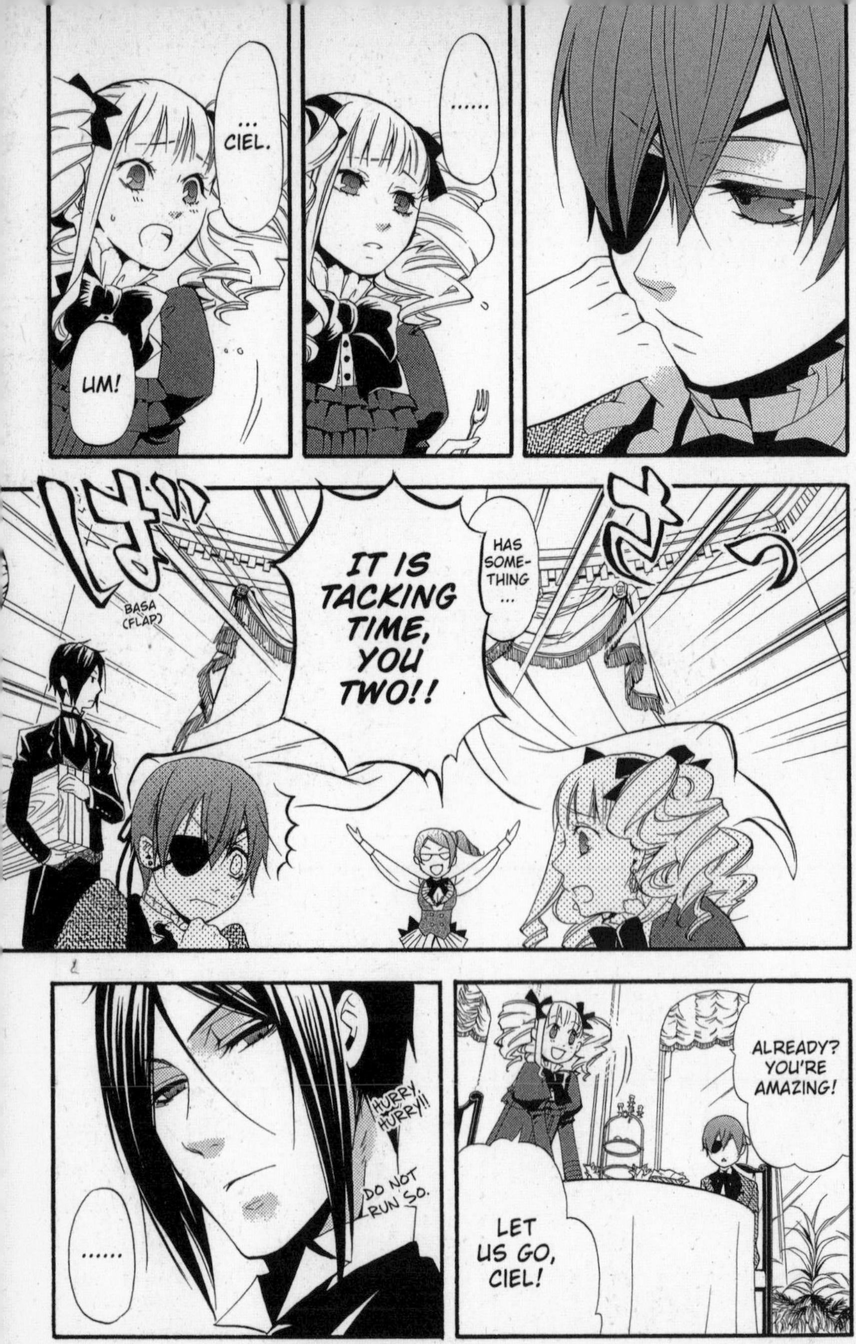
......
... CIEL.
UM!
さっ
HAS SOME-THING ...
IT IS TACKING TIME, YOU TWO!!
BASA (FLAP)
ALREADY? YOU'RE AMAZING!
LET US GO, CIEL!
HURRY, HURRY!!
DO NOT RUN SO.
......

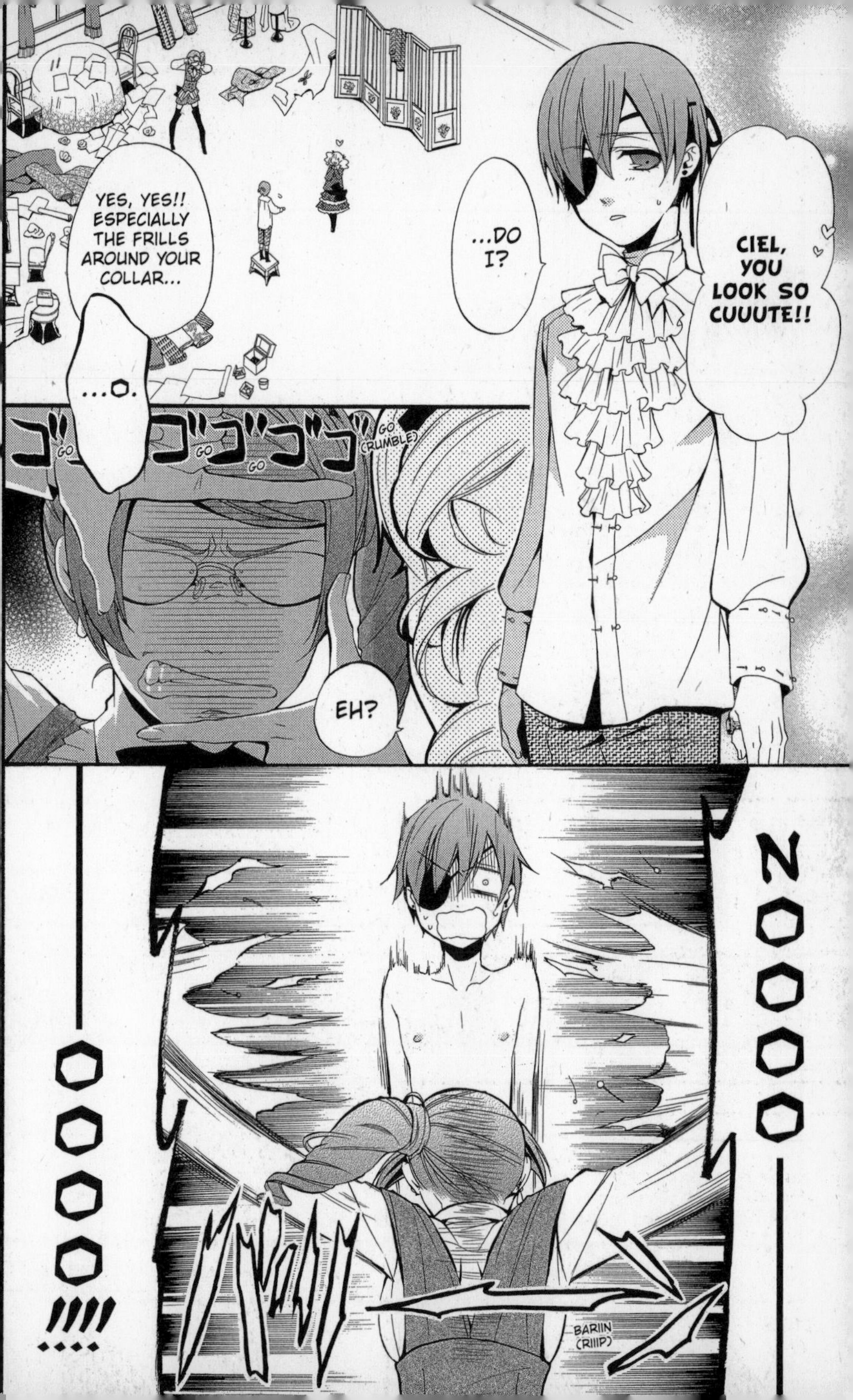
CIEL, YOU LOOK SO CUUUTE!!
...DO I?
YES, YES!! ESPECIALLY THE FRILLS AROUND YOUR COLLAR...
...O.
GO GO GO GO (RUMBLE)
EH?
NOOOO——
——OOOOO!!!!....
BARIIN (RIIIP)

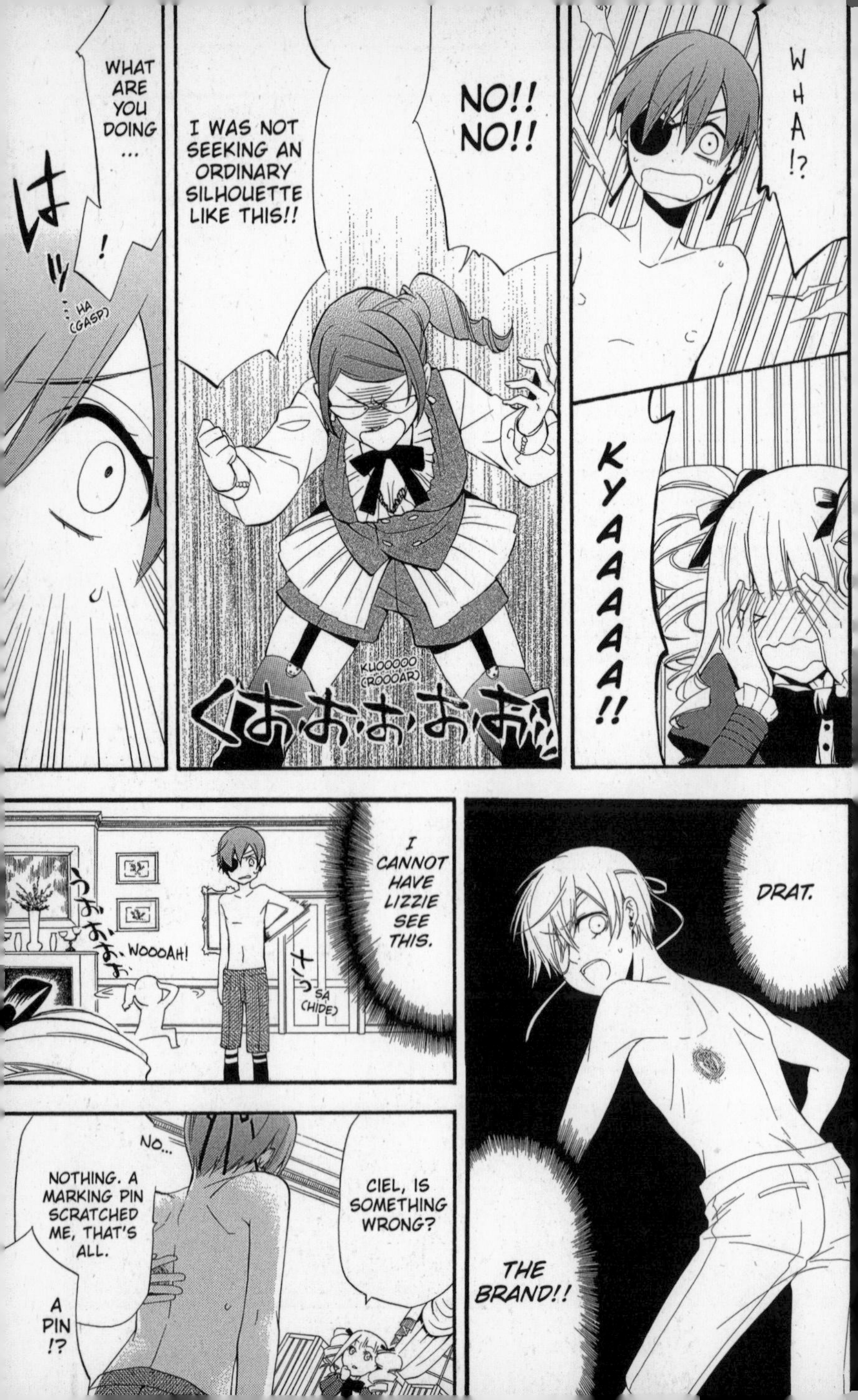
WHA!?
KYAAAAAA!!
NO!! NO!!
I WAS NOT SEEKING AN ORDINARY SILHOUETTE LIKE THIS!!
KUOOOOO (ROOOAR)
WHAT ARE YOU DOING...
!
HA (GASP)
DRAT.
THE BRAND!!
I CANNOT HAVE LIZZIE SEE THIS.
SA (HIDE)
WOOOAH!
CIEL, IS SOMETHING WRONG?
NO...
NOTHING. A MARKING PIN SCRATCHED ME, THAT'S ALL.
A PIN!?

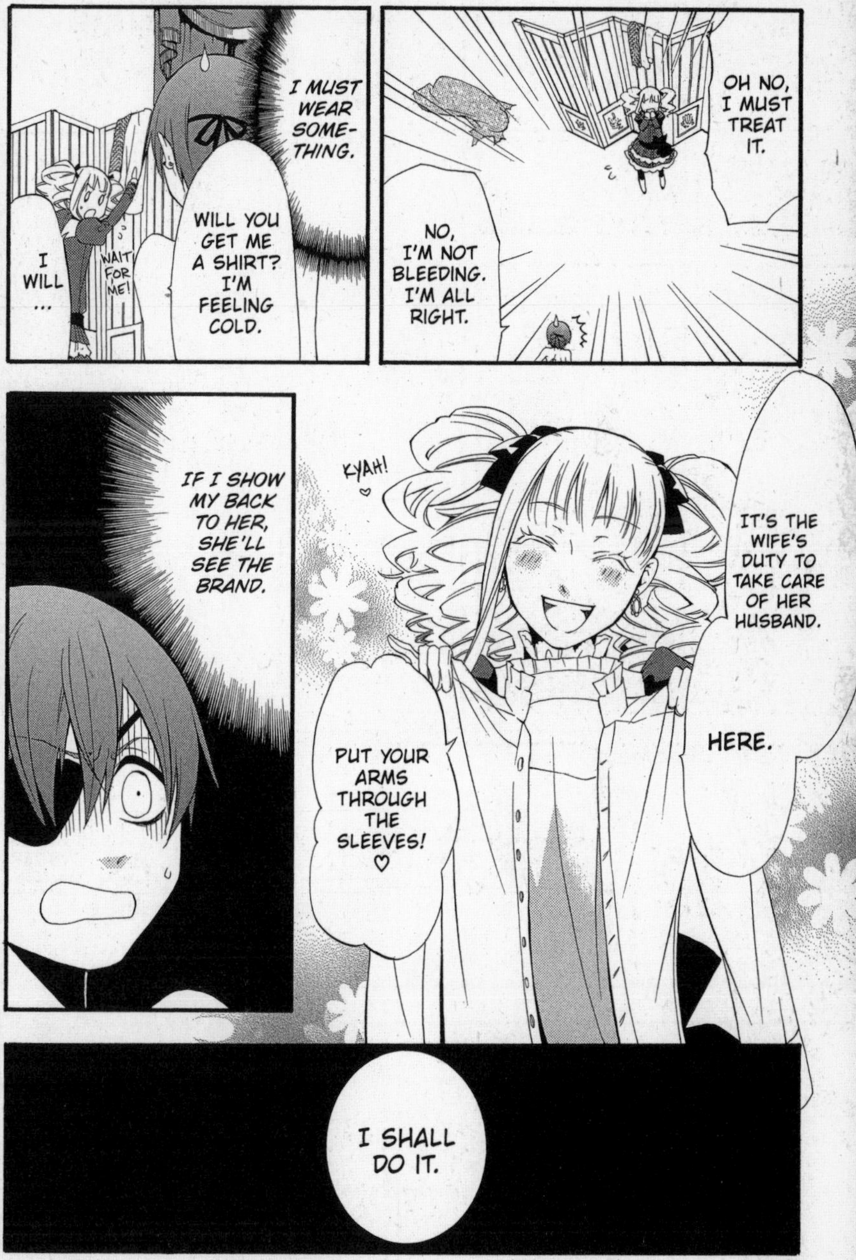
OH NO, I MUST TREAT IT.
NO, I'M NOT BLEEDING. I'M ALL RIGHT.
I MUST WEAR SOMETHING.
WILL YOU GET ME A SHIRT? I'M FEELING COLD.
WAIT FOR ME!
I WILL ...
IT'S THE WIFE'S DUTY TO TAKE CARE OF HER HUSBAND.
HERE.
KYAH! ♡
PUT YOUR ARMS THROUGH THE SLEEVES! ♡
IF I SHOW MY BACK TO HER, SHE'LL SEE THE BRAND.
I SHALL DO IT.

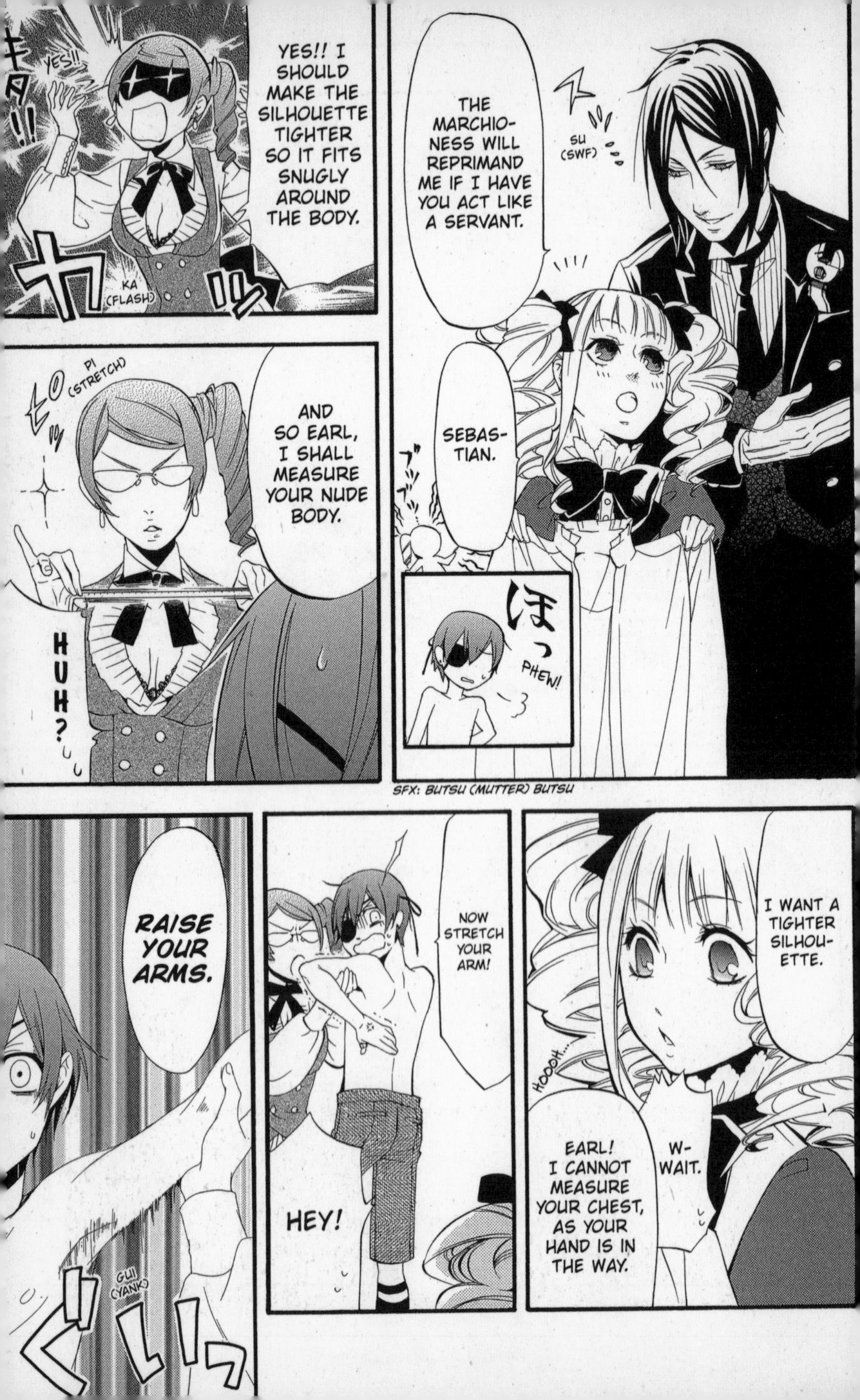
SU (SWF)
THE MARCHIONESS WILL REPRIMAND ME IF I HAVE YOU ACT LIKE A SERVANT.
SEBASTIAN.
ほっ
PHEW!
SFX: BUTSU (MUTTER) BUTSU
YES!!
YES!! I SHOULD MAKE THE SILHOUETTE TIGHTER SO IT FITS SNUGLY AROUND THE BODY.
KA (FLASH)
PI (STRETCH)
AND SO EARL, I SHALL MEASURE YOUR NUDE BODY.
HUH?
I WANT A TIGHTER SILHOUETTE.
W-WAIT.
EARL! I CANNOT MEASURE YOUR CHEST, AS YOUR HAND IS IN THE WAY.
HOOOH...
NOW STRETCH YOUR ARM!
HEY!
RAISE YOUR ARMS.
GUI (YANK)

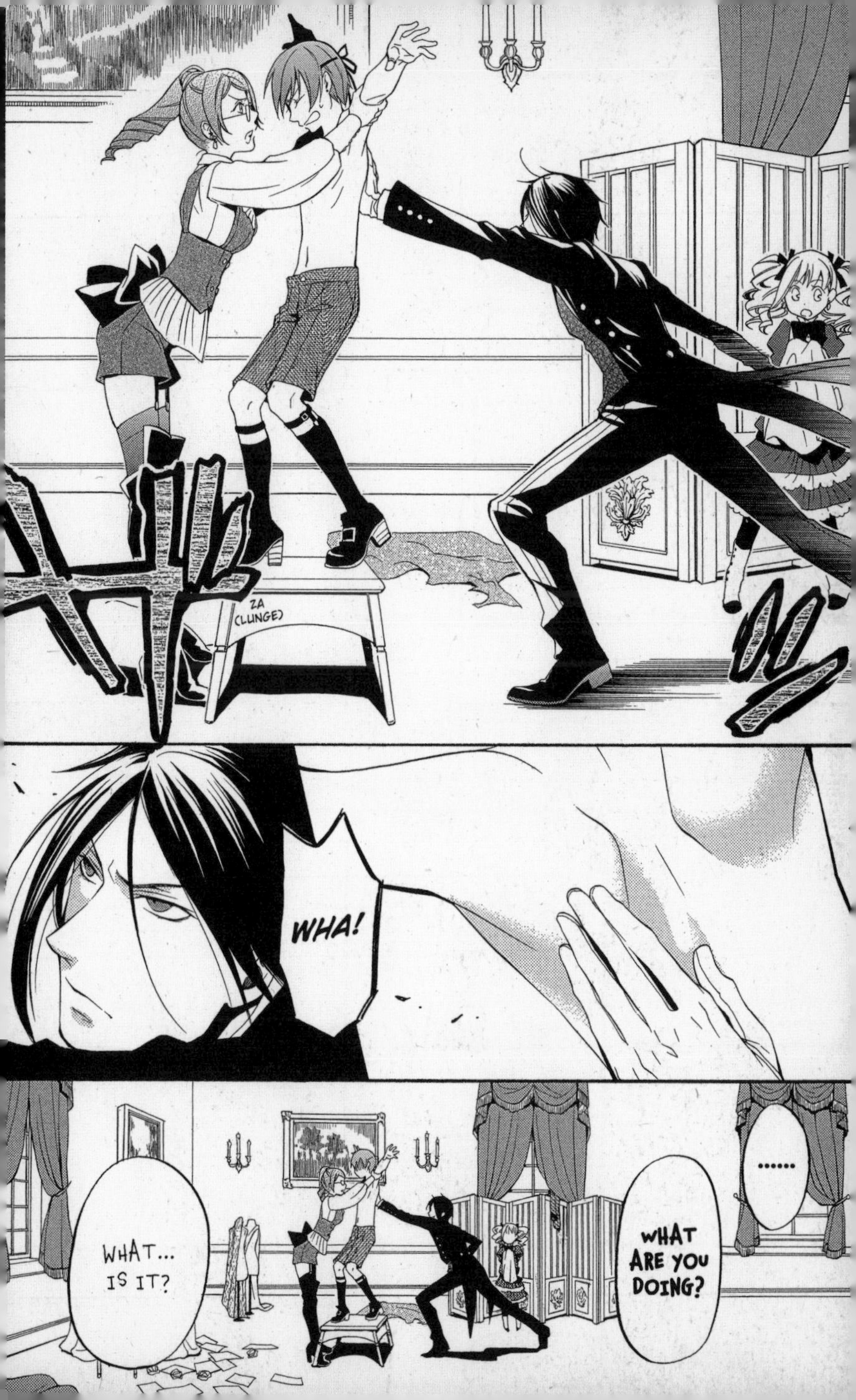
ZA
(LUNGE)
WHA!
......
WHAT ARE YOU DOING?
WHAT... IS IT?

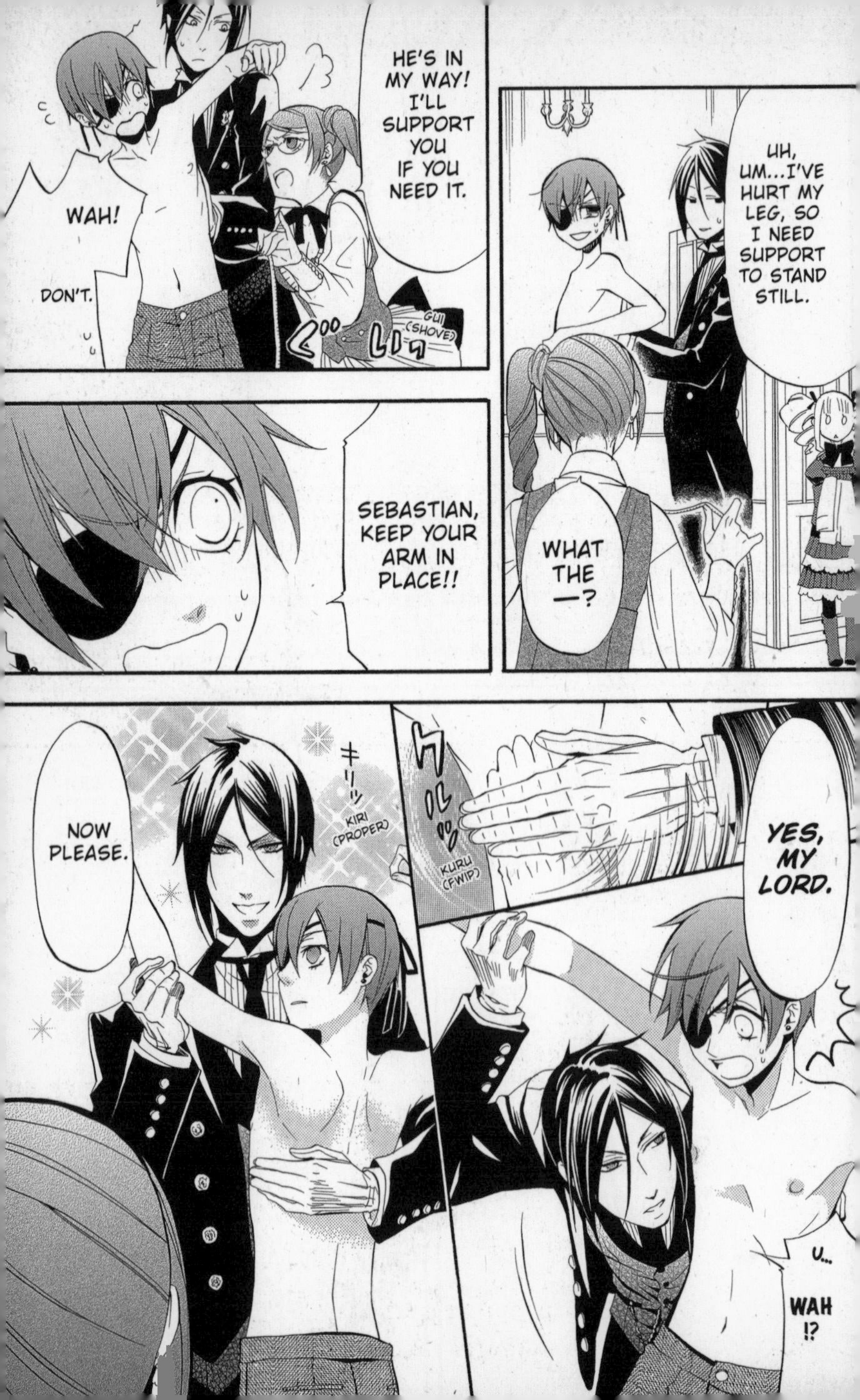
UH, UM...I'VE HURT MY LEG, SO I NEED SUPPORT TO STAND STILL.
WHAT THE—?
HE'S IN MY WAY! I'LL SUPPORT YOU IF YOU NEED IT.
WAH!
DON'T.
GUI (SHOVE)
SEBASTIAN, KEEP YOUR ARM IN PLACE!!
YES, MY LORD.
KURU (FWIP)
U...
WAH !?
NOW PLEASE.
KIRI (PROPER)

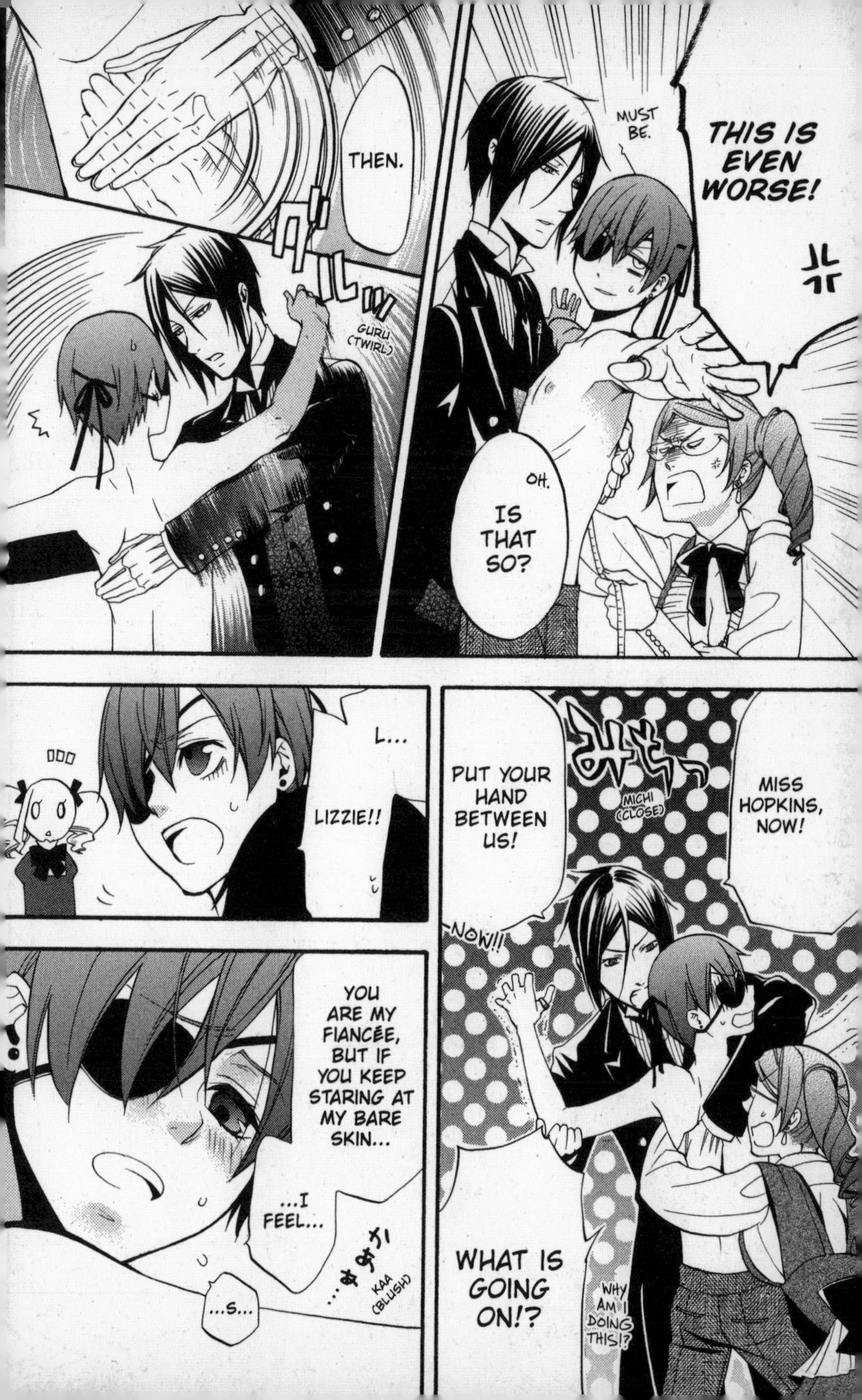
THIS IS EVEN WORSE!
MUST BE.
OH.
IS THAT SO?
THEN.
GURU (TWIRL)
MISS HOPKINS, NOW!
PUT YOUR HAND BETWEEN US!
MICHI (CLOSE)
NOW!!
WHAT IS GOING ON!?
WHY AM I DOING THIS!?
L...
LIZZIE!!
YOU ARE MY FIANCÉE, BUT IF YOU KEEP STARING AT MY BARE SKIN...
...I FEEL...
KAA (BLUSH)
...S...

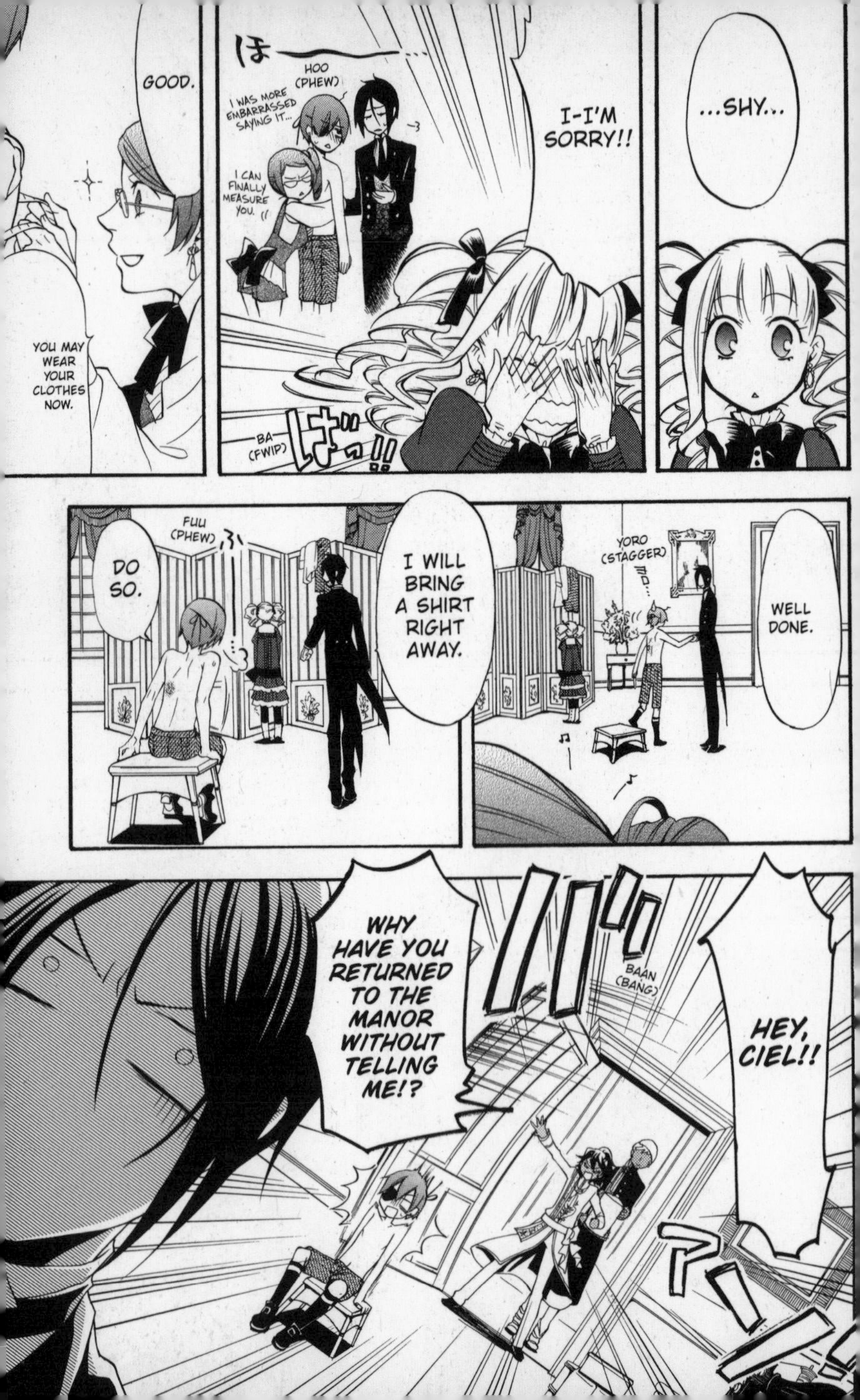
...SHY...
I-I'M SORRY!!
ほー…
HOO (PHEW)
I WAS MORE EMBARRASSED SAYING IT...
I CAN FINALLY MEASURE YOU.
BA (FWIP)
ばっ!!
GOOD.
YOU MAY WEAR YOUR CLOTHES NOW.
WELL DONE.
YORO (STAGGER)
I WILL BRING A SHIRT RIGHT AWAY.
DO SO.
FUU (PHEW)
ふ
HEY, CIEL!!
BAAN (BANG)
WHY HAVE YOU RETURNED TO THE MANOR WITHOUT TELLING ME!?

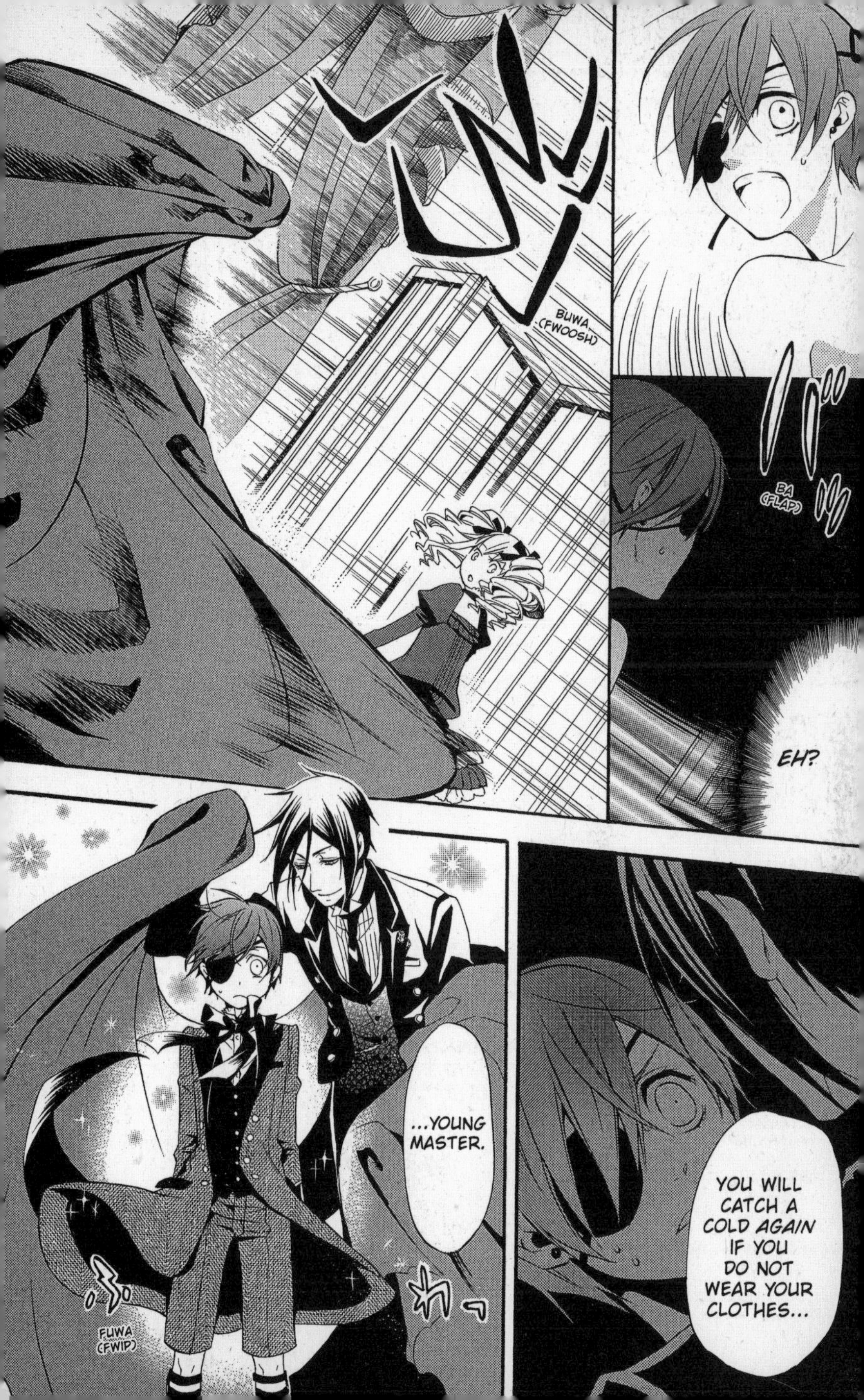
BA (FLAP)
EH?
BUWA (FWOOSH)
YOU WILL CATCH A COLD AGAIN IF YOU DO NOT WEAR YOUR CLOTHES...
...YOUNG MASTER.
FUWA (FWIP)

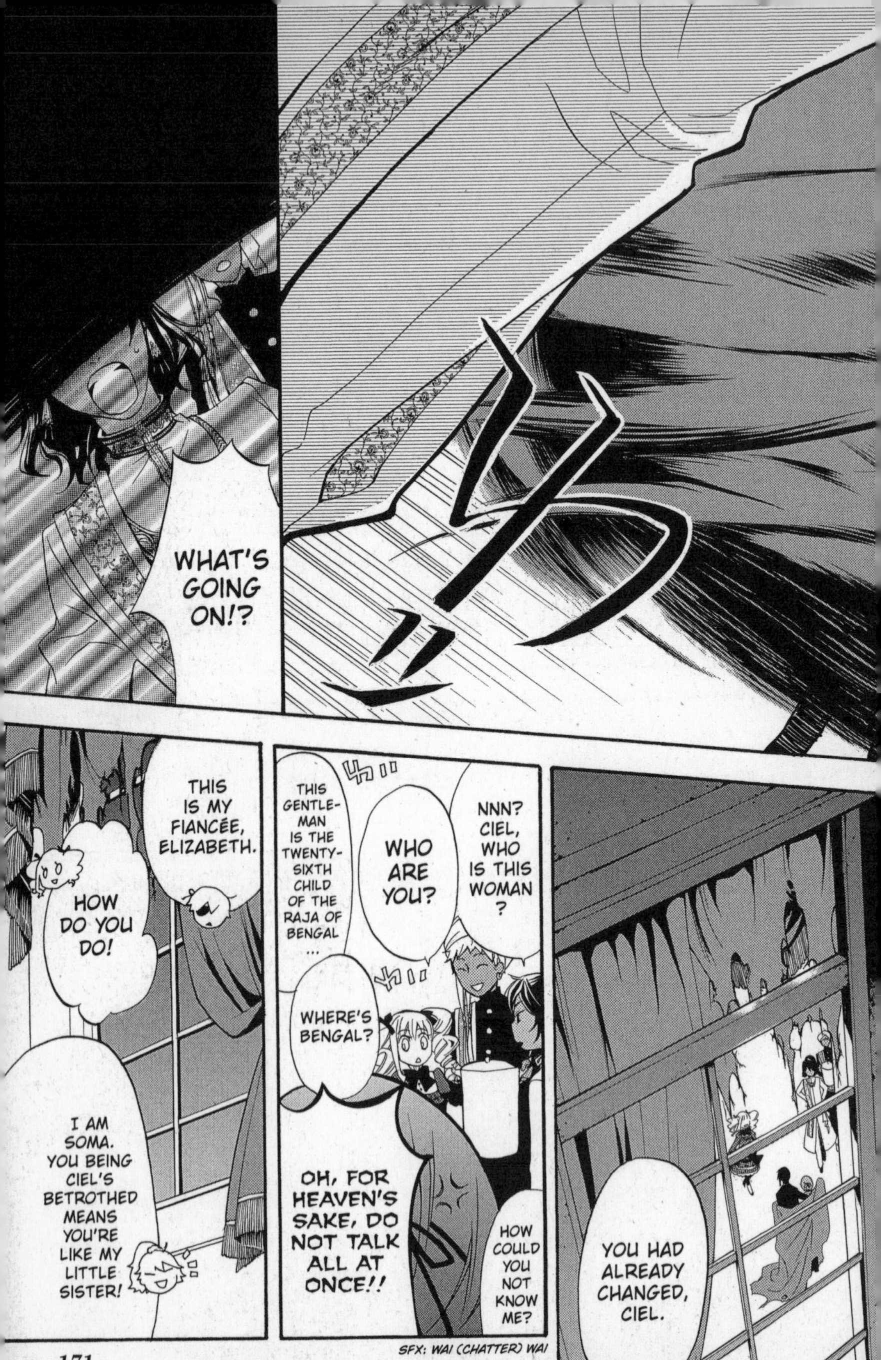
WHAT'S GOING ON!?
YOU HAD ALREADY CHANGED, CIEL.
NNN? CIEL, WHO IS THIS WOMAN?
WHO ARE YOU?
THIS GENTLEMAN IS THE TWENTY-SIXTH CHILD OF THE RAJA OF BENGAL ...
WHERE'S BENGAL?
HOW COULD YOU NOT KNOW ME?
OH, FOR HEAVEN'S SAKE, DO NOT TALK ALL AT ONCE!!
THIS IS MY FIANCÉE, ELIZABETH.
HOW DO YOU DO!
I AM SOMA. YOU BEING CIEL'S BETROTHED MEANS YOU'RE LIKE MY LITTLE SISTER!

SFX: WAI (CHATTER) WAI

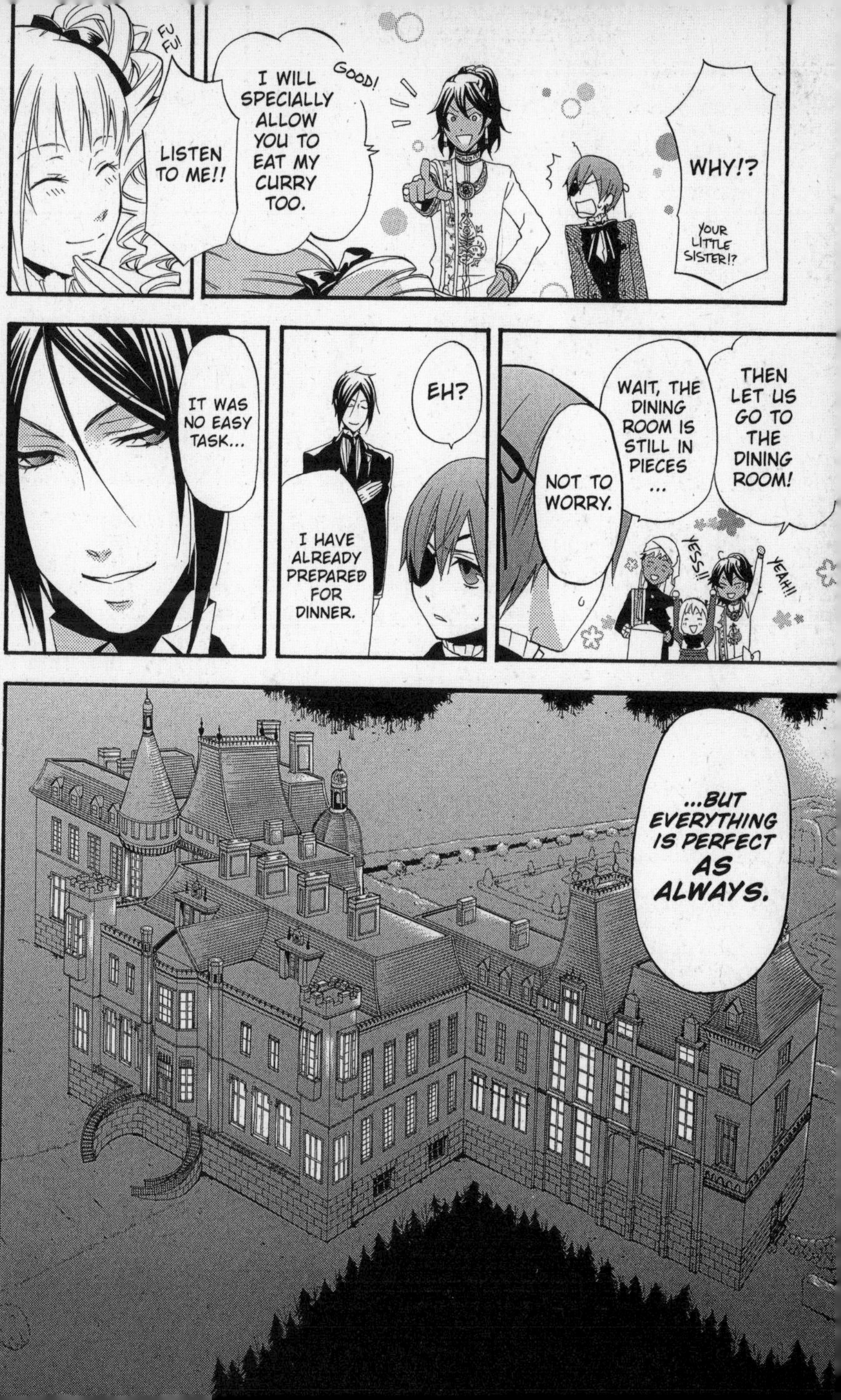
WHY!?
YOUR LITTLE SISTER!?
GOOD!
I WILL SPECIALLY ALLOW YOU TO EAT MY CURRY TOO.
FU FU!
LISTEN TO ME!!
THEN LET US GO TO THE DINING ROOM!
YEAH!!
YESS!!
WAIT, THE DINING ROOM IS STILL IN PIECES ...
NOT TO WORRY.
EH?
I HAVE ALREADY PREPARED FOR DINNER.
IT WAS NO EASY TASK...
...BUT EVERYTHING IS PERFECT AS ALWAYS.

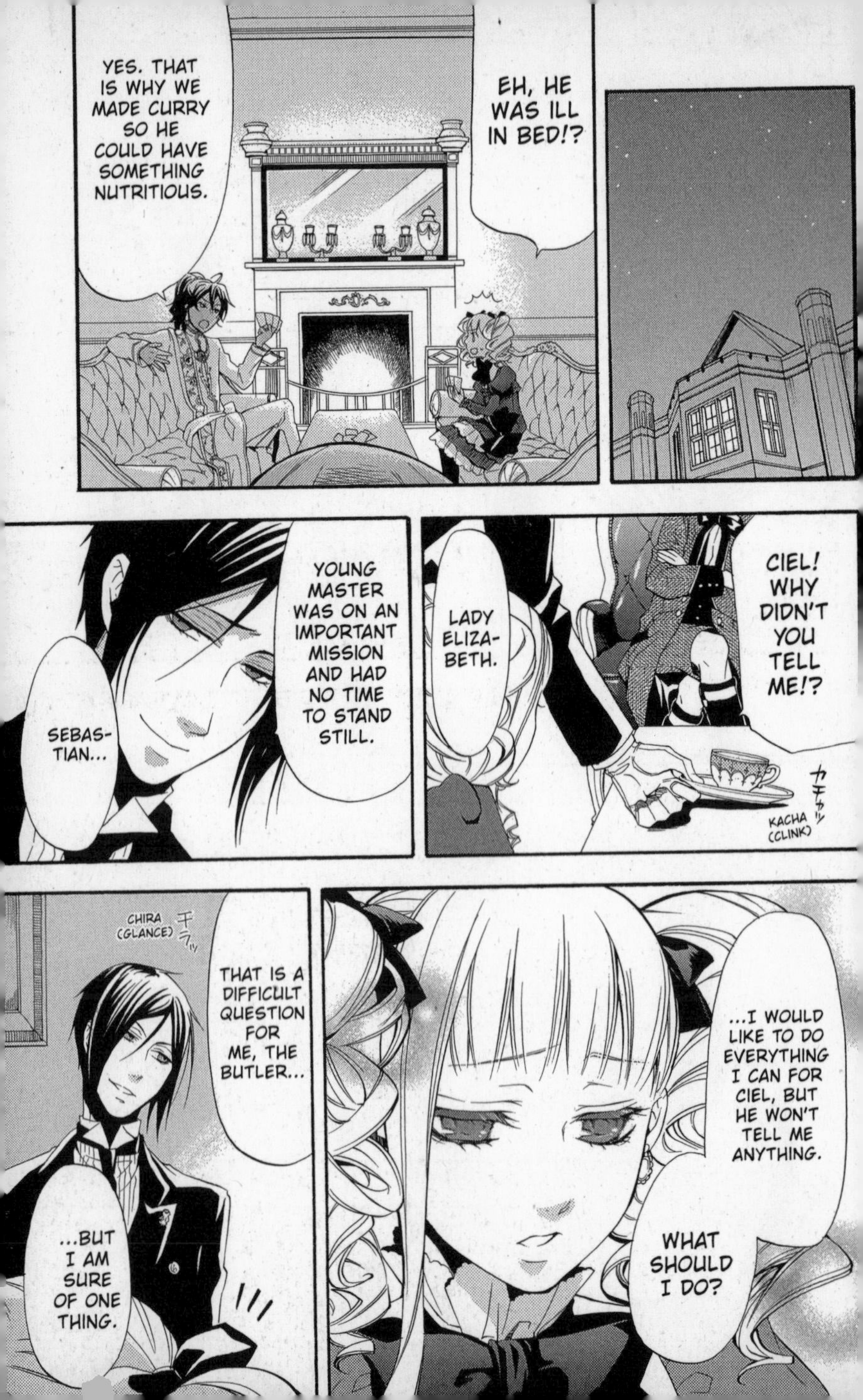
EH, HE WAS ILL IN BED!?
YES. THAT IS WHY WE MADE CURRY SO HE COULD HAVE SOMETHING NUTRITIOUS.
CIEL! WHY DIDN'T YOU TELL ME!?
カチャッ KACHA (CLINK)
LADY ELIZABETH.
YOUNG MASTER WAS ON AN IMPORTANT MISSION AND HAD NO TIME TO STAND STILL.
SEBASTIAN...
...I WOULD LIKE TO DO EVERYTHING I CAN FOR CIEL, BUT HE WON'T TELL ME ANYTHING.
WHAT SHOULD I DO?
チラッ CHIRA (GLANCE)
THAT IS A DIFFICULT QUESTION FOR ME, THE BUTLER...
...BUT I AM SURE OF ONE THING.

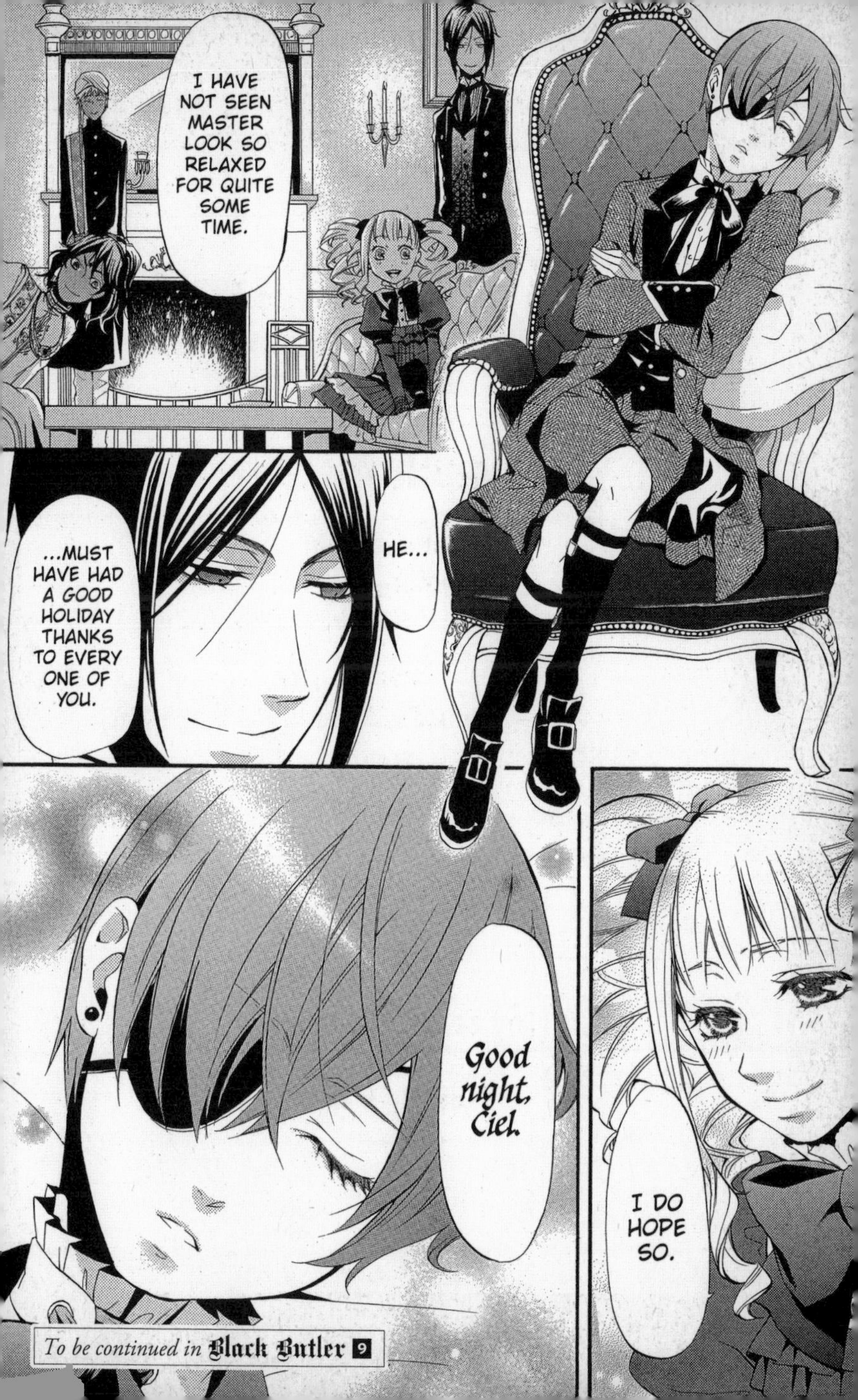
I HAVE NOT SEEN MASTER LOOK SO RELAXED FOR QUITE SOME TIME.
HE...
...MUST HAVE HAD A GOOD HOLIDAY THANKS TO EVERY ONE OF YOU.
I DO HOPE SO.
Good night, Ciel.

To be continued in **Black Butler 9**

❖ Black Butler ❖

黒執事

✦

Downstairs

Wakana Haduki

Suke

7

Kiyo

Yuka Fujikawa

*

Takeshi Kuma

*

Yana Toboso

❖

Special Thanks

Yana's Mother

for You!

Translation Notes

PAGE 24
Solomon Grundy
An English nursery rhyme first recorded in the nineteenth century. It reads, "Solomon Grundy / Born on a Monday / Christened on Tuesday / Married on Wednesday / Took ill on Thursday / Worse on Friday / Died on Saturday / Buried on Sunday / This is the end / Of Solomon Grundy."

PAGE 40
The Great Mill Disaster
Baldroy is referring to an actual fire that took place in Minneapolis, Minnesota in 1878. The Washburn "A" Mill, which was heralded as the largest flourmill of its kind at the time, was the site of a fire that started from a spark igniting the flour dust in the air. There were eighteen fatalities and the land around the mill was terribly damaged.

PAGE 84
Ronald Knox
There was an actual historical personage known as Monsignor Ronald Knox. He was born in England in 1888 and was a well-known preacher and literary man. Interestingly, he was a member of The Detection Club, a collective of English detective novelists, which was put together around 1928, and even penned a handful of detective stories. Furthermore, he also wrote a satirical essay entitled "Studies in the Literature of Sherlock Holmes."

PAGE 85
Ronald Knox's speech
In the original, Ronald occasionally adds -ssu to the ends of certain sentences. This speech pattern is often used by athletes, team sports types, and people who practice the martial arts.

PAGE 87
Group date
The Japanese term used in the original is goukon. During such an event, an all-male group and an all-female group meet (usually over drinks) to make new friends or boyfriends/girlfriends.

PAGE 89
Roger
This term came into use in the 1940s, with the use of radios in military communications.

PAGE 159
You cannot make an omelet without breaking eggs.
The original Japanese saying is "Unsown seeds never grow."

PAGE 165
Raise your arms
In the original, Nina says banzai.

INSIDE BACK COVER
96422
The number on Mey-rin's tag can be read in Japanese to sound like Kuroshitsuji, the original title of Black Butler.

Yana Toboso

AUTHOR'S NOTE

It's been decided that a second season of the **Black Butler** TV anime will be created!

Thanks to that, I was made to recognise the wonder of the power that people hold.

It wasn't the creators who made this decision, it was thanks to everyone who cheered on that the second season will be made.

Your powers are amazing. It made me feel that nothing is impossible. Everyone, thank you for creating **Black Butler**. And that's what I am feeling with Volume 8.

BLACK BUTLER ❽

YANA TOBOSO

Translation: Tomo Kimura • Lettering: Alexis Eckerman

BLACK BUTLER Vol. 8 © 2009 Yana Toboso / SQUARE ENIX CO., LTD. All rights reserved. First published in Japan in 2009 by SQUARE ENIX CO., LTD. English translation rights arranged with SQUARE ENIX CO., LTD. and Hachette Book Group through Tuttle-Mori Agency, Inc.

Translation © 2012 by SQUARE ENIX CO., LTD.

Yen Press
Hachette Book Group
237 Park Avenue, New York, NY 10017

www.HachetteBookGroup.com
www.YenPress.com

Yen Press is an imprint of Hachette Book Group, Inc. The Yen Press name and logo are trademarks of Hachette Book Group, Inc.

First Yen Press Edition: January 2012

ISBN: 978-0-316-18965-1

10 9 8 7 6 5

BVG

Printed in the United States of America